SQUANDERED
VICTORY

THE AMERICAN OCCUPATION AND THE BUNGLED EFFORT TO BRING DEMOCRACY TO IRAQ

LARRY DIAMOND

AN OWL BOOK

HENRY HOLT AND COMPANY • NEW YORK

Owl Books
Henry Holt and Company, LLC
Publishers since 1866
175 Fifth Avenue
New York, New York 10010
www.henryholt.com

An Owl Book® and 🛡® are registered trademarks of
Henry Holt and Company, LLC.

Library of Congress Cataloging-in-Publication Data
Diamond, Larry Jay.
Squandered victory : the American occupation and the bungled effort
to bring democracy to Iraq / Larry Diamond.—1st ed.
p.   cm.
Includes bibliographical references and index.
ISBN-13: 978-0-8050-8008-7
ISBN-10: 0-8050-8008-2
1. Iraq War, 2003.   2. Postwar reconstruction—Iraq.   3. United States—
Foreign relations—Iraq.   4. Iraq—Foreign relations—United States.   I. Title.
DS79.76.D53 2005
956.7044'31—dc22   2005043074

Henry Holt books are available for special promotions
and premiums. For details contact: Director, Special Markets.

Originally published in hardcover in 2005 by Times Books

First Owl Books Edition 2006

Designed by Victoria Hartman

Printed in the United States of America

1   3   5   7   9   10   8   6   4   2

Praise for *Squandered Victory*

"A scathing critique . . . [a] clear explanation of the internal characteristics of Iraq . . . deeply disturbing." — *Washington Monthly*

"Diamond's vivid, passionate, and fascinating firsthand account of the postwar effort in Iraq is immensely instructive." — *The American Prospect*

"[Larry Diamond's] eyewitness experience bolsters this vivid critique of the current administration's foreign policy cornerstone."
— *Publishers Weekly*

"A compelling story." — *Commonweal*

"Larry Diamond gives the most vivid account of life behind the T-walls, combining a gripping first-person narrative with the intellectual detachment of a professor." — *The Chronicle of Higher Education*

"Larry Diamond, one of America's foremost experts on democracy, has studied the process of democracy-building in dozens of countries across the globe. When offered a chance to assist in the effort to establish democracy in Iraq he did so—and was surprised and horrified by the mixture of arrogance and incompetence which characterized the American occupation. In this well-written book, Diamond explains what went wrong and why. In my view, a democratic Iraq remains a noble, important, and achievable goal. But it has been made so much more difficult and costly by America's squandered victory." —Fareed Zakaria

"A vivid, intimate, and unblinking view of the American occupation of Iraq. Larry Diamond takes us with him into Baghdad's Green Zone for an unprecedented look at good intentions run amok. *Squandered Victory* offers the clearest explanation to date of how the U.S. government miscalculated the real price of victory in Iraq." —Rick Atkinson

"Cautiously pessimistic but also optimistically cautious regarding Iraq's longer-range democratic potential, and sparing in its criticism of the high-handed manner in which top U.S. officials micro-governed occupied Iraq, troublingly informative about the confused character of the U.S. occupation, Diamond's book provides a remarkably incisive dissection of Iraq's tortured political realities." —Zbigniew Brzezinski

"Larry Diamond combines deep academic knowledge about democratization with hands-on practical experience of our nation-building effort in Iraq, to provide a stark critique of the U.S. effort there. It is a disquieting analysis that is rich in lessons for future American foreign policy." —Francis Fukuyama

"Larry Diamond, a believer in a democratic Iraq, earned his skepticism about the American effort there the hard way—by trying to make it work. This is an extremely valuable insider's account of idealism, illusion, and failure." —George Packer

SQUANDERED VICTORY

To my students:

May they learn from our mistakes.

CONTENTS

SQUANDERED VICTORY

★

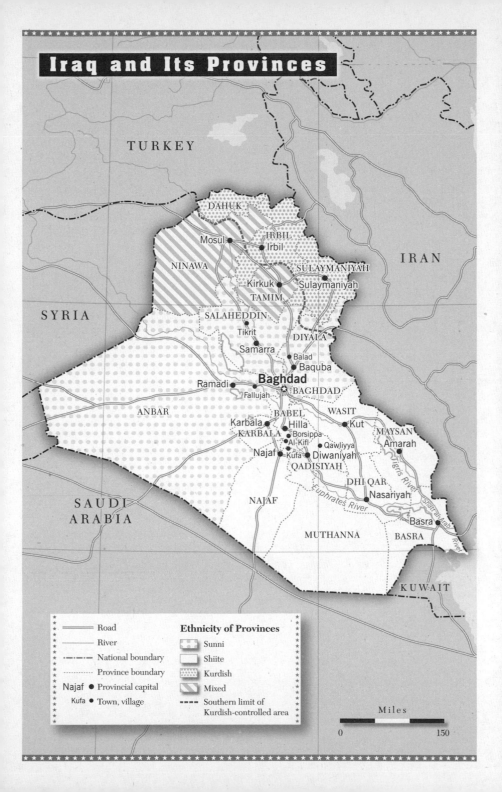

Iraq and Its Provinces

Ethnicity of Provinces

- Road
- River
- National boundary
- Province boundary
- Najaf ● Provincial capital
- Kufa ● Town, village

- Sunni
- Shiite
- Kurdish
- Mixed
- Southern limit of Kurdish-controlled area

Miles

0   150

INTRODUCTION: THE VIEW FROM BABYLON

★

High on a hill in the desert of Iraq stand the brick remains of a once-glorious tower. Twenty-five centuries have weathered the last remaining wall of this tower so that it appears from a distance as twin towers, like two trees growing from a common stump, bent and stunted from the wind. There is an eerie and magnificent view of these ruins from a Shiite mosque, Maqam Ibrahim, on a mountaintop a few miles away. It reportedly marks the site of the house where the biblical patriarch Abraham once lived in Borsippa over three thousand years ago, before he emigrated to Canaan, in what is now Israel. From that distant, opposite height, the twin towers emerge precariously from a huge, rounded, barren hill, which sits atop a shallow plateau of elevated, creviced earth, itself surrounded by miles of brown, empty dust. The scene is utterly arid and mysterious.

As one draws closer, the crevices become pathways, leading to the remains of an ancient civilization. The plateau is a series of excavations, themselves abandoned and chaotic, of layers and layers of settlements and religious shrines. The mound atop the plateau is not an earthen hill but the decay of millions of mud bricks, forming seven terraces that once rose 231 feet high. Scattered among the dirt and loose bricks along the pathways are fragments of clay tablets with cuneiform script, containing precious clues to this lost civilization.

This is the ziggurat—the temple tower—of Borsippa and, by local legend, the Tower of Babel, though in reality it dates from a much later epoch than its biblical namesake. It was one of the most magnificent ziggurats built by Nebuchadnezzar, the Babylonian ruler of the sixth century B.C. who ordered the destruction of the ancient Jewish temple in Jerusalem. Nebuchadnezzar had dedicated this temple, the best-surviving ziggurat in Iraq, to Nabu, the god of science and learning in Mesopotamia and the king's protector. In search of a myth to justify his own bid for greatness and immortality, Saddam Hussein had fashioned himself as a modern-day Nebuchadnezzar and the Iraqi people as the descendants of the ancient Babylonians, "the cultural heirs of the ancient Mesopotamian civilization."[1] No less a megalomaniac than the ancient Babylonian tyrant, Saddam had borrowed Nebuchadnezzar's vain practice of stamping his name on every possible building brick.

With the dangers and controversies of Baghdad seventy-five miles and a world away, I stood in March 2004 with several of my colleagues from the Coalition Provisional Authority (CPA) at the top of the ziggurat and looked out over the cradle of civilizations. This was the heart of ancient Mesopotamia, part of the rich alluvial plain between the Tigris and Euphrates rivers that was once one of the most fertile farmlands in the world. Now all of that lushness was gone. The empty brown expanse stretched for miles to the horizon. From many vantage points, we did not seem to be in the middle of the ancient Fertile Crescent, possibly very near the site of the Garden of Eden, but rather at the end of the earth, or on the moon. The barrenness and decay symbolized the fate of Iraq itself, a once-rich country now in ruins, sapped of life and prosperity.

Yet, as I looked around more carefully in the distance, I could see on each side of Borsippa a long faint trail of green: some rows of date palms and, here and there, a field of crops. Perhaps it was supplied with water from an underground river, perhaps by irrigation. But the fertility, the possibility, the hope had not been fully drained from this land. And that, I felt, was true for Iraq as well. That is what my colleagues and I were finding as we met with Iraqis, heard their stories, felt their aspirations, and assisted their organizations. The social soil of this land, traumatized by the blood of hundreds of thousands of martyrs slaughtered by Saddam and killed in his pointless wars, had not been turned irretrievably to desert. It could be irrigated and brought back.

★

A few miles from Borsippa, midway between the cities of Hilla and Najaf in the Shiite heartland of Iraq, lies the town of al-Kifl (Arabic for Ezekiel). We had visited there on the way to Borsippa to fulfill a promise I had made to myself, and to the mayor of the town, a leader of the Bedouin Bani Hasan (Sons of Hasan) tribe. He had implored me, on a visit to Hilla two months earlier, to come see his town and its proudest historical site, the Shrine of the Prophet Ezekiel and His Six Companions. According to the chronology in the Old Testament, Ezekiel preached to his fellow Jews during the Babylonian captivity, from 593 B.C. to 563 B.C. This region of Babylon was the oldest area of continuous Jewish settlement in the world, producing some of the most sacred texts of Judaism, including the Talmud and parts of the Torah. For 2,500 years, Jews lived side by side here with Arabs, Persians, and other peoples in a cultural mosaic. Then, upon the establishment of the state of Israel in 1948, Jews were expelled across the Arab world, and virtually all of Iraq's 100,000-plus Jews left the country in airlifts.[2] My guide throughout the day was a brilliant forty-six-year-old American diplomat named Michael Gfoeller, who was the regional coordinator of all CPA reconstruction efforts for the six provinces of the South Central region, and a man deeply knowledgeable about the language, culture, and history of the region. He explained to me that until 1948, the Jewish synagogue at the shrine in al-Kifl had been the oldest in the world in continuous use.

Al-Kifl's mayor, Sheikh Ahmad Khabut al-Abbasi Bani Hasan, led us through the town's dusty streets, through the thousand-year-old covered Market of David (Suq Da'ud), with its ancient brick arches and vaults, and into an open area full of dirt and debris (some of it damaged from the war). Dominating the landscape was an intricately decorated minaret dating back to the tenth or eleventh century, its six-story height leaning slightly from the weight of time. Here once stood an Islamic

university, now in ruins. Just beyond the mosque was a courtyard that
had been the site of a caravanserai, where, over a thousand years ago,
the caravans had stopped for food and supplies, mingling Arab and Jew
in commerce. Rising above the decaying brick walls, at the corner of
the yard opposite the minaret, was a ziggurat-like structure, several stories high atop an ancient building. This pyramidal tower had been the
house of the rabbi; beside it stand the ancient synagogue, library, and
tombs, all connected through passageways.

Removing our shoes, we were led through the green wooden door
of the complex by Sheikh Ahmad, who was also guardian of the Shrine
of Ezekiel. He explained that his forefathers in the Bani Hasan tribe
had promised the Jews when they fled in 1948 that they would guard
and preserve the synagogue until the Jews returned. According to
Sheikh Ahmad, the Babylonian Talmud was composed in this synagogue. For him, the juxtaposition of the ruined Islamic university and
Jewish synagogue signifies the vanished alliance between Jews and
Arabs in Iraq, which he hopes will one day be restored. To this day, the
tribe still refers to the complex as the Jewish temple, and awaits the return of the Jews. "Can you bring the Jews back?" the mayor asked
Gfoeller. "They are as Iraqi and Arab as I am. We have been keeping
the temple for them for the past fifty-five years." At one point, it is believed, there were half a million Jews in Iraq; in ancient times, Babylon
was probably home to as many Jews as were the lands that now comprise Israel and Palestine.

The temple and tomb complex is dark and worn, but some of the ancient Hebrew writing on the walls and above the arched passageways is
discernible, and it is still possible to imagine the splendor of this small
but historically precious temple, with its vaulted ceiling, elaborate wall
designs, multiple altars, and stone prayer benches. The ancient
Torahs—dating back hundreds of years—are now gone, seized, with all
the ancient manuscripts of the library, by Saddam Hussein in 1979.
One of the Torahs, says the tribe, had been written by Ezekiel himself,
and the Jews of the town would parade with it in ceremonial pro-
cessions during holidays. Before 1948, every year on the holiday of
Shavuot, thousands of Jews from Baghdad and elsewhere made a pil-

grimage to the shrine. Proceeding through the rooms, one arrives finally at a large crypt containing the stone tombs, covered in wood and fabric and surrounded by beautiful carpets, of Ezekiel and his companions. At the base of the wooden cover is a small opening, where, kneeling to the ground, one can see the actual stone tomb of Ezekiel.

Sheikh Ahmad, the guardian of the shrine, explained that he would like to open up the site to religious tourists, but it would require several million dollars to restore the ancient temple and mosque complexes to the point where they could handle long lines of visitors. In fact, that is not the biggest obstacle. Militant Shiite militias want to seize control of the complex, and the area is now too insecure. The militia leaders had threatened the sheikh with death; he had threatened them back. As Gfoeller explained to me, "The sheikh is a quiet, polite man, until he is pushed too far." Like his fellow tribesmen, he knows, and is prepared for, the dangers he confronts. The sheikh provided several armed guards for this local tour, and we had our own as well. Saddam's regime had executed his father and brother some two decades earlier, using one of its favorite, most horrific methods—injection of acid into the cranial cavity.

Only a few weeks prior to our visit, on February 5, another mass grave had been discovered near the town, dating back from the Shiite intifada (uprising) following the Gulf War, in 1991. That April, Saddam's regime systematically slaughtered hundreds of thousands of Iraqi Shiites and buried them in mass graves, while the United States stood by. "They drove busloads of people in, they dug ditches with bulldozers, and then machine-gunned them in industrial fashion," Gfoeller said. "Others had their arms tied behind their back and were just buried alive. Many of the bodies we saw in these mass graves had no obvious bullet wounds." The killing and terror were protracted. Whole families were murdered when they went to the fresh sites of mass graves, looking for their relatives. By the time I visited Hilla and al-Kifl at the end of March, 280 mass graves had been discovered. One of the leaders of the uprising lost thirty-six family members to the slaughter. Virtually no family in the region was left untouched by the violence. So many Shiite men were executed during this period, or died as cannon fodder during the war Saddam recklessly launched with Iran during the 1980s, that in many Shiite communities today, few men in their forties remain, and the ratio of women to men is now something like 60 to 40. Says Gfoeller, "Ask a group of people in this region, 'How many of you lost a family member in the April 1991 uprising?' and there are very few hands that do not go up."

★

During the time I spent in Iraq working for the Coalition Provisional Authority, in the early months of 2004, I was often startled by the contradictions. How could such a rich country have become so impoverished? How could the cradle of civilization, a country historically of great culture and learning, have descended into such horror and misery? Why did the United States topple Saddam's regime in 2003, on the basis of dubious evidence that he threatened America's national security, and not twelve years earlier, when he was actively engaged in the mass murder of his own people, a crime against humanity? Was it possible that we could help this country, so steeped in tyranny and bereft of the experience of freedom, become a democracy?

It was the last question—which I considered a moral imperative—that had drawn me to Iraq with equal measure of hesitation and conviction after I received a call asking for my assistance. By the autumn of 2003, the war was over. The United States and its coalition partners had been occupying Iraq for more than half a year. American soldiers and civilians—as well as a much larger number of Iraqis—were dying in the effort to rebuild the country politically, economically, and socially. I had opposed going to war, but I supported building the peace. Having conquered Iraq, we had an obligation to help reconstruct it as a democratic, prosperous, and decent place. And now that the whole world was watching and the jihadists were pouring in, the fate of Iraq had become vital to our national security to a degree well beyond what was true before the war.

As I traveled to al-Kifl and Borsippa on the afternoon of March 31— what would prove to be my first and only tourism in Iraq—I did not know that the American occupation of Iraq was slipping into a new phase of crisis and violence that it would never overcome. On the same day, four American contractors were ambushed and murdered in Fallujah, their charred bodies hung from a bridge like hunting trophies. Within a few days, a full-blown insurgency would break out in the very Shiite heartland through which we had been touring. The ragtag Mahdi Army of the firebrand young Shiite cleric Muqtada al-Sadr seized the nearby cities of Najaf and Karbala, with their sacred Shiite shrines, challenging the authority of the occupation and the credibility of its transition program.

None of this should have come as a surprise. We had had plenty of warning signs. CPA officials had been pleading for months for action against Sadr, and against other militias as well. That very morning, I had visited one of Sadr's most bitter and effective enemies, a moderate Shiite cleric, Sayyid Farqad al-Qizwini. ("Sayyid" is a term of honor signifying a direct descendant of the Prophet Muhammad.) With his unruly black beard, flowing clerical garb, and retinue of religious followers, Qizwini could easily be mistaken for just another radical Shiite mullah. However, he was preaching the compatibility of Islam and democracy—indeed, the *necessity* of democracy for Islam. In the former presidential mosque in Hilla—a majestic, towering structure of stone and marble where Saddam had never allowed the impoverished Shiite masses of this ancient region to pray—Qizwini had established a university with American assistance after the Gulf War. In front of it, he built a moving artistic tribute to the martyrs of the 1991 uprising. His students—men and women—learn not just about Islam but about all the world's great religions, and the principles of democracy as well. In a section of the sprawling mosque complex, a dozen Iraqi linguists translate a variety of works on democracy into Arabic. In another, a new radio station broadcasts teachings about democracy.

On the grounds behind the mosque, I saw the fruits of millions of dollars in U.S. assistance that were going to construct a regional democracy center, men's and women's dormitories, and a cafeteria. Dedicated earlier that month, with a plaque quoting President John F. Kennedy ("ask not what your country can do for you . . ."), the gleaming new center had been built in a matter of months by Iraqi contractors who had worked with an intensity that put the big American corporations to shame. Boasting a conference room, two state-of-the-art computer rooms with thirty-six computers, more than a dozen offices, and a two-hundred-seat auditorium, along with the dormitories, the center would enable Iraqis throughout the region to receive intensive training in the ideas, values, and techniques of democracy.

On a rough woven mat, under a huge tented *mudheef* (the traditional reed-frame guesthouse), my colleagues and I sat that morning with Sayyid Qizwini on the roof of his mosque and university while he poured out his concerns. In the days before our visit, Muqtada al-Sadr's organization had been widely distributing a leaflet denouncing Qizwini and ten of his leading supporters as "pigs and dogs" who had defiled Islam and needed to be "stopped and silenced." Qizwini had been living under the threat of assassination for months, but now this pseudo-religious call for his murder had raised the stakes. The menace of radical, Iranian-backed armed militias—not only Sadr's Mahdi Army but the Badr Corps of the Supreme Council for the Islamic Revolution in Iraq (SCIRI), which had been based in Iran until Saddam's overthrow; the militia of another Islamist party, Da'wa; Hizbollah; and many smaller groups and factions—had been mounting rapidly through the early months of 2004, even as the leaders of their sponsoring political parties were sitting in Baghdad on the Iraqi Governing Council, signing democratic declarations and professing sweet moderation and restraint to the Americans.

The threat was in fact quite proximate. On the way to Qizwini's university, our armored SUV had passed by a very different center of activity. In the courtyard of a nondescript building, the followers of Muqtada al-Sadr were training for their new war in Iraq. There, in virtually open view of the occupation authorities, they learned how to handle firearms, assemble bombs, and kill infidels. Like Qizwini, Sadr had a fiery black beard and an ability to organize and move the masses. And his father, like Qizwini's, had been murdered by Saddam's regime during the 1990s, along with two brothers and an uncle. But there the resemblance ended. Saddam had meant to kill Muqtada's father, who had a wide following. The car bomb that killed Qizwini's father had been meant for Qizwini himself, a leader in the underground resistance.

Qizwini found his vision expressed in these words, which he had seen on a wall of the Jefferson Memorial, in Washington: "I have sworn upon the altar of God eternal hostility against every form of tyranny over the mind of man." Sadr's vision was of a new, religious tyranny, an Iranian-style Islamist dictatorship in which he would have the ultimate power. Qizwini had been building a peaceful movement of farmers, tribal sheikhs, moderate Islamic clerics, women's-rights advocates, and urban professionals called the Iraqi Democratic Gathering, while Sadr had been using massive inflows of Iranian money and arms to mobilize an army of marginalized, angry young men.

As we sat under the *mudheef* on March 31, Qizwini implored the United States to act immediately. "These militias will turn Iraq into a dark age of bloodletting if they are not stopped soon. Any decision to dissolve the militias should be implemented in the next week." At that moment, I thought Qizwini's statement a bit hyperbolic in its urgency. For several weeks, I had been coming to a similar conclusion about the danger of the militias and the need for the Coalition to act energetically, comprehensively, and soon. But I did not realize that the dam was just about to burst, and that this dramatic day would essentially mark the end of my involvement with the American occupation.

1

THE CALL

When the call came on Tuesday, November 11, 2003, I was in Mexico, speaking at the University of the Americas about the global spread of democracy. The sweet, soft, southern drawl of the assistant to the president's national security adviser informed my office answering machine that Dr. Condoleezza Rice wanted to speak with me, and asked me to please return the call as soon as possible. There followed two more calls, increasingly urgent in tone. The last came from the office of my friend Coit Blacker, who had been one of Rice's closest friends at Stanford and was now the director of Stanford's Institute for International Studies. If Rice was calling her old pal Blacker to try to find out where I was, this was a serious matter.

I retrieved the three messages as soon as I landed in Denver the following night, to participate in a three-day dialogue on U.S.–China relations. I was darting from one continent to another, with a trip to Taiwan planned for the following month. The Middle East was not on my travel agenda, but Iraq had been on my mind. With my colleagues at the National Endowment for Democracy, I had organized a strategy session in Washington the previous Friday to consider how we might offer support and technical advice on the process of drafting a democratic constitution for Iraq. The day before that, I had been in attendance when President George W. Bush marked the twentieth anniversary of the NED with an eloquent speech advancing "a forward strategy of freedom in the Middle East." To vigorous, emotional applause, the president had declared, "The establishment of a free Iraq at the heart of the Middle East will be a watershed event in the global democratic revolution."

I was all for the effort to build a free Iraq, and I wanted to help—but not *in* Iraq. I had been reading and watching the news, which was filled with the steady drumbeat of violence, insurgency, and troubles. Seven months after the overthrow of Saddam Hussein and the end of major combat, the violence in Iraq seemed "to be growing in intensity and effectiveness, rendering all plans uncertain,"[1] according to an article that week in the *New York Times*. In fact, the American military commander in Iraq, Lieutenant General Ricardo Sanchez, had acknowledged in early October that the resistance was becoming more dangerous and that it would continue to worsen. A public opinion poll that month found that two-thirds of Iraqis regarded the U.S.-led coalition as "occupying powers," while only 15 percent viewed them as "liberating forces."[2] November 2 had been the deadliest day for Americans since the inception of Operation Iraqi Freedom on March 19, as sixteen American soldiers were killed when a helicopter came under missile attack outside Fallujah. By then, more American soldiers had died in the postwar occupation than in the six-week war itself.

It was not only American soldiers who were being attacked. On October 26, the al-Rashid Hotel, in the supposedly impregnable Green Zone, which headquartered the American occupation, was hit by rocket fire while Deputy Secretary of Defense Paul Wolfowitz was staying there. Wolfowitz escaped uninjured, but a senior U.S. Army officer was killed and seventeen people were wounded in a "brazen strike at the core of the U.S. presence in Iraq."[3] The next day, the Baghdad offices of the International Committee of the Red Cross were attacked, killing more than a dozen people. The strikes were part of a coordinated series of attacks by suicide bombers in Baghdad, on the first day of the Muslim holy month of Ramadan, that killed at least thirty-four people and wounded more than two hundred. The following day the deputy mayor of Baghdad was murdered, and members of the U.S.-appointed Iraqi

Governing Council criticized America's failure to achieve security in Iraq. On November 1, the last of the UN international staff pulled out of Baghdad; most of its members had been withdrawn earlier, following a massive truck-bomb attack on August 19 that had killed 22 people and injured more than 150. On November 8, the Red Cross announced that it would close its Baghdad and Basra offices because of the increasing violence.

With the bloodshed rising and the plans for political transition in Iraq floundering, Ambassador L. Paul Bremer III, the Administrator of the Coalition Provisional Authority—in essence, the American occupation in Iraq—flew back to Washington on November 11 for urgent consultations with the senior Bush administration national security team, and with the president himself. As I returned to the United States on November 12, the *Washington Post* was reporting that these consultations were "to save the troubled political transition in Iraq by accelerating the hand-over of power."[4]

Thus I had a sinking feeling when I listened, in succession, to the three phone messages, with their rising tone of urgency. I had known Condi Rice for nearly twenty years, and we had become academic colleagues and friends at Stanford. Despite our differences in party affiliation and in our views of the world, we liked and respected each other, and we were able to laugh about our political differences. Rice had a way of engaging her more liberal friends in the academy, and during her Stanford years she impressed her friends and colleagues with her intellect, reason, moderation, open-mindedness, and good humor. She was also a stunningly effective and popular teacher. I had seen her occasionally in Washington since she became the president's national security adviser in 2001. But I didn't think the call was to chat about the old days at Stanford. By the time I was able to return her call, it was well past 9 P.M. in Washington, and there was no answer. As I put away my cell phone, I issued a silent prayer, "Lord, please don't let her ask me to go to Iraq."

★

Early the next morning, I tried again and was put through almost immediately to Rice. As it turned out, my hotel was a stone's throw from her alma mater, Denver University, where she had earned her B.A. and her Ph.D., inspired and tutored by one of the leading specialists on the politics of the Communist world, Josef Korbel—Madeleine Albright's father.

We exchanged a few pleasantries. "You wouldn't believe this," I said, "but I'm talking to you from your alma mater in Denver."

She laughed heartily. "Say hello to them for me," she answered.

Then she turned more serious. The U.S.-led effort to bring democracy to Iraq was about to take a new turn. On November 15, a more concrete, faster-paced plan for political transition would be announced. It would begin with the drafting of an interim constitution, and the administration felt it was vital that the document be as liberal and democratic as possible. Then the plan would move on to the holding of indirect elections for a transitional parliament, and a handover of governing authority on June 30, 2004. The White House needed an expert on democratic development to go to Iraq and advise on the political transition. Could I go?

Her question knocked my breath out. It was what I had anticipated since the previous night—and dreaded. I was honored by her invitation. I felt a call and a certain obligation. But I kept thinking about the violence, the insecurity, the danger, the many mistakes and miscalculations we had already made, and the way my family and friends would react. I wanted time to think about it. I almost hoped the request would just quietly slip away.

"How much time do I have to decide?" I asked her.

She laughed again, in a friendly, joking way—but she wasn't entirely kidding. "Oh, a few minutes."

I knew the situation was urgent. The American occupation of Iraq—and Iraq's prospect for any kind of democratic postwar order—was reaching a turning point. There were over 100,000 Americans in Iraq, most of them military, taking risks and making sacrifices far greater than anything that was being asked of me. I knew the situation in Iraq was difficult, that things were going much worse than the advocates of the war had expected. But I did not think it was hopeless. Having studied, observed, and assisted democracy-building efforts in some twenty countries over the previous two decades, I felt I could make a contribution. Yet I also felt that the task was daunting, that the odds were long, and that we had already made a number of profound mistakes in Iraq.

In fact, I had opposed going to war in early 2003, arguing in a published essay that the greater danger to the United States at the time was not Saddam's programs to develop weapons of mass destruction but "our own imperial overreach and the global wave of anti-Americanism that it is already provoking." I had favored, instead, "a patient and consultative process of international coalition building," using "the legitimacy of the United Nations." Since there was not yet compelling evidence that Saddam had flouted his obligations to disarm, I thought the UN-sponsored weapons inspections should continue until we could demonstrate more convincingly that he was lying to the international community. "We will pay a heavy price," I warned, "if we decide unilaterally, without convincing evidence, that he is in 'material breach' and then launch a war that the U.N. Security Council has not authorized and that our most important allies in Europe and the Middle East do not support." In the same essay, I expressed concern about America's plans to administer Iraq as an occupied territory, as General Douglas MacArthur had done in Japan: "An extended, unilateral American military occupation of Iraq would legitimize widespread regional defiance. American soldiers would quickly turn from liberators to occupiers and come under frequent attack from snipers and terrorists." I urged, instead, the rapid construction of an interim Iraqi government "through a transparent and legitimate process of dialogue, working alongside an international coalition that would include the United States but not necessarily be led by it."[5] On both the war and the postwar, the Bush administration pursued policies very different from what I had favored.

By November, however, I was conflicted. I still thought the war had been a strategic miscalculation, but the postwar imperative seemed obvious: to build a decent, lawful, and democratic political order in Iraq. I believed that if we failed there, Iraq would become what it had not been before the war: a haven for international terrorism and possibly a direct threat to America's national security. Part of me responded to this imperative from a sense of duty and conviction. Part of me was excited by the challenge. Part of me was still critical of the Bush administration's arrogant, unilateral approach. And part of me was terrified.

Sucking in my fears, reservations, and insecurities, I told Rice, "Okay, I'll do it."

Early the next morning, Ambassador Bremer called me in Vail, Colorado. It was the first time I had talked to him, and the conversation left me deeply impressed. He had a rich, resonant voice (already familiar to me from his many television interviews), and he spoke with conviction and confidence. He explained that the first priority in the new plan would be to draft an interim constitution, although it would be called a "fundamental law." This document would lay down the structure and principles of the transitional government that would rule Iraq until a permanent constitution was written and a government elected under its rules. Bremer expanded upon what Rice had told me. The fundamental law would not only be a transitional document; it would also likely provide some basis for a permanent constitution. It was vital for the future of democracy in Iraq that this law specify as many principles of democracy as possible, particularly regarding individual rights, the separation of powers, and federalism. The drafting would be a fairly quick process, with the hoped-for completion date of February 1, 2004. Already, Bremer was pressing the Iraqi Governing Council to appoint a committee to draft the document. I would be heavily engaged in consulting on the drafting. But the American role, he stressed, was to be advisory.

"We need to let the Iraqis take the lead—visibly," Bremer said. "It has to be their document." Under the new plan, a constituent assembly was to be elected early in 2005 to draft the permanent constitution. "We have to think about how much international help we want to and can give them." Then he added something that would stick in my mind for a long time: "Our maximum ability to influence the course of events in Iraq is now. We will be gone in two years."

He and I then talked about timing and logistics. I told him his proposal was very sudden, and I needed a couple of weeks to get ready. He said it would be fine if I could get out there after Thanksgiving. I also said that I was willing to consult for as long as necessary but that I could not drop all my other obligations on such short notice. It was not so much my university duties at Stanford; most of those could be deferred. But I had ongoing commitments as coeditor of the *Journal of Democracy* and codirector of the National Endowment for Democracy's studies center in Washington. So we agreed that I would commute between Stanford and Baghdad over the coming months, spending significant blocks of time in Baghdad between December and June in a consulting role.

Unfortunately, December came and went, as I fell into a bewildering maze of painfully slow processing and conflicting messages from the bureaucracy at the Pentagon. In Baghdad, Bremer's administrative deputy, Ambassador Patrick Kennedy, had moved on the appointment rapidly, but once it got to the Washington side, things slowed to a tortoise-like pace. I had hoped to be on a plane to Kuwait by the end of November, but it was not until December 2 that I got the "deployment guide" with the necessary "request for country clearance" that I had to fill out. Then I was to experience the same waiting and confusion that I would later find most of my CPA colleagues in Baghdad had also had to endure. With a military-style, can-do spirit, the deployment guide cheerfully advised:

> Our team members overseas badly need your skills and abilities to get this difficult mission accomplished, and they needed you there *"yesterday!"* If you follow the procedures in this booklet, most of your questions will be addressed and the road to Iraq will be faster and smoother.

I followed everything literally, but the road was neither fast nor smooth. First I was told that I needed to go to Fort Bliss, Texas, or Fort Belvoir, Virginia, to be trained and equipped. Then, later, it turned out I did not need to go. I needed a visa to enter to Kuwait. Then I did not need a visa. (In the end, all I would need to get through Kuwait was a certain type of government photo ID that would become my most precious piece of plastic in Iraq.)

On paper, the bureaucracy seemed to have thought of everything. The deployment guide finished with a handy "suggested packing list," one for women and one for men. For men, the clothing list read:

- 1 or more business suits, depending on your scope of duties
- 5 pairs of cotton pants (Dockers or jeans) and a belt

- 5 light shirts, with sleeves
- 5 pair, or more, of athletic socks (to wear with your boots)
- 1 or 2 pairs of casual shoes (walking shoes, sandals)
- 1 pair of shower shoes/clogs
- 2 pair of pajamas (sleep wear) and robe
- Light jacket or coat
- Hat or cap; for sun protection
- Scarf for blowing sand protection
- Sufficient number of washable undergarments (at least 5-day supply)
- Exercise clothing and tennis shoes, swimsuit optional

The list of recommended personal items was twice as long and included such things as moisturizers, a sewing kit, and Ziplock-type baggies. I quickly went to work rounding up a duffel bag, backpack, sunscreen, towels, sheets, caps, medications, "washable undergarments," and so on. I decided to forgo the recommended "butt pack." And then I continued to e-mail and wait, and e-mail and wait again. Finally, a colleague in Washington shared my frustration with a member of Bremer's staff in Baghdad, who got hold of Rice's office, and in early December, things began to move, but not fast enough to get me there much before Christmas. By then, much of the Baghdad CPA office would be back in the United States on staggered leaves, for some badly needed rest and reunion with families. We revised my departure date to January 3, 2004.

★

When I told my family members, friends, colleagues, and students that I was going to Iraq to advise on the transition, I encountered a variety of reactions. Several people were instantly and completely supportive. To my great surprise, some of the most enthusiastic were my students at Stanford, who were awed by the challenge and moved by the opportunity, even if they personally opposed the war. Two students asked me, in all seriousness, "Can I go with you?" Some friends and relatives were torn but understanding. Some were worried but accepting. Some were truly scared for my safety and wondered why I had to be the one to go.

Occasionally, I met an explosion of anger and fear, as in: "Are you f——ing crazy? Have you lost your mind? They have totally f——ed up the situation over there and now they are asking you, who didn't even support the war, to rescue them and save the president's ass? Call her back and tell her you can't go!"

Once I said yes to Condoleezza Rice, I never questioned my decision—not before my departure, not when I was in Iraq, and not since then. But I knew that it was going to be a formidable challenge to build a democracy in Iraq, and the effort was swimming against mighty currents of history, culture, and politics.

As someone who had studied the conditions for democracy for my entire academic career, I was deeply sobered by the difficulty of the mission. Earlier in the year, when the war was under way, I had written:

> It is possible—just possible—that Iraq could gradually develop into a democracy, but the task is huge and the odds are long against it. Only a frank recognition of the obstacles and dangers, and a sober reflection on the lessons of post-conflict reconstruction, can make a democratic transformation possible. It will require a prolonged and internationalized engagement with Iraq, costing billions of dollars over a number of years. We must not repeat the mistakes of our post-war engagement with Afghanistan, which has been ad hoc, haphazard, inadequately funded, tardy in reconstruction, and utterly unwilling to deploy and utilize the military force necessary to secure the new political order.[6]

Over the preceding few decades, scholars had built up a huge body of knowledge and research on the conditions that foster stable democracy. In its early form, this literature emphasized the need for economic development; democracy was much more likely to emerge and become stable where there was reasonable prosperity, limited inequality, a strong middle class, high levels of literacy and education, a productive market economy, and a vigorous civil society. Indeed, the level of a country's economic development had proved to be one of the best predictors of durable democracy. Yet in recent years, the pattern changed somewhat. Beginning in 1974, a new wave of democratic expansion began to sweep the world, and the proportion of the world's states that were democracies climbed dramatically, from a little over one-quarter in that year to about 60 percent in 1994.[7] Democracy expanded to encompass many more poor, troubled countries in Africa, Asia, Latin America, and the former Communist states that did not have the classic "conditions for democracy." These trends raised the prospect that democracy could emerge where the social scientists would least expect it. After all, if democracy could take root in a dirt-poor nation like Mali—a country in the harsh Sahelian region of Africa, in which the majority of adults are illiterate and live in dire poverty, and the life expectancy is forty-four years—then why could it not emerge just about anywhere?[8] Indeed, Mali was one of a number of predominantly Muslim states demonstrating some sustained experience with democracy in this period. Just as Catholicism and Confucianism had proved not to be the obstacles to democracy they were once assumed to be, so a growing amount of political experience and careful argument was suggesting that Islam and democracy could also be compatible.[9]

And yet it was not simply its level of economic development and the structure of its society that made Iraq a challenging case. It was the trajectory of the country's subjugation and decline over the past half century. Almost everything seemed to conspire against the prospects for a viable democracy. Although Iraq had a tradition of liberal thought, which thrived in exile among a network of Iraqis who had advocated and strategized passionately for a free country, the nation was coming out of a long period of brutal dictatorship. Iraq's economy and society had been devastated by forty-five years of authoritarian rule and, in particular, by the last twenty-four years of murder, plunder, and terror under Saddam Hussein. The dictator had plunged his country into two devastating, needless wars (with Iran in 1980–88, and with the United States in 1991), which had left some 150,000 Iraqis dead, a similar number captured, and more than a quarter of a million wounded. Dictatorship, war, international sanctions, and steady economic decline had driven millions of Iraqis into exile and had devastated the middle class; annual per capita income had fallen by well over half to about $1,000; educational and health levels had declined sharply; child mortality rates had increased several times over; infrastructure had deteriorated; and the country had piled up a staggering foreign debt, estimated at $200 billion. More than 40 percent of Iraqi adults were illiterate, and the population was very young (40 percent were under age fifteen) and growing rapidly. A young, burgeoning, increasingly urban population, in the context of pervasive joblessness and disruption of services, meant that postwar governance would confront a boiling cauldron of expectations that would be difficult to fulfill.

Worse, the effort to bring democracy to Iraq was unfolding in a hostile regional environment. When the Berlin Wall came crashing down in 1989, the former Communist states, in contrast, found a welcoming, supportive group of democratic neighbors in the West. Indeed, the desire to join an expanding European Union became one of the most powerful incentives for countries, from the Czech Republic to the Baltic states, to institutionalize democracy and the rule of law. On the other side of the globe, as democracy spread to the Philippines, Korea, and Taiwan in the late 1980s, the richest country in the region, Japan, was already a consolidated, liberal democracy. In Latin America and Africa as well, democratization took place in the 1980s and 1990s in areas where some democracies already existed, and a number of countries were moving, more or less simultaneously, toward democratic rule. In the Middle East in 2003, there were only two democracies among the nineteen states, and those two—Turkey and Israel—were culturally distinct and distrusted by most Iraqis, incapable of serving as a model or bulwark for Iraqi democratization. The sixteen Arab states of the Middle East constituted the only major cultural and regional group in the world that did not have a single democratic government. Indeed, three of Iraq's neighbors—Syria, Iran, and Saudi Arabia—were highly authoritarian states (despite the veneer of elections in Iran) that would feel threatened by a democratization process in Iraq and could be expected to sabotage it in one way or another.

Iraq was also a deeply divided society, and some even questioned whether it could be called a nation. To begin with, it was not entirely an Arab land; about one in five Iraqis were Kurds, most of whom shared with another fifth of the Iraqi population the religion of Sunni Islam but who had their own language, culture, national identity, and aspirations.[10] The Iraqi Kurds had been subject to violence and discrimination, most brutally under Saddam, who expelled them from their homes in the hundreds of thousands and then bombed them with poison gas, kidnapped, tortured, and murdered them during the notorious *Anfal* (spoils) campaign of the late 1980s.[11] Since the end of the Gulf War, in 1991, the Kurds had enjoyed political autonomy from Baghdad, under the shield of American military protection, and despite tensions and rivalries within the Kurdish community, they had conducted democratic elections; constructed representative government; established two universities and a vibrant, pluralistic press; and enjoyed more freedom, dignity, and protection than at any other time in their modern history. As a consequence, by 2003 most Iraqi Kurds did not think of themselves as Iraqis and preferred to formalize the independence they had effectively enjoyed for more than a decade. By then, in the words of the American diplomat Peter W. Galbraith, "For the older generation, Iraq [was] a bad memory, while a younger generation . . . [had] no sense of being Iraqi."[12]

The Kurds were not the only aggrieved identity group in Iraq. So were the much smaller minorities of Turkoman and Christians, along with the Arab Shiites, who made up an estimated 60 percent of the Iraqi population. Since the time of the founding of the modern Iraqi state in the 1920s, the Shiites had been marginalized and victimized, as the Arab Sunni minority monopolized power and wealth. Under Saddam's rule, the Shiites lived with a sense of ongoing subjugation and persecution. Basra and other southern, predominantly Shiite cities had suffered the brunt of physical destruction during the Iran–Iraq war, and had fared poorly (to the point of destitution and humiliation) in the distribution of development benefits relative to the Sunni center of the country—despite the fact that most of the country's oil wealth lay in the south. In response to a Shiite uprising after the Gulf War, Saddam had assaulted the southern marshes and had had them drained, driving a quarter of a million Shiite Arabs from their homes and wreaking an ecological catastrophe. The Shiites had also seen many of their religious and political leaders tortured or assassinated because of their opposition to Saddam.

Adding to the gloomy picture was the predominance of oil in the Iraqi economy, a factor that in other developing countries has proved to be more of a curse than a blessing, severely distorting their financial and political systems.[13] Where oil dominates the economy, ambitious individuals seek to benefit from the massive flow of money pouring into state coffers; the easiest way to capture this wealth has been to corner political power and, in essence, to steal the funds. Governments in oil states have tended toward staggering excess and waste, as the oil revenues are not invested to create a diversified economy and a productive, educated workforce capable of sustaining genuine development—and democracy. As a classic petro-state, with one of the world's largest proven reserves of oil, a tradition of corruption, and few other sources of foreign exchange, postwar Iraq would be likely to suffer these problems in spades.

Moreover, Iraq confronted the particular difficulties that afflict states that have collapsed after war or long periods of political decay. In order to have a democratic state, a country must first have a state. Where the state has broken down entirely, its authority and capacity must be reconstructed if competitive elections and basic freedoms are to be feasible. Rebuilding the state is typically a slow process that requires an extended transitional period of rule by—or with the extensive support of—the international community. A RAND Corporation study reviewing the U.S. role in such nation-building efforts since World War II found that such enterprises have succeeded only with enormous investments of labor, money, and time—five years at a minimum.[14]

History imposed further heavy burdens. How would Iraqis view an effort to implant democracy under the aegis of an American occupation, especially one in which Britain, the former colonial ruler, would play a significant role? The proud, nationalistic Iraqis would surely not welcome a renewed occupation, and certainly not by its onetime colonizer. There were also problems with the United States, which was distrusted and resented by most Arab Iraqis for its longtime support of Israel to a degree they felt was contemptuous of Palestinian and broader Arab rights and sensitivities. Beyond this, the Shiites in Iraq were embittered by the failure of the United States to come to their aid when they rose up after the Gulf War—partly at the urging of President George H. W. Bush himself—in an effort to overthrow Saddam. This left many (if not most) Shiites feeling that the United States could not be trusted, while the Sunnis now feared a U.S. effort to strip them of their power and privilege.

Finally, Iraq had had no prior experience of democracy as a system of government, in which the people can select their leaders and hold them accountable in regular, free, and fair elections. However, some fragments of democratic institutions and practices had been put in place under British colonial rule and had developed over the subsequent three decades. In 1924, the Iraqi Constituent Assembly adopted a constitution that stood for more than thirty years, providing for an elected parliament under a monarchy, some political competition and opposition, and some means for the political integration of, and cooperation among, Iraq's diverse ethnic and communal groups. A pluralistic press with a "tradition of questioning and criticizing" the government had also emerged during this period, even amid efforts at censorship.[15]

Weighing the social, political, economic, and historical conditions that Iraq confronted—and which America was to face in Iraq—as well as the Iraqi people's strong feelings of nationalism, I had worried, back in March 2003, about the daunting challenge of reconstructing Iraq as a democracy—and the likelihood that we would fail if we did not resist what I called "the imperial temptation in the triumphalist, unilateralist visions of what America's role should be in the post–September 11 world."[16] Now, nine months later, the words of Rudyard Kipling's imperialist poem "The White Man's Burden" kept ringing in my mind:

> Take up the White Man's burden—
> No tawdry rule of kings,
> But toil of serf and sweeper—
> The tale of common things.
> The ports ye shall not enter,
> The roads ye shall not tread,
> Go make them with your living,
> And mark them with your dead!

As I prepared to leave for Iraq, I could not know how much of Kipling's dire vision I would see materialize during the journey that was about to begin.

2

IN SEARCH OF A PLAN

★

On November 11, 2003, as Ambassador Bremer flew back to Washington, senior White House officials indicated to reporters that President George W. Bush was dissatisfied with the pace of progress in Iraq. High-ranking British aides were likewise worried that Bremer's existing seven-point plan for transition—which seemed to involve an eighteen-month timetable for drafting a constitution, choosing an Iraqi government, and ending the American occupation—was "too slow and cumbersome."[1] In fact, the government of Prime Minister Tony Blair was "pressing the United States to hand over power to an Iraqi government within a year or risk a full-scale uprising against the military occupation."[2] The British—who brought a historical perspective to the experience of governing Iraq, having faced a Shiite rebellion against their colonial occupation in 1920—feared that the violent resistance would spread south from the Sunni Triangle to the majority Shiite section of the country, spelling doom for the occupation.

The anxiety was underscored by a Gallup poll of the Iraqi people conducted two months earlier. Iraqi suspicion of the American occupation was rife. Only 5 percent of Iraqis surveyed thought the United States had invaded Iraq "to assist the Iraqi people" and only 1 percent believed it was mainly to establish democracy in Iraq; almost half thought it was "to rob Iraq's oil." Iraqis seemed evenly divided about the seriousness of Washington's intentions to bring democracy to Iraq, but they were almost universally frustrated with the failures of security. Fully 94 percent of Iraqis said Baghdad was "a more dangerous place than before the invasion," and 86 percent said that they or a family member had recently feared going out at night for safety reasons.[3]

The pace of political transition needed to be speeded up. The Iraqi Governing Council had been dragging its feet on preparing "a timetable and program for the drafting of a new constitution for Iraq and for the holding of democratic elections under that constitution," which the UN Security Council had asked it to submit by December 15. Instead, leading members of the Governing Council were pressing, as they had been for months, for the appointment of a provisional government that they would lead. Some Shiite members, following the religious ruling of their spiritual leader, Grand Ayatollah Ali al-Sistani, were demanding that the members of any constitution-drafting body be directly chosen by the Iraqi people—a process the CPA was resisting out of concern that a free and fair election simply could not be organized anytime soon. An ineffectual body rife with political divisions and machinations, the Governing Council was the object of increasing frustration by CPA and administration officials, even as polls showed that three-quarters of Iraqis believed that their country was controlled by the CPA. Things were adrift.

Adding to the worries was the steadily worsening violence. On November 12, as Bremer was meeting with top Bush administration officials, including the president and Vice President Dick Cheney, a truck bomb destroyed the Italian military police compound in the southern city of Nasariyah, killing eighteen Italians and nine Iraqis, and injuring some eighty others. Moreover, a CIA report leaked to the press stated that a growing number of Iraqis, confident that the United States could be defeated and driven out of the country, were joining the insurgency.

On November 15, not long after he arrived back in Baghdad, Bremer announced an agreement between the CPA and the Governing Council that defined for the first time a detailed transition timetable, with specific steps and deadlines. The plan significantly accelerated the transfer of sovereignty back to the Iraqi people. In Bremer's initial plan, the occupation was to have concluded only at the end of the process of constitutional drafting and elections, which might stretch over eighteen months or longer. Now the Iraqis were to regain "full sovereignty" by June 30, 2004, less than eight months hence. Before that date, an interim constitution would be written and adopted by the Governing Council; an interim government would be chosen through a complex, indirect system of caucuses; and a constitutional assembly would be directly elected. After June 30, a permanent constitution would be drafted and approved by the elected assembly and ratified by popular referendum; elections would be held for a permanent government by the end of 2005.

The November 15 plan marked a promising turning point for the occupation. But the seven-month path leading up to it had been littered with mistakes and misjudgments that would dog the American presence in Iraq.

★

As has been documented in a number of excellent investigative reports, the United States invaded Iraq without a coherent, viable plan to win the peace. But the absence of a plan did not mean that no preparation had been done. State Department planning for a possible transition in a postwar Iraq had begun as early as October 2001, in what became known as the Future of Iraq Project. Directed by a savvy, energetic career officer, Thomas Warrick, the project drew together the disparate Iraqi exile organizations in a series of conferences, dialogues, drafting sessions, and ultimately seventeen working groups on key problems that would confront the postwar order in Iraq.

In November 2002, as part of that project, the Democratic Principles Working Group produced a report titled "The Transition to Democracy in Iraq." While not offering a coherent or finished blueprint for the postwar political order, it did produce a generally viable strategy for filling the vacuum of authority and launching a transition to democracy, or at least a transition to a considerably more representative, accountable, and responsible government than Iraq had known for many decades. What is striking, in retrospect, is the lack of any reference in the report to an extended political occupation of Iraq by the

United States or any other international actor. The overarching concern of the thirty-two Iraqi exiles who made up the working group was to establish an Iraqi transitional authority as soon as possible, and to define and strictly limit its scope of authority and its time in office.

The report recognized that a huge political and security vacuum would open up with the fall of the regime and that this vacuum would need to be filled immediately. Thus it recommended that an Iraqi transitional authority "be on the ground and capable of operating as soon as the [Saddam Hussein] regime begins to disintegrate."[4] This process would not entail a handover of power to some Iraqi strongman, anointed by the United States, but rather to a broad-based coalition (including an executive and a national assembly) elected from the roughly three million Iraqi expatriates and the roughly four million Kurds living relatively freely in Iraqi Kurdistan. For this authority to have even temporary legitimacy, the report argued, it would have to be elected from a "large and representative body of Iraqis convened" at a conference of the Iraqi opposition, outside the country and in advance of the war; it would have to pledge to expand its membership to include Iraqis inside the country once it took control in Baghdad (and identify a credible means by which this would be accomplished); it would have to be "visibly inclusive" of Iraq's social and political diversity; and it would have to limit its time in office to a maximum of two to three years. The envisaged transitional authority would act as both a provisional government (to be restrained as soon as possible by an independent judiciary) and a constitution-drafting body. But it would not begin the latter task until the national assembly elected from Iraqi exiles and Kurds had doubled in size to include an equivalent number of Iraqis elected or chosen from the remainder of the country.[5] The November 2002 report also emphasized the urgency of establishing legitimate governance from the ground up, and suggested that local elections (with international support, training, and monitoring) be held throughout Iraq within a year of the fall of Saddam's regime.

A number of U.S. government agencies had a variety of visions of how political authority would be reestablished in Iraq. Vice President Cheney and his office, and Pentagon neoconservatives like Deputy Secretary Wolfowitz, Undersecretary Douglas Feith, and Harold Rhode, a key figure in the Office of Special Plans under Feith, were looking to hand power over fairly quickly to Ahmed Chalabi, the best-known but also most controversial Iraqi exile opponent of Saddam's regime. Chalabi was the leader of the Iraqi National Congress, a darling of American neoconservatives, and a brilliant, dynamic, and voraciously ambitious politician. The CIA had its own favored Iraqi exile leader, Ayad Allawi, a former member of the Baath Party who had defected in the 1970s, survived an assassination attempt in London by Saddam's henchmen, and attempted to organize coup attempts to overthrow Saddam. Now he headed a group called the Iraqi National Accord. Chalabi and Allawi had been receiving large sums of money from the Pentagon and the CIA, respectively, for many years. By some rumors, the State Department favored yet another Iraqi exile, Adnan Pachachi, a secular nationalist and a sophisticated, liberal thinker who had served as Iraq's foreign minister and UN ambassador before the Baathists seized power in 1968. But key State Department figures also saw the need for a political process that would enable Iraqis to come together and define a process for choosing a broadly acceptable Iraqi interim government.

In the bitter, relentless infighting among U.S. government agencies in advance of the war, none of these preferences clearly prevailed. One Iraqi American who participated in some of the chaotic interagency discussions to plan Iraq's postwar political order recounted to me, "There was never any discussion of *how* the Pentagon would implement their plan, or anybody else's. There was never any dialogue on it. Each group had its own plan, but nothing ever got done or decided because of the infighting. Each plan had its good aspects, but the president needed to get behind one plan and say, 'This is going to be it.' He never did."

What the president did decide was to designate the Pentagon as the lead agency in charge of postwar Iraq, although many nongovernmental organizations and outside experts with long experience in reconstruction had been pushing to have that authority based in the State Department. "It was the first time since World War II that the State Department would not take charge of a post-conflict situation,"[6] the *New York Times* noted, and Secretary of Defense Donald Rumsfeld and his inner circle of civilian officials took the decision as a mandate for policy monopoly. To head the postwar American administration of

Iraq, Rumsfeld chose retired general Jay M. Garner, who had successfully commanded Operation Provide Comfort to assist the Kurds at the
end of the Gulf War in 1991. Garner began working from the Pentagon
in an operation that would eventually be named the Office of Reconstruction and Humanitarian Assistance, or ORHA.

By the time Garner was appointed, on January 20, 2003, the war was
less than two months away, and he began scrambling to put together
the core of some two hundred occupation officials he would bring to
Baghdad. One of the first people Garner sought out—naturally—was
the person who had directed the Future of Iraq Project, Tom Warrick.
But Garner later stated that he was ordered by Rumsfeld to remove
Warrick from his staff and to ignore the Future of Iraq Project.[7] According to the original conception of Garner's postwar administration
structure, the State Department was supposed to oversee civil administration, but Douglas Feith vetoed every nominee the State Department
put forward for that crucial role. By the time State could finally get its
nominee into the mix, the Pentagon had already filled the civil administration post with Feith's choice, his special assistant and former law
partner, Michael Mobbs. But lacking any appropriate experience for
ORHA's single most important function, Mobbs was not able to get a
new civil administration off the ground in Iraq.

Still scrambling to get someone from its ranks into ORHA's senior
leadership, the State Department contacted one of its top regional experts, Barbara Bodine, a former ambassador to Yemen who was a
diplomat-in-residence at the University of California, Santa Barbara.
Bodine flew to Washington in late February to meet Garner. He had as
yet no career diplomats on his senior team, no one with real expertise in
the region, and no one able to speak Arabic. Bodine filled all three of
those needs, but Garner asked her only two questions: Are you married? Do you have children? When she answered no to both, he said,
"Good. You are deployable."

Rumsfeld zealously opposed any role for career State Department
experts, whom he regarded as too soft for the hard job of remaking
Iraq, and whom his subordinates assumed (incorrectly) to be uniformly
dismissive of the prospects for democracy in Iraq. Initially, Rumsfeld
apparently did not know who Bodine was, but he and his senior staff

were nevertheless uninterested in her expertise. When Bodine briefed the defense secretary in mid-March, just before the war began, she explained the urgent need to figure out a way to make sure Iraqi civil servants got paid in the aftermath of the war, so that government services could continue and opposition could be preempted. The operating assumption had been that the Iraqi civil servants would be in their offices after the war, ready to work, and that the occupation would have a fully functioning Iraqi government within a matter of days. Rumsfeld insisted that it didn't matter whether Iraqi civil servants got paid. "They can wait two weeks or two months," he said. What mattered, he said, was that the American taxpayer wouldn't stand for the United States paying Iraqi civil servants. When someone suggested that there would be riots in the streets if the civil servants didn't get paid, Rumsfeld replied that this could be used as leverage to get the Europeans in to pick up the burden.

Deputy Secretary Wolfowitz pressed his own radical vision for Iraq. Why not redraw all the provincial and district boundaries? he suggested. Bodine told him, "Look at the road network. This is the way the roads go. This is the pattern that has evolved over centuries. This is how the Iraqis see themselves." The prospect of Western powers once again drawing lines in someone else's sand seemed to echo the debacle of the 1916 Sykes-Picot agreement, when France and Britain secretly agreed to carve up the Ottoman Empire into exclusive zones of influence (a French "blue area" and a British "red area"), an act of presumptuous imperialism that still rankled the Arab world. Bodine left her Pentagon meetings unnerved. "It was the second week of March, the war was about to begin, and we weren't ready," she later recalled. Meanwhile, the appointment of senior American advisers to oversee the Iraqi ministries was being held up for weeks, even after the end of the war, in the now all-too-familiar interagency turf wars. In mid-May, after only three weeks on the ground in Baghdad, Garner acknowledged his difficulties, in testimony to Congress: "This is an ad hoc operation, glued together over about four or five weeks' time." He added that his team "didn't really have enough time to plan."[8]

★

Garner thought the American occupation of Iraq should be brief and brisk, and he told reporters he was giving himself three months to complete the job of assembling an Iraqi interim authority.[9] This approach no doubt reflected Rumsfeld's desire to avoid an extended period of U.S. rule in Iraq. From the moment he arrived in Baghdad on April 21, Garner insisted that the United States would leave as soon as possible, that his contract ran out in August, and that he would be gone by then, along with the American occupation. The statements were well intentioned—to signal to the Iraqis that the United States did not plan to impose a protracted occupation upon them. But what the Iraqis observed was a bungling, wavering American presence, in which no one was really in charge. One of Garner's senior civilian staffers finally got through to him that the Iraqis were fearful of a repeat of 1991: "Sir, what the Iraqis are hearing from you is a second betrayal—that we are going to bug out on them and leave them to the thugs, criminals, and Baathists." But by then it was too late. Maladroit from the start, largely ignorant of the country and its culture, Garner would not listen to anyone except Rumsfeld, and had around him precious little expertise on which he could draw. Bent on appearing publicly in open-necked shirts when a greater degree of formality and respect was required, Garner cut a poor image for the United States. Hobbled, as well, by an inadequate and poorly prepared staff, which was riven by the same political and interagency divisions that plagued the administration in Washington, ORHA quickly established a reputation for being dysfunctional.

To the extent that Garner had a transition plan in mind, it was simple and swift. Shortly before departing his Kuwait headquarters to assume responsibility in Baghdad, Garner told some visitors from Washington how he intended to complete the transition to a permanent Iraqi government within four months. First, his team would go into Baghdad and appoint an Iraqi interim government. Second, it would select an Iraqi constitutional convention, which would write a democratic constitution, which would be ratified. Finally, it would hold elections and hand over power to a sovereign Iraqi government by August.

There was dead silence. An astonished listener stammered, "By what year?"

"Well, by this August, of course," Garner confidently replied.

Later, one of his senior staffers confronted him. "Jay, it takes a little longer to do democratization than three or four months in the summer in Baghdad," the adviser said. "You can't do it that fast."

"Oh yes we can, and we will," Garner shot back.

Garner's timetable matched the military instructions that the Pentagon issued in early May to its top commander in Iraq, General David McKiernan, to accelerate redeployment plans in order to make possible an August withdrawal. And his desire to quickly establish an Iraqi government reflected what high administration officials were also promising. In an April 13 interview on *Meet the Press*, Rumsfeld defined the challenge as enabling the Iraqi people to "come together in one way or another and select an interim authority of some kind. Then that group will propose a constitution and a more permanent authority of some kind. And over some period of months, the Iraqis will have their government selected by Iraqi people."[10] On the same program, Ahmed Chalabi predicted that Garner's job of restoring basic services would be done within a few weeks, and then an interim authority "of Iraqis, chosen by Iraqis," would take power. In subsequent weeks, a steady drumbeat of other officials—including Rice, Wolfowitz, and President Bush himself—reiterated that an Iraqi interim government would be constituted as soon as possible.

With that in mind, Garner and his staff sought to begin a dialogue with Iraqis. Even before establishing his occupation headquarters, Garner flew into Iraq on April 15 to meet with some seventy-five Iraqi community and exile leaders to discuss the country's political future. However, that meeting, near the city of Nasariyah, was roundly denounced by major Shiite political and religious figures—including the leaders of the two most important Shiite political parties, Da'wa al-Islamiyah (the Islamic Call Party) and the Supreme Council for the Islamic Revolution in Iraq—for failing to include them adequately. A meeting of Iraqi factions in Madrid on April 25 discussed transitional issues but also failed to agree on any plan for an administration. This gathering was followed by a broader, more ambitious conference of some three hundred Iraqis chosen by the Pentagon, the State Department, and the CIA in Baghdad on April 28, which featured "Shiite and Sunni Muslim clerics in robes, Kurds from the north, tribal chiefs in

Arab headdresses and Westernized exiles in expensive suits," according to one press report.[11] The stormy session saw a number of heated outbursts and demands, including repeated, urgent appeals for Coalition forces to repair the breakdown of law and order in the country.

ORHA's lack of preparation and command was apparent at the Baghdad conference. In a symbolically disastrous move, Garner dismissed his four professional, Arab American translators and drafted a career American diplomat, fluent in Arabic, to translate for him. The professional translators were among the State Department's best, whom the department had just sent out to plug an astonishing gap in ORHA's operational capacity: it had landed in Baghdad with no professional translators and interpreters, despite a prior estimate that it would need two hundred of them. When asked by a tribal sheikh, "Who's in charge of our politics?" Garner replied, "*You're* in charge."[12] The obvious absence of any mechanism for making it so left mouths agape. Garner spoke to the assembly and then left, not bothering to stick around to hear what Iraqis were saying. Papers were presented by distinguished Iraqi democrats in exile, such as Kanan Makiya and Rend Rahim Francke, but most of the audience was not listening. An Iraqi American participant recalls: "The conference was run like an Oprah Winfrey show, very open and spontaneous—something that Iraqis were not used to. But it became chaotic. Speakers were getting up saying we have anarchy in the streets, looting, we don't care about a constitution right now, we need order. One tribal leader got up and declared [to the American chair, Zalmay Khalilzad], 'We need a decision maker. We need you to appoint a government that can determine our future. We can't have this chaos. It is up to you to appoint somebody to do something.'" Then the meeting began to fall apart in a cacophony of voices, as American participants who supposedly spoke Arabic scrambled to understand what was being said from the floor.

Ultimately, the ten-hour Baghdad conference resolved to hold a national conference about a month later to select a postwar transitional government for Iraq. Behind-the-scenes negotiating began to crystallize around the idea of an Iraqi interim government of technocrats nominated by the "big seven" mostly exile parties: Chalabi's Iraqi National Congress (INC), Allawi's Iraqi National Accord (INA), the two leading Kurdish parties—the Kurdistan Democratic Party (KDP) and the Patriotic Union of Kurdistan (PUK)—SCIRI, Da'wa, and the Communist Party. But Garner was already moving to appoint a number of councils, with the apparent aim of constituting an Iraqi interim government soon thereafter, which probably would have been headed by Ahmed Chalabi. A senior official in ORHA from outside Garner's tight Pentagon circle learned of the plan, alerted the State Department, and it was derailed. But the question remained: Why go through the sequences of conferences and consultations if Garner was just going to appoint an interim government from the top down?

As the situation rapidly slipped in Iraq, it was becoming widely apparent that Garner was ill suited for the job of steering a political transition in Iraq. His heart was with the Kurds, and politically he was close to Chalabi, but otherwise Garner appeared disconnected from the Iraqi scene, without the will or the ability to learn quickly on the job. One of the few Americans in ORHA who knew the region and the culture tried hard from the start of the occupation to get Garner to reach out to Ayatollah Sistani, the Shiite religious leader, and meet with him. Garner wasn't interested. "Why?" he asked. "Who is this person?"

The lack of knowledge of, or interest in, Iraqi politics was characteristic of much of Garner's coterie. This was first evident on April 10, when Abdul Majid al-Khoei—Iraq's most outspoken pro-democratic Shiite cleric, the son of Sistani's predecessor as the leading grand ayatollah in Najaf, and America's best hope for a moderate, truly democratic Shiite religious interlocutor—was stabbed to death. A senior American official with Garner in Kuwait was alarmed by the assassination but soon found this feeling was not shared by others. The official later recalled,

> One of the [retired] generals said, "Oh, it's just them killing each other." There was aggressive disdain for the significance of it. . . .
>
> The civilians among us would get together once in a while and bang our heads in unison because we just could not believe what we were seeing. They [Garner and his fellow retired generals and Pentagon colleagues] were getting their orders from OSD [the Office of the Secretary of Defense]. This had nothing to do with the Iraqis. If it did, the local governance plans would have been put into effect immediately. We did what suited us, on a timetable that

suited us, and predicated on the assumption that the Iraqis would be passive. Not only passive, but gratefully, happily passive. For a while they were grudgingly passive. The assumption was that they would wait for us to establish a timeline, for us to arrange everything. I am not sure who would put up with that, but to imagine that the Iraqis would is just nonsense.

The Iraqis knew they did not have a voice. The dialogue was only for show. They had a sense that "they, the Americans, did not want to talk to us, didn't understand our culture, and had no learning curve because there was no interest in learning." The Iraqis figured that out fast.[13]

In late April, not long after he arrived on the ground in Baghdad, Garner received a call from Secretary Rumsfeld informing him that he was being replaced. On May 1 the Bush administration announced that Paul Bremer would oversee the selection of an Iraqi transitional government; five days later, Bush named Bremer as the new civilian administrator of postwar Iraq. At the time, "Iraq was in a state of near anarchy. . . . Garner had no control over anything," according to Fred Barnes's later assessment in *The Weekly Standard*.[14] As a former ORHA adviser explained, "Under Garner, people were pulling in different directions. And the president wasn't leading on this. It was felt that they needed a real administrator, so Bremer was brought in."

★

Ambassador L. Paul Bremer III was in many ways a logical and impressive choice to take command of the floundering American occupation. A tough-minded, politically conservative, widely experienced diplomat, Bremer had been one of the fastest-rising stars in the State Department during the 1970s and 1980s. He became an assistant to Secretary of State Henry Kissinger at age thirty-one, executive secretary to Secretary of State Alexander Haig at thirty-nine, and ambassador at large for counterterrorism at age forty-five, before leaving the foreign service in 1989 to become managing director of Kissinger Associates and one of the leading civilian experts on terrorism. In 2001, he cochaired the Heritage Foundation's Task Force on Homeland Security. A skillful, take-charge leader, he would quickly come to be seen in Baghdad as a man in control. The contrast to the inarticulate, laissez-faire Garner could not have been more striking.

Bremer arrived in Baghdad on Monday, May 12, to assume his new role. Massoud Barzani, the leader of the Kurdistan Democratic Party, expressed his disappointment at the replacement of his good friend Garner, but he acknowledged that the American civil administration had made mistakes under his leadership. As he and other Iraqi political leaders would do repeatedly in the coming weeks and months, Barzani reiterated his desire for a rapid handover of power and urged that a strong Iraqi mayor be appointed immediately to run the capital city. It was expected that Bremer would meet with Iraqi leaders in a day or two to discuss the formation of an Iraqi interim government, which Iraqis were seeking by the end of the month. However, on May 16, the new American administrator announced a bombshell. Implementing a decision made in the White House shortly before his departure, Bremer told Iraqi leaders that an interim government would not be formed by the end of the month—and that the idea of an interim government with real sovereign authority had been indefinitely postponed. Instead, the Americans and their allies would remain in control of Iraq under the newly formed Coalition Provisional Authority, led by an administrator (Bremer) who would exercise all executive, legislative, and judicial power, manage ministries, and supervise the drafting of a constitution. The longer-term American occupation, which many Iraqis had warned against and which Garner himself resisted, had begun.

Almost immediately, Iraqi leaders (both former exiles and internals) were warning of potential resistance if an interim government was not established soon. "This . . . gives fuel to all those extremists who said the U.S. had a secret agenda to occupy Iraq and exploit its oil resources," one Iraqi warned.[15] Shiite religious leaders loyal to the militant young cleric Muqtada al-Sadr brought out some ten thousand protesters to the streets of Baghdad on May 19. Chanting "No to foreign administration" and "Yes, yes to Islam," the protesters called on the United States to surrender power to an elected government and criticized America for favoring exile groups (particularly Chalabi). In a foretelling of what was to come, one of the protesters told an American journalist, "This is an occupation and we don't accept it. After a week, after a month, there will be armed resistance against the Americans. This land is sacred."[16] The next day, a number of moderate Iraqi leaders, meeting in Baghdad with a representative of Britain's Tony Blair, again demanded the formation of an interim government and warned that an extended occupation would only confirm Iraqi fears of a takeover of their country and its oil by Western powers. What Iraq was being offered, Chalabi told the emissary, was "far less than you gave the Iraqi government when you occupied Iraqi in 1920."[17]

Two days later, on May 22, the United Nations Security Council explicitly recognized United States and Britain, under international law, as "occupying powers" in Iraq. Security Council Resolution 1483 called upon America and Britain "to promote the welfare of the Iraqi people through the effective administration of the territory," while creating the conditions for Iraqis to "freely determine their own future."[18] The Bush administration saw the resolution as a major step forward, one that blessed its postwar engagement with Iraq, ended thirteen years of sanctions on the country, enabled it to sell the nation's oil and get the economy started, encouraged international cooperation with the reconstruction, and requested the secretary-general to appoint a UN special representative for Iraq. However, Iraqis viewed it differently. Now the United States and Britain were clearly established as occupying powers in Iraq. "It was a tremendous moral victory for the Iraqi opponents of the American intervention," a liberal Iraqi democrat told me later. "The U.S. was already bound by the Geneva Convention and the laws of war. But to formalize the occupation was a huge mistake." It was not long before Bremer would cite Resolution 1483 as justification for sidelining the plans to constitute an Iraqi interim government and exercising governing authority directly. At every step, the United States and its allies would underestimate the force of Iraqi nationalism.

One U.S. official who did not do so was General John P. Abizaid, who was then the deputy commander of the U.S. Central Command (Centcom) and would, that summer, succeed General Tommy Franks as commander. A Lebanese American fluent in Arabic, with a master's degree from Harvard, a year's fellowship at the Hoover Institution, and command experience in Bosnia, Kosovo, and the Kurdish region of northern Iraq (during the 1991 Gulf War), Abizaid was probably more knowledgeable than any other officer in the U.S. Army about the Arab and Muslim world and the challenges of peace building. He was also one of the first high officers to acknowledge publicly that we were fighting a guerrilla war in Iraq. In a March 2003 meeting at Centcom with visiting Pentagon officials, Abizaid reportedly advocated a rapid transfer of power to an Iraqi interim authority and the use of Iraqi forces to help impose order, cautioning: "We must in all things be modest. We are an antibody in their culture."[19]

★

If Garner's operation had been loose and drifting, and Abizaid's watchword had been modesty, Bremer arrived as an American viceroy in the tradition of MacArthur in Japan, determined to assert control and to purge Iraq of any vestige of Saddamism or Baathist rule. The problem, as one ORHA adviser observed (echoing a pervasive complaint), was that "he not only wanted control, he had to be involved in every decision." Within days of his arrival, Bremer announced two major decisions—both of which Garner had deliberately resisted—that would have fateful consequences. On May 15, Bremer disbanded the 400,000-strong Iraqi Army—a decision that had no doubt been discussed and cleared (if not mandated) in Washington before he flew to Iraq. The formal order, which also dissolved the intelligence services and other repressive organs of the state, gave ordinary soldiers and junior officers one month's severance pay, and senior officers nothing. At the same time, Bremer dismissed from government service and banned from future government employment all senior members (the four highest grades) of the Baath Party—some 30,000 to 50,000 individuals, though the number actually affected may have been much higher. The two decisions were criticized at the time by many Iraqis and outside experts who predicted that expelling so many people so suddenly from the postwar order would generate a severe backlash. A number of American generals worried specifically about the surge of unemployment and frustration that would result from the formal dissolution of the Iraqi Army. As one U.S. official later commented, "That was the week we made 450,000 enemies on the ground in Iraq"[20]—and over a million more, if one counted their dependents. In the ensuing months, violence increased significantly and grew—as experts had predicted it would—into a well-organized and well-financed insurgency.

Undaunted by the controversy, Bremer plunged forward in late May, promising a national conference of Iraqi political leaders in July but not clearly indicating whether it would produce a provisional government (and hence some real sharing of power) or instead a more limited interim authority. A wide cross section of Iraqi leaders assumed that the conference would produce some kind of transitional Iraqi government that would at least be given immediate authority over ministries not related to security. Nevertheless, as was becoming clearer every day, Bremer did not mean to transfer real power anytime soon. By the beginning of June, key Iraqi figures were advancing a detailed plan for a conference of about three hundred political, ethnic, religious, and tribal leaders, most of them to be selected from the provinces in numbers proportionate to each province's share of the country's population.[21] Iraqi and American newspapers were reporting, however, that Bremer was talking about canceling the July national conference and just appointing a twenty-five- or thirty-member advisory council. Even the prospect of limited self-governance was evaporating. With the situation deteriorating, the Americans and their British partners now felt that they needed to take charge of the country, restore order and get basic services and the economy operating again, and delegate some responsibilities to Iraqi technocrats, before transferring governing authority back to an Iraqi body. They worried, as well, that an early exercise in democracy, even at a conference, could rip open the deep ethnic, sectarian, and political (exile vs. internal) divisions in the country. Their plan was to select, some months later, an Iraqi body or conference that would draft a new constitution.

Before being relieved of authority, Garner had appointed the seven-member Leadership Council, comprising the heads of the key parties behind the Baghdad conference in April: the two principal Kurds, Barzani of the KDP and his rival, Jalal Talabani of the PUK; the leaders of the two best-organized Shiite parties, Abdul-Aziz al-Hakim of SCIRI and Ibrahim al-Jaafari of Da'wa; and the two most important exile group leaders, Chalabi of the INC and Allawi of the INA (both of them also Shiites). Concerned to include a Sunni Arab as well, the United States chose Naseer Kamel al-Chaderchi, a lawyer, businessman, and head of a small secular party, whose father had been active in the democratic movement before the Baath Party came to power in 1968, but who lacked a strong base of support among Sunni Arabs.[22] Garner's council was probably a step on the way toward the administration's original goal of establishing Chalabi as the effective interim head of Iraq. But its members' desire for an Iraqi interim government was widely shared throughout the country.

Through June and the first part of July, Bremer held frequent discussions in search of a formula to widen the initial Leadership Council into a broader Iraqi advisory council. However, he faced steadfast resistance from Iraqis who kept warning of the dangers of an extended occupation and demanding, instead, real governing power, as they claimed was required under Resolution 1483. The political maneuvering was intense, as Iraqi leaders lobbied one another and the Americans in an effort to establish positions and find an acceptable formula. On June 4, Massoud Barzani traveled to Najaf for a historic meeting with Ayatollah Sistani and the SCIRI chief, Ayatollah Mohammed Baqir al-Hakim, the brother of Abdul-Aziz al-Hakim (whom Mohammed had deputized to represent SCIRI on the Leadership Council). For the first time, Sistani spoke publicly about the political situation, calling for the constitution to be produced by an elected national assembly, rather than by an appointed national conference (as Bremer reportedly wished). The announcement by Sistani was a serious setback, because of the authority he commanded among the Shiites. On June 7, SCIRI threatened to boycott Bremer's proposed political council, and U.S. forces raided a SCIRI office in Baghdad. Ahmed Chalabi repeatedly warned that the Bush administration was making a mistake that would foment resistance if it continued to project the image of American occupation rather than give Iraqis more authority over their country. To the chorus of objections was added the respected liberal voice of Adnan Pachachi, the former foreign minister who was viewed most favorably by the State Department. Pachachi asked Bremer to allow Iraqis to take the lead in forming an interim government, and he sharply criticized the aggressive military sweeps through civilian areas of Iraq. Bremer nevertheless pressed on, vowing, on June 23, to name soon a political council that would assist in managing Iraq's government but would have authority only to recommend policies on some issues.

By early July, as electricity blackouts returned and anger with the U.S. occupation rose, the United States faced a guerrilla war in Iraq against a much more entrenched enemy than it had anticipated. Increasingly, America's top generals in the field were acknowledging this while its Iraqi allies were making even more dire warnings of trouble if the American presence crystallized into a long-term occupation. A Pentagon advisory panel just back from Baghdad reported that the war had "entered a new phase of active resistance" and that Iraqis felt "that the window of opportunity for the CPA to turn things around in Iraq is closing rapidly."[23] But for Bremer, every surge in violence showed that the resistance was getting more desperate. Schools and clinics were reopening and commerce was reviving. "This is not a country in chaos," Bremer insisted.[24]

Much of Bremer's first two months in Iraq was spent negotiating with the seven Iraqis on the Leadership Council (whom the Americans sometimes called "the magnificent seven"). The new viceroy faced a difficult challenge. He had ambitious plans for the rebuilding of Iraq that clearly required more than a few months of direct U.S. rule. Bremer brought with him a bold agenda of free-market economic reforms: to reduce taxes and subsidies, streamline regulation, open up trade, foster competition, and launch a "wholesale reallocation of resources and people from state control to private enterprise."[25] He did not want to surrender real power to govern—and remake—Iraq, but he needed to include prominent Iraqis so as to have at least a fig leaf of legitimacy. Thus was born the Iraqi Governing Council. In his regulation establishing the Governing Council, which he announced on July 13, Bremer promised that the body would "consult and coordinate on all matters involving the temporary governance of Iraq." The negotiations on the membership of the council had been intense, as groups pressed for and vetoed rival candidates. (As the price of their participation, SCIRI leaders vetoed some Shiites who were too liberal for their taste, including Sayyid Farqad al-Qizwini, the pro-democracy cleric from Hilla.) Finally, a numerical balance was agreed upon that would be replicated in each batch of appointments, beginning with the ministers. The Shiites, who constituted a majority of the population, would have a bare majority on the Governing Council—thirteen of the twenty-five members— and there would be five Kurds, five Arab Sunnis, one Assyrian Christian, and one Turkoman.

When the Governing Council was announced, the country learned who had been chosen to serve. In addition to Pachachi and the core seven from the Leadership Council, the group included Dara Noureddine, a former Iraqi Kurdish court of appeals judge, who had once ruled one of Saddam Hussein's edicts unconstitutional and had spent eight months in Abu Ghraib prison for his crime; another independent judge, Wael Abdul Latif, who had been disbarred and imprisoned by Saddam and had recently been elected by the provincial council as governor of Basra; the relatively liberal senior Shiite cleric Muhammad Bahr al-Uloum; Ezzedine Salim, a writer, thinker, and activist from Basra who, with Ibrahim al-Jaafari, was a leader in Da'wa; Mohsen Abdul Hamid, a Sunni Arab Islamic scholar and secretary-general of the Iraqi Islamic Party; Ghazi Mashal Ajil al-Yawer, a Sunni Arab civil engineer from Mosul who was a member of the Shammar, one of Iraq's largest tribes (and one of the few that spanned the Sunni–Shiite divide), and who had spent many years in Saudi Arabia; Hamid Majid Musa, the leader of the Iraqi Communist Party (who had lived in the Kurdish-controlled north); and Mowaffak al-Rubaie, a neurologist who had practiced for many years in London but was active in the Shiite overseas religious and political opposition.

The members of the Governing Council spent their first two weeks arguing over their leadership structure. Unable to agree on a single president (or even a three-person presidency), they finally resolved, at the end of July, to rotate the presidency on a monthly basis among nine men (there were also three women on the council). It was in many respects an exquisitely balanced group. However, it was top-heavy with exiles (who had thwarted the CPA goal to give "internal" Iraqis a majority on the council), and so it provided a fairly easy target for the likes of Muqtada al-Sadr, who denounced it as an arm of the American occupation. On July 20, some ten thousand of Sadr's supporters poured into the streets of Najaf to protest alleged harassment by U.S. forces. Five days later, before a crowd several times larger, Sadr vowed to form a religious army to drive U.S. troops from Najaf.

Beyond the question of how, how soon, and to what extent Iraqis should be involved in the governing of Iraq was the issue of when elections would be held, and for what. Ignoring Ayatollah Sistani's call for an elected constitutional assembly, Bremer pressed ahead with his plan for an appointed body. Defying Sistani had far-reaching, ominous implications, for he was the most revered moral authority in Iraq. Reflecting a widespread sentiment among Iraqi Shiites, a businessman from Basra told an American journalist, "Sistani represents Islam. I will follow his call."[26] Bremer's early failure to grasp the wide popular support for Sistani's demand for elections would cost the occupation dearly in time and credibility. On June 30, four weeks after his initial public statement about elections, Sistani issued a fatwa—a legal pronouncement by an authority in Islamic law, which becomes incumbent on all believers—declaring Bremer's plan for an appointed body "fundamentally unacceptable" and ruling that "general elections must be held so that every eligible Iraqi can choose someone to represent him at the constitutional convention that will write the constitution," which would then have to be approved by the people in a referendum.

Sistani's ruling stemmed from a philosophical conviction, deeply embedded in his religious teachings, on the importance of a contract in social relations. He thus could not endorse as legitimate any form of rule that was not freely arrived at—that had been arranged by or under a political occupation.[27] In fact, it took a lot for Sistani to issue a fatwa on any political matter; although he had expressed "great unease" over the occupation and had refused to legitimate it by meeting with American officials, he had not yet condemned the occupation itself with a fatwa. Many in the U.S. government thought Sistani might be an Iraqi version of Ayatollah Ruhollah Khomeini, the architect of Iran's Islamic revolution; like Khomeini, Sistani had been born in Iran into a long line of religious scholars; mastered the Koran early; studied in the Shiite holy city of Qom, in central Iran; and was now a revered religious authority. However, Sistani strongly opposed Khomeini's philosophy of *vilayat al-faqih* (rule by religious jurist) and was considered, instead, a "quietist," who believed that the most that Islamic religious authorities could do politically was to offer general advice and guidance. That was more than many Americans would feel comfortable with, but it was a lot less than establishing himself as a Khomeini-style supreme leader. "As long as I am alive," Sistani told a Shiite intellectual who frequently engaged the Americans (and who was himself secular), "the Iranian experience will not be repeated in Iraq." When this Iraqi conveyed Sistani's words to me during a February 2004 meeting in Baghdad, he added, "You should consider Sistani a heaven-sent gift."

Bremer's response was to ignore Sistani's fatwa and press ahead with his own plans. At the same time, Bremer was reversing or vetoing plans put forward by local CPA officials to hold municipal elections in various localities. In mid-June, Bremer canceled American military plans to conduct elections in Najaf, a city of one million that was home to Sistani and to two of Shiite Islam's holiest shrines. The cancellation, which came after extensive preparations and the onset of voter registration, occasioned loud popular demonstrations. Later in the month, Coalition military commanders halted elections in other cities and towns across Iraq, using instead the CPA's preferred methods of consultation and indirect election to select local mayors and councils.[28]

★

With the Governing Council seated, Bremer renewed his search for a transition plan. "The timing of how long the Coalition stays here is effectively now in the hands of the Iraqi people," Bremer told the new body in mid-July.[29] It was up to the Governing Council, he said, to propose a plan and a timetable for selecting a constitution-drafting body and then writing the constitution. Once a constitution was prepared and national elections held for the government under it, he indicated, the CPA would cede power and go out of business. In his public comments, Bremer did not rule out elections for the constitutional assembly. He did, however, express justifiable skepticism about the logistical difficulties of organizing a national election anytime soon, and he suggested that the city and town councils could select delegates to a constitutional conference.[30] Later in the month, he suggested that elections could be held, and the political occupation ended, by the middle of 2004. However, some Iraqi and American officials were suggesting it might take twice that long.

The CPA's refusal to consider early elections raised concern among many observers, including the United Nations. The UN envoy in Iraq, the Brazilian diplomat Sergio Vieira de Mello, who had been hearing a rising chorus of protests from Iraqis over the slow pace of the political transition, felt keenly the aspirations of Iraqis to elect the members of any constitution-drafting body. In a report to the UN Security Council on July 22, Secretary-General Kofi Annan remarked on Iraqi frustrations and underscored the "pressing need to set out a clear and specific sequence of events leading to the end of military occupation." As Annan noted, de Mello was proposing that a voter registration drive begin "in the near future to demonstrate [that] tangible steps are being taken to pave the way for elections."[31] But that recommendation was a nonstarter for Bremer.

In fact, the UN's engagement with Iraq—which had grown to number some three hundred staff members—was about to suffer a shattering blow. On August 19 a suicide bomber destroyed the UN's lightly protected compound in Baghdad, wounding over one hundred people and killing twenty-two, including de Mello and many of his top aides. The assault was part of a rising tide of deadly terrorist violence. Earlier that month, on August 8, a car bomb at the Jordanian Embassy in Baghdad killed seventeen people and wounded scores more, in the deadliest attack, to that point, against civilians since the overthrow of Saddam. Speculation was that the Jordanian Al Qaeda terrorist mastermind, Abu Musab al-Zarqawi, had organized the bombing of the UN headquarters, possibly in collaboration with an Iraqi extremist group, Ansar al-Islam, which Kurdish security forces believed was infiltrating back into the country across Iraq's porous border with Iran (despite repeated warnings from Governing Council members of the potentially disastrous consequences of failing to seal the borders). On August 29, a car bomb exploded outside the Imam Ali Mosque in Najaf, killing at least eighty-five people and wounding several hundred others. Among the dead was the leader and founder of SCIRI, Ayatollah Mohammed Baqir al-Hakim, which suggests that the bombing had been a well-planned assassination of a major cleric who had been steering Shiites toward cooperation with the CPA. In addition to these high-profile terrorist bombings were a steady stream of small-scale assaults on police stations and other facilities, and exceptionally high levels of crime (with the murder rate in Baghdad about ten times that of Washington, D.C.).[32]

In the face of the devastating violence, Bremer soldiered bravely on. His reaction to the August 27 bombing was typically Churchillian in its defiant resolve: "Once again the terrorists have shown they will stop at nothing in the pursuit of their aims, but they shall be stopped," he declared. "We will stop them, we shall combat them and we shall overcome them."[33] Four days after the UN bombing, he told a Baghdad press conference, "Those yearning for the return of Ba'athism will be disappointed, and those seeking the imposition of some fresh tyranny will fail. They may pull off an operation or two, or maybe ten, but they will fail." He went on to detail "the swelling tide of good news" beneath the surface: a Baghdad water main repaired in record time, the restoration of a sewage treatment plant and of four public health clinics, distribution of five million math and science textbooks, and so on.[34] Many Iraqis admired Bremer's eloquence and pluck. However, they were not consoled by these fragments of progress. Increasingly, they would hold the Americans responsible for the failure to protect them and secure the postwar order.

On September 8, Bremer had an op-ed article in the *Washington Post* in which he laid out his clearest vision of the political transition, a seven-step plan for "Iraq's Path to Sovereignty" (as the article was titled). Early elections, he reiterated, were simply not possible; there were no voter rolls, no election law, no law on political parties, and no electoral districts. He argued, moreover, that "electing a government without a permanent constitution defining and limiting government powers invites confusion and eventual abuse." Nevertheless, he wrote, three of his seven steps had already been completed—the appointment of the Governing Council in July, its naming of a constitutional preparatory committee in August, and its naming of twenty-five ministers. The fourth step would be the writing of the constitution, once the Governing Council and its preparatory committee recommended a means to do so. Next would come a popular referendum to ratify the constitution, following a broad public debate; then the election of a government on the basis of that constitution; and, finally, the handover of power and the dissolution of the CPA.

Bremer's concerns about the logistical difficulties of arranging elections were valid, but they were not the whole story. Had a major effort been launched, by the early summer of 2003, elections for a constitutional assembly could probably have been held by the spring of 2004, using the existing provinces as multimember districts, or forgoing districts altogether. With adequate provisions for security, the United Nations could have helped prepare such elections. However, the United States (as well as some Kurdish and Sunni Arab political leaders) feared that early elections would give an advantage to radical Islamist political forces, which were better organized initially than their more moderate or liberal opponents. While some in the CPA viewed SCIRI and Da'wa as moderate Islamists who would play by the rules of a democratic game, others were skeptical, seeing their commitments and alliances as purely tactical. In truth, there was no way the Americans could know for sure what these parties really stood for.[35]

Also unsettling was an August poll of Iraqi public opinion commissioned by the United States. While Iraqis overwhelmingly endorsed such basic democratic principles as free and fair elections and free speech (even equal rights for women), they wanted religious groups to share power in government (87 percent) and religious leaders to play a role in politics (56 percent). One-third of Iraqis polled in Basra and Baghdad, 43 percent in Fallujah, one-half in Ramadi, and 92 percent in Najaf favored an Islamic state, and about one-quarter of those surveyed overall favored "a unique mix of democracy and Islam." Only a minority preferred simply "a democracy." In addition, most Iraqis seemed unfamiliar with the new crop of politicians; eighteen of the twenty-five members of the Governing Council were so obscure that two-thirds or more of Iraqis did not know enough to offer an opinion on them. Of those who were known, the two leading Shiite Islamist politicians, Ibrahim al-Jaafari of Da'wa and Abdul-Aziz al-Hakim of SCIRI, and the moderate Shiite cleric Muhammad Bahr al-Uloum were the most liked, while Ahmed Chalabi was the only one whose unfavorable ratings exceeded his favorable ones.[36]

In delaying elections, American officials did not have only the situation in Iraq in mind. One of the major lessons from the study of post-conflict nation building was that rushed national elections could strengthen extremists and diminish prospects for democracy and peace.

Of course, the CPA could have conceded national elections for a constitutional assembly while proposing some other means to form an interim government while the constitution was being drafted.

Neither was Bremer entirely sincere when he pledged that the constitution would be written entirely by Iraqis, reflecting "their culture and beliefs." To a great extent it would be so, even with American advice, but the question was *which* Iraqis would be drafting the document. As one CPA official succinctly put it, "On balance, we believe it's better to have a representative group of experts instead of a bunch of people with no particular credentials other than the fact that they won an election."[37] The U.S. government's concerns about the outcome of an early election were spelled out in October by New York University law professor Noah Feldman, who had served as a senior adviser on constitutional issues to the CPA from April to July 2003. "The end constitutional product is very likely to make many people in the US government unhappy. It's not going to look the way people imagined it looking," he said. "Any democratically elected Iraqi government is unlikely to be secular, and unlikely to be pro-Israel. And frankly, moderately unlikely to be pro-American."[38]

In the absence of imminent elections or any clear deadlines, the transition preparations stalled, as the Governing Council deadlocked over who should lead the drafting of the constitution and how the document should frame crucial issues like the role of religion in government. As the process slowed, the Bush administration grew impatient. On September 25, Secretary of State Colin Powell said the United States would set a six-month deadline for Iraqi leaders to write a constitution. The deadline was welcomed by many in Iraq and the Arab world as the first tangible sign that the occupation would indeed be limited in time. However, the United Nations, like many Iraqi political leaders, pressed for the transfer of sovereignty to an Iraqi interim government in the next few months, and on September 30, Secretary-General Annan set this as a condition for a renewed UN political role in Iraq. The wrangling intensified through the first half of October, as the Bush administration pushed for a new Security Council resolution that would mobilize broader international support behind the transition in Iraq. According to Annan, the way to reduce the violence was to constitute an interim government first and then proceed with constitution drafting and other phases of the political transition. American officials countered that such a government would lack legitimacy, and thus would do nothing to stem the violence. But they were not yet factoring into their calculations the possible boost to legitimacy of an elected constitutional assembly. Bremer kept imploring the Governing Council to come up with a timetable for drafting a constitution and then electing a government. When Resolution 1511 was adopted, on October 16, 2003, it set December 15 as the deadline for the Governing Council to submit such a plan to the Security Council.

The situation left no one satisfied. The Americans wanted the Governing Council to stop bickering and come up with a transition plan. The politicians on the Governing Council wanted the Americans to end the occupation and transfer power to them. The United Nations also wanted a rapid transfer of power to Iraqis—but not just to those hand-picked by the Americans. By October, relations between Bremer and the Governing Council were fraying, as Bremer chastised the members for taking independent decisions in his absence and reminded them repeatedly that he held the supreme authority in Iraq.[39] What Bremer and his colleagues never understood was that the Governing Council lacked a genuine incentive to exercise responsibility when it was Bremer himself who held the real power.

By early November, four contradictory trends were vying for dominance. First, there was the deadlock in Baghdad over a political transition plan. Second was the mounting violence and carnage: an average of thirty-five attacks per day on American forces (up from twelve per day in July), and a succession of car bombings and assassinations that were killing and terrorizing Iraqis cooperating with the occupation. The besieged Iraqi police, grossly lacking in guns, cars, equipment, body armor, and protection for their headquarters, were becoming a particular target. Beneath these gruesome headlines was the third factor: reconstruction efforts were beginning to be felt in the revival of economic, educational, and cultural life, and in the issuing of a new currency, without Saddam's fearful image. Yet beneath these currents of progress and normalization was the fourth element: a burgeoning Iraqi resistance to the occupation, which was crystallizing into an extensive, heavily financed, well-coordinated guerrilla insurgency, whose popular support was growing. An Iraqi tribal elder told Patrick Tyler of the *New York Times* that the violence against the occupation was not about bringing back Saddam or about religion, but rather—ironically, given how President Bush was then justifying the American mission in Iraq—about freedom. "The Americans should walk with us in freedom without pointing guns at us, and if they don't we will keep resisting until we force them to leave the country."[40] A survey in early October showed this sentiment to be widespread: two-thirds of Iraqis saw the Coalition forces as "occupying powers," while only 15 percent viewed them as liberators.[41] When the war ended, six months before, the Iraqi public had been evenly divided (46 to 43 percent) on the question.

It was in this context that Bremer flew back to Washington on November 11 to meet with Bush and his top national security advisers to present a new CPA plan for transition. During Bremer's brief visit, the Bush administration settled on the new plan, which Bremer brought back and essentially imposed on the Governing Council on November 15.

The November 15 agreement contained many promising aspects, and in its promise of a more rapid return to sovereignty with an interim government, it figured to have some appeal to the Iraqis on the Governing Council. The plan consisted of a number of deadlines and steps for an interim government and then a transition to a democratic government under a permanent constitution. By February 28, 2004, the Governing Council would draft and approve a basic constitution for the interim period, what was being called a transitional administrative law. By March 15, 2005, direct national elections would be held for a constitutional convention. This body would draft a permanent constitution, which would be publicly discussed, adopted, and ratified in a national referendum in time to hold national elections by December 31, 2005, for a permanent Iraqi government. Until then, from June 30, 2004, authority would rest with a transitional government chosen indirectly in two steps. First, by May 31, local caucuses would be held in each of Iraq's eighteen provinces, through a complicated tiered system, to choose a transitional national assembly. In parliamentary fashion, the assembly would then elect a transitional government to assume power on June 30, at which time the CPA and the Governing Council would go out of business. By March 31, 2004, the CPA and the Governing Council were also to conclude "security agreements to cover the status of Coalition forces in Iraq."

Finally, it seemed, the American-led occupation had settled on a clear, viable plan for transition. It had acceded to Ayatollah Sistani's ruling that only an elected body would have the legitimate authority to draft a constitution. At long last, a sense of optimism pervaded the Coalition effort. Now the effort to construct democracy was moving to the forefront of the occupation agenda. A reduction in the violence would follow, once the transition gained momentum. And the United States was turning a corner, where one could see—though no one ever dared use the term—the light at the end of the tunnel. A resolute Bremer was insisting that this was it—the final plan. It was into this climate of hope, purpose, and resolve that I was being recruited to advise on the drafting of the transitional law and the implementation of the transition program.

As I would soon discover, however, the November 15 plan would not survive in its original form. The plan had been developed without much input from the Governing Council, and many of its members resented having it imposed on them with little scope for discussion or revision. "The presentation was so rude," one source close to the Governing Council would tell me. Though the Kurds were delighted with the plan, the Shiites were wary, sensing a trap. While reluctantly agreeing to the plan, key Shiite members of the Governing Council went to see Ayatollah Sistani in Najaf, to sabotage it. Meanwhile, the Americans still had no strategy for dealing with Sistani, and no reliable means of engaging him. Once again, the Iraqis would complain that the Americans were dictating, rather than building a consensus. Just as this was not the first time (or even the second) that the United States had to redesign its agenda for Iraq, so it would not be the last.

3

MEDIATION EFFORTS

★

In mid-November, soon after Condoleezza Rice asked me to go to Baghdad, an old friend of mine who was working for the UN Development Program urged me to get in touch with Jamal Benomar to draw on his invaluable store of political knowledge on Iraq.

A senior adviser to the UNDP on governance in postconflict countries, Benomar had become one of the UN's best-informed experts on Iraq. As a young man, he had been a human rights activist in his native Morocco, until he was arrested in 1976, tortured, and imprisoned for eight years. Then he escaped from house arrest and went to Paris, where he worked at the National Center for Scientific Research. Later, in London, he worked for Amnesty International, and then at the Carter Center, in Atlanta, to head its human rights program. In 1993, Secretary-General Boutros Boutros-Ghali sent him to Geneva to head the advisory program of the new UN Center for Human Rights, and in 1999 he moved to the UNDP in New York. In recent years, however, he had spent much of his time working for the secretary-general's office, first on the transition process in Afghanistan, with the UN special representative Lakhdar Brahimi, and then on Iraq. At the beginning of June 2003, he went to Iraq with Sergio Vieira de Mello to help establish the UN office in Baghdad, and had conducted discussions with a wide range of Iraqi political actors. By a twist of fate, Benomar had managed to escape the August 19 blast that destroyed the UN compound in Baghdad and killed de Mello and twenty-one others (Benomar had traveled home on leave to see his wife and four small children).

The UN's experience in Iraq in the summer of 2003 had been unpleasant and dispiriting, to say the least. When de Mello and his team arrived in Baghdad on June 2, Ambassador Bremer informed them that he intended to establish a "political council" to consult on the administration of the country and the political transition, and he asked de Mello to be a member of the council or an observer on it. While they mulled over that offer, de Mello and his team plunged into a whirlwind of meetings with a diverse range of Iraqis. These consultations enabled the UN team to capture a broader lay of the political landscape than could the CPA headquarters, which was relatively isolated inside Saddam's former Republican Palace. But Bremer did not seem particularly interested in their views. Later that month, de Mello and an aide met in Najaf with Ayatollah Sistani, who had refused to meet with any representatives of the United States. Upon returning to Baghdad, they advised Bremer that Sistani's opposition to an appointed constitution-making body had to be taken seriously, but Bremer was dismissive of Sistani's importance. Then a powerful group of former Iraqi military officers approached the UN mission, demanding payment of their salaries and pensions, and reconstitution of the army. They were making threats, but the UN team felt they were also looking for a way out of a dead end. At one point during the summer, the officers organized a violent demonstration in front of the CPA headquarters. "At that point," says a member of the UN team, "we were convinced they would create havoc in the country. Bremer was not concerned; he thought he could get away with it." Bremer had set out on a decisive course—establishing the American political occupation of Iraq, dissolving the Iraqi Army, and instituting a sweeping process of de-Baathification—and he did not want to be steered off this course.

De Mello and his advisers were alarmed by Bremer's unilateralist approach and called his attention to the text of Security Council Resolution 1483, which recognized the United States and Britain as "occupying powers" in Iraq. The resolution called for "the formation, by the people of Iraq with the help of the Authority [i.e., the Americans and British, collectively] and working with the Special Representative [i.e., de Mello], of an Iraqi interim administration." This was to be "a transitional administration run by Iraqis, until an internationally recognized, representative government" could be established and assume full power. De Mello was authorized to work "intensively" with the CPA, the Iraqi people, and others to help "restore and establish national and local institutions for representative governance." To de Mello and his staff, the wording implied a substantial role for the UN in helping to structure and guide the transitional process. To Bremer and his staff, it meant that the UN mission was welcome to be in Baghdad, as long as it supported what the CPA was doing. As one member of de Mello's staff later summarized the situation, Bremer's attitude was, "Okay, you are here, good. From time to time, you issue a press release saying we welcome this and we welcome that."

After consulting with a wide range of Iraqis, de Mello urged Bremer and the CPA to construct an interim government rather than an advisory council—what later became the Governing Council. De Mello tried to persuade Bremer, in the words of *New York Times* reporter Patrick Tyler, "to trust the Iraqis to rule themselves during the transition to a new state." When Bremer insisted that the council have only an advisory role, de Mello, in turn, urged Iraqi political leaders to accept the offer, despite their reservations, telling them that once in the council, they could seize effective power because "Bremer will not be able to stop you."[1]

Divisions also ran within the UN mission itself. Before, during, and after the war, three options for the administration of postwar Iraq had been debated in the corridors of the UN. One, favored by many European governments, was direct UN administration of the country, as had taken place after the conflicts in Kosovo and East Timor. This strategy, UN senior officials felt, was wholly unrealistic, since Iraq was at least ten times the size of Kosovo, and twenty-five times the size of East Timor. The United Nations had never directly administered a postconflict territory anywhere near the size and complexity of Iraq. The second option, direct U.S. administration, was also viewed as inadvisable for an extended period of time, because of the likely resistance from the Iraqi people. This left a third option, widely favored by senior UN specialists in postconflict transitions: the creation, as soon as possible, of an Iraqi provisional government.

Most of de Mello's advisers supported the third option. Resolution 1483, they felt, had not envisioned an extended American occupation. Their discussions with diverse Iraqi groups were indicating that a prolonged occupation—in combination with the steps Bremer had already taken to dissolve the Iraqi Army and institute an aggressive campaign of de-Baathification—would lead to a violent uprising. The UN conveyed these concerns to CPA officials, including Bremer, but, in the words of the de Mello staff member, "The CPA had a plan and they were going to implement it, regardless of what the UN thought."

Within the cramped quarters of the three-story Canal Hotel, which had been converted into the headquarters of the UN mission, heated discussions ensued. The participants agreed that the United States could not be the referee in Iraqi politics—it was too much of an interested stakeholder to play that neutral role. Only the United Nations could arbitrate. But the issue was how and to what degree the international body could play that role. Jamal Benomar argued that establishing an American administration of Iraq was a bad idea and that sovereignty should be returned, as quickly as possible, to the Iraqis: an interim government should be established immediately, through a process facilitated by the United Nations, that might include a broadly representative national conference. De Mello seemed to agree with this analysis, but after his discussions with Bremer, he concluded that it was not possible to get an interim government—the United States had set itself upon a course of occupation, and the most the United Nations could do was to limit it. Though some on his staff wanted de Mello to take a stronger position against Bremer, he did not want to confront the American administrator with an ultimatum. Instead he decided to see what he could do to push Bremer's concept of a "political council" in the direction of a provisional government. He persuaded Bremer to change the name of the body from "political" to "governing" council, and to give it the right to name Iraqi ministers. (Bremer had wanted Iraqi "advisers" only at the apex of the ministries.) He convinced Bremer that the body had to have a representative from SCIRI, the power-ful Shiite Islamist organization, and that Bremer should also appoint the secretary of the Iraqi Communist Party, Hamid Majid Musa. But he was unable to persuade the American administrator to include any rep-resentatives of the Arab nationalists, or to give the body more than to-ken power.

In the end, his staff felt, de Mello embellished Bremer's plan for an Iraqi council and made it "more marketable," but he was not able to get the other countries of the region to buy into it, nor did he succeed in getting the UN Security Council to endorse the new structure. When a three-member delegation from the Governing Council appeared be-fore the Security Council in New York on July 22, it was greeted with respect but not formal acceptance as representatives of a legitimate government. Moreover, once the Governing Council was formed, de Mello found himself marginalized in Baghdad, his usefulness to the Americans largely finished. A high-ranking official at UN headquarters told me that de Mello "was feeling frustrated by the end. He was used to help choose and sell the GC, and that's it." A member of de Mello's staff put it more bluntly:

> After the GC was formed, he [Bremer] really didn't see any value to the UN mission. For a couple of weeks thereafter, de Mello was received, because they [the Americans] wanted him to legitimize the GC. Then they dropped him. By the time he died, he was very bitter, feeling that he had been used, then dropped.

The truck bomb that killed Sergio Vieira de Mello and twenty-one others did more than destroy the UN compound.[2] It shattered the UN's self-confidence, exposed deep political and organizational fissures within the institution, and essentially drove the international body out of Iraq. Back in New York, UN officials were appalled, enraged, and personally wounded. Kofi Annan had lost one of his most able and ad-mired senior officials, a friend and close confidant, who was widely spec-ulated to be a leading candidate to succeed him as secretary-general. In addition, Undersecretary-General Kieran Prendergast lost a valued per-sonal aide. Other senior UN officials also had close friends among the sixteen UN staffers who were killed. The United Nations had suffered the most devastating tragedy in its history—and for what? Many felt that the organization had taken great risks and made huge sacrifices, while having next to nothing in the way of authority or responsibility. It was, these UN officials felt, a massive, pointless loss, and they vowed it would never happen again.

Though Jamal Benomar shared in the sense of trauma and angst that gripped the UN after August 19, he was convinced that democratic progress in Iraq required that the world body continue to play an independent mediating role. In late August, he drafted a candid internal memorandum calling for a comprehensive reassessment of the UN role in Iraq. The UN could not simply resume its mission, nor could it administer Iraq on its own, he argued. But it needed to find a way to reengage on the most important front, where it could play a unique role: the search for political solutions to the most vexing issues of transitional governance. A small political team might maintain contact with the CPA and follow up on previous commitments to provide electoral and constitutional assistance. But the urgent priority was "much more intense engagement with Washington" at multiple levels of the U.S. government in an effort to convince the United States to explore alternative ways of moving the political process forward in Iraq, and to show how these alternatives would serve America's national interest. The strategy was a bold position at the time, because it flew in the face of the prevailing sentiment at UN headquarters.

With the UN mired in grieving and soul-searching, with Secretary-General Annan determined not to authorize any new UN mission without proper security and a clear purpose, and with communication between the CPA and the UN now severed, little came, initially, of Benomar's memo. Annan continued to speak frequently with Secretary of State Powell, but Powell lacked clout within the Bush administration, and Annan was beginning to break more emphatically from the administration's policy on Iraq. Early in October, the secretary-general publicly signaled his desire for the CPA to hand over power to an Iraqi interim government that would administer the country during the transition to an elected, constitutional government. As the negotiations over what would soon be adopted as Resolution 1511 reached a climax in mid-October, Annan made clear that any resolution would still leave authority in the hands of the occupying powers, and that "as long as there is occupation, the resistance will grow."[3] In a private meeting that month in Geneva with the five permanent members of the Security Council, the secretary-general called explicitly, for the first time, for an Iraqi interim government in Baghdad, taking the Americans by surprise. None of this was music to the ears of the Bush administration. The prospect of UN reengagement with Iraq seemed dim.

It was in this context that I got in touch with Benomar, and in late November we talked repeatedly, and at length, over the phone. I found his knowledge of the Iraqi political scene, and of the geopolitics surrounding the troubled Iraqi transition, outstanding. Soon enough I realized, however, that the UN adviser had much more to offer than simply a briefing on the issues and actors. What particularly intrigued me was Benomar's interest in finding a way for the UN to renew its involvement in Iraq. The institution was still shaken and divided, he cautioned, and its participation would not be easy to achieve; the initiative could not come from the UN. But if the United States requested a specific, meaningful role for the UN to play in Iraq, Benomar thought, the UN could perhaps be persuaded to return. Indeed, it was even conceivable that Ambassador Brahimi—who was then involved in the most sensitive, and we all hoped conclusive, phase of the constitutional negotiations in Afghanistan—might be recruited (albeit reluctantly) to undertake the mission. We both understood what the core of that mission had to be. Just two weeks after it was announced, the November 15 plan was already in serious trouble. Ayatollah Sistani had made clear his opposition to an unelected transitional assembly. Many observers—including several key figures in the UN—worried that the plan did not provide for the widening of the political process to bring in the excluded elements, such as Sunni Arab nationalists and the followers of Muqtada al-Sadr. Sistani would not talk directly to the United States, but he would talk to the UN. The same might be true for some of the radical forces that were estranged from the transitional process. What Benomar and other UN staffers in Baghdad had concluded back in the summer seemed truer than ever: the United States could not serve as referee in a political dispute to which it was an active party. But the UN might well be able to mediate and find a solution.

Other outside experts on Iraq I consulted during the latter half of November and in early December essentially reinforced what Benomar was telling me. The process was deadlocked, and if we simply ignored Sistani, it would be at our peril. We needed to reach out beyond the Governing Council to broaden the political process, bringing in Sunni tribal forces that were now estranged, and, if possible, al-Sadr and his following as well. Since the slow turning of the bureaucratic wheels was delaying my departure for Baghdad until early January 2004, I decided to use the second week of December to visit Washington, and I accepted Benomar's invitation to pay a visit to the UN as well.

On a personal trip to New York on December 8, I met at length with Benomar and talked, as well, with two senior officials to get a clearer sense of the institution's concerns. The United Nations welcomed several aspects of the new plan for Iraq. Finally, a timetable for transition had been established (as required by Resolution 1511). Now, at the UN's urging, the constitution was to be drafted and elections for a government under it were to be held *after* the transfer of sovereignty, rather than under occupation. However, the UN still had a number of concerns, some of which matched my own. The November 15 timetable was unrealistic; in particular, the March to December 2005 schedule was too short to allow for a participatory process of drafting and adopting a permanent constitution, and then electing a government under it. The problem would be all the more serious if, as envisioned in the plan, the fundamental law would not be subject to any amendment. UN officials were also worried about the drift in Iraq toward the "Lebanonization" of politics, with deals—as in the composition of the Governing Council—that meted out positions in rigid quotas for different ethnic and religious groups. They wanted more time for the emergence of political parties that would cut across these divides. One reason the UN had pushed for the early appointment of an interim government, it was stressed to me, was that it would have provided more time to write a permanent constitution, develop political parties, and then hold elections. UN officials shared the CPA's judgment that Iraq was far from ready, administratively or politically, for national elections. But, like many outside observers, the UN was also concerned about the complicated caucuses for choosing members of the transitional national assembly—a process that, in giving control to the local and provincial councils appointed by the United States and to the U.S.-appointed Governing Council, missed the opportunity to broaden support for the transition. There was also concern that the fundamental law would alter the tradition of a strong central government by introducing federalism, which was deeply controversial not only in Iraq but throughout the region. The UN wanted to leave as many issues as possible open to negotiation by Iraqis, and not have issues preempted or preordained by the United States.

Senior UN officials were cool to renewed involvement in Iraq in the near term but did not close the door altogether. UN assistance to help administer (and legitimate) the caucuses seemed out of the question, but once an interim government was installed, a more active, visible UN role could again be possible. Benomar was more hopeful about the near term, and more candid with me. The UN, he said, had always been open to participating in Iraq. The problem was that it had run up against the U.S. desire for nearly total control, in which the United States would establish the process and the UN would then tinker around the edges and support it. The world body, he made clear, could not return under that arrangement. It wasn't worth the risk to its people or to its credibility. If the UN was to come back, it would need to have more responsibility, and the United States would need to loosen its grip. If the real objective was to constitute, by June 30, an Iraqi interim government that would be representative of and acceptable to Iraqi society, the UN, he was confident, would help in that task—provided that the United States would be more flexible about how the government might be established. After all, the United States and the UN had worked closely and well together in Afghanistan.

That evening I flew on to Washington, where I had a meeting with Condoleezza Rice scheduled for December 12. In the intervening days, I talked with other experts on Iraq and with officials who had spent time there working with the CPA. And I prepared a lengthy memo for

Rice. In it, I argued that our plan for political transition in Iraq was critically flawed—that we had to "confront the contradiction between our aspiration for democracy . . . and our impulse for unilateral control. . . . If we do not pursue a better balance, we will lose both control and democracy, as the transition spirals down into distrust, stalemate, and violence." The transition, I argued, was centered on two illegitimate bodies—the CPA and the Governing Council. Participation must be widened both in the drafting of the fundamental law and in the selection of the transitional national assembly. We needed to consult broadly on the latter process in particular, and be open to revision of the system of indirect election prescribed by the November 15 agreement. I suggested, next, that fixing the transitional process would require renewed UN involvement, led by a special representative who would advise on the drafting of the fundamental law; consult widely with Iraqis on the process and criteria for choosing the transitional assembly; and monitor and help administer whatever process was chosen for selecting the assembly. A small UN team might also engage in dialogue with representatives of some of the armed groups (which were already making contact with UN officials) to identify conditions that might bring them into the political process and reduce the violence. If the right person could be found for this role—someone of real stature, from the region, experienced in dealing with postconflict issues and in working with the United States—the special representative might be able to break the stalemate, make the political process more inclusive, and create opportunities for international cooperation as well. I did not say so in my memo, but there was one obvious person who met all of these requirements: Lakhdar Brahimi.

It would have been hard to imagine a more talented mediator for the Iraqi political stalemate than the seventy-year-old Brahimi, who had spent his adult life in international diplomacy and had been honored by the Harvard Law School in 2002 with its annual Great Negotiator Award. Along with the late Sergio Vieira de Mello and the secretary-general himself, Brahimi had been among the UN's most widely experienced, accomplished troubleshooters. During his two years as the UN special representative in Afghanistan, he had been hailed for his successful mediation of both the 2001 Bonn conference, which established the post-Taliban interim government, and the historic 2003 constitutional settlement. Moreover, he had served a previous stint for the UN in Afghanistan, in the 1990s, and had been the world body's special representative in Haiti and in South Africa, where he led the 1994 Observer Mission that helped build confidence in that country's first democratic elections. He had also undertaken special missions for the UN in Zaire, Yemen, Liberia, Nigeria, and Sudan, and, as undersecretary-general, had chaired an influential study of the UN's peacekeeping operations. Brahimi had his critics and detractors, mainly among some former Iraqi opposition groups and American neoconservatives who felt that during his time as an Arab League official (1984–91) and Algerian foreign minister (1991–93), he had looked the other way in the face of Saddam's atrocities. Yet in Afghanistan he had, through his consummate skill and integrity as a diplomat, won the respect of the bitterly hostile Afghan factions and of the Bush administration as well. Urbane and eloquent in Arabic, French, and English, the silver-haired Brahimi moved gracefully, spoke softly, and listened intently. But beneath his courtly demeanor were a creative mind and a shrewd, tenacious will. Novelists would have difficulty conjuring up a more suitable intermediary between the two strong-willed protagonists in the Iraqi drama, Bremer and Sistani.

I was squeezed into Rice's schedule on a hectic Friday, two weeks before Christmas. The waiting room of the West Wing had a beautiful Christmas tree, and there was already an atmosphere of holiday in the air. The president's national security adviser greeted me warmly. I had not seen Rice in many months, and I was amazed to note how well she was holding up under the strain of being on call in every international crisis. She seemed as fit and graceful, well tailored, and poised as ever. She called her principal assistant for Iraq, Robert Blackwill, into the room, and I summarized for them the key points of my memo, which I also gave her. My bottom line took them by surprise, and they listened intently. I thought we should get the United Nations back into Iraq to arbitrate the controversies over the November 15 agreement, and I had gathered from discussions with people in the UN that it might be possible to do so. Though there was internal conflict and deep ambivalence at the highest levels at the world organization, I sensed that it might be persuaded to return if a specific mission could be defined. I had worried that Rice and Blackwill would react coolly to my suggestion, but they both welcomed it. They had seen what UN assistance and cooperation had achieved in expediting the political transition in Afghanistan, and they seemed open to some kind of UN brokering role in Iraq. Then I added a point not in my written memo: I thought it might be possible to persuade Brahimi himself to lead the mission. At this, Rice and Blackwill became enthusiastic and animated. It was clear that beyond the general appreciation they had for the role the UN could perform in breaking the deadlock in Iraq, they saw in Brahimi someone special: a skilled, honest, and trustworthy diplomat, respected in the region but respectful of American power, who could navigate artfully among the interests of diverse constituencies and reconcile what did not seem reconcilable. They were grateful to have been informed of these possibilities, and when I left Rice's office, I sensed that she intended to find a way to bring the UN back in.

If we were going to get Brahimi, it would not be immediately, because he still had to complete his work in helping to mediate the Afghan Constitutional Loya Jirga (Grand Council), which, after difficult negotiations, adopted a constitution on January 4, 2004. Once this task was finished, he would need (and, after two intense years, richly deserve) a break. But Brahimi was worth waiting for, and, in any case, the wheels of government moved slowly. I thought perhaps a resumption of the UN's participation in Iraq might be announced by the time I was scheduled to arrive in Baghdad on January 5, but the return of the United Nations could not take place without the say-so of Bremer and key members of the Governing Council. So a meeting was set in New York for January 19.

★

My December discussions led me into another sensitive but promising area. A UN staff member told me that, a few days before the capture of Saddam Hussein, on December 13, the aide had been contacted by groups involved in the Iraqi insurgency who were, as he recounted the situation to me, "keen to open a dialogue with the coalition, through the UN." They were indicating a readiness, a desire, to come out into the open and become political. They wanted to talk to the United States directly. The UN was not in a position to respond on its own but was conveying the information to the Bush administration. The staffer had surmised that there were two blocs to the insurgency. One was composed of Baathist elements (apparently including army officers) who had broken with Saddam after he was chased from power in April. The second consisted of several Sunni Islamist groups who had common origins in the old Muslim Brotherhood. Each bloc was a coalition in which some favored dialogue with the United States and some did not. The most ominous development was that the two blocs seemed to have begun coordinating their resistance activities with one another. "We have nothing to lose," the staffer said, "to understand who they are, what their agenda is, and what it will take to bring them in." If they were not included in the political process, he felt, they would continue acting as violent spoilers of the effort to build a new Iraq. The feelers could provide an opening for a political dialogue that might diminish the insurgency. Of course, for that to happen, the United States would have to be prepared to offer them some role in the political process, some assurance that they would be part of the new Iraq. This would be impossible if the Baathists were among the most-wanted regime officials (from the infamous "deck of cards") who were still at large. But the staffer judged that that was not who these people were.

A week before Christmas, I sent a second memo to Rice and Blackwill, reporting everything I had learned in the conversation. I urged them to follow up with the UN about this matter, and I made my point as forcefully as I could, with italics: "If these Sunni rejectionist forces remain outside the process, they will seek to undermine it through violence. If they are brought in, and given a vision of a future Iraq in which they will have some meaningful role, they may be persuaded to give up violence as an option, *and Iraqi and Coalition casualties may decline significantly, saving many lives in the coming months.*"[4]

The memo also discussed, more broadly, the need for Sunni outreach and inclusion. A common theme that had emerged from my talks with academic and policy experts on Iraq was that the Sunnis now feared they would be victimized by the very exclusion they had visited on the rest of the country. They wanted some guarantee of power and resources. In fact, some experts predicted that the same provisions for devolution of power and resources (and for mitigating pure majority rule at the center) that would reassure and protect the Kurds would help to give the Sunnis a stake in the new system. We needed a strategy, I suggested in the memo, to bring in the major Sunni Arab tribes and to talk, as well, with Council of Ulamma, the body of predominantly Sunni Muslim clerics. Some of the tribes were probably behind some of the recent violence against the Coalition, but I had the sense that these were practical actors who might be brought into the process through negotiations.

As I prepared to leave for Baghdad right after New Year's, I was carrying with me more than just the items on the suggested packing list. There was a chance that my discussions in New York and Washington might lead, in time, to a new role for the UN and a clearer path toward democracy for the Iraqi people.

4

THE PALACE

★

After almost two months of waiting, and of working the Pentagon bureaucracy, I finally made my way to Baghdad at the beginning of
January—but not directly. To get into Baghdad, I had to pass through
Kuwait, which had become a giant transit point and military encamp-
ment to support the American invasion and occupation of Iraq. For Coalition officials and soldiers entering and exiting Iraq, the stop in
Kuwait blended fantasy, luxury, and eccentricity: an airport surrounded
by layer upon layer of concrete bunkers and razor wire, yet whose ter-
minals featured the highest-end designer shops and hot-pink direc-
tional signs; flat, newly blacktopped highways, stretching far into the
desert night while gas flared into mammoth eternal flames in the distance; a constant stream of Americans coming and going (many entering the country with no passport and no paperwork, only a U.S.
government identification card), while elegantly robed Kuwaiti princes
lived a life of leisure, sipping coffee, reading the newspaper, strolling
past shop windows. Here was one of the richest countries in the Persian
Gulf, with an annual per capita income of nearly $20,000 (slightly
higher than Greece), and there was no automated system of passport
control. I stood at the immigration desk, jetlagged and bleary-eyed,

while an official fiddled with a manual hand stamp, trying to reset the date by moving the rubber digits.

I was driven in from the airport by a burly Vietnam veteran with shaved head and bulging tattooed forearms, one of thousands of civilian workers who had signed up with Kellogg, Brown, and Root (KBR), a division of the giant multinational Halliburton, to cash in quickly on the Iraq bonanza. Here, in the deserts of the Persian Gulf, an American driver could make well over $100,000 a year—most of it tax-free. This provision applied to all employees of private contractors working in Iraq or in Kuwait in support of our operations in Iraq. (I would soon discover this financial arrangement to be a major source of resentment on the part of the U.S. government employees, many of whom made much less money than the contractors and had to pay taxes on it.) My driver was hoping to earn enough on two tours in Kuwait to set his wife up in a janitorial business. A couple he knew had retired to Florida as millionaires after providing janitorial services, for some years, to a U.S. military base.

After a long wait, we were driven from the airport to the Kuwait Hilton Resort, through which most CPA civilian officials, and many American and British officers and soldiers, passed as they headed into and out of Iraq. For months at a stretch, the Hilton was also home to the KBR staff who drove, billeted, scheduled, and supported the constant stream of transiting officials, and who equipped us with the standard-issue desert boots, helmet, and flak jacket—which, I would later learn, could not stop an ordinary bullet. A sprawling, luxurious complex on a sandy cove, across the bay from a massive oil loading station that was constantly feeding the world's largest tankers, the Hilton offered travelers a last good meal, shower, and swim before they headed off to Iraq, or home to the States. The CPA had rented forty presidential villas on the Hilton's exclusive beach, at $9,000 per week per villa. Each villa had four bedrooms (each with two beds), six more cots under the staircase, and a large color TV in the living room. The beds were rarely empty, and the cots were often full.

Yet it was not until I was driven out to the military airport the next morning—past the heavily fortified military checkpoints, lookouts, and bunkers, and the rows and rows of huge white tents that held thousands of American soldiers—that I began to comprehend the scale of the

American intervention. Kuwait was merely the tail end of a massive U.S. military presence in the Persian Gulf. As I checked in at the British Royal Air Force office for my flight to Baghdad, waiting alongside a mix of Pentagon, CPA, and British officials, I was gripped by a sense of awe and unease. I had never served in the military, nor had I worked in government. Now I was becoming a part of the nation's most ambitious overseas venture since Vietnam.

For security reasons, the American and British air forces can never say precisely when the flights to and from Baghdad will take off and land. So the practice is to check in early and wait, and wait. Even if one has plenty to read, the anxiety builds up in advance of the first trip. It was not until mid-afternoon that we boarded the RAF C-130 military transport plane, each of us taking a spare, metal-framed jump seat. The C-130 is principally a cargo plane, with a huge back door that lowers down into a ramp for the rapid offloading of weapons and equipment. The detachable seats line up in four rows going lengthwise down the body of a plane, so that most passengers stare into the guts of the aircraft, with wires hanging down in all directions. A slow propeller-driven workhorse, the C-130 is so noisy that the crew hands out earplugs to spare the passengers' hearing. I had been warned that the plane might execute a corkscrew landing in Baghdad as one of several possible measures to avoid enemy fire, but in the end we came down with the wings tilting back and forth sideways in a somewhat less alarming maneuver. I was fortunate to have a view through one of the few windows, and all I could see as we neared the ground was a brown, utterly desolate landscape, dotted with the carcasses of burned-out tanks. This was not Baghdad, I soon learned, but the southern city of Amarah, near the border with Iran. With the engines running and the propellers spinning, the crew pushed out some pallets of supplies and equipment, and then we were off again. By late afternoon, with our plane firing flares to counter possible enemy fire, we had landed at the sprawling base—now used by the United States and its military partners here—that had once been Saddam Hussein International Airport.

Fortunately, I did not have to make the trip alone. George Adair, a staffer from CPA's Governance Office who had arranged my logistics, met me in Kuwait and flew back with me to Baghdad. During my brief layover in Kuwait, George began to prepare me, in his sardonic way, for the eerie world I was about to enter. Better than almost any other civilian I would meet on the CPA staff, George grasped the strange angles and deep ironies of our engagement in Iraq: the purpose and the waste, the discipline and the recklessness, the idealism and the opportunism, the nobility and the venality. An army veteran who had served in Korea, he knew enough about guns to see no point in carrying one inside the Green Zone—the protected enclave in central Baghdad where the CPA had established its headquarters—and to fear the casual machismo of the many untrained civilians who were ostentatiously "packing heat." His slow, soft southern drawl masked a keen eye and a sharp wit. And his down-home charm helped him make friends among Iraqis, opening doors to precious information. Within the Green Zone, George was unique. No one was better able to secure the difficult item, be it a car or a bottle of Johnnie Walker Black. During the occupation, he was the only American official to get married inside the Green Zone. In fact, his fiancée, Sheryl Lewis, had come to Iraq with him from the Pentagon, and their December wedding on the Republican Palace grounds had been a rare cause for extravagant celebration: an honor guard of Nepalese gurkhas, bayonets drawn; bridesmaids in traditional Iraqi dresses; a throng of CPA staffers, partying in the ornate ballroom of the al-Rashid Hotel; and the beautiful blonde bride herself, photographed before the ceremony in flowing white gown, with a shiny black M-16 automatic rifle lying across her lap. It was the kind of contradiction George instinctively appreciated.

George and I were met in the parking lot, just off the tarmac, by a couple of armed officials from CPA who would drive us back. One was a spunky, petite airman first-class with long blond hair, a pistol in a shoulder strap, and a name I would never forget, Dreama Sweeting. The other, Ty Cobb (no relation to the baseball legend), was a young lawyer from Nevada who was working on civic education and often volunteered to serve as a "shooter" when a trip like this needed to be made. These were the three people who brought me to the palace.

★

When our SUV pulled up at the front entrance to the Republican Palace—the headquarters of the Coalition Provisional Authority—at the end of the day on Monday, January 5, I did not have time to tour the building or find my trailer and get settled. Ambassador Bremer had just begun meeting with Scott Carpenter, the top official from the Governance Office, and Carpenter's deputy for democracy assistance programs, Judy Van Rest, to review a proposal for the delivery of democratic assistance to Iraq over the next six months. I was ushered straight into the meeting. Bremer sat with his aides around a low, inlaid traditional coffee table, leaning back in the kind of oversized, gaudy furniture one would expect to find in a bad replica of an eighteenth-century European palace. Dressed casually but crisply in his characteristic white shirt, khaki pants, and desert boots, Bremer cut an impressive and commanding figure, even in an informal setting where his fleece vest substituted for a blue blazer and tie. Brash, tireless, and athletic, he was a man of strong views, big aims, eloquent words, and supreme self-confidence. Looking much younger than his sixty-two years, he exuded leadership. In some striking stylistic respects, Bremer came to remind me of John and Robert Kennedy: in his extraordinary energy, powerful ambition, youthful athleticism and good looks, intense balance of pragmatism and conviction, deep Catholic faith, and unflappable courage in the face of constant danger of assassination. As the windows rattled and the curtains shook from the thuds of mortars landing in the distance, Bremer listened, oblivious and unruffled, while Carpenter and Van Rest outlined an ambitious plan to spend tens of millions of dollars in the next six months (and beyond) to establish the infrastructure of democracy in Iraq. The comprehensive program would do the following:

- train and assist Iraqi political parties, women's groups, youth groups, and other civic organizations
- fund civic education efforts in support of democratic values, the constitutional process, and the November 15 agreement
- build up the production facilities and professional capacity of the mass media
- support the caucuses that would select the transitional national assembly by the end of May 2004
- help recruit, staff, and train a new electoral administration for Iraq

- provide training and technical assistance to the transitional assembly as well as the provincial and local governments

Bremer was impressed, enthusiastic, and impatient. He wanted immediate action to get these assistance programs under way. "We have 175 days left, and then we're out of here. We have to get this done," he said.

Jerry Bremer—as he was universally known—was a man in a hurry, and also a man on a roll. The occupation had scored what many felt was a huge moral, political, and strategic victory the previous month when it captured Saddam Hussein, hiding pitifully in a hole in the ground. When Bremer breathlessly announced, "Ladies and gentleman: We got him!" on December 14, 2003, his stature among many Iraqis had soared to mythic proportions; indeed, the morale of the occupation had been boosted immeasurably. Widespread Iraqi fears of a return to the brutal past would now fade, CPA officials felt, while confidence in the future would grow. Preparations were also moving forward to put the November 15 transition plan into effect. In a conference-call briefing to security experts in the United States just before Christmas, a top American military commander had acknowledged the continuing violent resistance in the Sunni Triangle, west and north of Baghdad—particularly in Fallujah and Ramadi—but predicted that the combination of Saddam's capture, the "rolling up" of mid-level insurgent leaders, and the implementation of the transition plan would cause a number of Sunni figures sitting on the sidelines to come into the political process. As I settled into my new job and surroundings, the American mission seemed to be on an upward arc. That sense of optimism and resolution would not last long, but at the moment it was infectious and even a little intoxicating.

There was also a certain fascination to being inside the palace, until recently one of the most infamous contemporary symbols of tyranny. The 1.7-square-mile complex was now surrounded by so many layers of army checkpoints, watchtowers, bunkers, razor wire, chain-link fences, M-1 Abrams tanks, and heavily armed soldiers ready to shoot, and was so strictly limited to occupation officials and soldiers, that for anyone else to enter, without authorization, was, as one CPA insider confided to the journalist George Packer, "like a jailbreak in reverse."[1] Beyond the immediate palace complex, the wider boundaries of the Green Zone were sealed off from penetration by T-Walls—ten-foot-high, blast-proof, reinforced concrete slabs—and more layers of razor wire, checkpoints, tanks, Bradley fighting vehicles, and Humvees with 0.50-caliber machine guns on top. The palace itself was a sprawling maze of marbled halls, carved and gilded doors, dusty chandeliers, Persian carpets, soaring ceilings, gold-plated fixtures, and generally grotesque excess, making it riveting to behold but a difficult place to work. Even in the mild Iraqi winters, its cavernous spaces were cold and drafty, particularly in the long corridors and noisy alcoves that often had to double as meeting places. For a building with tens of thousands of square feet of space and some 250 rooms, the paucity of smaller, functional conference areas spoke volumes about the regime's style of operation. In Saddam's highly centralized, personalistic regime, there was little need for staff consultation. There were two or three conference rooms, including Saddam's cabinet room, but they were almost constantly in use by senior CPA and military officials.

What the palace had in abundance was large ceremonial spaces—including a massive ballroom and a huge dining room—where Saddam would receive adulation and deliver punishment and vindication. I was told that Saddam himself used this palace only twice a year, when he would gather his party minions around a large V-shaped dining table.[2] The vast ballroom, stretching three stories high to the ceiling, had, at one end near the top, an ornately carved wooden viewing chamber, the traditional location, in Arab Islamic architecture, where women could congregate unseen to men. From there, Saddam could look down on his legions of servile subordinates and decide who would be promoted and who would die because they might have betrayed or displeased him.

The blue-domed Republican Palace was only one of some eighty-eight presidential palaces—each more monstrously opulent than the next—that Saddam accumulated as monuments to his greatness and symbols of his absolute control. Unlike most of the other palaces, this one had been built well before Saddam's time; but during the 1990s, a massive renovation more than tripled the size of the complex by attaching semicircular wings to each side, in a neofascist style of architecture whose pillars were crowned by four identical, twenty-foot-high helmeted busts of the martial Saddam. On the insistence of staffers, Bremer had finally commandeered some cranes and had the busts removed, in December, to widespread celebration within the Green Zone.

My place of work was the Governance Office of the CPA—a long, narrow, tiled room that had once been the kitchen serving the ballroom of the palace, across the hall. At one end of the rectangular room, huge aluminum exhaust fans still hung from the ceiling, useless and disconnected, and below them stood more than a dozen desks and computers, along with a television, refrigerator, and supply cabinet. The location was the political nerve center of the civilian occupation, coordinating the CPA's interactions with the Governing Council and the ministers, as well as the negotiations over the transitional administrative law and the overall process of restoring power to the Iraqis.

I was given a desk in the middle of the room, set up with an e-mail account, and basically left to find my footing and figure out what was going on. My job description was vague. I had been brought out to advise the Iraqi drafters of the interim constitution and to counsel and assist the CPA on various other aspects of democracy promotion, but no one (least of all Bremer) ever spelled out what my role and responsibilities were, to whom I reported, and who, if anyone, reported to me. Eventually, it became apparent that I was officially to report to and through the head of the Governance Office, Scott Carpenter. I could write to Bremer through Scott, and I could see the administrator when I felt I needed to do so. I also inferred that I was probably a "senior adviser on governance," since most people who were working for the CPA at similar levels were senior advisers on something. So I took that title, and others used it as well, even though I never had any official designation as such.

I went down the hall to the other section of the Governance Office, where Judy Van Rest managed a dozen people working on programs to promote democracy, and I retrieved some of the boxes of books I had shipped from Stanford—books on democracy that I was hoping to donate to Iraqi universities and scholars as I got the chance to engage them. In one of the boxes was a thick wad of bubble wrap that I assumed had been inserted to hold the books in place during their long passage to Iraq. More alert than I, Dreama Sweeting retrieved from inside the bubble wrap a miniature likeness of George W. Bush: a plastic Ken doll of the president dressed in full flight gear, as he had landed, in the copilot's seat of a navy fighter jet, on the USS *Abraham Lincoln* on May 1, 2003, in the waters off California, behind a banner that declared MISSION ACCOMPLISHED. Accurate down to the green flight suit and the white helmet that the president carried as he strode from the plane, the doll had been ordered for me as a surprise gift from my assistant back at Stanford, and it would stand on my desk for the remainder of my stay in Baghdad. For many of my coworkers and other CPA colleagues, the Bush aviator doll symbolized pride in and dedication to our political mission, which was not yet accomplished, and support for a president they deeply believed in. Others observed merely a pilot in a flight suit standing on my desk. A few saw nothing at all, or nothing they would share. Now and then, over the course of my time there, some used the doll as an opportunity to express other feelings during late-night bouts of drinking. These sentiments would become apparent the next day, when I would find the aviator president in less than dignified and victorious positions.

Night had fallen by the time I made my way from the office, past the palace gate, through a dark and muddy field, to the trailer that would be my home for the next few weeks. Mine was one of dozens of trailers in a clearing outside the inner grounds of the palace, down the street from the gym, beyond which stood another vast field of trailers. All the trailers were identical: two rooms, each about five by twenty feet, separated by a shared bathroom in the middle, each room with two beds, two wardrobes, a linoleum floor, and very little else. The trailers, housing both civilians and officers, were constantly under construction, as the CPA struggled to keep up with the surging numbers. The signs of a swelling international presence were everywhere. The lines at the mess hall were lengthening dramatically, to the point where some people would bring reading material for the wait to reach the chow. The palace was constantly under construction, as workers threw up wooden partitions to mark off the expansive spaces of the palace into makeshift offices and cubicles; indeed, the entire ballroom, the size of a football field, had been carved up into a warren of military offices. We were also running out of cell phones and computers. With people pouring in faster than new trailers could be built, most of the arrivals spent their first days (or, if unlucky, weeks) in bunk beds and cots strewn across the floor of the chapel, off the dining room. A cavernous, domed room, about the size of a large circus tent, the chapel housed more than three hundred people and their most minimal belongings. In keeping with the gaudy themes of the palace, it featured decorative tiles, gilded fixtures, a painted ceiling, and a giant mural on the left wall depicting Scud missiles taking off to defend Iraqi honor and (presumably) destroy the state of Israel. Not exactly a bedtime lullaby, but most of the occupants had stopped noticing.

What no one could miss, however, was the distinctly military character of our operation. Although Bremer, a civilian, was in charge, and the majority of the more than one thousand CPA officials inside the palace were civilians, civilians and soldiers were, in fact, intertwined in virtually every aspect of the CPA's operations, and the palace was also the headquarters for CJTF-7—the Combined Joint Task Force Seven—the military side of the occupation. The palace complex served as a large military base, housing hundreds of officers and soldiers, who worked in the palace and provided security in and around the Green Zone. For anyone (like me) who had never lived before on a military base—much less a tense, active one in the middle of low-intensity conflict—the immersion among soldiers, light and heavy weapons, high-tech communications gear, and heavily armed checkpoints made for a dramatic experience. I was struck immediately, as I would be repeatedly, by the dedication and calm professionalism of the soldiers, the political sophistication of many of the officers, and the integrated character of the military, not only in terms of race but also of gender. There were women working in military administration, women loading airplanes, women driving huge forklifts, female soldiers working out at the gym, and certainly lots of them carrying M-16s.

★

Early January 2004 was a hopeful, crucial time for the Coalition Provisional Authority. We had a plan for political transition that would lead to a transfer of power in less than six months. Teams were at work around the country to refresh the provincial and local councils—consulting with each community to purge the councils of unpopular, corrupt members and to make the bodies more representative and acceptable. The crime rate was falling in major cities as authority took hold and more Iraqi police were trained. Economic life was beginning to recover, with more goods in the markets and more cars on the streets. The supplemental appropriation approved by Congress the previous November contained $18.4 billion for economic and political reconstruction in Iraq, and soon the country would see a mighty river of assistance dollars flowing in—the most intensive infusion of postwar reconstruction assistance since the end of World War II. As one of his major priorities, Bremer had been working to get electricity generation up from 4,200 megawatts per day in October to meet the estimate for full demand, 6,000 megawatts, before June 30. Now, with the projected upsurge in economic activity, Bremer was looking for the resources—an estimated $1 billion—to add 1,000 megawatts to that goal. In a January 8 meeting of regional military commanders and regional and provincial civilian coordinators, the outgoing Polish commander of the multinational division in the central-southern region, General Andrzej Tyszkiewicz, lavishly praised Bremer's leadership and concluded movingly, "I remain confident that our goal of a free, democratic, and independent Iraq will be realized." Thanking him, Bremer underscored the multinational goal of building a country that was "democratic, stable, and at peace, with itself and its neighbors." Democracy, he vowed, would make Iraq a dramatic example for the entire region. But stability was still an imperative, and much more had to be done to beef up the elements of the new Iraqi security institutions. Bremer was particularly worried about the persistence of armed militias, especially SCIRI's Badr Corps, which was waging a private campaign of de-Baathification at the point of a gun, and the followers of the radical Shiite cleric Muqtada al-Sadr, who we believed were responsible for much of the murder and mayhem. On the peace front, the process of reconciliation had begun with the capture of Saddam Hussein, and now a tribunal would be set up to try him and to stimulate Iraqis to think about their past. "I encourage all of you to get started on this process of reconciliation in each of your provinces," Bremer said.

In early January, the CPA was just getting back to full speed after a lull in which many key staffers had gone home for a badly needed break over the holidays. The ambitious schedule of the November 15 agreement was looming on the not very distant horizon; we had less than two months to get the transitional administrative law written and adopted, and not much longer to begin organizing the complicated system of caucuses that would select the members of the transitional assembly. Bremer and two of his younger governance staffers, Meghan O'Sullivan and Roman Martinez, were beginning to engage the Kurdish leaders—Barzani, Talabani, and their deputies—in delicate, detailed discussions on their future place in the Iraqi state. If these negotiations failed, everything else we were seeking in Iraq could unravel. By helicopter and other means, O'Sullivan and Martinez traveled repeatedly to the north for dialogue with the Kurds, at one point making a dangerous road trip to Mosul in a dilapidated school bus, under the guard of the Kurdish militia, the *pesh merga*. Negotiations to bring the United Nations back into Iraq were also reaching a pivotal stage, with Bremer and several representatives of the Governing Council due to fly to New York to meet with Secretary-General Kofi Annan on January 19. My CPA colleagues did not know that I had been heavily involved, since the end of November, in getting the United Nations back into Iraq to mediate the deepening dispute with Ayatollah Sistani over the November 15 agreement, which Sistani had denounced for its plan to constitute a transitional assembly without elections. But Bremer and his top governance aides were skeptical of renewed UN participation if it meant any serious alteration of the November 15 plan. They felt they had already given Sistani direct election of the constitutional assembly, and that should be enough. Clearly they did not understand who and what they were dealing with.

Even so, by the time I landed in Baghdad, discussions were already under way between the Bush administration and the United Nations about a possible UN role in Iraq. Rice and Blackwill had followed up on my memos and were succeeding in getting the United States to draw the UN back into Iraq. Bremer and his governance team had to figure out how to respond. From their standpoint, UN involvement later on, in managing elections for the constitutional convention (due by March

2005) and then in supporting the process of drafting the permanent constitution, made sense. The problem was how to limit UN participation during the coming months until the transfer of sovereignty. (I also brought Bremer up-to-date on my thoughts about the disgruntled Sunnis. He was wary but willing to learn more about what the Sunni groups could contribute to the transition. The UN was authorized to have further discussions, which revealed what we were already surmising on the ground: that the insurgents were more resourceful, more sophisticated, and better coordinated than we had imagined. But they were also willing to talk. And yet nothing tangible ever came of these inquiries. U.S. officials were skeptical that the Iraqi groups issuing the feelers were able or willing to reduce the violence, and the Iraqi groups did not get the direct negotiations they were seeking. To say that there was a huge gulf in trust between the two sides would be a vast understatement. The insurgency grew more violent.)

In the face of Sistani's opposition, the November 15 agreement was now in serious trouble. In early January, much of the time and energy of the senior CPA staff was consumed with the question of how the plan could be implemented with no more than minor adjustments. The key problem was how to have Iraqis choose a transitional assembly through some kind of representative means that did not entail direct elections. Inside the CPA, and among most external experts on post-conflict transitions, there was widespread agreement that Iraq would not be ready for national elections anytime soon, for several reasons. First, it would be many months before an Iraqi electoral administration could be appointed and organized to register voters and certify the eligibility of parties and candidates to contest the elections. Second, elections would require a legal architecture defining the means by which representatives would be chosen and establishing criteria for the registration of parties and candidates and for access to the media during the campaign. The third, more serious obstacle was the security situation. Free and fair elections could not be held without a much greater level of security in the country, which meant the demobilization of the party and factional militias. Finally, there was the political problem. In immediate postconflict conditions, insecure citizens often turn to nationalist, ethnic, and other identity-based parties to protect their interests, and the more moderate parties tend to get squeezed out. CPA officials and outside analysts felt that time was needed, in Iraq, to allow the moderate, secular, and democratic parties to develop their identities and capacities. It was not merely a political judgment that imminent elections would favor Islamist parties—though that concern existed—but the principled belief that for elections to be fair, a level playing field would have to be established for the competing parties. Some of us were also aware of the experience of other postconflict countries, like Angola and Liberia, where premature, poorly prepared elections had inflamed tensions in a downward spiral toward renewed civil war.

The November 15 agreement called for selection caucuses to be held in each of Iraq's eighteen provinces (formally called governorates). The caucuses would then elect the province's representatives in the assembly. Once the size of the assembly was established by the interim constitution, each province would be assigned a number of representatives proportionate to its share of the population. The urgent challenge before us concerned the selection caucuses. How were they to be organized and chosen? How large would they be? What method would they use to elect the province's representatives? The November 15 agreement offered an answer only to the first of these questions, and even then a partial one. In each province, the CPA would supervise the establishment of a fifteen-member organizing committee to choose the members of the selection caucus. Five of the fifteen members were to be appointed by the Governing Council, five by the provincial council, and the remaining five by local councils (one by the council of each of the five largest cities in the province). To ensure that a narrow majority on a provincial organizing committee did not stack the selection caucus with members from a particular faction or group, the agreement required each committee to solicit nominations "from political parties, provincial/local councils, professional and civic associations, university faculties, tribal and religious groups," and it mandated that any nominee to the selection caucus would have to be approved by an eleven-vote supermajority of the organizing committee. This latter provision was meant to mollify the Governing Council (which had wanted more direct and thorough control of the process), ensuring its members that an organizing committee could not act without support from at least one of the Governing Council's nominees.

In theory, this strategy would provide for a broadly representative gathering of some one hundred to two hundred notables from throughout a province, who would, in turn, elect (from among their ranks) representatives who would reflect the ethnic, religious, professional, and political diversity of the province. But in the atmosphere of endemic suspicion and intense political maneuvering that prevailed in postwar Iraq, not many outside the CPA had confidence that the process would be transparent, inclusive, and fair. In fact, the procedures were so complicated that even many within the CPA had trouble understanding how they were going to work. Moreover, many Iraqis felt that because the local and provincial councils had been appointed by the CPA (or by commanders of the U.S.-led military coalition), they would be manipulated to produce a pliable assembly. One of my CPA colleagues succinctly expressed the dilemma we faced: "to figure out how to get a group that is considered illegitimate [the organizing committees] to produce a legitimate body." Iraqi critics of the occupation and the Governing Council (which was seen largely as a pawn of the occupation) saw a plot by the CPA to control the entire process. After all, they argued, the CPA had appointed the Governing Council, and it had also appointed the provincial and local councils. It didn't help that Bremer and his top governance staff were deliberately resisting calls and even vetoing plans for direct elections of some provincial and local councils, including a call by Sistani and other ayatollahs for direct election of the provincial council in Najaf. With control over the appointment process, the CPA could, Iraqi critics feared, stack each provincial organizing committee with its Iraqi allies, who would then keep all dissenting voices out of the selection caucus, thereby ensuring that opponents of the occupation were largely shut out of the assembly. The Governing Council, however, was also not pleased with the arrangements. Its goal was to manage the process entirely, by choosing all the provincial organizing committee members. In fact, the Shiite group within the Governing Council—what came to be known as the Shiite house—wanted to proceed directly to elections if the Governing Council could not control the organizing committee entirely.

Partly because of their history and culture, and partly because the CPA did so poor a job of engaging them, Iraqis generally suspected the worst of the Americans. The suspicions were somewhat misplaced, as the CPA intended to organize as democratic and open a process as was possible at the time—which meant free and fair *indirect* elections. In a January 8 meeting with his civilian regional and provincial coordinators and regional military commanders, Bremer was emphatic about this: "It will be the responsibility of each of you to ensure that the process is transparent and fair. Every single element of your command must work on this, with town hall meetings, consultations with NGOs, and so on. It is vital that you seize it and work it hard. It is just as important as the money you are spending on CERP [the military Commanders' Emergency Response Program] and on the schools. In the long run, it is more important."

If Bremer was sincere in wanting to bring democracy to Iraq, it was at his own pace and in his own way. Gradually I realized that Bremer and his most trusted CPA advisers simply did not grasp the depth of Iraqi disaffection, suspicion, and frustration, even among many of our partners and philosophical allies within the Iraqi political class. Thus they simply imposed a transition plan on the Iraqi people and political class, rather than engaging in an open, broad-based dialogue that might have generated wider consensus. As I ventured outside the palace, by the middle of January, I encountered candid and even sympathetic critics that I felt Bremer should heed but did not. One of the first such Iraqis I met, and consistently one of the most thoughtful and creative, was the political scientist Ghassan Al Atiyyah, who had returned the previous year from a long exile in London to establish the Iraq Foundation for Development and Democracy. Atiyyah was an intriguing figure not only for his intellect and political savvy but for the range of his social and political ties, which spanned many of the deepest ethnic, sectarian, and political divides in the country. I admired his sheer invention: when he fled Saddam's rule for exile in London, he built a false wall in his Baghdad home to protect his vast personal library, and when he returned, two decades later, it was there waiting for him, sealed and intact. During a three-hour discussion with me and Judy Van Rest at his home in mid-January, Atiyyah chided the United States for its mistakes:

failing to plan for the postwar transition and then insisting on drafting a constitution before holding national elections, thereby prolonging both the occupation and the legitimacy deficit. There were three key words to solving the problem of Iraq, he insisted: *legitimacy*, *democracy*, and *elections*. We, the CPA, should have committed, in September 2003, to elections by the following June, under UN supervision. Instead, we had settled on a convoluted, opaque system of caucuses to choose a transitional assembly. "If you continue down this road," he said more in sadness than in warning, "I will have nothing to do with it. You will alienate the Kurds, who are disenchanted with their two leaders. You will alienate the Sunnis, who fear [that] a list of cronies will be imposed on them. You will alienate Baathists, who will be completely marginalized. You will alienate all the progressive people, who want democracy. If all these people boycott the process, you will have *more* organized opposition. You will have more problems than you can imagine." He suggested that we return to square one, by having the UN convene a large, broad-based national conference, like the Afghan Loya Jirga, that would designate, by consensus, a framework for choosing the transitional government. (In fact, this approach approximated what the UN had wanted to do the previous summer.) Then, as a secular Shiite who had met Sistani several times, he told us what I had heard, and would continue to hear, from many Shiites, religious and secular: "Compromise with Sistani. He is not Khomeini. He simply wants an elected government. He does not want confrontation with the Americans. He wants compromise."

Bremer and his key staffers also wanted to avoid another confrontation with Sistani. However, as they had been the previous summer, they were handicapped by the lack of an authoritative, coherent intermediary to the grand ayatollah, who would not meet directly with Bremer or any other American official. Increasingly, in Baghdad and in Washington, the Americans were looking to the United Nations to rescue the situation, albeit with different expectations. In Washington, decision makers in the National Security Council and especially the State Department were eager for a substantial, high-level UN mission. In Baghdad, Bremer was wary both of the risk of diluting or ceding some of his authority and of the danger that a UN mission might radically revise the method for choosing a transitional national assembly. He was willing to have the world body tinker around the edges, perhaps adjusting the composition of the organizing committees; he would also agree to hand over the administration of the caucuses to a UN team. But he did not want any fundamental reconsideration of the plan. In particular, Bremer and his top advisers were worried that if a UN mission were given a broad mandate, it might recommend either a national conference to choose an interim government or an election. A conference, Bremer and his inner circle felt, would have no more legitimacy than the provincial caucuses, and risked spinning out of control. And elections would certainly force a postponement of the June 30 date for transferring sovereignty to an interim government. To Bremer and everyone else in the CPA, that date was now sacrosanct—the indispensable element that was keeping a lid on Iraqi frustrations. Bremer would consider UN involvement and was willing to fly to New York for the January 19 meeting to discuss a possible UN role, but he insisted that Secretary-General Annan first put down on paper what he had said the week before, that direct elections would not be possible before June 30. Bremer and his top aides believed—based as much on hope as on any evidence—that Sistani might be looking for a graceful way to abandon his insistence on direct elections for a national assembly; a letter from the secretary-general explaining that national elections were not technically possible by June 30 would give Sistani cover to back down. After discussions with New York, it was agreed that a letter would be addressed from the secretary-general to Adnan Pachachi, in his capacity as chair of the Governing Council, and that Pachachi would deliver it personally to Sistani as part of a scheduled trip to Najaf on January 11.

The letter was conveyed to Pachachi, who then shared it with Sistani. Sistani's reaction, however, was not what the CPA, or Pachachi, had hoped for. In his statement rejecting the caucus system, Sistani had said that he would reconsider his decision only if a UN delegation came to Iraq and judged for itself that such elections were not possible. Now, with the United Nations offering a cursory judgment by letter, the ayatollah felt that the United States was manipulating the world body and presenting him with a fait accompli. What he expected, he acidly explained in his meeting with Pachachi, was not a fatwa from New York

but a UN team to come to Iraq and review the options, then make recommendations. Sistani further denounced the Governing Council as illegitimate and the caucus system as "treasonable." Then, in a carefully
worded public statement issued after his meeting with Pachachi, Sistani
reiterated his position that a transitional assembly should be chosen
through a direct election, "which," he said, "many experts believe is
possible to hold within the next months and with an acceptable level of
transparency and credibility."[3] In a statement whose significance the
CPA also grossly underestimated, Sistani called for the interim constitution to be approved by the elected transitional assembly.

Sistani's flat rejection of Annan's letter on January 11 sent the CPA
back to the drawing board. Two days later, in an elegant cabinet room
where Saddam had once grilled his ministers, Bremer sought the views
of CPA officials from the southern provinces. While respectful of Sistani's influence and esteem, the CPA field coordinators nonetheless
recommended pressing forward with the caucus plan. Even another
fatwa from Sistani would not necessarily doom the November 15 plan,
they suggested. Sistani was important, but he was only first among
equals in the realm of the four grand ayatollahs ministering to Iraq's
Shiite majority. We need to show our respect, they said, but changing
our plans just to satisfy Sistani would diminish our credibility. The regional and provincial coordinators debated among themselves and with
the governance staff what Sistani's agenda really was. One argued that it
was the Governing Council's role in appointing five members to each
provincial organizing committee that Sistani objected to. Others said,
no, it was the appointment powers of the local and provincial councils
that he could not swallow: he had been told that the councils were not
representative, that they were filled with Baathists (who were indeed
present on some councils), and that even in the Shiite south, some of
the councils had a significant presence of Sunnis (particularly in Basra).
Or maybe, someone speculated, Sistani worried that the United States
would manipulate all three forms of selection of the organizing committees. Another staffer said that what Sistani really cared about was for
the Shiites finally to achieve a majority in government, so they would
never be tortured again; if the price was delay of the handover of sovereignty another six months, Sistani would pay it. No, another insisted,

Sistani's goal was to destabilize the occupation long enough for Iran to penetrate the country, buy up property throughout the south, and develop a sphere of interest that would extend all the way to the Shiites of northern Saudi Arabia. According to yet another staffer, no one knew what Sistani really thought, so we should just follow our instincts. Amazingly, no one considered the most obvious interpretation, derivable from the serious study of Sistani's writings and philosophy: a sincere belief in the political legitimacy of a social contract between rulers and ruled. Of course, this principle coincided with the practical inevitability that elections would give power, for the first time in Iraq's modern history, to the country's Shiite majority.

The CPA field coordinators recommended that Bremer exploit the sudden surge of political capital and moral prestige he had recently accumulated from being, in the eyes of Iraqis, "the guy who got Saddam." They wanted him to give a major television speech soon (which they thought could defuse or even preempt a fatwa from Sistani), explaining the CPA's plan for caucuses to choose the transitional national assembly. One reason the CPA field coordinators were bullish about moving forward was that they were fed up with the strong-arm tactics of the two Islamist parties from the Governing Council—SCIRI and Da'wa— who would mobilize the core of popular support behind any new fatwa from Sistani. In much of southern Iraq, SCIRI in particular was unpopular. But SCIRI had one huge asset besides its Islamist credentials: a 15,000-man militia, the Badr Corps, which had been built up in Iran, during twenty years of exile, to fight Saddam Hussein's regime, in part by infiltrating secret resistance cells into the country. Bremer worried that any confrontation with Sistani would throw SCIRI and its militant fighting force, along with Da'wa, into open political conflict with the CPA—and possibly armed confrontation as well. Some of the field coordinators were not so sure that such an outcome would be a disaster, given how hated SCIRI was among many Shiites for its religious militancy and crude bullying tactics, as well as its strong identification with Iran. But the governance staff—and, behind us, our nervous superiors in Washington and London—had other concerns as well, which were not so visible from the distance of the field offices. The CPA's hold over the Governing Council remained tenuous. We had been warned that if

Sistani issued a fatwa denouncing the November 15 plan, the Shiite members of the Governing Council would feel compelled to resign en masse. Moreover, we understood that Sistani could reach the Iraqi people more rapidly and effectively than could the CPA, with its cumbersome communications machine, and that the international media would portray a second fatwa from Sistani as a disaster for the CPA and its transition plan. "Our ability to communicate with the Iraqi people is much less than his," warned one top governance staffer. "And he has the simpler message: 'We want elections.' The bottom line is that the Shiites are a majority and they fear the caucus system will take it away from them."

The meeting broke up in a familiar state of irresolution. We did not want to alter significantly the November 15 plan. It was our last best program for transition. But it was also our route out of Iraq. One of my CPA colleagues—a career diplomat who was a bit more jaded than the younger political appointees—confided to me at the time: "Washington has no stomach to extend the deadline. We have lost sight of the objective and are just trying to get out now as ugly as need be. We are going to preserve the timeline at all costs." Still, we knew we risked a crisis if we tried to fly in the face of all-out opposition from Sistani. We needed a deal. We needed the United Nations.

★

On January 15, two days after the meeting of coordinators and CPA staffers, Bremer left for Washington, and then flew to New York for the January 19 discussions at the United Nations. His departure gave the governance staff an opportunity for a breather. Fridays were slower in any case, as Friday was the Muslim day of prayer and so Iraqi government offices were closed. People had been working at their usual impossible pace and had vowed to take the morning off. The office was quiet, almost abandoned, when I stopped in late that morning. Deciding to get better acquainted with this historic edifice that so intensely gripped my curiosity, I climbed the two flights of stairs to the roof on an unseasonably warm, brilliantly blue-sky winter day. Toward the east, across the Tigris River, over high-decibel loudspeakers in the distance, I could hear the voice of a mullah imploring the faithful in Arabic. I cursed my inability to understand a single word he was saying. Was he denouncing the American occupation, or simply reciting the call to prayer? I would never know. Far on the horizon a tower of fire was flaring off natural gas. Just below me, the physical expanse of the American military presence extended across the near horizon: crowded in among the dusty palm trees, row after row of heavily sandbagged trailers, from which soldiers came and went slowly on an uneventful day. Farther down the road I could see the corner of the palace swimming pool, and for the first time, a fountain of water spouting twenty feet into the air, at the curving indent of the kidney shape. The gleaming pool, surrounded by date palms, chaise longues, and, on one side, a green lawn that shimmered amid the concrete and dust, was the most beautiful part of the palace complex, and as the days grew warmer and sunnier, it became the social center of palace life. During the spring days, before the onset of the brutal, searing heat, CPA officials would bring out their cafeteria trays to catch a brief glimpse of daylight, while the young soldiers and contractors stripped down as far as possible and grabbed whatever sun they could in their spare time. At night, the pool area was the site of spirited parties, intimate conversations, sentimental singing, and sometimes bawdy drinking. As the days grew warmer, people flocked to the water. The one thing I shared with Saddam was a love of swimming, and the palace pool, with its gentle curves, crystal-blue water, and deceptively long stretches (fifty meters in one direction, twenty-five in another), offered a spectacular swim. When I finally braved its waters in mid-February—on a mild winter day—I discovered that the pool was also deceptively deep and thus retained the winter cold to a degree that gave a paralyzing shock to the unaware. After five minutes of furious swimming in a desperate bid to ward off hypothermia, I had to exit in a breathless rush. As I said in a letter home that night, I hoped that the United States would not do the same in Iraq.

I crossed the roof to the west side, stepping gingerly over a sprawling tangle of wires, cables, metal braces, and cigarette butts. The spot was a favorite smoking-break hangout of the soldiers. At almost any time (and this was no different) one could find there a soldier or two, staring out into the distance, guns at their sides, listening to their MP3 players and thinking of home. I felt embarrassed to be there—an intruder. The west side overlooked the front entrance of the palace. Three soldiers, in full gear, stood in the vast empty space of a fountain, now drained and forlorn, posing for pictures with one another. Off in the distance I could see the devastated headquarters of the Baath Party, sheared in half by the American bombing during the "shock and awe" of the first night of the war. Next to it stood the control tower for a helicopter port that Saddam and his circle used as a way to evade the Baghdad traffic. It was one important thing that Saddam left behind, unwittingly, for the American occupation: plenty of helicopter landing pads in the Green Zone.

Wanting to see more, I took George Adair up on his offer to show me around the Green Zone. There isn't much in the way of tourism in this four-square-mile area. But two must-sees are Saddam's military parade grounds and the nearby Tomb of the Unknown Soldier. A five-minute drive from the palace, the parade grounds were, in Saddam's era, one of the most photographed sites in all of Iraq. The quarter-mile-long route is framed at each end by a pair of awesome sabers, each about forty yards long, which cross in the sky at about one hundred feet. Emerging from the ground and holding each saber is a muscular forearm and fist, said to be modeled after Saddam's own. The arms alone are some fifty feet long, and inside one of them is a staircase, rising through the metal forearm to a cramped platform in the fist, from which one can look down on the parade ground. At the base of the forearm is a small, macabre monument to Iraq's great victory in its grinding, pointless, eight-year war with Iran during the 1980s. From a huge steel basket, tied to the saber, cascade down to the ground hundreds of helmets collected off dead Iranian soldiers. Now frozen permanently in the concrete, these helmets appear, from a certain angle, still to be falling, eternally, into a muddy field of Iraqi victory. Yet now, on close inspection, the helmets convey another military victory, in handwritten black letters bearing such words as "Sgt. Murdoch. 86th Signal Battalion. U.S. Army. TEXAS ROCKS." And: "PFC Martinez. 26 Aug 2003. Viva Mexico." And "11-17-03: Susan, AJ & Travis, I Love You."

From a pair of reviewing stands around the midpoint of the long concrete parade route, several thousand Baath Party officials and military elites would watch as their soldiers goose-stepped by in the best imitation of the Fascist armies of the past, while tanks, missiles, antiaircraft guns, and other heavy weaponry rolled along behind them. In the middle of the two stands is a separate, half-domed building in which Saddam would sit, with his most favored military officers and cronies. High up in the center of the building stood a throne, where the modern-day Babylonian tyrant would watch from his position of absolute power, and in front of it a podium, from behind which he would fire his famous rifle in defiance of the world and in celebration of being Saddam. Now it was all in disrepair. Saddam's throne had been torn out. The drab concrete stands looked like half of a minor league sports stadium long since abandoned and waiting to be torn down. Two rows of stadium lights still lined the parade route, to no effect. Lurking around the historic site was a small clutch of self-appointed guides ready to offer the visiting Americans a cheap tour of Saddam's secret quarters in the domed building behind the central reviewing stands. It was yet another place that Saddam used for receiving people, holding meetings, staging parties, dictating orders, procuring women, and sleeping—one of scores of such sites, which he could get in and out of quickly by helicopter. The guide took us upstairs to the living complex. An elaborate rotunda, now in marble ruins, had been the formal entryway. Another room—with marble walls on all sides—had served as a personal bedroom for Saddam. We looked up at the ceiling and saw cheap chrome lights. No taste. The carpet stunk. The room had been stripped bare. The power to the building was out. The place was dark, broken, and filthy. On the walls of the reception area were the familiar scrawled signs of American military conquest: "Tom loves Julie," "Ben + Sarah," and so on, in huge black letters on the dusty marble. Saddam's bedroom opened out into a huge reception hall and dining room (and, off to its side, a restaurant-sized kitchen), with a view of the parade grounds and an artificial lake and palm trees in the distance. From a pair of helicopter pads in back of the building stretched a great vista of the city, and yet another palace that was under construction (the cranes still in place) when the war broke out.

From there we drove the short distance to the Tomb of the Unknown Soldier, a massive, circular concrete structure visible for miles away and clearly distinguishable on satellite photographs. Three huge concrete driveways (signifying Iraq's three great rivers—the Tigris, the Euphrates, and the Shatt al-Arab) rise up in a triangle to an elevated mound. Atop a weird rectangular structure, with metal sculpted over red glass, sits a gigantic half dome, tilted open at a forty-five-degree angle. The red glass, we were told, holds the unknown soldier, sleeping. The huge half dome is supposedly in the shape of a soldier's beret, but if anyone was inspired to film a sequel to the movie *ET*, the dome could better serve as the top hatch of a giant spaceship. From the edges of this huge mound lie more great views of the city—mosques, palaces, hotels, office buildings, springing up in the distance, across a stretch of immediate horizon that is, for a city of six million people, stunningly barren of people and buildings, and yet of real green space as well.

★

Like most of my colleagues, I quickly fell into an obsessive, workaholic routine inside the palace. The reality of life in the Green Zone was that there was not much to do other than work, and occasionally work out. And there was a staggering amount of work to do. Despite the soaring numbers of Americans, every office was understaffed. The scale of what we were trying to achieve—an imperial occupation to remake a country, and now with less than six months until a transfer of power—was daunting, even perhaps absurd. But we knew our longer-term efforts to foster democracy and an open society could not succeed unless power was transferred reasonably soon; and although our engagement and assistance would presumably continue for years to come, a breathtaking range of tasks had to be accomplished before the end of June. No office was under greater pressure than Governance, which had to make the political transition happen. As a result, most of us worked until late into the night, and some—like Meghan O'Sullivan, Roman Martinez, Scott Carpenter, and Irfan Siddiq (a brilliant young British diplomat, fluent in Arabic)—seemed to average two workdays in one, with a few hours off for sleeping, eating, and working out. Most people came back to the office after dinner. Some would knock off at a reasonable hour now and then to watch the nightly film shown in a makeshift basement theater, or one of the DVDs our office manager loaned out from a small private library. Time off for me was going to the gym—a state-of-the-art facility with dozens of weight machines, free weights, floor mats, running machines, bikes, and elliptical trainers, packed almost constantly with sweating civilians and trim, muscular soldiers. I also enjoyed reading the U.S. newspapers on the Web, or watching Lou Dobbs on CNN, which we were able to tune in on our computers. We all found it helped now and then to have a reality check of independent news—any news. From inside the palace, CPA staff members often had to call home to the United States to ask family and friends about what had just happened only a mile away by means of mortar, rocket, or car bombings near the Green Zone.

If you didn't venture out into dangerous places, life in the Green Zone was surprisingly simple. The quarters were spartan and cramped. But even as it worked to push Iraq's transition to a free-market economy, the Green Zone was for its staff a kind of socialist outpost. Everything of a practical nature was taken care of. Meals were served in the mess hall three times a day (plus the late-night snack). Generally you could have as much food as you wished, and though it was hardly restaurant quality, the meals were wholesome, and KBR made some gesture to variety. If you needed equipment, you called Facilities. Soft drinks were available from the mess hall. If you needed a car, you grabbed the keys from the office motor pool. For gas, you drove the car to the filling station. You could take your clothes to the laundry and pick them up three days later. If you wanted to call someone—down the hall or in the United States—you just pulled out your cell phone, which conveniently had a U.S. area code (for suburban New York) and talked to whomever you wanted, for as long as you wanted (provided the circuits were not overloaded). None of these services required any expenditure of money, and most of them did not entail much effort or time. For those special needs—cookies, CDs, DVDs, underwear, a serrated hunting knife, or a four-way holster—the PX was close by and tax-free.

The late nights and youthful age profile of the staff created an atmosphere that sometimes resembled a college dormitory. Our office was said to have a rule that you were supposed to leave the office the same day you came. But I routinely worked past midnight, and rarely without several companions. With his baggy clothes, ubiquitous MP3 player and headphones, and boisterous sense of humor, Roman Martinez—the closest on our staff to being just out of college (Harvard) by, I guessed, about three years—helped to sustain the air of a late-night college cram. "Just for the record, we are now into Wednesday," he would declare as we banged away at our computers, trying to finish the next memo to Bremer or the distillation of the day's meetings. Then the beer would break out from the refrigerators, the table full of baked goods from home would be raided all over again, discussion would en-sue over the day's political crisis, until finally we would all go back to our computers. Sometimes a soccer ball would appear and get kicked pretty hard across the length of the former kitchen that was our office. Miraculously, midnight soccer practice never took out one of our com-puters, not even when it was kicked by one of the spiked high heels of a visiting NSC staffer in a tight black dress, perhaps because we had, in Irfan Siddiq, someone who knew when and how to subdue and dribble the ball, in play as much as in diplomacy.

In truth, I liked wandering the palace at night. During the day, the halls would be swarming with people of every nationality and race, mil-itary and civilian, moving intently with their briefing books and cell phones, pistols strapped to their thighs or M-16s draped over their shoulders. Iraqi workers would be painting the walls or cleaning the floors, splashing water that would then be stepped on by muddy boots, creating a mess. At night, things were slower, simpler, and quieter, but by no means inactive. Between eleven o'clock and midnight, the kitchen staff would lay out a late-night buffet of leftovers from dinner, cold cereal, cookies, and of course coffee and tea. There was a constant supply of caffeine in the palace. As I made my way down for a fix of Sugar Smacks, I would meet big American soldiers in their desert fa-tigues and full, loaded battle gear—a fearsome sight—carrying huge plates of leftovers they would consume before going out on night pa-trol. I would see other senior staffers who were also having to crank out the next memo, but would still have some minutes to talk. And I would notice features of the building that were not apparent in the hurly-burly of the day—like the twenty-five chandeliers that adorned the ceilings of the halls leading from my office down to the dining hall.

Inside the Green Zone, there were a few options for cutting loose.

The most popular was the Green Zone Café, a flimsy metal lean-to run by Iraqis that served burgers, chicken, falafel, and plenty of beer. Here staffers and contractors would drink and unwind, after being cautioned by a sign to empty their weapons before entering. Overmuscled body-guards, eager young political appointees, veteran crisis and relief work-ers, and prematurely jaded diplomats would drink, unwind, and flirt, perhaps while puffing away on a giant water pipe that the waiters were eager to load with different flavors of tobacco. Late at night, when the place was packed with gun-toting civilians smoking the hookahs and downing large quantities of beer, the place began to resemble the bar scene from *Star Wars*.

For those who sought a more upscale option, there was the bar at the al-Rashid Hotel, still inside the Green Zone, if a bit on the edge. The ho-tel's second-floor disco had been shut down, along with most of the rest of the upper floors, after the mortar attack the previous October. But the basement bar was still functioning during limited hours. George Adair wanted me to meet the bartender there, an Iraqi named Jimmy whom he had befriended. Short, bald, and sociable, always immaculately dressed in a white shirt and black bow tie, Jimmy could have been straight out of casting for *Casablanca*. He did not have much English, and what he had was heavily accented, but he loved to talk to the Americans. I learned that he was from Tikrit and had been a waiter at Saddam's palace there. I asked him what it was like to work in Saddam's palace. Terrible, he said. Frightening. "Women," he said, and drew his finger across his throat in a slashing gesture. "Men," and he mimicked murder once again. Finally, he fled Iraq and escaped for a while to Syria, returning after Saddam fell. I was beginning to realize that every Iraqi had a story about life under Saddam, and most of the tales were filled with fear and horror.

That was not the case, however, with another Iraqi whom George wanted to introduce me to at the al-Rashid, Hassan al-Tikriti, the gen-eral manager. Meeting Tikriti was a shock for almost any American, be-cause with his tall frame, thick black mustache, and facial features, he looked as if he could have been Saddam's brother. And indeed, he was part of a powerful clan from Tikrit, Saddam's hometown, who had risen to positions of power and wealth throughout the regime. The al-Rashid was not just another hotel. It was *the* hotel in the forbidden zone of power, owned and operated by the Iraqi state. It was also the inn where, after the Gulf War, Saddam had ordered the traditional mosaic on the entryway floor to be ripped up and replaced with a portrait of the first President Bush, so Iraqis could step on him upon entering and leaving. I assumed that, as general manager of the most favored hotel at the epicenter of power, Tikriti had to have been an enthusiastic supporter of Saddam and the Baath Party. But somehow he survived the regime change, and he now seemed as eager to please the Americans as he must have been before to please Saddam. He gave me a custom tour of the building, showing me a room near the top floor where, looking out through the thick haze, one could see the dusty expanse of downtown Baghdad and the eerily rising hatch of the Tomb of the Unknown Soldier. Then he escorted us back down to the ballroom where George had celebrated his wedding the previous month. George pointed to what looked like a long mirror near the ceiling of the ballroom on one side. This is where Saddam's demented, sadistic son, Uday, would stand concealed, watching guests eat and dance at wedding parties, and pick out the women whom he would rape, beat, and often murder. But there were also lighter aspects to the al-Rashid, including the only decent tourist shop in the Green Zone, where one could buy Iraqi artwork, military artifacts, worn, pathetic postcards, and watches and defunct currency with Saddam's smiling face.

When I arrived in Baghdad, it was with the promise to my close friends and family that I would be safe, because I would be living, eating, and working in the heavily protected environs of the Green Zone. Soon enough, however, I realized that people were venturing out not merely for work but for meals and socializing as well. Occasionally we would eat at an excellent Iraqi restaurant, with superb hummus, pita, and falafel, in a hotel not far from the Green Zone. The spot was located in a mini-bubble of concrete barriers, razor wire, and heavily armed security guards, so I felt relatively safe in going there. As I grew more comfortable with the situation, and more desperate for interaction outside the Green Zone, I would accompany Iraqi and American friends deeper into the city for meals at restaurants that were considered safe, or for an evening at the sandbagged and guarded rental home that served as living and working quarters for an American newspaper.

My friends assured me these various expeditions were safe, but then they would confess, fatalistically, that their office had recently been cased by suspicious cars and they were thinking of moving, or that the night before a mortar had landed near where we were eating.

I had my heart in my throat when I ventured out at night in a "soft" (unarmored) car with no body armor, no "shooter," and no weapon. In fact, there was always a certain element of unspoken unease and shared drama in these nighttime meetings, which everyone knew, deep down, were tempting fate. Our only protection in those circumstances was our anonymity. People who were not CPA employees, even American journalists and NGO workers, had a tough time getting into the Green Zone without clearance, so I would sometimes meet them at the "red zone" side of an inconspicuous checkpoint. To get through the checkpoints on foot, one had to negotiate a maze of concrete barriers, sandbagged fortifications, razor wire, and no-nonsense, armed American sentries, whose flashlights stared down intently and skeptically at my plastic identity cards, my lifeline to reentry. Out on the Baghdad streets at night, our cars were sometimes stopped at makeshift police checkpoints, and I asked myself, How do we know that these are really Iraqi police and not terrorists wearing the uniform? In fact, a number of Westerners and Iraqis would later be murdered and kidnapped on the highway at fake checkpoints. Outside the Green Zone, I felt naked and exposed, with no protection; when I came back in March from a break back home, it was with a $1,200 custom-made bulletproof vest that I had ordered over the Internet. If insurgents tried to kill me in a public meeting or a restaurant, or on a road trip, the vest would give me a fighting chance of stopping some ordinary bullets. I liked the fact that the vest fit under my clothes, since there was no way I (or any of my colleagues) would sit in a public meeting or restaurant draped in a bulging, ceramic-plated exterior vest of body armor—even if we had been issued one. For the remainder of my time in Iraq, I wore my concealed vest every time I exited the Green Zone to socialize, meet, speak, or travel. I had a blue blazer that was cut generously enough to accommodate the extra bulk, and it became my uniform. The vest was awkward, stiff, and uncomfortable, but no one seemed to notice.

I did not yet have that layer of personal protection in mid-February, when the Governance Office organized a good-bye dinner for one of our staffers who was heading back to the States, and then eventually to a plum European diplomatic posting that she had richly earned. She was a funny, savvy, and capable colleague, and everyone wanted to give her a warm send-off. So nine of us walked across the street to the palace parking lot and piled into two of the sedans that belonged to the Governance motor pool. I was nervous about this excursion, because it involved the entire senior staff of the Governance Office going out together into Baghdad at night, with no security. But I respected my colleagues, and I figured they knew what they were doing. We proceeded on what can only be described as a thirty-minute joy ride through the darkened streets of the war-torn capital, turning suddenly one corner and then another, searching for a particular Italian restaurant that had really good pizza. Our lead driver thought he knew where the restaurant was, but we quickly became lost as both drivers and other would-be navigators exchanged hunches and instructions between the two cars via cell phones. As we wound through the streets of the upscale Arasat neighborhood, we passed the ruined hulk of a building, now largely rubble. This, my colleague told me matter-of-factly, had been the Nabil Restaurant—until a car packed with four hundred pounds of artillery blew it up at a New Year's party on December 31, killing eight people (including three American journalists) and wounding over thirty. Now, I thought, we are really tempting fate. Here we were, a few weeks later, in the neighborhood where a suicide bomber had blown up a holiday party packed with Iraqis and Westerners. Shortly we found the Italian restaurant, and we arranged ourselves around a long table covered in a red-checked plastic tablecloth. We were the only customers in the joint, and throughout the meal I ate in a private turmoil thinking that one phone call from one Iraqi waiter to one insurgent group could bring in a guy with a machine gun who could wipe out the CPA's entire political transition program. I was furious. The next day I told my senior colleague that if he wanted to put his life in jeopardy, that was his business, but the previous night's escapade had better be the last time he endangered our entire mission just so that we could get a good pizza.

★

In my obsession to catch up with the months of preparation that had preceded my arrival, and to get as much done as possible in the limited time I would have, I often brought lunch or dinner back to my desk and ate while working. But I also made a practice now and then of picking someone new, at random, to dine with in the palace mess hall. Over meals, I met a wide range of interesting, talented, hopeful, and frustrated men and women. In this way, I met a number of army officers— smart, well educated, pragmatic, and robust. None of them thought we had enough troops in Iraq, and many complained about the lack of resources. Here I also got to know more of the Iraqis who were working for the CPA. One of them, Mohammed (not his real name), was just getting off his six-hour translating shift when I met him at dinner. His six hours at the palace followed six hours of work every morning at a nearby hospital. As a doctor he earned $100 per month, four times what he was making before the war but only a quarter of his monthly pay as a translator. We talked about a lot of things—his hopes for Iraq, his family, and the difficult state of the economy. I told him I had just bought a wad of the old currency, with Saddam's picture, to hand out to my friends. He told me he gives the worthless currency to his daughter to draw on. His little girl saw the picture of the smiling Saddam and cried out, "Uncle." No, her father explained, it was a very bad person. Then she corrected herself: "Bad uncle."

Like our other Iraqi translators, Mohammed had to hide his work at the CPA from all but his closest family and friends; otherwise his life would have been in danger. The insurgents knew that our inability to work in Arabic was part of the soft underbelly of the CPA, and they regularly harassed, threatened, and murdered our Iraqi translators, many of whom were torn between the desire to serve, the need for the income, and the fear of violent death. We had, in the Governance Office, a superb Iraqi translator (I will call him Rashid) who, like many of the Iraqis who worked for the CPA, was underutilized and underappreciated but fiercely committed to the job. Despite his hint of a British accent, he had never left Iraq, and in fact his specialty before the war, while teaching at an elite military language academy, had been American English. His wife and oldest daughter were schoolteachers. As he accompanied me in my lectures and tours in Baghdad and we built up a kind of friendship and trust, Rashid began to share with me his fears and frustrations. A number of our Iraqi translators were being assaulted and threatened. A translator in the Ministry of Justice had gone to the military force responsible for security in the Green Zone and was told simply, "We can only protect you in the Green Zone." He did not come to work the next day. Another was badly beaten but came to work anyway. Not long before, Rashid himself received a note that read, "If you don't quit working for the Americans, we will kill you." He told me in a chillingly flat tone, "If it is our destiny, it will happen." But he also complained bitterly that the American forces were unable to do more to protect him—or at least permit him to shape his destiny a little more actively. He had a gun and wanted a license to carry it, to have a fighting chance if he was attacked. But the U.S. Army—not wanting to deal with an Iraqi entering the Green Zone with a weapon—refused him. Rashid didn't think that the American forces "really care about us." When we spoke one day in mid-February, he had arrived at six in the morning at the Fourteenth of July Bridge, one of the major points of access for Iraqi workers to enter the Green Zone. But because of the danger of car bombs and sabotage, every vehicle had to be checked laboriously; he did not enter the Green Zone until ten. For four hours he sat there, turning his engine off and on, bored and aggravated, tortuously creeping up a car at a time, utterly exposed—a target.[4]

I suppose one could say it was Rashid's six children (ages three to twenty-one) and the $100 per week (a good salary by the standards of a devastated postwar Iraq) that kept him coming back each day in the face of the mortal dangers and the indignities. But I felt as well—as I did with most of the Iraqis who worked with us—a sincere sense of conviction, gratitude, and solidarity with what we were trying to do. These were good, decent, brave, and ethical people who had quietly survived thirty-five years of Baathist dictatorship. I did not see how we could leave them, cavalierly, standing in line outside the Green Zone for hours each day, waiting for the next car bombing. Alarmed, I asked the senior CPA civilian figure in charge of administration if we couldn't find some way of processing these Iraqi workers each day that didn't leave them standing, or sitting in their cars, exposed outside the Green Zone, easy targets. He expressed sympathy, but no change was instituted during my time there.[5] Rashid was assassinated in January 2005 while continuing to work as a translator for the U.S. embassy.

★

For the most part, we all felt safe inside the Green Zone, but now and then we were jolted into sharp awareness of the violent world around us. That happened to me at eight in the morning on a quiet, foggy Sunday, January 18, when the walls of my trailer shook with a mighty force. A mile away, a 1,000-pound car bomb exploded at one of the main gates into the Green Zone, aptly nicknamed the Assassin's Gate, killing twenty-five people (including two American civilian employees of the Defense Department) and wounding more than a hundred. Most of the dead were Iraqis, and quite deliberately so; the bomb had been timed to kill, maim, and terrorize the maximum concentration of Iraqis—manual laborers and highly educated translators alike—who lined up each morning to be cleared to enter the Green Zone and then the palace, where they worked in support of the CPA. It was the deadliest car bombing, to date, in Baghdad, and although no American CPA officials were among the casualties, we were nevertheless devastated. The terrorists had struck, literally, at the gates of our operation, and many of us had friends and coworkers among the Iraqis killed and wounded. Nor did I think it was a coincidence that the bombing took place on the eve of the meeting at the United Nations to discuss the possible return of a mission to mediate the standoff over the political transition in Iraq.

In mid-March we would get a different kind of scare. Sometime on the night of March 13, a CPA military staff member was attacked and critically injured from stab wounds to his body, head, and neck as he walked back to his trailer. Military patrols then went from door to door in the trailers, hunting for the assailant and advising people to lock down their living spaces, but no suspect was ever apprehended. Rumors quickly flew through the palace, as they often did. An Iraqi terrorist had penetrated the Green Zone and would strike again. An Iraqi brother had avenged the honor of his sister and would not strike again. Somebody got caught up in a love triangle. In reality, nobody knew anything. Minds were not set at ease when an All Hands notice went out to every computer in the palace the next day, warning people to lock their trailer doors, utilize the buddy system while traveling back to the trailers at night, and, in the event of an "incident outside," to "stay in the trailer and defend your space." For several days thereafter, civilian women were accompanied to their trailers late at night and those with weapons made sure they were loaded when they headed back to the trailers. Having loaded weapons inside the palace or its immediate grounds was strictly forbidden, however; anyone carrying a gun had to ensure that its chamber was empty by firing it into a sandbagged area before entering the grounds. I had heard that there had been an "accidental discharge" inside the palace, landing the offender in serious hot water.

There was also the ever-present danger from rocket and mortar attacks, which came mainly during the nighttime, when insurgents could unload their launchers on a street across the river, fire away, and be gone before American forces could track them down. Like most of my coworkers, I quickly became inured to the thuds and rattles from these assaults, because in their relatively rapid, blind aim, the attackers never managed to actually hit the palace, and we had a lot of work to do. But when the attacks came too close, too fast, the sirens would sound, and we were all supposed to grab our helmets and flak jackets and head for the bomb shelter in the basement. My helmet and flak jacket were back at the trailer, and when I was under pressure of a tight deadline, I found the prospect of racing down to the basement a time-consuming annoyance. On several occasions, I just stayed at my desk and worked, along with some of my colleagues. But one night in March, the walls and windows shook with a vengeance I had not experienced before, and even the most hardened veterans of palace life became alarmed. Before the sirens sounded moments later, everyone in the office was gathering up some belongings or papers and heading quickly down the hall to the nearest basement entrance. It was my first visit down there, and I was awed by the spectacle of the bulk of the palace staff, high and low, military and civilian, standing around against the walls of the basement halls while troops in full battle gear with weapons ready raced past us to their stations. During my time in the palace, nothing was more unsettling than the sight of those American soldiers dashing down the crowded palace corridors. It was as if this last bastion of quiet and security was under imminent assault. The emergency exercise did provide an opportunity to meet new people, however, and I struck up a conversation with an Iraqi American woman from the Kurdish north who was working on reconstruction. She described to me her experiences there, and the poison gas attacks on the Kurds by Saddam's troops. She and her family, friends, and neighbors had to flee for their lives during one of those attacks. As people were running to escape Saddam's onslaught, an exhausted mother carrying her baby in her arms dropped the infant and could not go back to fetch the child. At this point, the woman who was telling me this story burst into tears and was unable to continue. She apologized for losing her composure, but I felt it was instead we, the Americans, who had stood by while Saddam gassed and slaughtered the Kurds, who owed an apology to her.

5

PROMOTING DEMOCRACY

★

During my first weeks, I was itching to get outside the palace and engage Iraqis. It was a season of optimism, and the CPA had great ambitions for promoting democracy. Beyond advising on the drafting of the interim constitution, I had come to the CPA with a vague, broad mandate to do just that. My mission gave me standing to inquire about and participate in a range of activities to assist civil society organizations and to educate Iraqis about the ideas and institutions of democracy. Over the previous two decades, I had spent a good deal of time working with and learning from nongovernmental organizations around the world that were struggling to build democratic values and structures. I had also spent the last quarter of a century teaching and lecturing about democracy to university students and other audiences. I very much wanted to undertake these activities in Iraq, and I asked Judy Van Rest and her democracy programming staff to set up whatever meetings and seminars they could.

On January 15, I got my first opportunity: a seminar with university students and recent graduates from three Iraqi NGOs. My seminar was organized by Van Rest's office and a democracy assistance unit with which it worked closely, the Office of Transition Initiatives, or

OTI, a division of America's foreign aid instrument, the Agency for International Development. OTI was only one part of the massive USAID presence in Iraq, which occupied a sprawling expanse of modern office space in the Convention Center, just across from the al-Rashid Hotel. For democracy building, though, it was a precious asset. It had been established in 1994 as a vehicle for responding quickly to the political reconstruction challenges that arose suddenly when dictatorships fell, states failed, and civil wars ended. Since 1990, USAID had been growing dramatically beyond its original mission of economic development to include a substantial program (with half a billion dollars in budgeting) to promote democracy around the world. But USAID was notorious for the slow, deliberate pace and complex contracting requirements of its traditional work. Situations like the one we were now confronting—a regime had suddenly collapsed and civic groups needed aid and inspiration fast—needed a leaner, more adaptive, and more rapid response, through an organization that was not afraid to take risks and could make grants quickly to small, indigenous organizations, without the usual ponderous trail of approvals. That was what OTI did.

Among the Iraqi organizations OTI had helped to fund were the three groups of Iraqi young people that I was about to meet. One was Just Read, a circle of university students from Baghdad who had come together to learn about the principles of democracy and to teach those principles to fellow Iraqis. Just Read, which had assisted OTI with the production of a handbook for training workshops, was about to reproduce and distribute copies of the Universal Declaration of Human Rights. Its founder, a thirty-four-year-old Iraqi whom I will call Omar, had deserted the military after being drafted in the mid-1990s, spent a year in prison, and escaped in 2000 to Jordan, where he worked with the Iraqi Free Officers Association. Omar's boss at the association rode back into Iraq on an American tank, and had invited Omar to join him. Instead, he quit the group, which he felt suffered from the same authoritarian mentality as the Baathists, telling his former supervisor that the Iraqi people would remember how the exiles returned to the country. So he rented a car and drove back in, and quickly reengaged with Iraqi youth. His philosophy was that people should be encouraged to write out their complaints and that people in authority should "just read" them and respond. The Iraqi people also needed to "just read" (and think for themselves), to trust facts and data, not slogans.

The second group funded by OTI was the Contemporary Visual Arts Society, which drew together about 250 young Iraqi specialists in a wide variety of visual media—painting, photography, sculpture, theater, cinema, caricature, and digital art—to deploy their talents in a campaign to publicize democratic values. In the preceding few months, with OTI assistance, they had put up several thousand posters around Baghdad, promoting a vision of a peaceful, prosperous future through art and poetry, and they had staged workshops in Sadr City (the Shiite slum of Baghdad) and Fallujah, teaching three thousand children not just the techniques of painting and drawing but the idea of free expression through art.

The third group receiving OTI assistance was the Al-Salam Association for Development of Youth, which worked with OTI to distribute leaflets describing the November 15 agreement. Like Just Read and the Contemporary Visual Arts Society, Al-Salam and its members had a passionate desire to live in a free society and recognized that freedom would require a widespread change in values and expectations. Indeed, the Just Read organization had as its motto: "Iraqis must learn that the man sitting behind the desk is now the servant of the man standing in front of the desk."

When I walked into our conference room in the cavernous Convention Center, I encountered a scene that resembled meetings at almost any college in the world. Young men and women were laughing and gossiping. The men were dressed casually in jeans and slacks. Most of the young women were Western in appearance, but a few wore headscarves and were conservatively clad. A number of latecomers (mostly the young men) were rummaging around for seats. People were drifting in slowly because the group members had to clear the formidable layers of security surrounding the Green Zone. There was a faint trace of nervousness in the air as the professor waited to meet the students, the students waited to engage the professor, the men flirted with the women, and everyone wanted to make a good impression on everyone else. As we waited for the latecomers to arrive and find seats, I used the same technique that I had in classrooms back at Stanford. I picked some nearby individuals and started talking with them. This set the room at ease and got us going informally.

After a short wait, Omar introduced me and I began speaking in English. Only some of the participants had a good command of the language, so an interpreter was provided. It took me a while to adjust to the rhythm and pace of consecutive translation, which works best if one speaks in short clips, pausing often for the interpreter. I also had to struggle to find the right pitch. I had been asked to speak about basic principles of democracy, to help these young people to shape the content of their civic education efforts. I did not quite know where to begin. How much did they know about democracy as a system of government? If I overestimated their understanding, I risked veering toward the arcane and missing the big principles they were looking for. But if I underestimated them, I risked boring them or, worse still, insulting them.

I decided to speak only briefly and to leave most of the allotted time for questions and comments. As I would do in later seminars and speeches, and in a variety of civic education materials that I drafted, I emphasized two basic principles of democracy: rule by the people and rights of the people. Democracy is a system of government in which the people can choose their leaders—and replace their leaders—in regular, free, and fair elections, I began. It is a government of laws, not individuals. In a democracy, the people are sovereign and government functions with the consent of the governed. Many people think of this system as "majority rule," I said. But there are a number of ways of structuring democracy, and a fundamental element of any democracy is protection of the rights of minorities and of individuals. People must be free to think, worship, speak, write, organize, assemble, and petition the government. Groups must be free to practice their religion and culture. Democracy is as much about minority rights as majority rule. And it is also about the rule of law. I explained that real democracy requires independent courts, equality before the law, and constitutional limits on the powers of government. It establishes independent institutions to control and punish corruption and abuse of power. Successful democracy depends on a culture of tolerance, negotiation, compromise, and restraint. Citizens must not only exercise their rights but respect the rights of others.

Conceptually, this information was not new to the young people in the hall, but they seemed to welcome having it presented in this way. They had many questions, which they had been struggling with and debating among themselves. What were the virtues of parliamentary versus presidential government? Does democracy require the privatization of state industries? (No, I said, but the economy would become more vigorous if capitalism was eventually adopted.) They also wanted to express their ideas and frustrations and, in a way, to educate me. "How do we make people feel free after thirty years of dictatorship?" one student asked. I conceded that I didn't know the answer; the shift in perception would happen only gradually and through the practice of democracy, not just the spreading of ideas. Another chimed in, "People aren't ready to jump to democracy. Over the last thirty-five years [since the Baath Party came to power], all sorts of authoritarian ideas were imposed on us. They established dictatorship even in the primary schools, where one child would be singled out as the leader of the class. So we feel the superiority of our leaders." A few raised concerns about what democracy would bring in the near term. "How can I be sure of fair elections if the majority of people are poor?" one person asked. The implication was that poor, uneducated Iraqis would vote as their tribal chief or imam instructed them. Another young man was more explicit: "Elections are purposeless now. People will just vote for their own group. Kurds will vote for Kurds."

All these young Iraqis agreed on democracy as the long-term goal. They understood that the commitment would require a profound change in the mind-set of Iraqis, who for thirty-five years had been taught to submit unquestioningly to authority—to "look to the president as a demi-God." But they were deeply worried about the practical challenges and obstacles. "The Americans didn't take into account that all the neighboring states are nondemocratic. There will be a campaign against democracy here." Indeed, another conceded, such a campaign was already under way, and democrats in Iraq were losing the media war. They felt isolated and overwhelmed. "For the last seven months, we have been trying to contact the outside world," said one of their leaders. "We have no passports, no Internet, no telephones, and independent groups in the U.S. can't contact us." They wanted help from the CPA to build Iraqi civil society, and they thought democracy should

emerge gradually, so that Iraqis could become educated about a free
society and the culture could be transformed. Some of them simply
wanted my encouragement and reassurance. "Professor, will democracy be successful in Iraq?" a young woman asked. Another young person answered her, "We had a democratic process from the 1920s to
1958. We were standing, someone pushed us down, and we need to
stand up again. I am sure democracy will succeed in Iraq with international support." Our session went on for more than two hours, but I
could not offer a better response to the young woman's question. I left
the seminar both concerned and inspired.

★

Back in the palace, planning was going forward on a number of aspects
of a comprehensive campaign to assist the development of democracy.
In Judy Van Rest's office, down the hall from the main Governance Office, sat an enthusiastic crew of foreign service officers, political appointees, military officers, and postconflict specialists, all working on
programs of outreach and assistance to political parties, civic groups,
women's organizations, and universities. On many initiatives, there were
cross-functional task forces drawing, as well, from USAID; the offices of
the senior advisers to the various ministries; Strategic Communications,
our enormous and cumbersome public relations operation, which
everyone called Stratcomm; and CJTF-7, the military command. One of
the task forces had recently been set up to craft a comprehensive program for civic education in Iraq. I was asked to join the group, to help it
explain, in simple terms, the principles and institutions of democracy.

Our goal was straightforward but disarmingly ambitious. We wanted
to educate the Iraqi public about freedom and democracy. We wanted
them to understand—for the first time—the rights and obligations they
had as citizens of a democracy. For many of my colleagues, the task was
a challenge; while they had grown up in a democracy and worked in
myriad ways to advance the institution, they had never had to explain
what democracy is and how it works. I, in turn, had been doing so for almost twenty years—but to university students, not to people with as little as a fifth-grade education. And while I had lectured about
democracy well beyond the United States—for a year to students in

Nigeria, and to students and civic activists in Asia, Latin America, eastern Europe, Turkey, and other parts of Africa—I had never before engaged a society that was so recently emerging from such a long and brutal authoritarian reign. Where to begin?

First we had to map out a sequence of themes—the various elements of democracy, which would be introduced one by one over several months. Each week we would distribute (in both Arabic and Kurdish) up to a million leaflets and 40,000 posters. By early February, OTI had approved six grants to the Contemporary Visual Arts Society, totaling over half a million dollars, to cover the design and printing costs of the first three leaflets and posters. On one side of the leaflet would be the weekly theme in big bold letters, followed by a short question and then a brief, one-sentence answer, below which would be an eye-catching illustration. For example: "Citizens' Rights. What Rights Do Citizens Have in a Democracy? Everyone Has Basic Human Rights That the State Cannot Take Away." On the other side of the leaflet would be a more substantial, but still concise, one-paragraph explanation. The posters would be large enough to combine the two design elements, with the short paragraph appearing at the bottom, below the illustration. Beginning in mid-February and stretching through to the handover of power at the end of June, we would release one leaflet each week. Distribution would depend heavily on CPA regional and provincial offices, Iraqi NGOs, and—not least, given that they had by far the greatest capacity—the (predominantly American) Coalition military forces. Little did we know then how much of an ordeal this project would become.

I suggested that we start with an overview of what democracy is— that government flows from the people and is based upon their consent—and then move on to citizens' rights and the rule of law as the next two themes. This subject could be followed by judicial independence as the bulwark of the rule of law, and by such other attributes of democracy as participation, minority rights, transparency, unbiased media, civil society, political parties, free and fair elections, legislative representation, and civilian control of the military. We would also need to explain what federalism is, and the different ways of structuring and limiting executive power. We exchanged ideas and elaborated the list, and since I had the greatest expertise in this area, my recommendations were generally accepted. One important change was made from above, however. Because our campaign was due to be launched in mid-February, just two weeks before the interim constitution, the transitional administrative law, was to be finalized, it was decided that the project would begin with the four key themes of the public relations effort to promote the interim constitution: Citizens' Rights, Federalism, Separation of Powers and Judicial Independence, and the Structure of Executive Powers. It says a lot about the priority CPA gave to federalism in the interim constitution that it was designated as the second theme in the campaign (I had initially imagined it would come weeks down the line). The leaflet on executive powers would explain how parliamentary systems work and why even in some parliamentary systems some power can be exercised by the presidency.

The second step was to devise appropriate wording for each theme. Some preliminary drafting had been done, but it was not precise, concise, and instructive enough, and I decided to start from scratch. I approached the task with some unease, because my teaching and writing about democracy had not prepared me to engage a general Arab public, many of whom had not attended high school, much less college. Of course, all the paragraphs were going to be translated into Arabic—that was the third step, and it would require more than just literal translation. The rendition of meaning from one language to another is not simply a technical exercise. It is an art, requiring the translator to preserve the substance while finding a style of wording that appears as authentic and familiar as possible. The process was a challenge because some Western democratic concepts lack a natural parallel in Arabic. OTI was thus arranging to have some Iraqis review the translated material to ensure that it was expressed in a voice that would ring true.

In delineating the themes and content of the democracy campaign, I was helped greatly by the Center for Civic Education, a nonprofit corporation founded in 1969 to advance democratic civic education in the United States but which had become increasingly international in its work with the global democratic revolution of the 1980s and 1990s. Over the previous several years, the center had developed a comprehensive international framework for democratic education titled *"Res*

Publica,"[1] from the Latin phrase (meaning "the public thing") from which the word *republic* is derived. Although it did not provide democracy lessons in the simple language we were looking for, it did present (for teachers, textbook writers, policy makers, and civic groups) the core ideas and elements of democracy, valid across nations and cultures. The center's Web site was loaded with instructional materials and strategies as well. Beyond this, the center's executive director, Chuck Quigley, and its international curriculum guru, Chuck Bahmueller, responded expeditiously by e-mail to my requests for help. It never ceased to amaze me that I was able to obtain so much valuable help from experts in democratic development around the world, while sitting at a computer in Baghdad in the former kitchen of Saddam Hussein's Republican Palace.

During the second week of February, I created a series of nine paragraphs that would carry the campaign from its opening, with Citizens' Rights, in mid-February through to Due Process of Law, in mid-April.[2] The leaflet on the rule of law read:

WHAT IS THE RULE OF LAW?

Laws and Procedures Apply Fairly and Equally to All Citizens

Democracy is a system of rule by laws, not individuals. In a democracy, the rule of law protects the rights of citizens, maintains order, and limits the power of government. All citizens are equal under the law. No one may be discriminated against on the basis of race, religion, ethnic group, or gender. No one may be arrested, imprisoned, or exiled arbitrarily. No one may be denied freedom without a fair and public hearing by an impartial court. No one may be taxed or prosecuted except by a law established in advance. No one is above the law, not even a king or an elected president. The law is fairly, impartially, and consistently enforced, by courts that are independent of the other branches of government.

The leaflets and posters were only one dimension of a bold, mutually reinforcing, multimedia campaign. A major part of the project was to unfold over radio and television. OTI had made another grant to

Evini Films, an Iraqi video production company based in the Kurdish north, which had recently produced a moving documentary on Iraq's mass graves. Evini was now to produce, in Arabic and Kurdish, public service announcements that could be broadcast over the Iraqi television network, Al-Iraqiyah, as well as on local television stations throughout the country. Each week the nationally broadcast public service announcement would distill and dramatize the content of the week's civic education leaflet. Once the Transitional Administrative Law was finalized, an even larger advertising campaign would roll out in a media blitz to sell the document to the Iraqi public.

The leafleting and media efforts were to be complemented by a third, crucial component: face-to-face democracy dialogues and town hall meetings. The CPA team, which included USAID officers with experience in civic education, understood that education for democracy must not be merely passive and abstract. The design of the program had absorbed the lessons of previous efforts in emerging democracies. If civic education is to be successful, it must be linked to what is actually happening in the political process, and to the concerns that citizens have in their daily lives, communities, and organizations. Further, it must focus not just on individuals but on groups and communities, including large numbers of women. And it must be action-oriented, providing repeated opportunities for individuals to participate (with the encouragement of indigenous trainers) in elements of the democratic process, including discussion, negotiation, and formulation of issue agendas.

On the basis of these operational principles, the CPA drafted an elaborate plan for a series of public meetings, large and small, at which the Iraqis would discuss not only what democracy is but what they wanted it to produce. The dialogues would take place on many levels. In communities throughout the country, citizens would exchange views about the key themes of our civic education campaign, and of the new interim constitution, with the aid of an Iraqi facilitator who would direct, stimulate, and mediate the discussion. A private USAID contractor, Research Triangle International (RTI), had been enlisted to hire and train local Iraqi facilitators for this purpose, and the facilitators' supervisors were put through an intensive, five-day training course. In the process, the effort would develop capabilities among Iraqi NGOs, from which many of the facilitators would be recruited, and would cultivate the skills and habits of active citizenship. On a much larger scale, a series of national agenda conferences would bring Iraqis together across geographic, ethnic, and religious lines, on the basis of shared functional or professional interests—for example, women, young people, lawyers, business leaders, academics, journalists, farmers, and the physically handicapped. For each sector, an Iraqi civil society organization (such as the bar association) would be asked to sponsor a series of local discussions and workshops, culminating in a two-day national conference. These meetings went well beyond civic education to foster democracy in action. The intention was for the various sectors of society to craft an agenda of political and social concerns that they would then present to political leaders, to the caucuses that would be held to select the transitional national assembly, and to the new assembly itself. There was also to be a series of town hall meetings at which the members of the Governing Council and other experts would explain the political program, including the Transitional Administrative Law. All these activities were meant, in the words of one planning document, "to encourage Iraqi ownership of the Transition to Sovereignty and the upcoming political process."

The strategic plan was conceptually impressive and exciting. For some months, the demand for written materials about democracy had been rising, as Iraqi groups and local CPA officers were taking the initiative to conduct civic education efforts. Some of the infrastructure for the democracy education and dialogue project was in place as a result of the work that RTI had done to develop and staff a local governance program. But we still faced formidable hurdles. We would need to recruit and train another five hundred to six hundred Iraqis (university students, NGO staff, teachers, and others) to facilitate the dialogues—especially people who had the education and values that would enable them to be trained quickly, and who would be likely to stick with the program as it seeped into the schools and the local governance. There was also a demand for educators—ideally Iraqis, but if necessary international staff—who could give lectures, around the country, on the elements of democracy and citizenship, and on the interim constitution

and the transitional program. Political science had been a grossly underdeveloped and ideologically politicized field in Iraq; only a few of
the members of the Governing Council exhibited much enthusiasm
for engaging their supposed constituents; and the CPA headquarters
was seriously understaffed; as a result, it was not clear where these lec-
turers would come from. (I was finding myself drafted into the role.)
Finally, there was a tension between the desire to generate active citizens who would assemble their interests, formulate their demands,
and take ownership of the process, on the one hand, and the reality of
a political vacuum, on the other. "We need to be careful about having
the national agenda dialogues generate policy recommendations," one
governance staffer warned at a meeting, "because we have no one to
implement them."

In mid-February, as the dialogues were getting started, I sat down
with a group of the Iraqi facilitators near RTI's high-tech, heavily fortified headquarters in downtown Baghdad. They were well educated, optimistic, and highly motivated, and they offered several rationales for
the work they were embarking on. They wanted to build a decent society and to "find solutions to our suffering" that would show "how we can
participate in repairing Iraq." Of course, they wanted to teach their fellow citizens their rights and responsibilities and "to promote a culture
of public service." Their efforts would give citizens the confidence to
speak freely and share their ideas, to unlock the initiative of "a very talented people" who had been beaten down for a generation. But they
also hoped "to see things from different sides," and to encourage Iraqis
to do so as well, to "solve problems without violence and to deal with
each other as human beings." If the dialogues could go forward with
these messages as planned, I thought, they could begin the process of
reshaping Iraq's political culture. But none of us was calculating then
how much this information might be muted or overshadowed by the
outbreak of a second war.

★

The democracy dialogues were building on a program of local government development that had been under way for months, through the

work of CPA officials in each of the provinces and through the large contract USAID had granted to RTI, which had over a thousand Iraqis—many of them teachers, doctors, and engineers—working in seventeen of the eighteen provinces and in four regional hubs. For decades, local governance had been dominated by the center. Now the CPA's Local Government Program was seeking to reverse that. It sought to train and empower local and provincial councils to assume more responsibility in the era of decentralization; to cultivate norms of accountability and responsiveness to the local populace; and to reform (the term used was "refresh") the councils so as to make them more inclusive and legitimate. None of these goals would be easy to achieve.

The challenges for decentralization were simple: the councils had no formal authority, no money, and questionable legitimacy. A decree specifying the powers of provincial and local governments had been under preparation by the CPA, but the Governing Council and many in the occupation authority felt it should not be promulgated until after the completion of the Transitional Administrative Law, which would define the constitutional parameters of government authority below the center. Thus, in late autumn of 2003, the CPA had put on hold plans for a new policy to allow provincial ministry offices to reallocate funds they received through the central ministries. Even so, the CPA's provincial coordinators and the local Coalition military commanders wanted the councils to begin exercising some responsibility, so that Iraqis could establish ownership of the reconstruction process, and so that the councils could develop legitimacy through their performance. Advisers were urging the CPA to give the councils real authority over resources (perhaps a portion of the budgets of selected central ministries) and over technical department heads, who were historically responsible only to the central government ministries. But money and authority were simply not flowing downward—sending an unfortunate mixed message. One CPA provincial coordinator later commented to me, "City council members were not being paid for months and months. Neither were police officers. We had local government without any resources and power. We kept raising these issues with CPA headquarters. We were trying to empower local government, but we couldn't pay them and they had no power." Sometimes military commanders would step in to fill the financing breach with their own funds, through the Commanders' Emergency Response Program, which had been set up to enable local U.S. commanders to respond quickly to urgent humanitarian and reconstruction needs. But these funds were not intended to pay the monthly salaries of Iraqi local government officials, and in any case that well was also running dry.

The "refreshment" process, we hoped, would broaden the representation on local and provincial councils, to reflect tribal, ethnic, religious, political, and occupational diversity; bring women into the system; remove corrupt, discredited officials and representatives; weed out anyone subject to de-Baathification (any member of the top four levels of the Baath Party)—and thereby give the councils, and the mayors and provincial governors elected by the councils, more legitimacy. Between May and November 2003, provincial and local councils had been constituted by a variety of means. In a few cases, councils had simply been appointed by the U.S. military commander; in others, CPA officials and civil affairs officers of the Coalition's local military command negotiated (even shuttling between rival factions in search of a compromise) to find the right balance. In some provinces, council members had been elected by a caucus of representatives and notables identified by the CPA.[3] At its most elaborate, in Baghdad, this method had chosen eighty-eight neighborhood councils, which elected representatives of nine district councils, which in turn elected members of the City Council. The only method that had been explicitly ruled out was direct elections, despite the call of many Iraqis, and the preference of several CPA officials in the provinces, for that approach. (However, in a few small towns, direct elections were conducted, using the food ration card as the basis of family registration.)

As the process gained momentum toward late 2003, some in the CPA were appealing again for direct elections. One major external adviser urged the CPA to reconsider holding elections for provincial councils soon, "so that Iraqis perceive the next step in the transition to be in the direction of greater Iraqi control, not a movement away." The councils were "all the Iraqis (and we the Coalition) have for the next few months to serve as a potential source of legitimacy," something that

Iraqis could feel "they own, can influence and can control." This potential was at risk because of the Iraqis' lack of a democratic mandate, their perceived ineffectiveness and powerlessness, and the prospect that they might be "caught up and captured entirely by the selection process for the transitional national assembly." The process proceeded through January, bringing in more women, more ethnic minorities, and representatives from beyond the provincial capitals (some of them elected by the local councils). In all, more than six hundred neighborhood, city, district, and provincial councils were established and in many cases reconstituted. Some were asked to advise on CPA reconstruction projects, or given small budgets to fix schools, promote public health, or control traffic. But for the most part, the deficits of resources and authority persisted, and with no plan to hold direct council elections for another year, the legitimacy deficit was expected to widen again soon.

★

On January 21, 2004, I made my first trip out of Baghdad, to speak in Hilla at the University of Scientific, Humanistic, and Theological Studies. The visit had been requested and arranged by Michael Gfoeller, our area coordinator for the South Central region (which mainly covered the Shiite heart of the country, including the holy cities of Najaf and Karbala). Because of Gfoeller's extraordinary energy, vision, and organizational skills, South Central (known to Iraqis as the Middle Euphrates) was the region under CPA administration that was furthest along in the promotion of democracy. He was in the process of setting up a network of eighteen democracy centers in the region's six provinces; but the brightest star in this firmament was the university— and the associated regional democracy center, in Hilla, which the CPA regional office was then in the process of building. Shortly after the war, the CPA had turned over the magnificent former presidential mosque in Hilla to the moderate Shiite cleric Sayyid Farqad al-Qizwini, for his university, which was part of a bold intellectual, theological, and political effort to reconcile Islam and democracy, and to reestablish the roots of Islam as a religion of tolerance.[4] Qizwini was not only educating Shiite men and women and conducting Islamic services in his mosque; he was creating a political movement of farmers, clerics, merchants, and tribal leaders called the Iraqi Democratic Gathering. Gfoeller wanted me to come down to Hilla to lecture on the meaning of democracy, and to spend some time with Qizwini and his colleagues.

It had taken some thought to organize the trip. Would we obtain an armored car and an elaborate escort—thereby exchanging our anonymity for tighter security—or would we fly under the radar screen, using sedans from our car pool, purchased because they looked like ordinary vehicles? This was a question that CPA officials struggled with whenever they had to travel outside Baghdad—or even outside the Green Zone. With sedans, one was much less likely to come under attack from an ambush, a drive-by shooting, or a roadside bomb, but more likely to die if attacked. Since armored cars and professional security details were in scarce supply, and since I had the sense that the lower profile might actually be the safer of the two alternatives, I opted for simplicity. We would need two cars, however, and we would have to recruit some shooters to give us a chance of repelling an attack if one came. As was so often the case, people volunteered without hesitation or complaint. Ty Cobb, who had picked me up at the airport, was among those who offered to escort me, along with a colonel from our Governance Office and a couple of retired military officers working on contract.

Exiting the Green Zone early that morning, we passed long lines of people and cars waiting to enter over the Fourteenth of July Bridge—just three days after the enormous car bomb at the Assassin's Gate checkpoint had killed twenty-five people. As we crossed a second bridge, mist rose off the Tigris on a cold, sunny winter morning. In the distance stood the four tall smokestacks of a power plant, one of them billowing thick black exhaust that trailed off across the horizon in a long wisp, like the emission from an old train. From the elevated freeway over the southern section of Baghdad, we could see palm trees and minarets protruding above a flat expanse of one-story homes and buildings, punctuated occasionally by a modest high-rise. We passed the sprawling al-Rashid vegetable market, where a tangle of trucks fought to get in and out, then a massive junkyard strewn with ruined vehicles and burned-out tanks, and fields of dirt and muck that looked like raw sewage. The gray, smoky sky, dotted with palm trees, reminded me vaguely of Nigeria (where I had taught and conducted research over many years), except that there was no moisture in the air, and virtually no other green on the ground. Cars floated in and out of lanes, as if drugged, and our calm, experienced Iraqi driver did his best to maneuver around them. As we darted past traffic, most of it backed up in the other direction, coming into the capital, I tried to keep my head down, to avoid advertising my American face. I wished I had worn my flak jacket; I did not yet understand that it would have done me little good if someone had starting pumping automatic weapons fire into the soft metal skin of our car.

We continued driving south, past a Shiite mosque with a primitive, earthen dome resembling a beehive, and into the town of Mahmudiyah. Every so often we had to stop at a police checkpoint; there would be four on the two-hour trip. We drove by fruit stands and horse-drawn carts, then a makeshift bus station for vans taking people into Baghdad, and sped onto another stretch of highway, passing ramshackle houses, abandoned half-finished buildings, straw huts, rusted metal shacks, and an occasional mansion surrounded by high walls. Thirty miles out of Hilla, the traffic thinned and we sped past miles of barren brown land littered with pools of sludge, mounds of trash, and twisted wreckage. It was the stark landscape of a broken, wasted country.

We arrived in mid-morning at the Babylon Hotel in Hilla, which served as the South Central regional headquarters of the Coalition Provisional Authority. The Babylon was a seedy structure that had once been a Baathist hangout. Mike Gfoeller offered us a brief orientation. Hilla, the capital of Babel Province, had been a center of the Shiite resistance to Saddam, and Sayyid Qizwini had been a leader in the underground resistance. Qizwini's family had been prominent in the Middle Euphrates region for four centuries.[5] A few years earlier, Saddam's regime had tried to assassinate the cleric by planting a bomb in his car. But that day the younger Qizwini lent the car to his father, the founder of the university, who wound up being killed by the bomb, along with one of Qizwini's brothers. The presidential mosque from which Qizwini now operated had been built in the early 1990s at a cost of some $25 million. Saddam never prayed in it, and when Iraq was liberated, in April 2003, the mosque had been locked up for a decade, except for the occasional Baathist dinner party. The situation was a grievous insult to the pious, impoverished people of Hilla, who were in need of a decent place of worship.

We piled into Gfoeller's huge armored SUV, accompanied by a heavy security detail, and made our way to the mosque. The drive took us through a dilapidated city, now jammed with traffic. We passed a building in total ruins that had once been the local Baath Party head-quarters and now provided shelter to squatters. Mobs had looted and destroyed it after Saddam fell. I noticed a stream of graffiti scrawled in huge Arabic script on the outer wall. Gfoeller translated it for me: "The house of the oppressor is in ruins." The heavy traffic, Gfoeller explained, resulted from the revival of the economy. The CPA had pumped $65 million into South Central since July, as much money as the rest of the country combined, feeding a boom in construction, much of it locally driven. Kilns were pouring out bricks using the area's rich clay deposits. Homes were being rebuilt, salaries paid, shops opening, and more food harvested. "This is Mesopotamia," Gfoeller said, "some of the finest land in the world. You can grow almost anything here. It was a food ex-porter until 1958." Dates, grains, livestock, and fish farming were all re-bounding. Gfoeller had high hopes for the future. "The economy of this area will run on agribusiness and tourism. Oil will be an afterthought." The area was littered with ancient archeological sites, and Gfoeller's re-gional office was spending money to protect them against tomb raiders and other thieves—a means not only of preserving the past but of pro-tecting the economic future. A few miles south lay the ziggurat of Bor-sippa, in the heart of ancient Babylon, and an hour south of that was Nippur, which had served for thousands of years as the religious capital of Mesopotamia. This area could make Iraq one of the greatest tourist destinations in the Middle East. "Maybe 5 percent of Babylon has been looked at," he said. "Most still lies underground, unexcavated."

Gfoeller was as animated in talking about the ancient past as he was in discussing the Iraqi present or future. He had been an avid enthusi-ast of archeology since he was a child, hearing his father recite Homer in Greek. After his service as deputy chief of the U.S. mission in Arme-nia, Gfoeller and his family had established a private foundation to sup-port archeological research in the Caucasus. Gfoeller himself reads

Greek, Latin, and Coptic—and speaks German, French, Russian, Polish, Romanian, and Arabic. Before joining the Foreign Service in 1984, he studied Islamic history, philosophy, and theology at the famous al-Azhar University, in Cairo, going on to earn an M.A. summa cum laude in Middle Eastern studies from Georgetown. With seven previous postings in the Middle East and the former Communist states, he came to Iraq as one of the rising stars in the Foreign Service, and as one of its best Arab linguists—which I would soon discover when he frequently corrected the interpreter during my sessions with Qizwini.

Soon we arrived at the gated compound of the former presidential mosque, where Sayyid Qizwini was waiting for us. The site of the powerful Shiite cleric greeting his friend Gfoeller in traditional Arab style was a memorable one. Both men were larger than life, and they shared an evident rapport, respect, and even affection. With his black turban (the mark of a Sayyid), flowing black outer robe, ample girth, huge hands, thick black beard, and six-foot, six-inch frame, Qizwini towered over his Iraqi students, colleagues, and followers—and over his American visitors as well. Inventive, indefatigable, and at home in this milieu, in his trademark safari jacket and olive fedora, Gfoeller—or Mr. Mike to his Iraqi interlocutors—called to mind, in turn, "a soft-spoken, Midwestern version of Indiana Jones" to a reporter from *U.S. News & World Report* who would accompany him a few weeks later around the South Central region.[6] Behind the Sayyid on the steps of the mosque stood an assemblage of black-robed Shiite clerics in white and black turbans, joined by local political officials, community leaders, and tribal sheikhs in traditional dress. It was an amazing scene. The clutches of clerics were, in appearance, indistinguishable from the radical mullahs who had run Iran into the ground. I wondered what I was in for.

The mosque was a soaring, magnificent sight, a gleaming complex of sculpted stone walls, enormous arched entries, and delicately chiseled pillars, finished above with golden lines of Arabic script on blue tiles, then crowned by a massive, blue-inlaid dome and two perfectly proportioned minarets. The interior ceiling rose several stories high, sustained by gigantic marble columns, beneath which hung chandeliers and rich wooden doors, framed by intricate marble patterns. It was the most beautiful building I had seen, or would see, in Iraq.

Gathering inside for my lecture were perhaps a thousand people, seated in chairs that completely filled two long interior spaces that met in a right angle in the rotunda, just outside the main hall of prayer—the largest and most stunning part of the building, capable of accommodating three thousand people. But first the Sayyid wanted a private chat.

We walked to Qizwini's personal office in a corner of the mosque complex. I presented him with several of my books on democracy, which I thought might be useful for his library. His face quickly lit up; he had a better idea. With support from the CPA, his university was just beginning an ambitious effort to translate, into Arabic, a number of Western books on democracy. "Yours will be the first," he declared. I called his attention to the collection I had helped edit from the *Journal of Democracy*, titled *Islam and Democracy in the Middle East*. This immediately provoked him to explain why Islam and democracy are in fact compatible. In Shiite Islam, he said, leadership comes from Allah, but Allah will not choose directly. When the people elect a leader, he will be the man selected by Allah. "So there is no contradiction between Islam and democracy," he said. "This is the mistaken understanding of those whose thinking is in the Middle Ages, who have a dictator in their hearts." Then he uttered a statement that I would hear over and over in my interactions with Iraqis, and which he would repeat to the crowd in introducing me: "We must get rid of the little Saddam in each of us." Off to the side, Al-Jazeera television was silently flashing images of John Kerry winning the Iowa caucuses and George W. Bush delivering his State of the Union address, while a headline crawled underneath in Arabic, "Gephardt withdraws from presidential race." Paying no attention, Qizwini poured out his views while the interpreter struggled to summarize them for me. He wanted to see Iraq develop an ideology that combines Western and Islamic versions of democracy. There could be room in democracy for Islamic principles such as *zakat*, the obligatory giving of alms to the poor. The result would be a synthesis, but with real democracy, not the kind of sham that exists in Iran. His deep contempt, even loathing, for the Iranian regime quickly became apparent. Indeed, one thing that united the several thousand tribal sheikhs and local notables from around the country who had joined his movement was resentment at the Iranian effort to penetrate and control Iraq's emerging politics—something that worried Gfoeller as well. The people who had come to my lecture wanted to understand and achieve democracy. That is why two thousand came when a thousand were invited, Qizwini said.

I could not know how many people were really in the mosque (the CPA press release said "more than 1,500"), but the two huge hallways that converged on my podium were packed and the interest was intense. In a back section of one of the chambers, perhaps two hundred women were seated, separate but included. Qizwini began with a spirited introduction, in which he appealed to Iraqis to respect the role of women and to "put love and friendship between us again. Let us each have the freedom to express ourselves, but let us respect each other. Let us not turn on each other. Let us not create another dictator that will oppress us. Together we can build a new, free and democratic Iraq." I gave the speech I had prepared, titled "What Is Democracy?" In it, I articulated more fully the principles I had conveyed to the students the previous week. I identified four key elements of democracy: choosing and replacing the government through free and fair elections; active citizen participation in politics and civic life; protection of the human rights of all citizens; and the rule of law, in which the regulations and procedures apply equally to all citizens. I then explained that if democracy is to work, citizens must be bound by certain obligations: to respect the rights and the dignity of fellow citizens, to be open to compromise, to obey the law, and to reject violence. I closed with a personal appeal. I had been told that people in this area feared that the United States would abandon them again—as it had done heartlessly in 1991, when the Shiites rose up against Saddam with U.S. encouragement and then were left to be slaughtered by Saddam's army as the Americans stood aside. Many worried that the United States would walk away after the transfer of power on June 30. I assured them, "From my deepest conviction, this will not happen." I conceded that Americans were divided about whether we should have gone to war in Iraq, as they were in their political preferences. But the overwhelming majority supported our efforts to help build democracy in Iraq. In the coming months and years, there would be assistance to help Iraq revive its economy and establish democratic parties, legislatures, courts, governments, and NGOs.

If Iraqis embraced democracy, I said, we would be with them for the long haul.

The speech was well received, and occasioned an outpouring of written submissions. People had questions about how democracy works, as well as comments and personal reflections. Several wanted to know why elections were not possible soon. I explained that an election could be held at any time but that a free and fair ballot requires administrative, political, and civic preparation so that everyone can vote and every political group has a chance to compete. I did my best to answer all the questions. At one point, when a female lawyer asked whether it wasn't possible in Islam for women to be judges, Qizwini intervened directly, to indicate politely (and much to my chagrin) that this practice was not permitted in Islam but that a wide range of other political and governmental roles could be open to women. This response was a reminder to us all that the philosophical fusion Qizwini was seeking would not simply reproduce Western liberalism. Still, he seemed to endorse heartily my general arguments about democracy.

Following an elaborate, traditional feast, Qizwini summoned us back to his office to continue the conversation. He implored us to help the local agricultural economy, so rich in potential, which had been starved of services and investment under Saddam. He worried that after the CPA went out of business, on July 1, Islamic extremists would try to seize control of the mosque and turn his university into a fundamentalist madrassa. And then he returned to his favorite subject, Islam and democracy. "I will bring you fifty passages from the Koran, and fifty stories from the life of the Imam [Imam Ali] to justify democracy," he said. "I will even be a little naughty. I will turn the concepts of Khomeini around to justify democracy, not the system he established." Finally, he led us on a tour of the complex, the stone walls of the mosque glistening against the brilliant blue winter sky. The library was in ruins, but it was being refurbished. Qizwini was building a radio station to spread his ideas; a television station would follow. He showed me classrooms where students were studying the principles of all major religions, including Judaism, Christianity, and Buddhism. As we were leaving, he led us to the Monument to the Unknown Martyrs, in the front yard of the compound. It contained the bodies of seventy-five people who could not be identified—among the 15,000 bodies that had been discovered in mass graves in the area. The monument consisted of two giant metal cupped hands, holding figurative skulls and remains, out of which protruded seventy-five thin metal rods, symbolizing the spirits of the martyrs escaping their chains. In front of the focal sculpture, stretching out in long rows toward a white fist, were the tombs of the seventy-five martyrs. As we climbed into our vehicles to head back, Qizwini gripped my hand and implored me, "Remember, you said you would be with us until the end."

★

The program to develop effective, and ultimately democratic, local governance was an important complement to our effort to transform the national political system. But both of these initiatives had to be, and were, sustained by a bottom-up approach. CPA and USAID officials had been working for months to help organize, train, and support a new generation of Iraqi NGOs. Sometimes the effort involved helping local professional groups—for example, the bar association and a doctors' association—reorganize under leadership that was not an extension of the Baath Party. Sometimes it entailed support for new organizations, including a number of human rights and democracy advocacy groups. In most of the country, the CPA was working to encourage the formation of women's organizations, and to establish centers where women could receive instruction in computer and other basic skills. Here, female activists learned how to become more effective advocates for democracy and women's rights: how to use the Internet as a tool for advancing rights, how to draft a nationwide petition for women's representation. The project was part of a campaign to help NGOs by providing them with small grants and by developing their skills at organizing, reaching out to their constituencies, writing grant proposals, and marketing themselves to international donors.

A good portion of this bottom-up assistance was provided by democracy assistance NGOs from the United States. At its January 2004 board meeting, the National Endowment for Democracy approved $15 million in grants for work in Iraq. Some of the money went directly to Iraqi

NGOs, but most was allocated to the two institutes run by the Democratic and Republican parties, and to the Center for Private Enterprise, for private sector development. Both of the party institutes had been working on the ground for months in Iraq. The National Democratic Institute for International Affairs was organizing political party training sessions throughout the country, while gently encouraging Iraq's fragmented parties to coalesce. It was also conducting weekly meetings at which the local NGOs could share information, coordinate their activities, enhance their organizational skills, and network with international donors and the CPA. By January, these initiatives were receiving an enthusiastic response. At the same time, the International Republican Institute was supporting several projects, including the programs of the Iraq Foundation for Development and Democracy, the organization founded by the political scientist Ghassan Al Atiyyah after his return from exile in London. In one cramped section of its Baghdad offices, several people were working full time translating two of James Madison's most famous essays from *The Federalist*; Martin Luther King's "I Have a Dream" speech; a State Department brochure titled "What Is Democracy?"; and a variety of other documents downloaded from the Internet. The International Republican Institute had also done extensive opinion polling and convened a wide range of focus groups. The director of the focus group operation, Steve Moore, had invited me to come to the offices and meet some of the Iraqi group leaders, which I did the day after my visit to Hilla.

The focus group leaders included a thirty-year-old dentist, a twenty-four-year-old lawyer, a young doctor, and two middle-aged Iraqis, a man who had gotten a bachelor's degree in computer science in England in the 1970s and a woman who was a schoolteacher. They had enjoyed doing the focus groups around the country and had found Iraqis surprisingly eager to express their opinions and feelings. Almost universally, the group leaders found people appreciative of their freedom, eager to understand what democracy is, and "very glad to be rid of Saddam." Mixed with the exhilaration, however, was a great deal of resentment, fear, and suspicion. The Shiites wanted elections right away, because they felt elections would finally bring them power. Members of other groups favored more time, in order to guarantee people's rights.

The Kurds desired autonomy, if not independence. The Arabs in Mosul felt that the Kurds were trying to suppress them and were seeking to incorporate that mixed-population city into Kurdistan. The legacy of absolute dictatorship hung in the air. People were afraid that political freedom might lead to violence, or even civil war. Many Iraqis did not trust the police, who, they feared, were still dominated by Saddam loyalists; consequently, they shied away from informing on the terrorists. Someone heard of a person who disappeared after he went to the police with information. Among many Shiites in southern Iraq, the focus group leaders had encountered a determination (even among highly educated people) to do, unthinkingly, whatever Ayatollah Sistani instructed—particularly if his message came in the form of a fatwa. One Iraqi told his focus group leader that even questioning a ruling from Sistani would be a sin. Such obedience was part of an attempt by the Shiites, a focus group leader suggested to me, to fill the postwar political vacuum. But it ran deeper, to basic instincts of faith and fear. In one focus group, a Shiite religious cleric had questioned Sistani's stance and his supreme power; he was driven out of the group and was afraid to return. The group leader later asked another Shiite participant, "Why does everyone feel that they need to follow Sistani? Why not make up your own minds?" He replied, "We are afraid, if we disagree, of what might happen to our families." The schoolteacher told me a story from the time of the 1991 Gulf War. She knew a family with two brothers (both engineers), one of whom suddenly disappeared. The other brother went to the authorities to ask what had happened. He, too, disappeared. For six years, the mother was afraid to ask about them. Then, in 1996, a piece of paper arrived, informing her, without explanation, that both her sons had died. "I told my own kids," she continued, "'Don't say anything; even the walls have ears. If someone ever says something bad about Saddam, leave the room.'" Such personal experiences had left many emotional scars.

The next day I was the lone Westerner among a number of Iraqi intellectual and political leaders who presented papers at a conference sponsored by the Iraqi Foundation for Development and Democracy. The topic was Iraq's constitutional future, and Ghassan Al Atiyyah asked me to participate. Several themes resonated through the presentations and discussions, and I would hear them again and again as I engaged Iraqis directly in various settings. One motif was the hunger of Iraqis to chart their political future and to elect their leaders, including those who would write the permanent constitution. Such feelings sometimes accompanied an expression of resentment toward the occupation, but the Iraqis were emphatic in their desire for democracy. The loudest applause of the day followed this declaration from a Muslim cleric: "Authority should never again be put in the hands of one absolute leader." Another theme was the yearning for a genuine rule of law. One speaker noted that the only permanent charter Iraq had had in the past century was the 1925 constitution; all the others were "interim." At the same time, however, Iraqis were deeply divided over the issue of federalism. Here, as in many other public discussions, Kurdish leaders, and sometimes liberal and far-sighted Arab Iraqis, made a compelling case for a federal Iraq. My own remarks aimed (in part) to explain the nature of federalism, why it was increasingly being adopted around the world, and how it differed from confederal arrangements, which largely eviscerate the powers of the center. In advocating federalism, Dr. Mahmoud Othman, an independent Kurdish member of the Governing Council, spoke movingly about the suffering that had been visited upon the Kurdish people. He was interrupted by an angry protest, from the floor, that Iraq needed to be one country, not a federal system. Othman continued by saying that the existing Kurdish authority needed to be preserved in the new constitution, with a Kurdish parliament for the region. "We want Iraqi unity, but we want our lives to be protected," he said. As tension erupted anew, with people shouting that federalism would be a disaster for Iraq—likening it to a partitioning of the country—Al Atiyyah stepped in to appeal for tolerance. "We are here to build a new Iraq. I would like us all to accept other opinions at the same time as we give our own opinions." The announcement returned the three-hundred-member conference to some degree of civility, but it was clear that the room— and the country—remained polarized between the belief that each cultural group, or each geographic region, should have some right to determine its future, and the belief that "Iraqis are one people, one nation"—indeed, "an inseparable part of the Arab nation," and "nobody has the right to subjugate and divide them."

By January, conferences and public meetings on Iraq's political and constitutional future were taking place around the country, to examine the transition process, and to explore such issues as civil society, the role of women, religion and the state, elections, and federalism (which overlapped with the question of Kurdish autonomy). The larger town hall meetings, drawing from one hundred to three hundred participants, were often heated discussions that went on for three or four hours. But no issue drew more intense debate than that of federalism. I encountered this again when I spoke in mid-February to a daylong conference on decentralization. The conference mainly dealt with administrative challenges in decentralizing a political system that had long been hypercentralized. I felt my contribution would lie at a more theoretical level, in explaining how a federal system would serve the cause of democracy in Iraq. I explained that federalism was a way of holding a country together, not breaking it apart; that the United States was strongly committed to a unified, democratic Iraqi state; and that we Americans had fought a bloody civil war to prevent our nation from fragmenting, and we did not wish less for the Iraqi people than what we had achieved at so dear a price. Still, my remarks raised the familiar controversies. After the panel, the Iraqi minister who was presiding over the conference (herself a Kurd) said, only half-jokingly, that I had been a "troublemaker" for raising the issue of federalism at a conference on "decentralization."

This time the tension was eloquently dispelled by an Iraqi political leader, a Shiite member of the Governing Council, Mowaffak al-Rubaie. A British-trained medical doctor and moderate Islamist, Rubaie was part of the core Shiite caucus on the Governing Council, and sometimes served as an intermediary between the CPA and Ayatollah Sistani. Rubaie exhibited an ability to reach across divides that many other Iraqi political leaders lacked, and his skill impressed me. Laying aside his thoughtful, carefully reasoned paper on federalism, Rubaie offered a moving, extemporaneous endorsement of federalist decentralization. Decrying the past thirty-five years of power concentration, sectarian oppression, and racial discrimination (especially against the Kurds), he said:

There are certain things we have learned from the massacres, from the Arabization campaign, and so on. One is the need to acknowledge our cultural, confessional, and regional diversity. Either we engage in a bitter conflict over power, or we devolve power to the fringes.

The unity of Iraq and the borders of Iraq are sacred. . . . Yet within this unity, we can give power to the fringes at the expense of central power. There is nothing wrong with that.

Centralization is the source of our divisions. It has isolated Kurdistan. Southern Iraq never felt affiliated to Iraq. It was oppressed. . . .

The way to address the problem is to devolve powers. This would be a solution to a number of fears. Believe me, whatever fears the Iraqi people are experiencing are important. If I were a Kurd, I would fear central power might stage a massacre again. Shiites fear central power will come back again and unleash oppression again. If I were a Sunni Arab, I would fear I might be killed by the majority, that my status would be transformed from an oppressor to a victim of the majority.

We can't just forget these fears—or those of the Turks, the Assyrians, and the Chaldeans.

I am not asking for Arab versus Kurd, no. Let's base federalism on all the governorates. We can have a Basra State, or region, or province. Najaf. Karbala. Hilla. Diwaniyah. Baghdad State. Kurdistan State.

This is not a formula for division but for unity. . . .

It is terribly wrong to imagine that this federal solution is a Kurdish request. It is an Arab request as much as a Kurdish, from Basra and Baquba as much as Kurdistan. They all want to feel that they belong to where they came from.

At Al Atiyyah's conference, there had been another moment of spontaneous applause when a female participant raised the issue of the role of women in Iraqi politics. "Women are sixty percent of Iraq, but where is the *real* representation of women?" she asked. "Up to now, we have seen no significant role for women, not even in the Governing Council. You rarely find women in these conferences. This is wrong and we should acknowledge it. There will be a vital role for women in the next government." Women were, in fact, organizing to demand inclusion, as I discovered the next day when I met for two hours with twenty-five members of the Iraqi Higher Women's Council, an umbrella organization of groups that had formed the previous October. These women were energetic, astute, and determined to ensure the meaningful participation of women in politics. We discussed options for achieving that goal, including a statutory quota for women's representation in the transitional parliament and the constitutional convention. We briefly considered ways that a quota could be structured. I gave them a paper I had asked Pippa Norris, of Harvard's Kennedy School of Government, to prepare on alternative mechanisms (such as quotas and reserved seats) for increasing women's representation in Iraq; she drew on her knowledge of other developing countries, including Afghanistan, Jordan, and South Africa. Given the looming deadline of February 28 for completing the Transitional Administrative Law, I urged the women to formulate a proposal and present it to the Governing Council and the CPA as quickly as possible. They resolved to do so soon, and we agreed to meet again to discuss specific institutional options. Three weeks later, seven of their leaders met with Ambassador Bremer and presented to him a letter requesting a 40 percent quota for women in legislative bodies and the repeal of Decision 137, which the Governing Council had passed late in December (during a poorly attended session) to replace Iraqi civil law on family matters with the provisions of Islamic Sharia law, which are generally interpreted as strictly limiting women's rights to divorce and inheritance. They also wanted the interim constitution to bind Iraq to observe UN human rights covenants.

That night, after meeting with the women, I wrote a memo to Bremer on challenges we were facing with regard to democracy promotion and political transition. I was just about to leave for a brief trip to South Africa to attend, with a number of Iraqi NGO leaders, the third assembly of the World Movement for Democracy, an international gathering of networks and activists that was supported by the National Endowment for Democracy. Among other things, I wanted to press again, with the reluctant Bremer, the case for some kind of gender quota. I wrote:

Iraqi democracy will be better and stronger if there is significant representation of women. Beyond all of the obvious reasons why, another occurred to me today after watching these women interact with one another. This Higher Council is one of the few bodies that transcend ethnicity and religious confession with a genuine, cross-cutting interest. A significant presence of women in the TNA [Transitional National Assembly] might help to soften some of the raw sectional cleavages we have been struggling with.

Indeed, the women were a remarkable cross section of Iraq: Kurds, Sunnis, Shiites, and others, religious and secular, with covered and bare heads, from both privileged and modest backgrounds. In contrast to the shouting, bluster, and long dramatic presentations of the previous day's conference, I found, in these women, Iraqis who were pragmatic and cooperative, idealistic and savvy, respecting one another even while disagreeing. I thought, "If only this could be the future of Iraq."

★

But before we reached the future of Iraq, the CPA faced a more immediate challenge: convincing the United Nations to return to the country to aid in the transition to democracy. On January 15, Bremer and several of his most senior aides flew to the United States, for meetings in Washington with their superiors in the Bush administration and for meetings in New York with the secretary-general and his senior staff. Prior to Bremer's departure, my colleagues in the Governance Office strategized on possible scenarios for UN participation in the political process. In the most positive scenario, a new UN special representative would come to Iraq and determine that direct elections were indeed impossible before June 30, and would succeed in persuading Ayatollah Sistani of this reality. The UN team would then make suggestions to reform the caucus procedures in a way that would enhance their legitimacy without radically revising them or disturbing the transition timetable. Under this scenario, the CPA would be willing (we hoped) to accommodate a more extended UN role that would help oversee the transfer of sovereignty. In the worst-case scenario, the UN special representative would find it possible to hold direct elections by May, or would recommend a delay in the transfer of sovereignty to September or October. We worried that this "disaster scenario" would wreck the transition timetable and stir ethnic and political tensions. It seemed unlikely, but in his January 11 letter to Pachachi (which Sistani had rejected as insufficient), Secretary-General Annan had said that "there may not be time to organize free, fair, and credible elections" before the handover, and his use of "may" had raised anxiety within Bremer's team. I myself considered the disaster scenario remote, because it was obvious that anything approaching democratic elections could not be organized in four or five months in Iraq, and because I knew that the United Nations, having urged the U.S.-led coalition consistently, from the beginning, to *expedite* the transfer of sovereignty to an Iraqi interim government, was not now going to recommend any course of action that would delay the handover date.

The governance team judged the most likely scenario to be something in between. The special representative would probably conclude that direct elections before June 30 were not feasible but would not endorse the caucus selection method as envisioned in the November 15 plan. Instead, the world body might propose to appoint the members of a transitional national assembly itself, or to organize a national conference, or to add its appointees to the organizing committees to make them more representative. Such an approach, my governance colleagues worried, could be expected to bring in disaffected Sunnis and former Baathists, an outcome that would create serious problems for Sistani and for the Governing Council. In fact, they argued, we should alert the Governing Council delegation, in advance of their meeting with the UN, to this danger (and to the related possibility that the UN might propose to dilute the council's influence over the selection process), so that they would understand the possible costs of UN involvement. Throughout, Bremer's inner circle in the Governance Office worried that the UN would tilt the balance back too far to the Sunnis— failing to recognize that unless the fundamental flaw of Sunni marginalization was corrected, the transition would experience chronic violence. My colleagues, fearing that increased UN involvement risked creating a political impasse, recommended trying to limit the UN's mandate to the refinement and implementation of the November 15 agreement, ruling out any new proposals from New York. This is precisely what Bremer was resolved to do as he departed on January 15.

Back in New York, UN officials were debating scenarios of their own. Postponing the June 30 handover was, in fact, never an option. The UN was as committed to preserving that date as the United States was. As the January 19 meeting approached, the UN was now considering whether and how the caucus system might be revised to make it more credible and acceptable. In at least some provinces, it might be possible, senior UN officials speculated, to enlarge or otherwise restructure the organizing committees, so that they would include key figures (for example, Arab nationalist parties in Baghdad or representatives of Sistani in Najaf, if these groups were not adequately represented). But decisions could not—as Washington hoped—be taken at the January 19 meeting. A UN team would have to visit Iraq first and assess the situation.

Within the highest ranks of the United Nations, debate continued on whether the secretary-general should dispatch a mission to Iraq. Kofi Annan was by nature a cautious man, and he was still traumatized by the previous summer's bombing of UN headquarters, for which he felt some personal responsibility. He remained deeply concerned about the security situation in Baghdad, and he was uncertain whether the UN's recommendations on repairing the process would be taken seriously. Early talks with the Bush administration suggested that the Americans wanted the UN simply to monitor the process, not significantly revise it. That would not be enough responsibility, Annan felt, to justify the risk the UN would have to assume. In any case, Annan was not going to authorize a new mission on anything like the scale of the original one. Moreover, many senior UN officials were advocating that the world organization stay out of Iraq altogether until the transfer of sovereignty was completed, whereas others argued that Iraq was at a dangerous impasse, which the United States could not resolve on its own and which called for precisely the kind of mediation that the UN existed to perform. It was also clear, after the Annan letter fiasco, that Sistani needed to be engaged directly and given some space. Jamal Benomar believed that Sistani did not want to issue a fatwa against the transition plan; he had issued only one since the beginning of the American occupation. But if backed into a corner, he might do so again. On the other hand, if the UN came to Iraq, reviewed the facts on the ground, treated Sistani respectfully and reasoned with him, then he might well accept the need for a different approach. Indeed, a close associate of Sistani's had recently signaled through the press that the grand ayatollah might "change his opinion" if a UN delegation came to Iraq and determined that elections were not possible by June 30.[7] For such a mission to be credible and effective, however, the UN would have to play an independent role.

The January 19 meeting at UN headquarters was a large one, and covered a broad spectrum of issues relating to Iraq. Joining the secretary-general and his senior staff were eight members of the Governing Council (led by Adnan Pachachi), Bremer, his British deputy Jeremy Greenstock, Meghan O'Sullivan from the Governance Office, U.S. ambassador to the UN John Negroponte, two U.S. assistant secretaries of state, and Robert Blackwill from the national security adviser's office. The discussion went well, as Bremer and other American officials expressed the desire for partnership and cooperation that the UN wanted to hear, and the CPA promised to provide full security for a UN team. Both the CPA and the delegation from the Governing Council stressed that they would welcome a UN mission to assess the feasibility of holding elections before the handover, and that they would accept the UN's conclusions. Annan now seemed to be favorably inclined, but after the meeting he was noncommittal in public, and no immediate decision was forthcoming. Among UN staff members, there was still strong skepticism about American motives and resistance to renewed UN involvement before the handover. Hence, Annan had to build support within the UN. In doing so, he pondered whether to compromise between the pro and the con camps by initially sending a low-level fact-finding mission. I hoped he would not choose this course, because such a team would not have the stature to deliver an authoritative assessment. To sway the major actors, it would need to be followed by a weightier mission, and thus it would accomplish nothing except a time-consuming breaking of the ice. Time was not on our side. Because the Transitional Administrative Law had to be finished by February 28, the CPA had stated that any UN recommendation must come by the third week of February, so that, if it was accepted, it could be incorporated into the document. We needed a high-level UN mission soon.

Finally, on January 28, Annan announced that as soon as security arrangements were worked out, he would "send a technical mission to Iraq to establish whether elections . . . can be held before the transfer of sovereignty on 30 June, and, if not, what alternative arrangement would be acceptable." Moreover, he stated that the UN mission would consult "a broad spectrum of Iraqi society in the search for alternatives," and that it would look for a consensus among Iraqis. Although he did not immediately announce it, Lakhdar Brahimi, who had only recently returned from Afghanistan, had agreed to lead the mission. Now the initiative that I had discussed informally with Jamal Benomar and had worked for since the end of November was about to take place.

★

Although Bremer had been wary of the Brahimi mission, once the special representative arrived in Baghdad, on February 6, the CPA administrator was determined that it should have the space and independence to succeed. Whether Bremer had changed his stance because he had been ordered to do so by Washington, or because he had come to accept the importance and potential of the mission, I wasn't sure; probably both factors had played a role. Bremer sent instructions to all CPA staff that we were to give Brahimi's team (which included Jamal Benomar among its seven members) all possible cooperation and refrain from trying in any way to influence its deliberations. As the Brahimi mission progressed (and then later returned), taking care to coordinate closely with the Americans, Bremer gained confidence in the UN team and gave its advice and recommendations the kind of serious hearing he had not given to de Mello and his mission.

The members of the UN team lost no time in plunging into a wide range of meetings with key actors in the CPA, the Governing Council, and the wider party system and civil society. They talked to tribal leaders and religious leaders, women's groups and professional associations, journalists and academics, people inside the process and people who were alienated from it, including Arab nationalist parties and other stakeholders that the CPA had failed to engage. Repeatedly, they were frustrated by the perilous security situation, but still they felt, as they later reported, that they were able "to ascertain the views of a wide spectrum of Iraqis."[8] Most important, Brahimi and Benomar met Sistani and his aides for two and a half hours on February 12. The meeting went extremely well, as the two septuagenarians found, in each other, an intelligent, worthy, and stimulating peer. Brahimi had been carefully briefed on Sistani, his thinking, and his concerns. Sistani also appeared remarkably well informed and erudite, as he began the discussion with a reference to an article about Brahimi in an Egyptian newspaper. He seemed to be a thoughtful, reasonable man, open to persuasion by logic and facts. Brahimi mobilized both effectively in explaining to the grand ayatollah why the UN mission had concluded that credible elections could not be organized before the handover of power on June 30. Decent elections, he said, required not just some measure of security but a political consensus, a legal framework, and an administrative infrastructure as well. An electoral commission had to be chosen; political party and campaign rules had to be established; voters, candidates, and parties had to be registered; polling stations had to be designated; procedures for voting and counting had to be defined; equipment needed to be procured; voters needed to be informed about the procedures, the issues, and the candidates; and electoral observers had to be accredited and trained. The earliest the UN team felt Iraq could be ready would be December, if the right conditions were put in place. At the same time, Brahimi and his colleagues had taken seriously the widespread concerns about the CPA's caucus system for selecting members of the transitional national assembly. Brahimi asked the grand ayatollah whether he could accept a process in which the caucuses would be scrapped and an interim government chosen, with the TNA then directly elected by the end of the year, or no later than late January. The elected body would act as both parliament and constitutional assembly, thus delaying elections for the national legislature beyond the June handover but moving up elections for the constituent assembly (scheduled for March 2005) by as much as two months. As the UN envisioned it, the interim government would be a caretaker government, with limited authority for the few months until a parliament was elected under a permanent constitution. Sistani indicated that he would prefer to have the UN run a transitional administration for the interim period—an idea to which he appeared to have given some thought—but as this plan was not feasible, Sistani accepted in principle the core compromise that rescued the political transition: a postponement of elections for up to eight more months (beyond May), but with the understanding that the transitional national assembly would then be chosen through direct elections, not caucuses.

Brahimi's plan quickly gathered consensus support among key players. For the Sunni Arab and Kurdish leaders, it provided the delay in elections they felt would give more time to their political arms to organize. For the Shiite Islamist parties, who feared that the caucus system would deny them a victory they would otherwise win through elections, the plan at least promised to produce a transitional government through direct elections within a year. The CPA worried about who would select the caretaker government and how it would be restrained and held accountable without an assembly of some kind, but with the other participants on board and with a confrontation defused, the CPA had little choice but to accept Brahimi's compromise.

★

When Brahimi held his closing press conference in Baghdad on February 13, he did not reveal the outlines of what he had settled on, but he cautioned that holding elections before June 30 could inflame ethnic and religious tensions. His detailed recommendations, finalized during consultations with Secretary-General Annan and his senior staff, were contained in his written report, which the United Nations released on February 23.[9] Despite its account of success in forging the compromise with Sistani, the document noted with concern the rising levels of violence (including two devastating attacks on Iraqi security forces during their mission), "a growing fragmentation of the political class" along ethnic and sectarian lines, and "rising disillusionment and anger" over widespread unemployment and the limitation of the political arena to a narrow range of participants. The UN team found Iraq "a dynamic place, full of ideas and political arguments," but also of "expectations, fear, tensions and distrust" that represented the "potential for civil strife and violence" if the key actors did not address the most pressing political issues. Indeed, in his February 13 press conference, Brahimi had explicitly warned about the dangers of civil war if the politicians were not careful.

Brahimi had crafted an ingenious compromise, and with the public release of the report, it gathered an unusually broad and rapid consensus in Iraq. The deadlock between Sistani and the CPA had been resolved. Each side had given up something important: Sistani agreed to wait another seven or eight months for elections, and the Americans relinquished the complicated caucuses and agreed to an elected transitional parliament. But with all sides committed to the June 30 date for transferring sovereignty, two major issues remained unresolved: the precise provisions of the interim constitution, the Transitional Administrative Law; and the composition of the interim government that would rule Iraq for the six or seven months between the June 30 handover and the January 2005 elections. The wrangling over the interim constitution was well advanced and the divisions among ethnic and religious groups were playing out in what was becoming a contentious process of negotiations. The Governance Office was consumed by these complex talks, and the question of a caretaker government would have to wait until the interim constitution was approved. But one thing was clear: the maneuvering had only just begun.

6

CONSTITUTIONS AND COMPROMISES

A few days after I arrived in Baghdad, I had been given an early, partial draft of the Transitional Administrative Law (TAL), the formal name for the Iraqi interim constitution that, under the November 15 agreement, had to be adopted by February 28, 2004.[1] The preliminary version had been prepared by an Iraqi adviser to the Governing Council's drafting committee, chaired by Adnan Pachachi. Though promising in some respects and liberal in intent, the initial document was full of holes and left many issues still to be resolved. In particular, I felt, the draft needed stronger, more explicit, and more detailed protections for civil and political rights. Securing rights had been one of the principal concerns of Condoleezza Rice and Jerry Bremer when they asked me to go to Iraq to advise on the democratic transition. And given Iraq's brutal recent history of human rights violations, it seemed that the interim constitution needed to articulate its protections as explicitly as possible. I had similar worries about the treatment of due process, judicial independence, civilian control of the military, and prohibition of torture. For example, the draft ruled out torture of anyone "suspected of violation, misdemeanor or crime," leaving open the possibility that prisoners could be tortured once convicted, or that individuals could be tortured for other reasons.

Many other questions arose from the start. Some of these were related to the complicated process of choosing the transitional national assembly through caucuses, as the details of selection had still to be defined. Another group of issues focused on the structure of the government. A three-member presidency council harkened back to the three-member Sovereignty Council established in 1958 under the provisional constitution that followed the overthrow of the monarchy. I was concerned about how power would be divided between the presidency council and the prime minister. From my experience studying democracies worldwide, I favored a predominantly parliamentary form of government, with significant checks on the power of the prime minister. In light of Iraq's history of extreme concentration and abuse of power, I felt, the country would be better off with a system in which power was diffused among multiple centers, some with veto power, rather than concentrated in one office or branch. Unfortunately, the draft appeared to give sweeping decree authority to the presidency council, even as it seemed to anticipate a powerful prime minister. Furthermore, the draft envisioned a weak and passive parliament—a troubling provision for the same reason. I also felt the document should offer stronger provisions for judicial review, but under clear guidelines that would prevent the supreme court from becoming a runaway, unaccountable body, as it had become in Iran.

Then there was the question of timing. Putting into a document—which was supposed to be nonamendable—the ambitious deadlines of the November 15 agreement, I thought, could be looking for trouble. What would happen to the legality and legitimacy of the transitional government if having elections for a new government under a permanent constitution by December 2005 proved impossible? And finally, we were going to have to wrestle with the question of federalism. Iraq would need strong provisions for dividing power between the central government and the provincial and local governments, to assure the Kurds and other minorities that their rights would be protected. But when I arrived in Baghdad, the federalism issue was temporarily quarantined while Bremer and other top CPA officials negotiated directly with the Kurds.

Fortunately, most of my concerns were shared by a remarkable man who was assuming the lead responsibility for the TAL drafting process. Feisal Istrabadi was a brilliant forty-one-year-old Iraqi American lawyer from Indiana, who was often elegantly clad in custom-tailored suits and shirts, finished with French cuffs. He had taken a leave from his law practice to come to Baghdad in mid-December, at Pachachi's request, initially to translate the Arabic text of the TAL draft into English. However, in the process of translating, he identified many of the deficiencies in the document that I would find on reading the English version. When he raised these with Pachachi, the most liberal member of the Governing Council, the elder statesman invited the younger lawyer to propose changes. By the time Pachachi left with Bremer for New York and Washington in mid-January, he had given Istrabadi exclusive authority within his movement, the Iraqi Independent Democrats, to rework the TAL on his behalf.

As with so many political developments in Iraq, Istrabadi was initially drawn to Pachachi by family connections. He had known Pachachi since childhood; his grandmother and Pachachi's mother were friends. But he answered the call because he admired Pachachi as a democrat and a nationalist, a former foreign minister and ambassador who had also drafted the federalist constitution for the United Arab Emirates. For Istrabadi, and a number of other Iraqi intellectuals, Pachachi was the leader, in the democratic opposition, least motivated by personal considerations, the most credible bearer of a liberal design for Iraq's future. As Istrabadi later explained it to me: "Dr. Pachachi wants to create a modern liberal democratic state, with a rule of law, where the rights of the individual are guaranteed, and the emphasis is on the individual, not the group. His vision is not of what one group or another can get for itself, but what a truly unified Iraq might accomplish. He has a vision for serving the country. He has no desire to rule Iraq."

Istrabadi's own family had a long tradition of service to democratic principles in Iraq. His grandfather had been a member of the Constituent Assembly, which wrote the first constitution for Iraq, in 1923–24, and then went on to serve in Iraq's first senate. His grandmother was shot to death as she tried to help the prime minister escape during the 1958 military coup. The family stayed on in Baghdad for another eleven

years, until the consolidation of Baath Party rule in the late 1960s un-
leashed a deepening reign of brutality and terror. When the regime
hanged thirteen opponents in Liberation Square and a close family
friend and former minister emerged from a year and a half of imprison-
ment badly tortured, Feisal's father, the chair of the Department of
Civil Engineering at Baghdad Technical University, and his mother, a
professor of English at the University of Baghdad, realized there was no
hope for liberals under Baathist rule. The family left in 1970 for Bloom-
ington, Indiana, where his father took a teaching position while his
mother obtained a Ph.D. From the age of eight, Feisal grew up in the
American heartland, speaking Arabic at home and English in school (a
reversal of the family's practice in Baghdad). He went on to take his undergraduate and law degrees at Indiana University, and then to establish a highly successful law practice in Indiana and Chicago.[2]

Like many Iraqi intellectuals and politicians with whom I interacted,
Istrabadi was powerfully motivated by his understanding of the Iraqi
past. At one of our constitutional drafting sessions, he told me about his
grandfather's service in the Constituent Assembly, and then remarked,
"Now, eighty years later, here we are again. It's as if all the progress of
that period has been erased and we are back to square one. I hope my
own grandchildren do not find themselves in the same situation."

Joining Istrabadi as the other lead drafter of the interim constitution
was another forty-one-year-old lawyer trained in the United States,
Salem Chalabi.[3] Both Chalabi and Istrabadi had been active members of
the Future of Iraq Project, and of the Democratic Principles Working
Group, which had laid down an initial framework for Iraq's constitutional future. The two men also had a distant family bond: their grandfa-
thers had once been neighbors in Baghdad. More than Istrabadi, Sam
Chalabi (as he was called by his American friends) was tied to the transitional process by blood. The nephew of the powerful and ambitious
Ahmed Chalabi, Salem had a difficult balancing role to play. On the one
hand, he was one of the principal political deputies to his uncle, who was
widely known to aspire to the leadership of postwar Iraq and was willing
to cut all manner of Machiavellian deals in the quest for that goal. On
the other hand, Salem was, like Feisal, a liberal, secular Shiite, educated

at Yale and Northwestern Law School, who favored the same goals of democracy, individual rights, and the rule of law. Whereas Istrabadi's political and family ties impelled him in the same liberal direction as his personal beliefs, Salem was sometimes torn between his broad-minded, secular personal instincts and his periodic need, in representing an uncle who was bidding for the leadership of the "Shiite house," to gesture toward the Islamist and majoritarian concerns of the religious parties. This tension would play itself out in visible contradictions. In late February 2004, while standing in for his uncle on the Governing Council, Salem voted to repeal the decision to impose Islamic Sharia law on family issues. Yet when most of the Shiite members walked out of the meeting after being reversed on the issue, Salem walked out with them.

There were other differences, substantive and superficial, between the two drafters. Although he bore a striking physical resemblance to his dapper uncle, Salem often had a rumpled appearance, and was generally more informal than Istrabadi, who typically dressed as though he were ready to argue a case before the Indiana Supreme Court. More important, Salem was deeply influenced by the years in exile that he and his family had spent in Lebanon during the civil wars of the 1970s and 1980s. His experiences both deepened his Shiite identity and inclined him intellectually toward the Lebanon-style, ethnically based power-sharing formulas that he and his uncle would later push in Iraq. Though Istrabadi was also technically a member of Iraq's Shiite majority (by descent on his father's side), such rigid, predetermined distributions of power were anathema to him. Salem felt that the Lebanon-style formulas could facilitate an accommodation with Kurdish demands for regional devolution and power sharing at the center. While recognizing the need for a federal system, Istrabadi, like his patron Pachachi, believed that the power-sharing approach had failed miserably in Lebanon, and thus they were committed to avoiding the entrenchment of group identities and to preserving a strong center.

★

After several days of poring over the draft TAL and comparing notes with my governance colleagues, I had my first meeting with Istrabadi and Chalabi in the nondescript headquarters of the Governing Council.

A drab, three-story structure in the Green Zone, near the Convention Center and the al-Rashid Hotel, the Governing Council building provided offices and meeting rooms for the twenty-five members, but it was not a particularly charming or comfortable place. Five of us sat around a small table and began working over the document: Istrabadi, Chalabi, myself, and two of my younger colleagues from the Governance Office, Irfan Siddiq and Roman Martinez. Within the CPA, we had identified nine issues that we thought needed work in the document: human rights, the judiciary, federalism, the executive structure, legislative power, civil-military relations, the method of selection of the transitional national assembly, the office of public integrity, and the transition timetable. There was also the issue of whether to institute a provision, such as a fixed quota (for example, 20 percent), to ensure minimum representation of women in parliament. This was something that Tony Blair and his top diplomat in Baghdad, Jeremy Greenstock, favored, but which Bremer resisted, on conservative philosophical grounds that opposed all quotas. We resolved to focus on the first four issues in our first group meeting.

Some of the issues were technical and arose from problems in translating the document back and forth between Arabic and English, or from styles of language that differed among various legal and political traditions. For example, the draft of the TAL had declared, "Laws shall be issued in the name of the Presidency Council." This wording implied to us in the CPA the intention to give the presidency council sweeping powers of decree, while allowing little scope for lawmaking by the parliament itself. In fact, the language had been intended mostly as a formality of state procedure. More substantive was the question of what powers the presidency council would have and how it would make decisions. At a minimum, the council would have the authority to name the prime minister—who, as in any other parliamentary system, must then obtain a vote of confidence from the parliament for himself and his cabinet. But would the council also have the power to veto legislation, or to approve treaties? And by what means would this three-person body make decisions? The last issue was crucial, because we assumed that the council would include one person from each of Iraq's three principal groups—Shiite, Sunni, and Kurd. If the presidency made decisions by majority vote (2 of 3), the Kurdish member could be consistently overruled, and a key dimension of political protection for Kurdish interests could be vitiated.

The issue of rights would not prove controversial among our working group. Istrabadi and Chalabi, steeped in Western, liberal traditions of constitutionalism and the law, were keenly aware of the growing international architecture of human rights. Thus, they welcomed efforts to amplify this section of the TAL. Istrabadi would invest a great deal of his intellectual energy and legal craftsmanship on the elaboration of these provisions; before our first meeting, he had added to the draft a bold guarantee of human rights:

> The enumeration of the foregoing rights shall not be interpreted to mean that these rights are the exclusive rights enjoyed by the people. The people of Iraq enjoy all the rights which befit a free people in the exercise of their human dignity, including those rights secured by international covenants, agreements, declarations, and other instruments of international law to which Iraq is a party, to which Iraq has acceded, or which otherwise bind Iraq.

The addition was profound and ingenious, because it invoked and incorporated into the TAL the more far-reaching provisions of the International Covenant on Civil and Political Rights adopted by the UN General Assembly in 1966 and ratified by most countries in the world, including Iraq. In fact, working independently of each other over the previous several days, Istrabadi and I had consulted that document to see how the guarantees of individual rights could be further specified and entrenched, consistent with international standards. Within a week, the provisions on rights had grown, largely by Istrabadi's hand, from a few brief articles to several pages of precise, detailed, and comprehensive guarantees that would be—at Istrabadi's passionate insistence—unencumbered by any qualification that might provide grounds for abridgment by an aspiring dictator.[4]

The Iraqi drafters of the TAL, ever conscious of the Sunni-Shiite divide, were also determined to guarantee religious freedom.[5] The biggest religious question, however, concerned the place of Islam in politics and governance. This was one of the most sensitive of all issues, which we in the CPA had to address gingerly. Secular Iraqis, led by Pachachi, were responsible for drafting the TAL, and, early on, they reached a compromise with the Islamists, under which Islam was recognized as "the official religion of the state" and as "a source of legislation" but not *the* source (or "the primary source") of legislation, as many Islamists wanted. While respecting "the Islamic identity of the majority of the Iraqi people," the TAL also guaranteed "the full religious rights of all individuals to freedom of religious belief and practice." In the final negotiations over the TAL, the Islamist Shiites, inspired and pressured by Ayatollah Sistani, demanded more, and therefore a provision was later added forbidding the passage, during the transition period, of any law "that contradicts the universally agreed tenets of Islam." However, on Pachachi's insistence, language was also inserted that forbade laws contradicting democracy or fundamental human rights—leaving unanswered the question of what would happen if what were asserted to be the "universally agreed tenets of Islam" pressed in one direction while principles of democracy and rights pressed in the opposite direction.[6]

Istrabadi threw himself into extending other rights as well. As a lawyer, he felt strongly about due process, and by the time we were done, two brief clauses in the original draft had become a ten-point set of guarantees that occupied one full page of the nineteen-page document. In considerable detail, the TAL required state authorities to obtain a search warrant under all but "extreme exigent circumstances"; prohibited unlawful arrest and detention; guaranteed the right to "a fair, speedy, and open trial"; affirmed that the accused is innocent until proven guilty; and provided detainees the right to habeas corpus, to independent counsel, to remain silent, and to be notified of their rights—guarantees that would be familiar to citizens of any liberal democracy. In the end, the guarantees were too much even for the Bush administration, which sought to weaken the exclusionary rule (which rendered inadmissible in court any evidence gathered in an illegal search). The CPA pressed for wording that would allow illegally obtained evidence (including coerced confessions) to be admissible in court if the evidence "could have been obtained" without the use of illegal methods.

Istrabadi told the CPA, "If the exclusionary rule is good enough for the United States, it is good enough for Iraq." Fortunately, American liberal principles held out against American tactical interests, and Istrabadi's rigorous due process provisions would be preserved in the final version of the TAL.

Many of these measures were a direct response to the abuses suffered under Baathist rule, which Istrabadi, Chalabi, and other Iraqis who shaped the TAL were determined should never be repeated. One of these concerned the loss of citizenship. Having been capriciously stripped of their citizenship by Saddam after they fled his dictatorship, the returning exiles were determined that this right should never again be abridged. Istrabadi was ardent on the point, feeling that the deprivation of citizenship he and his family had suffered was the violation of a basic human right. He elaborated the draft's simple ban on withdrawal of citizenship into a seven-point article, guaranteeing all Iraqis their citizenship, including the right to dual citizenship and the right to reclaim citizenship that had been wrongfully withdrawn.

★

The articulation of a comprehensive bill of rights for the Iraqi people went smoothly and quickly, but other issues occasioned more debate. Istrabadi, for example, favored the establishment of a supreme court that could review the constitutionality of any legislation or executive act during the interim period. However, the Kurdish leaders, like Massoud Barzani of the KDP, worried that a constitutional court would not have sufficient authority to overrule laws that might undermine the autonomy of the Kurdish region. Early on, the Kurds had indicated that they wanted an even more powerful and political version of a constitutional review body, a joint panel drawn from the transitional assembly and the Kurdistan Regional Government to determine whether laws passed by the assembly would be applicable in the Kurdish-ruled provinces in the north. By contrast, Roman Martinez—a conservative Republican who projected an American template onto the Iraqi constitutional landscape—was skeptical of judicial review; he complained about what it had done in the United States, and argued for limiting it in Iraq. Although I advocated judicial review by an independent constitutional court, I worried that a supreme court could usurp power, and become an ideological force—or even, as in Iran, a veto instrument of religious hard-liners—if its scope of authority was not carefully circumscribed. After some discussion, we agreed (despite Roman's concerns) on a federal supreme court that would have broad power of constitutional review—but only on the basis of a specific complaint or a referral from another court. This, we felt, would help constrain the court's ability to weigh in politically on any issue that moved it.

The question then became how the court would be constituted. I argued for limiting the power of politicians to appoint whomever they wanted to the courts and the review bodies; as much as possible, I felt, appointments should be made on professional, not political, grounds. Istrabadi and Chalabi rallied to this position, both for its capacity to entrench judicial independence and for its potential to build on the surprising degree of judicial professionalism that had managed to survive Saddam's oppression. In fact, Chalabi had been working on issues of transitional justice and was familiar with the state of the Iraqi judiciary. He noted that before Saddam consolidated his grip on power in 1979, the Council of Judges had recommended jurists to the cabinet and the president had appointed them. He now proposed that this procedure be revived. Already, by mid-January, a CPA-appointed judicial review committee had assessed roughly 600 Iraqi judges, expelling 120 of them for incompetence, corruption, or high-level Baathist membership but ratifying the rest to continue in office. In addition, Chalabi had a list of 70 retired judges who were ready to return to the bench. The relatively low purge rate testified to an astounding reality: somehow, in one of the most brutal dictatorships on earth, a relatively decent judiciary had persisted. I wondered why this had happened, and guessed (with some affirmation from Iraqis) that Saddam might have been so contemptuous of the law that he ignored it whenever he wanted to. Saddam didn't need to transform the courts into a comprehensive instrument of oppression when he could simply try, sentence, and shoot any potential offender on the spot. "The reality is that a lot of the judges are good," Salem told us in our January 18 meeting. "And they have been independently vetted." Also working in our favor was the establishment, by the CPA, of a Higher Juridical Council (succeeding the old

Council of Judges), consisting of the senior judges of all the courts of appeal who had cleared this vetting process.

The procedure developed by Chalabi and Istrabadi affirmed the professionalism and neutrality of the judiciary. The Higher Juridical Council would appoint all the judges of the federal judicial branch below the supreme court; for the supreme court, the Higher Juridical Council would nominate three individuals for each vacancy, from which the presidency council would select one (or reject all three and request another panel of nominees). Initially, to constitute the nine-member supreme court, the Higher Juridical Council would propose eighteen to twenty-seven nominees, from whom the presidency council would select nine and name one to be presiding judge. This procedure, we felt, would inject an element of accountability and legitimacy into a body whose decisions would affect vital political interests in the country, but would ensure that all the supreme court nominees met high standards of experience and capacity. To establish the authority and prestige of the supreme court as the apex of Iraq's judicial system, Istrabadi added the provision that the presiding judge of the federal supreme court would also preside over the Higher Juridical Council.

As with the majority of the provisions we drafted, the structure of the federal judiciary as articulated by Istrabadi and Chalabi made its way into the final version of the TAL with little change. One alteration in this section, however, was indicative of the most sensitive issues in the drafting of the interim constitution: the rights and powers of the various levels of government, and in particular of the Kurdistan Regional Government. Our drafts had stipulated that a simple majority of the nine supreme court judges would produce a binding decision. In the final TAL, the measure was changed to require a two-thirds vote of the judges in all legal proceedings between the national transitional government and the regional governments and other lower-level administrations. It was one of many provisions insisted upon by the Kurds to protect their autonomy.

We also added a layer of institutional protection against the abuse of power. Bremer had made a high priority of establishing a strong infrastructure of transparency and accountability, and he had persuaded the Governing Council to draft a provision for a national public integrity commission, which was to function as a countercorruption body. The wording was adopted in January, followed by orders from Bremer in February, setting up an office of inspector general in each ministry, to examine government accounts; and in April, establishing a board of supreme audit to work with the inspectors general and the public integrity commission in detecting and deterring corruption, fraud, waste, and abuse. In addition to these bodies, Salem Chalabi and I favored the creation of an independent office of ombudsman to defend citizens' rights and to investigate and correct the abuse of power. The agency was a passion for Salem, who had given the matter a great deal of thought during his participation in the Democratic Principles Working Group, before the war. We accepted the detailed provisions he had drafted—creating an independent ombudsman, with extensive authority to investigate (and, if necessary, halt) any action by any level of government that might violate the dignity or rights of a citizen. We resolved on a method of appointment similar to that of the supreme court: selection by the presidency council from three names presented to it by the Higher Juridical Council. However, the CPA General Counsel's Office found the proposed scope of authority too wide-ranging and the office too powerful and, along with the Governance Office, requested that the long provision be radically condensed, which it was. Ultimately, the office of ombudsman was established as an arm of a human rights commission to investigate "an allegation that the conduct of the governmental authorities is arbitrary or contrary to law." Without the complex architecture we had originally agreed upon, there was less promise that the office of the ombudsman would amount to much, but the potential remained. Collectively, these various bodies and agents constituted a "fourth branch" of government, separate from and checking the other three.

★

By the third week of January, the five of us were meeting on an almost daily basis to work through the various issues and drafts of the TAL. Pachachi had hoped that a revision of the TAL could be completed by late January so that the full Governing Council drafting committee could review it, modify it, and then present it for discussion to town hall meetings in some Iraqi cities, well before the February 28 deadline. As was often the case in that period, we felt the pressure of time. We quickly shifted the site of our deliberations from the windowless conference room in the Governing Council headquarters to the home where Salem Chalabi was staying, inside the Green Zone. It sat along the Tigris River, with a beautiful view, from the balcony, of the river and the city beyond. Surrounding it was an exclusive neighborhood of fashionable homes and luxurious gardens, ponds, and swimming pools, laced with footpaths and generously sheltered by a lush array of palms and other exotic plants. All this property had once been part of Saddam's vast presidential compound, forbidden to ordinary Iraqis. The modern-style home we worked in had been built by the father of the Iraqi architect and democratic dissident Kanan Makiya, and then—like the other private homes in the district—was seized by Saddam and his cronies as they tightened their grip on power. The home had been given to Saddam's chief bodyguard, a relative named Yassin, who added an oversized bathtub and sauna on the ground level. Word had it that at one point, Saddam's son Uday was held there under house arrest after killing one of Saddam's bodyguards in a dispute. After Saddam fell, Makiya managed to reclaim his family's property, as did a few of the other rightful owners, but most of the homes in the Green Zone were now occupied by Iraqi power brokers, foreign contractors, and American generals. For a succession of days in the second half of January, we met around the dining room table of Makiya's home for hours at a stretch, wolfing down chicken sandwiches from the Green Zone Café while carving up drafts, section by section.

We were now coming down to some of the thornier issues, one of which involved the structure of executive power. The three-member presidency council was a given—though Istrabadi personally opposed it, as he did all rigid formulas for allocating positions on an ethnic basis. We still had to define the powers of the presidency, the prime minister, and the cabinet. The original draft of the TAL had been vague on the powers of the presidency, which were "to oversee higher national affairs" and "to oversee the various ministries," as well as to approve bills recommended by the ministries before submission to parliament. We felt this was at once too much power and too little. While both the Bush administration and the principal Shiite parties had been pushing for a strong—almost presidential—prime minister, Istrabadi saw the potential abuse of power as a greater danger than weak government. He therefore ensured that the TAL did not grant the presidency council or the prime minister the authority to issue decrees or declare a state of emergency—provisions that were common not only in Arab constitutions but in those of many emerging democracies around the world. Beyond this, Istrabadi took the lead to entrench checks and balances into the TAL. The most important was a provision for the presidency to veto legislation by the transitional assembly, which could then (as in the United States) override the veto by a two-thirds vote. At the same time, we removed the vague authorization for the presidency to "oversee higher national affairs," and crafted a system that would be parliamentary in nature. However, under the pressure of the Shiite parties and the Americans, with the Kurds agreeing for tactical reasons, Istrabadi's effort to generate more checks on the power of the prime minister, and to press the system more toward collective, cabinet government, failed. Thus, beyond the right to veto legislation, to nominate the prime minister, and to make certain other key appointments (of the supreme court judges and of high military officers, as well as of the director of the intelligence agency), the presidency council was largely a ceremonial body, acting as commander in chief of the armed forces only "for ceremonial and protocol purposes." As in other parliamentary systems, governing power would reside with the prime minister and the members of the cabinet, who were collectively and individually responsible before the assembly, which could at any time vote "no confidence" in any or all of them, thereby compelling their resignation. In a bid to strengthen the office of prime minister, the United States sought to eliminate the assembly's ability to withdraw confidence in an individual minister, but the Iraqi drafters prevailed on this point. In its deliberations, the Governing Council later reshaped the presidency council from a body of three equals (which would have had a rotating ceremonial head) to one of a president and two deputy presidents (with equal powers), reflecting a feeling that a rotational presidency had not worked well in the Governing Council over the preceding months.

There was also a host of issues that related to the provisional arrangements. These included the timetable for the transitional period, the system for election of the transitional assembly through the caucuses, the means of assuring women's representation in parliament, and the question of whether there would be any procedure for amending the TAL.

The timetable was essentially given by the November 15 agreement. But I worried that the plan, which included three elections during the calendar year 2005, was simply too ambitious and that the constitutional convention (which would not even be elected until March) would have difficulty drafting and adopting a permanent constitution in time to be ratified through a referendum and then have national elections held before the end of the year. It was not just a matter of drafting a constitution. We all felt that this founding document and institutional framework of Iraqi democracy must have broad public understanding and support. The experience of constitution making in other postconflict settings underscored the need for significant popular participation and consultation, through public hearings and submissions, town hall meetings, mass media programs, and civic education efforts.[7] This would all take time. As we projected the requirements of the constitution-making process and the other steps to complete the transition, we realized that there might not be enough time. If the convention was not elected until March 2005, it might not begin deliberating until April. Then, if national elections were to be conducted by mid-December, a referendum must be held by early autumn, and the constitutional draft would need to be ready several weeks before that. This schedule might give the convention no more than four months to be organized, choose officers and committees, draft the document, engage the public in discussion, and adopt a final draft—a formidable timetable.

We took a number of steps to deal with the problem. First, we determined that the deadline for electing a constitutional convention could be moved up to January 30, 2005. Then we set August 15 as the deadline for adoption of the draft constitution by the convention, and October 15 as the deadline for the referendum, with elections to follow by December 15. This calendar would allow six months for the convention to produce a constitution. Finally, we debated whether to allow an extension of the process. According to Istrabadi, doing so would open the door to the common curse of Arab politics: provisional governments that remain forever, never submitting themselves to a genuine constitutional and democratic test. Yet we all worried that even six months might not be enough for the convention to complete its work in a manner that involved the Iraqi public. We therefore decided, at Istrabadi's reluctant suggestion, to provide the option of a one-time, six-month extension of the deadline, but only under carefully circumscribed conditions that included approval by the presidency council and the transitional assembly, based on a judgment by each that work on the draft had been "substantially completed." To ensure that the politicians did not cavalierly delay the process, we also provided, again at Istrabadi's suggestion, that if the convention did not agree on a draft by September 15 (or if the draft constitution was defeated in the referendum), the convention would be dissolved and elections for a new transitional assembly would be held by December 15. The final version of the TAL retained this logic, and the August, October, and December deadlines, but streamlined the procedures. By then, the national assembly and the constitutional convention had been merged into one body, again to be elected by January 30, 2005. That assembly, by majority vote, was permitted to request, by August 1, a six-month extension of the drafting process, which the presidency council was obliged to grant, but the deadline could "not be extended again."

An issue also emerged about constitutional integrity. The November 15 agreement had declared that the TAL, as a purely transitional document, would not be subject to any amendment. This stipulation would focus the country and its politicians on the task of writing a permanent constitution, and would protect basic rights in the interim. It also suited the interests of the Kurds, who worried that an overwhelming Arab majority in the transitional assembly might erase whatever federalist guarantees they achieved in the TAL. However, our drafting committee worried that an absolute prohibition on amendment could, in fact, undermine the principle of constitutionalism, by leaving no means to redress an unanticipated defect that was widely acknowledged across ethnic and partisan lines. We therefore inserted a means for amending the TAL, but only by a formidable consensus of three-fourths of the transitional national assembly and unanimous approval by the presidency council—providing, in essence, a Kurdish veto over any amendment. And in any case, the TAL still prohibited amendment to such sensitive provisions as the bill of rights, the status of Islam, or the powers of regions and provinces.

Early on in our deliberations, we struggled with the issue of whether and how to provide for the representation of women in the transitional assembly. This was a matter that divided religious from secular Iraqis, while generating differences of opinion within the CPA. The Shiite religious parties were strongly opposed to any quota or standard for women's representation in parliament, not only on philosophical grounds but also because they worried that they might have difficulty fielding and electing women candidates. But progressive, secular Iraqis favored such quotas, and the Iraqi Higher Women's Council was pressing for a 40 percent quota for women's representation in parliament, thinking that at least they might wind up with 25 percent. Seeing the progressive implications for Iraq of such a quota, Istrabadi supported the 40 percent figure and wrote it into a draft of the TAL, with Pachachi's explicit support. Despite Bremer's philosophical resistance to quotas, a few of us in the CPA persuaded him of the need for an active approach. Without a quota or standard, we argued, few women were likely to be elected to the transitional assembly. And if they were largely shut out of the first parliament, I argued in a January 11 memo, this "birth defect" would likely be perpetuated in elections and institutional choices for some time to come, "diminishing the quality and legitimacy of democracy in Iraq and the potential for its transformative effect on the Arab world." With the support of the CPA and mobilization from women and other Iraqi liberal forces, a provision was added to the TAL mandating the electoral law to "aim to achieve the goal of having women constitute no less than one-quarter of the members of the National Assembly," as well as ensuring fair representation for the Turkoman, Chaldo-Assyrian, and other minorities. The language of "aim to achieve" was weaker than some had wanted, but after long discussion with experts from the International Foundation for Electoral Systems (working on an extended contract with the CPA), we became convinced that we could craft electoral system rules (based on list proportional representation) that would largely ensure this goal.

One of the most complicated issues concerned the method of electing the transitional national assembly. The November 15 agreement had broadly stipulated a caucus system, steered by the provincial organizing committees, but it did not specify how elections would actually take place inside the caucuses. During January, we immersed ourselves, in our drafting committee but much more so in the Governance Office back at the palace, in consideration of alternative scenarios for organizing the caucuses—or finding another method for selecting the assembly. The Governance Office, faced with Ayatollah Sistani's intractable opposition to the caucus method, examined a wide range of alternatives. By January 20, the office had produced a memo with nine options and several suboptions. The first option, still the preference, was to retain the caucus procedure but to give it a more palatable name, such as "indirect elections" or "elections by conference." The CPA could also build "various electoral features" into the process, such as public campaigning by candidates in each province, televised debates, and the use of some kind of list proportional representation within the caucus (systems of proportional representation award seats to political parties or lists of candidates in proportion to their shares of the vote). Or the November 15 plan could be revised more substantially, by allowing the UN to name five additional members to each provincial organizing committee, or by scrapping the committees altogether and having the newly "refreshed" provincial councils receive and vet nominations. We also weighed having the CPA or the UN convene the caucuses directly, but conceded that this strategy would only "replace the derivative illegitimacy" of the Iraqi bodies "with the direct illegitimacy of either CPA or UN involvement." Option 2 was to throw in the towel and give Sistani, and Iraq, direct elections for the assembly, but we estimated that this would delay the handover of power by at least three months, while risking violence and disadvantaging moderate parties that were only beginning to gain traction. Option 3 was open caucuses, in which any Iraqi could come to the provincial selection meeting and vote, but this procedure would be vulnerable to abuse and intimidation. Under option 4, "open, cascading caucuses," there would be an open caucus in each locality, to select representatives to a provincial caucus, which would elect the assembly members. But this approach was subject to the same abuses as option 3 and would require organizing something like 1,400 local caucuses across Iraq within a few months—an impossible goal. Option 5 was to have each of Iraq's 45,000 public distribution centers, in villages and neighborhoods around the country, choose a representative who would have the power to vote for the provincial assembly candidates. This scheme, too, was judged operationally infeasible and open to abuse. Under option 6, the caucuses would select or the UN (or the CPA, or the Governing Council) would appoint a slate of candidates, which Iraqis would then simply vote up or down (at either the national or the provincial level). Option 7 was to have the Governing Council simply expand itself into a temporary assembly, adding between 50 and 225 members to its ranks. Then direct elections for a new transitional assembly would be held in January 2005. Option 8, a variation of option 7, would have the CPA and/or the UN appoint the temporary assembly that would govern until the January elections. Option 9 was to hold a single national conference to elect the assembly, but this returned us to square one: by what means could the Iraqi delegates to the conference be legitimately chosen? (Not presented was a tenth option, advanced by an external adviser, calling for direct elections for provincial councils, which would then indirectly elect the transitional national assembly). Only option 2 was certain to satisfy Sistani, but several of the others were considered to have some potential to mollify him, by guaranteeing a Shiite majority in the assembly. Having nine options was clear evidence that this was a question without an easy answer and that the choice would have to be made at a higher level than the TAL drafting committee. Not until Brahimi's compromise with Sistani in mid-February would this Gordian knot be cut.

★

Perhaps the greatest source of friction between the United States and the Iraqi drafters of the TAL concerned security issues. Even prior to my arrival, CPA officials had been seeking a highly expedited procedure to enable the transitional government to adopt treaties. They began by suggesting that the prime minister be able to conclude and implement international treaties. To Istrabadi and many of the other

Iraqis, concentrating in one office the power to make binding international agreements was a nonstarter. By the time I entered the deliberations, the Americans were urging a simple majority vote in the transitional assembly to ratify a treaty. Istrabadi replied that a *transitional* national assembly was on dubious grounds ratifying a treaty in any case, but if it was to do so, it ought to be with a supermajority vote, like the two-thirds required for approval of a treaty in the U.S. Senate. Listening to Roman Martinez press the case over chicken sandwiches and soft drinks, I found it bizarre, disturbing, and politically unwise for the United States to be asking the emerging Iraqi democracy to accept a lower threshold for treaty ratification than the Founders of the United States had deemed appropriate. I was appalled, and at the same time amused, to see—not for the only time—the Iraqis taking the more democratic side of a constitutional argument with the United States. Privately, I told Istrabadi I sympathized with him and his colleagues, and hoped they would hold their ground. I also made my views known to my colleagues in the CPA, but the request for a low threshold for treaty ratification was being driven from Washington.

As the TAL negotiations struggled into the second week of February, the elimination of the two-thirds requirement for parliamentary ratification of international agreements rose to an A-level concern—one of Washington's highest priorities for the TAL. Although it was never spelled out in so many words, I understood that the Bush administration wanted to conclude a treaty with the Iraqi transitional government granting the United States long-term military bases in Iraq, and perhaps other concessions as well. I wondered how our government could be so myopic as to fail to see that *any* treaty with an Iraqi transitional government was bound to be of questionable legitimacy, but especially one that was approved by a narrow majority vote—and by representatives who had not been directly elected, at that! If we had been smart, we would have seen that a stronger majority would be necessary to confer legitimacy on any such agreement. But we were much more stubborn and arrogant than we were smart. Again and again, down to the final negotiations, the Americans insisted on simple-majority approval. "The fact that we keep mentioning this should tell you how important it is to us," Bremer's deputy, Ambassador Richard

Jones, told Istrabadi near the final deliberations. "And the fact we keep objecting to this should tell you how important it is to us," Istrabadi replied. In the end, American pressure prevailed, and the two-thirds requirement for treaty ratification was dropped from the TAL.

The United States was also vigorously pushing the Iraqi drafting committee to insert into the TAL a permanent renunciation of any development or possession of weapons of mass destruction—nuclear, biological, and chemical. Istrabadi sympathized with the goal, but not the timing or the means. On instructions from Washington, Martinez kept prompting the issue. Istrabadi resisted, explaining at one meeting, "Look, let's tread lightly on this and let the Iraqi people decide it later. If I were to be in the constitutional convention, I would advocate a total ban on developing and holding WMD—and even on using troops offensively abroad, as in the Japanese constitution—but this is the wrong place to do this." As a compromise, Pachachi crafted a provision requiring Iraq's transitional government to "respect and implement Iraq's international obligations regarding the non-proliferation, non-development, non-production, and non-use of nuclear, chemical, and biological weapons." The United States leaned on Iraq to "forswear" all such weapons and any associated equipment and technology, but the Iraqis held their ground, and their wording became the final language in the TAL.

One security aspect the United States did not follow up on was a status of forces agreement, which would officially recognize that the U.S.-led military operation was in Iraq with the consent of the Iraqi government and would define the rules under which it would function. According to the November 15 agreement, such a pact was to be concluded between the CPA and the Governing Council by the end of March 2004. Pachachi wanted a reference to the security agreement to be included in the TAL, to make it clear that the international forces were there at the invitation of Iraq, and were cooperating with Iraq, rather than being an occupying power. By February, however, it had become obvious that the United States no longer wanted a formal status of forces agreement, but preferred to rely on UN Resolutions 1483 and 1511, which gave the U.S. forces in Iraq unfettered powers. Pachachi and his advisers maintained that once there was a sovereign

Iraqi government, American and other international troops could no longer operate as an occupying force but would be governed by an explicit security agreement with Iraq. They did not want the UN resolutions mentioned in the TAL. Nevertheless, the Bush administration insisted on this point, and no status of forces agreement would ever be concluded, much less enshrined in the TAL. Istrabadi recalled to me later, "The American position was that they did not want any restrictions on their movements. And they wanted to make it clear that the Bill of Rights only applied to the Iraqi government. Only the Iraqi government would need an arrest warrant; the multinational force could break down doors."

★

The most vexing nexus of issues concerned the status of the Kurds and the future structure of the state of Iraq. From the beginning of discussions on Iraq's constitution, the CPA confronted a difficult choice. On the one hand, the United States felt a moral and political obligation to the roughly five million Iraqi Kurds, who had suffered greatly under Saddam and had been steadfast allies in the fight against the Iraqi dictator. Most American policy makers believed that the Kurds needed and deserved protections of their rights as a minority within Iraq, as well as continuation of the considerable autonomy they had exercised since the end of the Gulf War, in 1991, when the establishment of a no-fly zone had enabled them to establish a regional government in the north.[8] On the other hand, the United States was concerned that autonomy not constitute a slippery slope toward Kurdish independence, which would dismember Iraq and might destabilize Turkey, home to a large Kurdish population of its own. Thus, when Bremer declared his vision to be an Iraq that was democratic, unified, and federal, he was sincere, even though he was not above squeezing the democratic structures to fit America's perceived interests.

Early on in the deliberations on the interim constitution, it became apparent that the issues relating to the rights, powers, and protections of the Kurdish minority would be the most contentious, explosive, and difficult to resolve. Pachachi advised Bremer that the CPA should get more involved in this aspect of the negotiations. In fact, things had gone badly in December, with Washington informing the Kurds that there was no place for the Kurdistan Regional Government in the proposed federal system based on the eighteen provinces, and the outraged Kurds replying that the CPA was offering them less than they had been given under Saddam. In the Governing Council's drafting committee, the Kurds had been staking out maximalist, inflexible positions that carried the implicit threat of secession, and on December 21, KDP leader Massoud Barzani had published an article in a Kurdish newspaper declaring that "the Kurds will not accept less than their existing situation" of regional autonomy and warning that the "imposition of an unacceptable formula" could lead the Kurds "to resort to other choices."[9]

On January 2, Bremer and his British deputy, Greenstock, traveled to Irbil (one of the two Kurdish capitals) for the first serious discussions on federalism with the two Kurdish leaders Barzani and Talabani. Their task was a delicate one: to continue to press the CPA position in favor of purely geographic federalism (eighteen provincial governments, and no regional one), while reestablishing the trust that had been frayed and getting the Kurds to accept a set of powers for the central government. This was a circle that could not be squared. The CPA team understood that the preservation of the Kurdistan Regional Government was a fundamental priority for the Kurds, one they were unlikely to surrender. The CPA team thus decided to defer the question of geographic versus ethnic federalism until the end of the discussion, to preserve it as a bargaining chip to get the Kurds to agree to a strong central government that had built-in protections for them. In the meeting, Bremer expressed the Coalition's support for significant decentralization of power. But the Iraqi central government, he went on, would need sufficient power to hold the country together, and this would require exclusive authority over national defense, the country's borders, fiscal and monetary policy, and natural resources (read *oil*). Furthermore, all political-party and private militias—including, by implication, the *pesh merga*, the battle-hardened armed forces of the two Kurdish parties—would have to be demobilized, and Iraq would need to be a fully integrated state, not one like Lebanon, where power was divided along ethnic and sectarian lines. When Talabani insisted that a provincial-based federalism was unacceptable, they all agreed to lay that question aside and discuss the division of powers. On this question, the CPA and the Kurds made progress in assigning powers like defense, foreign policy, finance, and communications to the center, while allowing decentralization of authority in areas not explicitly reserved for the central government, like education and culture.

The January 2 meeting marked the beginning of more active CPA intervention in the drafting of the TAL, and in the negotiations with the Kurds over the future structure of the Iraqi state. During the next two months, Bremer and his governance team were engaged in frequent, frank, and extended conversations with the two Kurdish leaders and their deputies. From the start, Bremer made it clear that he wanted this to be a "conversation among friends," and not a negotiation. But delicate, difficult negotiations ensued, down to the final moments before the adoption of the TAL. The central tenet of the American position, laid out from the beginning and upheld to the end, was that the United States was sympathetic to the Kurds' desire to preserve their substantial autonomy but that it had to coexist with a viable central government. In other words, the United States was committed to a unified, federal Iraq. From an analytic perspective, and from my experience studying divided countries around the world, federalism made eminent sense. Indeed, it was hard to see how Iraq's deep regional, ethnic, and sectarian divisions could be managed in a democracy without constitutional guarantees of autonomy. Yet Iraq had always been highly centralized, and for many Iraqis, the unitary state was a bedrock principle of their nationalist identity. Many in Iraq and the Arab world did not understand what federalism meant, and saw the U.S. endorsement of it as part of a plot to weaken or even dismember the country, rather than as an indispensable instrument to hold the country together. High officials in the United Nations also felt that such a fundamental change as the introduction of federalism into a historically unitary state should not have been introduced during a transitional period, while Iraq was under international occupation. Thus, America's endorsement of federalism in Iraq was a controversial step.

For the Kurds as well, a federal Iraq was a big step, but in the other direction. What many Kurds wanted was outright independence. During more than a decade of autonomy, Iraqi Kurdistan had thrived as never before, and a whole generation of Kurds had grown up speaking no Arabic and feeling no identification with the Iraqi state. Most of the Kurdish population felt only a reluctant, pragmatic, and conflicted tug toward Baghdad. For them, Kurdish regional autonomy within a democratic and federal Iraq was acceptable, but it was still a second-best solution. A return to a unitary state, or failure to achieve meaningful protections within a strong federal system, was not simply a third-best outcome but an unacceptable one. What Kurdish leaders were now proposing was a "voluntary union with Iraq," conditioned on the preservation of their autonomy.[10] Moreover, the Kurds felt that the Americans owed them this, since they had been America's most loyal ally in the region and had joined American troops on the front lines of the effort to overthrow Saddam's regime.

In a follow-up meeting with Bremer on January 7, the two Kurdish leaders pressed home this point. The Kurds were firmly committed to a unified Iraq, but only if it was truly federal and democratic. Barzani objected to the American position favoring a federalism based on the provinces, which, he felt, failed to recognize Iraq's character as a state with two distinct nationalities, Arab and Kurdish. "We were expecting a reward, not a punishment," he told Bremer. Talabani said the Kurds could agree to have the central government control such national matters as foreign policy, defense, and economic policy. But it was not enough to have a system that devolved power to the eighteen provinces. The Kurds needed to retain a single autonomous government encompassing all the territory north of the Green Line, which included or cut across five provinces. They sought, as well, to have their linguistic rights recognized, their autonomy guaranteed, and Saddam's campaign of Arabization in the city of Kirkuk reversed.

No problem caused CPA officials more headaches than the status of Kirkuk, a city on the border between the Kurdish and Arab Sunni areas of settlement, which was rich in oil (controlling as much as 6 percent of the world's known reserves). In fact, the northern oil fields of Kirkuk and Mosul together accounted for about half of Iraq's production, and Kurdish control of them, by some reckonings, made independence a much more realistic prospect. For decades, Kurds had suffered periodic Arabizing pressure on the margin of settlement, in and around the city. The pressure escalated into a large-scale campaign of displacement and deportation under Baathist rule, and reached a level of ethnic cleansing during the last two decades of Saddam Hussein's dictatorship, when more than 100,000 Kurds were expelled from their homes and properties, which were then given to Iraqi Arab settlers. After the fall of Saddam's regime, tens of thousands of Kurds poured back into Kirkuk to reclaim their property; a like number of Arabs were now displaced from their homes; and the city came to be widely regarded as the most likely flashpoint for a civil war, if things were to take a disastrous turn.

The CPA's strategy for dealing with Kirkuk had three basic dimensions. First, Kurdish action to reverse Arabization by force and intimidation had to cease. On this point, Bremer was emphatic in the January 2 meeting, stating that the past injustices must not be compounded with new ones, and declaring the aggressive actions by Kurdish officials in Kirkuk irresponsible and inflammatory. Second, because it was the most difficult of all problems, the status of Kirkuk—like Jerusalem in the Israeli-Palestinian conflict—had to be postponed until the end of the transition. Third, a system of due process had to be established to sort through the various claims and grievances and to resettle displaced people according to the law, and not at the point of a gun. In their January 7 meeting, Barzani and Talabani agreed with Bremer on the need to establish the Iraqi Property Claims Commission to adjudicate these disputes, and the following week the statute for its creation was adopted by the Governing Council and signed into law by Bremer.[11]

As the discussion wore on, though, it became clear that the Kurds wanted a substantial degree of autonomy, with the Kurdistan Regional Government able to veto the application of national laws within the region, prevent the deployment of Iraqi troops within the region, and retain the *pesh merga* as an independent armed force organized by the Kurdish government, its ultimate defense against renewed oppression by Baghdad. The first demand would negate the concept of a central government, while the third directly contradicted the CPA position that all independent militias should be incorporated into a comprehensive plan for demobilization. In addition, the Kurds sought local control of national resources, while Bremer and the CPA insisted that oil and other natural resources be owned by all the Iraqi people. The Kurds also wanted their language to have equal status with Arabic at the center; Iraqi Arabs generally resisted this idea, and especially the larger notion of a binational state; to them, Iraq was an Arab state with a Kurdish minority. Pachachi strongly agreed that Iraq was a single national state, but he also felt that the Kurds had the right to use their language, and that giving Iraq's largest minority language equal status with Arabic would strengthen national unity. Resisting suggestions from Bremer and others that he use the language question as a bargaining chip, Pachachi agreed, early on, to accept Kurdish as a language of equal status and eventually convinced the Governing Council to go along.

Several big issues still remained to be resolved in less than two months, but in their early January discussions, Bremer and the Kurdish leaders had struck the outlines of a historic federalist bargain for Iraq's interim constitution. The Kurds accepted a number of significant powers for the central government, and the CPA, in turn, accepted the preservation of a unified Kurdistan region whose government would have autonomous powers far beyond those of the eighteen provinces.

Through patient and sympathetic engagement, Bremer and his CPA colleagues had drawn the Kurds away from their initial, untenable vision into a framework of federalism, which gave them substantial autonomy and veto rights while firmly planting Kurdistan back within the Iraqi nation. It would be one of Bremer's most important (and least appreciated) achievements as administrator of the CPA. Then, in the first half of February, things blew up. After weeks of noting, with no response, the CPA's cables reporting on the negotiations, the Bush administration sent instructions that reference to the Kurdistan Regional Government be stricken from the TAL and that federalism be based solely on the eighteen provinces. When Bremer dutifully conveyed this demand, the Kurds—most of all Barzani—became furious, and the negotiations plunged into crisis. Feeling they had, in essence, been double-crossed, the Kurds retreated to an extreme position on all the key issues: Kirkuk, regional powers, the *pesh merga*, control of oil revenue. CPA officials were frustrated and angry—but more with Washington than with the Kurds. In time, the CPA persuaded Washington that the preservation of the Kurdistan Regional Government was a necessity, and a certain equilibrium between the Kurds and the Americans was restored. Yet hard bargaining still lay ahead. During the second half of February, the Kurds continued to insist that they be able to keep the *pesh merga*, that they be guaranteed a share of oil revenue proportionate to their population, and that the boundaries of the autonomous Kurdish region be expanded to include Kirkuk and other areas below the Green Line that had heavy concentrations of Kurds. All of these proposals were nonstarters for the principal Sunni and Shiite interlocutors on the Governing Council, and for the CPA. Tension rose. "These are our rights—we fought hard for them," said Rowsch Shaways, a senior KDP leader and constitutional adviser. "The experiment of Iraqi statehood failed once before. We do not want to repeat the same mistakes." Even Mahmoud Othman, a moderate Kurdish member of the Governing Council, warned: "After all the Kurdish people have been through, the killings, the genocide, I cannot go to my people and tell them to accept the things the Americans are trying to force on us. The Kurdish people will not accept them."[12]

The notion of a powerful regional government proved attractive to more than just the Kurds. Shiites began to ask, If the Kurds can have it, why can't we? Although the Shiites, as the demographic majority and likely dominant group in a democratic Iraq, stood to gain from a high degree of political centralization, they had also been on the receiving end of much abuse by the central government under Saddam. The perspective of some Shiite political leaders was, therefore, to give the Kurds much of what they wanted—so long as the Shiites could have it, too. This attitude was most visible on regional powers and the control of oil revenue. Arguing that "anything the Kurds get the Shia must get," SCIRI's Adel Abdel Mahdi pressed for a provision that any three provinces outside the Kurdistan area (with the exception of Baghdad and Kirkuk) could form a region among themselves, with approval from the national assembly and (by referendum) of the peoples of the relevant provinces. Salem Chalabi then presented this proposal to the drafting committee. Istrabadi, representing the thinking of Pachachi and a key segment of Iraqi opinion that wanted to keep the center strong, objected to this proposal, arguing that so fundamental a reorganization of the Iraqi state should not take place in the transitional period, under an interim framework with limited legitimacy. "This will be read on the street as a template for the dissolution of the country," Istrabadi warned. When the idea gathered momentum, Istrabadi suggested the addition of a mechanism to discourage the formation of regions—for example, by creating an upper legislative house (a senate) in which each province or region would have the same number of seats, so that if three provinces united into one region, they would lose senate seats. His proposal went nowhere, and the popularity of the original idea increased. However, I shared Istrabadi's concern, as I had written my doctoral dissertation on the failure of the First Nigerian Republic in the 1960s, when the partition of the country into three powerful regions, largely along ethnic lines, fostered ethnic, party, and regional conflict that eventually led to civil war. Now I worried that if the divisions were consolidated mainly along Kurdish, Sunni, and Shiite lines, Iraq could meet the same fate. A strong sense emerged among Governing Council members for greater equality in the treatment of different parts of the country, so the proposal to allow any three provinces to create a region was written into the TAL. But because the procedure for establishing a region is politically cumbersome, and the transitional period would be limited, the implications of the measure may prove largely symbolic. Even so, the question of whether Iraq would continue to be a federal state—and, if so, how its constituent units would be delineated—remained a profound issue confronting the drafters of a permanent constitution.

In any federal system, a key issue is how to finance governments below the central level. In Iraq, as in Nigeria, this was an explosive matter, because it involved the distribution of the country's oil wealth. As in Nigeria, some sections of Iraq have oil and some do not; therefore, leaving control of oil revenue in the hands of local authorities might severely disadvantage the groups—the Sunnis in particular—from non–oil-producing regions. Yet it was, in fact, the Sunnis who had controlled the oil wealth for decades, under a succession of dictatorships, and had used it to steer resources their way while neglecting much of the rest of the country. Now, as a result, the Kurds and the Shiites believed that it was time to right a series of historic wrongs, by giving a significant share of oil revenue to the regions from which it derived, and by requiring that areas that had been underdeveloped receive special attention. To this recommendation, Istrabadi replied, memorably, in one of our protracted drafting sessions, "The whole damned country is underdeveloped. Everyone has been ignored for at least the last twenty-five years!"

In a meeting with the Kurds, Salem Chalabi proposed an ingenious compromise: Iraq's natural resources would be owned by companies in which the central government would have a majority share and the local governments (where the resources originated) would have a minority share. Other formulas were adduced as well, but Istrabadi and Pachachi were adamant that Iraq's natural resources belonged to all the people, and on this point the United States supported them. In the end, their view, and that of other national-minded Iraqis, won out. The central government was given, among its exclusive responsibilities, management of the natural resources of Iraq, which were declared to belong to all the people. It was enjoined to consult with lower-level governments, however, and to distribute the resulting revenues "in an equitable manner proportional . . . to the population . . . and with due regard for areas that were unjustly deprived . . . by the previous regime."[13]

The Kurds proved to be tough and savvy bargainers. Although they felt they had relinquished a number of cherished goals, their shrewd sense of what they needed, their repeated appeals to the atrocities they had suffered and the sacrifices they had made, and their patient, unified bargaining posture paid off handsomely in the final document. Many Iraqi Arabs wanted to establish Arabic as the sole official language of the country, while not preventing the use of other languages, such as Kurdish, Turkish, and Armenian. The TAL instead recognized Arabic and Kurdish as "the two official languages of Iraq" (the tongues of the smaller minorities could, of course, be spoken). All official documents and correspondence were thus required to be published in both Arabic and Kurdish, while members of parliament, ministers, judges, and conferees were permitted to speak and conduct official business in either language.[14] The provision went a long way toward symbolically enshrining the Kurdish vision of a binational state. The Kurds also received the right to "amend the application" in their territory of any federal law not in an area of exclusive federal competence. On the militia question, the *pesh merga* were to be formally integrated into a new Iraqi civil defense corps (and other Iraqi armed forces). Theoretically these were to be under central government command, but, in practice, their Kurdish command structures would remain intact. This arrangement helped to assuage Kurdish anxieties about the powers they were surrendering and the uncertainties of the future political order.

The Kurds also won a huge victory on the structure of the presidency council. For the Kurds, a seat on the council was a vital form of protection, since it would enable them to weigh in on crucial choices at the center, including the passage of legislation and treaties, the appointment of judges to the supreme court (the body they counted on to uphold their federalist guarantees), and the nomination of the prime minister. But much would depend on how the three members of the council would be elected and by what rule they would make decisions—majority or unanimous. We opted for the election of the presidency council as a single slate, because this method seemed most likely to lead to the kind of broadly inclusive balance (to put it baldly, a Shiite, a Sunni, and a Kurd) that was intended for the body. To ensure that the body would not be dominated by a single group, however, we considered requiring a supermajority for a slate to be elected. The Kurds insisted on, and won, the requirement that the council be elected by a two-thirds vote of the assembly. No less important, they won a rule for presidential decision making on which they had staked no small measure of their bargaining capital: the final version of the TAL stated that all decisions of the presidency council must be unanimous. (In our early drafts, we had specified only that the appointment of the prime minister be unanimous.) This provision gave the presumed Kurdish member of the presidency council the right to veto any decision of the body; it would, in turn, occasion bitter protest from many Sunni and Shiite Iraqis around the country. The irony, however, was that the requirement for unanimity actually diluted Kurdish power in one crucial matter: the ability of the council to veto legislation. Many Iraqis did not immediately realize that it took all three members of the presidency to *block* a law. Moreover, in return for this concession, the Shiite members of the Governing Council insisted that the presidency council be composed of a president and two deputies, rather than the original plan for a collective body. Since the Shiites were expected to have a majority of the national assembly, the possibility (indeed, among many, the expectation) was raised that both the head of government and the ceremonial head of state would be Shiite Arabs.

Through weeks of shrewd bargaining, the Kurds had emerged as the most successful players in the negotiations over the interim constitution, building on their friendship (strained though it sometimes became) with the United States and an alliance of convenience they had forged with the key Shiite actors on the Governing Council. The Shiites gave the Kurds significant regional autonomy, including the ability (in effect) to keep much of the *pesh merga* intact, and the veto at the center that they wanted; the Kurds, in turn, agreed to a strong prime ministry that the Shiites were destined to control. Thinking he would be the next prime minister, Ahmed Chalabi became the most articulate advocate for rescinding draft language requiring the disbandment of all militias and for allowing the Kurds (in effect) to keep the *pesh merga*. But according to savvy observers, the real victor in the center would, ultimately, not be Chalabi but the Shiite religious parties. Toward the end of the negotiations, a frustrated Iraqi liberal told a leading Kurdish negotiator, a top deputy to PUK leader Jalal Talabani: "The Kurds have made an alliance with the Shia. They think they will be exempt [from developments in the center]. But what happens in Baghdad will matter in the North." The Kurdish leader conceded the point, which was about to hit home much sooner than either of them had realized.

★

The bargaining between the Kurds and other members of the Governing Council, particularly the Shiite caucus, became tense and difficult as the February 28 deadline drew near. For weeks the CPA had been negotiating intensively with the Kurds as a group, and the Shiite members of the Governing Council, who were increasingly acting in unison as a group, felt neglected. They had issues they wanted to discuss with Bremer, including the role of Islam and the quota for women's representation in parliament, but they were told that Bremer would not deal with the Shiites as a caucus. On Friday, February 27, things finally unraveled. Dr. Raja Habib Khuzai, a female Shiite member of the council, moved to repeal Decision 137, which implemented Islamic Sharia law on family matters. Many Shiite members opposed repeal in general but sought to avoid dealing with the issue when the deadline for the TAL was so near. Pachachi, who was chairing the meeting, nevertheless ruled the motion in order, and the Governing Council voted 15 to 10 to repeal the decision and reinstate Iraqi civil law. At that point, one of the most crucial Shiite players, the SCIRI delegate, Adel Abdel Mahdi (standing in for his party leader, Abdul-Aziz al-Hakim), packed up and left the meeting, explaining to a colleague, "The majority wants to force things on us and does not operate by consensus. Let them do what they want." Eight Shiite delegates then met and decided to walk out of the deliberations together (including Salem Chalabi, who was so instructed by his uncle, Ahmed—to whose home the eight retreated). The Shiite walkout was a devastating blow, polarizing the sectarian divisions within the body to the point that one moderate adviser (a secular Shiite) told his colleague, "If there is ever a civil war in Iraq, this will be one of the remote causes."

The following morning, Saturday, February 28, the Governing Council was supposed to finalize and adopt the TAL, but the Shiites did not show up, and the meeting was not held for lack of a quorum. Bremer pressed for the Governing Council to meet and finish the document, but the Shiites were now demanding significant concessions, and for the first time, on Sunday, February 29, Bremer met with the Shiite caucus. Among their demands was the right of other provincial governments to form regions—a provision that had been in a draft of the TAL but was taken out. Skeptical about the provincial governors chosen under the CPA's procedures, they also wanted the central government to have the power to fire and appoint governors until elections could be held. Bremer refused on this count. And on religion, the Shiite delegates were willing to back away from their insistence that Islam be considered "the primary source" of legislation (rather than "a source")—as long as a provision was added that no legislation could contradict the tenets of Islam. This compromise had been cleared in advance with Ayatollah Sistani.

Bremer then called a meeting of the Governing Council for that evening to try to finish the document, a session that would last well into the following morning. In fact, it initiated a seventy-two-hour marathon struggle to conclude the interim constitution. The deliberations quickly broke down along ethnic/sectarian lines, pitting the Shiite caucus against the Kurdish leaders and the Sunni members.[15] The Shiite caucus read its demands, which included the ability of any three provinces to form a region of their own, and the allocation of a significant portion of the resources from the Basra oil fields to Basra and its neighboring provinces. While the Kurds could not object to either demand (since they were asking for similar provisions themselves, including a share of the proceeds from the Kirkuk oil fields), the Sunni delegates became upset. At one point, some of the Sunni members wanted to stage a walkout of their own. Pachachi refused to go along. "He was not willing to engage in brinksmanship," one of his aides later reflected. "He wanted a result, because he truly felt the burden of having the fate of a country in his hands—a burden I don't think any other member of the Governing Council quite felt." In the end, the Sunnis stayed put, and the TAL moved toward completion.

Meetings continued throughout the next three days, around the clock, to work through the document and resolve the remaining substantive issues and nuances of language. One of the contentious matters was whether Baathists would be able to run as candidates in the elections. The Shiites wanted the same strong de-Baathification provisions as Bremer had decreed for state employment, while the Sunni delegates wanted looser restrictions. In the end, they reached a compromise under which high-level Baathists, those who had been members at the division level or above, remained excluded. At 4 A.M. on March 3— the key Iraqi players and CPA observers had been up for three days, with little or no sleep—they came to the last substantive provision of the TAL, Article 61, which prescribed the procedures for drafting and adopting the permanent constitution. Then, Kurdish leader Massoud Barzani proposed an amendment to Article 61(c)—that ratification of the permanent constitution in the national referendum should require an additional threshold beyond a simple majority of the votes. The constitution would be defeated if it was rejected by two-thirds of the voters in three or more provinces. The punch-drunk, bleary-eyed Governing Council members adopted the change without giving it much thought, and believed that they were done.

What had seemed an innocent, last-minute consideration was in fact a brilliant tactical maneuver, planned long in advance, to achieve the Kurds' remaining vital interest in the making of the interim constitution. To that point, the Kurds had achieved most of their minimum goals. They had a powerful regional government, with control over police forces and internal security; the right to impose taxes; and a wide range of other authorities not assigned to the center. Their government could veto the application, in the Kurdistan region, of any federal law that lay outside the areas of exclusive federal jurisdiction (such matters as fiscal and monetary policy, and customs). They seemed likely to have a veto over any action by the presidency council. Kurdish was recognized as a national language equal in status to Arabic. They were given the opportunity to preserve much of their *pesh merga* intact, under the guise of integration into the Iraqi armed forces. None of these provisions in the TAL could be changed without their assent. Almost all had initially been opposed by other members of the TAL drafting committee, and by the United States. It was a remarkable political victory. But what about their longer-term security under the permanent constitution? How could they be confident that the federalist protections they had won in the interim would not be taken away from them in the permanent document? That would depend on the makeup of the transitional assembly (which, with the compromise agreement brokered by UN envoy Lakhdar Brahimi, was to be both a lawmaking body and a constitutional convention).

The problem was that the Kurds could not be confident of their representation in the national assembly, since the system of election for that body had yet to be specified. Neither would a higher national majority in a referendum easily assure the Kurds, because with only about 20 percent of the population, they could lose out even if a two-thirds majority was required for ratification. Thus, Barzani's deputy, Rowsch Shaways, hit upon an ingenious innovation: to base the veto on voting in the eighteen provinces, three of which were predominantly Kurdish.[16] If the draft constitution was seriously objectionable, the Kurds could defeat it with a two-thirds vote in each of their three provinces.

With the clarity of a night's sleep, the implications of the last-minute, hastily adopted provision began to dawn on Shiite leaders. In a meeting of senior party deputies the next day, March 4, Adel Mahdi suggested that the language of Article 61(c) be modified, but Shaways said that the Kurds could not agree to such a change. One of the key Shiite members of the Governing Council, Mowaffak al-Rubaie, then traveled to Najaf to brief Ayatollah Sistani's son, Mohammed Reda al-Sistani, on the development. The younger Sistani was livid, and vowed that the grand ayatollah would denounce them all if Article 61(c) was included in the TAL. In a phone conversation with the Shiite caucus later that day, Sistani refused to endorse the TAL if the new version of Article 61(c) was included. He further requested that the structure of the presidency council be changed to a five-member body (which would presumably give the Shiites three seats), with no right of veto for an individual member. Together, the two demands went to the heart of the philosophical and political cleavage in Iraq: the Shiites' quest for majority rule versus the Kurds' demand (which was also beginning to grow on many Sunnis) for minority rights.

By Friday, March 5, the Shiite leaders on the Governing Council were in a serious bind. In a foggy, sleep-deprived blur, they had agreed to Article 61(c) and the country had finally adopted an interim constitution. It was to be signed later that day in an elaborate ceremony before a throng of international media and officials at the Convention Center. The event had already been delayed once, from March 3, as a result of a wave of terrorist attacks the day before, on Shiite pilgrims in Baghdad and Karbala, which killed more than 180 people. But the most important Shiite religious leader was flatly opposed to the provision, and the two Kurdish leaders, Barzani and Talabani, were refusing to consider any further change.

For much of the day on Friday, the five Shiite leaders remained huddled in Ahmed Chalabi's office at the Governing Council headquarters, while the other twenty members were left stewing in the body's official chambers, one floor below. The signing ceremony was set for 4 P.M. A block away, at the Convention Center, as the hour neared, a traditional Iraqi musical ensemble stood by in the wings and three hundred guests waited and conversed. Twenty-five blue and gold pens (one for each council member) sat on an antique desk that had once been used by Iraq's first monarch, King Faisal, installed by the British in 1921. In one of the most embarrassing moments that the CPA suffered during its fourteen months of administering Iraq, the five Shiite leaders refused to show up, and the occupation authorities were forced to cancel the event. The relevant dispute was "a technical matter related to minority rights," said the ever-upbeat CPA spokesman Dan Senor. "Democracy is an inherently messy process."[17] Privately, one of my depleted senior governance colleagues had a different assessment: "We've truly snatched defeat from the jaws of victory."

The entire constitutional agreement now seemed at risk of unraveling. The five Shiite leaders were demanding changes in the TAL along the lines requested by Sistani. Kurdish leaders, suspecting a plot to erase their autonomy, were threatening to reopen the entire process if the Shiites insisted on revisiting Article 61(c). Some suggested that the five Shiite holdouts were exhibiting a greater loyalty to Iran than to Iraq. In fact, most of the other twenty council members—as well as the key officials in the CPA—were deeply disturbed that the five Shiites were reneging on an agreement they had reached, whatever their state of exhaustion at the time. After another twelve hours of bitter discussions that stretched until midnight, the five Shiites agreed to take the matter back to Sistani and try to persuade him to accept the TAL as it was, while a new signing ceremony was scheduled for Monday, March 8. The next day, Saturday, they traveled down to the holy city of Najaf, where, after much back-and-forth discussion, they won Sistani's reluctant assent to proceed. On Sunday, the five Shiites said they would sign the document "as it stands."

The next day, the signing ceremony took place as it had been originally staged, with a moving musical performance by Iraqi children, and the same long row of blue and gold pens at King Faisal's old desk, which each of the Governing Council members took, one by one, to sign a poster-sized version of the endorsement statement. Muhammad

Bahr al-Uloum, the Shiite cleric who was acting as president of the council for the month, declared it "a decisive moment in the history of Iraq." Switching from Arabic to Kurdish, Barzani recalled the suffering of the Kurdish people, and then gushed: "This is the first time we Kurds feel that we are citizens of Iraq."[18] Adnan Pachachi—who had done more than any single member of the council to bring it about—called the TAL "a document we can justly be proud of," taking particular pride in the bill of rights. Speaking in English after remarks in Arabic, he declared:

> Some may say that the Bill of Rights is copied from the West; my answer: these rights and values are not exclusively the property of the West; they are universal and should be respected and imple-mented everywhere. This law is aspirational in character. We have not legislated for the present, but we have put up a high standard so that the people in the future will always try to reach. It is thus a beacon of light and hope for future generations.[19]

The high ideals and lofty spirits were soon brought down to earth. Shortly after the ceremony, one of the most powerful of the five Shiite leaders, Ibrahim Jaafari, read a statement on behalf of twelve of the thirteen Shiite council members, declaring their intention to amend certain provisions of the document that they considered undemocratic. They had signed the TAL, he said, to preserve the unity of the country, but they would seek changes in it before the June 30 transfer of power—even though there was no legal or constitutional mechanism for them to do so. "There is a mistake in some of the articles," Adel Mahdi said. "We have to fix them." Later that afternoon, Ayatollah Sistani released a religious decree declaring, "This law places obstacles in the path of reaching a permanent constitution for the country that maintains its unity, the rights of sons of all sects and ethnic back-grounds." He further warned that the TAL would lack legitimacy until it was approved by a democratically elected national assembly. His words again reflected his philosophical position, which he had reiterated for many months, that an unelected body could not bind an elected one.

I considered Sistani's statement an ominous warning, because it signaled the possibility of a profound constitutional crisis at the birth of the Iraqi democracy. Once it took effect, the TAL could be amended only through a prohibitively difficult process, over which the Kurds could exercise a veto. But if the TAL did not legitimately take effect until the elected transitional assembly approved it, then the new assembly could amend it at will—and presumably by any majority that it designated. Unless a new constitutional consensus was fashioned before that moment, I felt, everything we had tried to achieve could unravel.

7

SALESMANSHIP

★

As the Transitional Administrative Law (TAL) was being signed on March 8, I was preparing to return to Iraq after a short break to attend to work in the United States. I had been alarmed by the crisis that had almost derailed the signing of the interim constitution, but now that it was done, I was feeling cautiously hopeful about the task ahead. With Brahimi's artful intervention a few weeks earlier, it seemed that we had resolved the biggest problem, the deadlock with Sistani. In the press, the TAL was widely praised for its liberal provisions and democratic structures. I would be lecturing throughout Iraq about the provisions of the TAL and the principles of democracy, and I was looking forward to being a part of the democracy dialogues that were unfolding across the country. Back at CPA headquarters in Baghdad, the Governance Office was arranging an ambitious schedule for me. I was excited to be returning.

Then, as I was just about to depart for Baghdad, I got the news that Fern Holland had been killed. A bright, idealistic, vivacious thirty-three-year-old lawyer from Oklahoma, Holland had been working with Iraqi women's and human rights groups as a CPA civilian staff member at the South Central regional office in Hilla. She had been traveling back to Hilla on the night of March 9 from a women's center in Karbala when several gunmen posing as Iraqi police officers stopped the car carrying Holland, regional press officer Robert Zangas, and an Iraqi translator and coworker, Salwa Ali Oumashi, at a makeshift checkpoint. All three were murdered in cold blood. Holland and Zangas were the first two American civilian officials of the CPA to be killed in Iraq. I had met Holland briefly during my visit to Hilla in January, which she had helped arrange. Everyone who worked with Fern Holland was impressed with her dedication, energy, and charm.

The murders of Holland, Zangas, and Oumashi were shocking and sobering at many levels. Within the CPA, they would prompt a reevaluation of security measures. A few days after the event, Ambassador Bremer issued a memo to all CPA employees, cautioning them to vary the times and routes of their travel, and he now required that all travel outside the Green Zone be conducted "with a minimum of two vehicles during hours of daylight" and that we carry cellular or satellite phones and wear "all regulation gear including helmet and body armor." Some of these protections might have spared the three CPA employees from their fatal ambush, but we all knew that assaults on Coalition civilian staff and contractors were mounting, that there were not nearly enough satellite phones for everyone who needed them, that the insurgency was becoming more adept, that traveling around visibly with a helmet on was an invitation to attack, and that all travel was becoming more dangerous, especially in unarmored—soft—cars. I had already seen the evidence from CPA armored cars that had been shot at and survived with only bullet scars. And I had taken note of the fact that while all British staff (as well as USAID staff) were issued and required to wear the highest-grade personal body armor, most of the American civilian employees had only flak jackets. For this reason, I was taking back with me to Baghdad a bulletproof vest that I had ordered over the Internet and had managed to get made and shipped in a matter of days. With the heavily reinforced metal plates in the front and back, the vest would stop a round from an AK-47. I had gotten the vest even before I heard about Fern Holland's murder.

The tragedy also forced me to revise my standards for traveling outside Baghdad. Over the preceding week, I had been in touch via e-mail with Derek Berlin, an undergraduate senior on leave from Columbia

University who had replaced George Adair as our Governance Office assistant—the guy who could organize trips, find transportation assets, and make things happen. Derek had begun arranging my travel according to my instructions—to use either armored SUVs or nondescript vehicles, like the ones we had taken to Hilla in January. Now, following the assault on Holland and her colleagues, I felt that traveling long distances in soft cars was out of the question. I sent another e-mail to Derek: tell them it has to be armored cars, or flying. (Soon after my return to Baghdad, a high-ranking USAID official would give me a similar, very strong word of advice: "Move around only in armored vehicles. We would have lost several people already if we hadn't made this a standard practice.")

I hadn't even thought about getting to the Green Zone from the airport, however. That trip was also becoming more dangerous, to the point where people in the palace were (quite wisely) losing their enthusiasm for making the trip out to pick up their friends and colleagues. So I was left to wait for a bus that made the run in each direction two or three times a day. I figured it would be fine. The bus was armored and was escorted by heavily armed Humvees in front and back. But when I got on the bus, I realized that it was not armored. So I was heading back to the palace in a huge tin can with wheels, which might as well have had a bull's-eye on it for rocket-propelled grenades and automatic weapons fire. At the time I could do nothing about the situation except console myself with the facts that there was still some daylight, we had some kind of military escort, and the odds were low that this would be the particular time they hit the bus. I was right about the odds, but the insurgents eventually hit a bus making the airport run, in a bloody assault. Later I would shake my head in disbelief as I heard of more and more contractors and soldiers, traveling in such conspicuous vehicles with even less protection on even more dangerous roads. Many of them were killed, or kidnapped—and then killed.

★

I arrived back to a palace that was in a kind of campaign mode. We had just completed the first milestone on the path of political transition in Iraq—the interim constitution—and now we had to figure out a way to sell it to the Iraqi people. Lectures, dialogues, and town hall meetings were being arranged around the country to explain the provisions of the TAL, the basic principles of democracy they embodied, and the remaining steps of the transition program. These were billed as dialogues and discussions, but it was not really dialogue that we were interested in, since the document was now completed and could not be amended. What we wanted for the TAL was understanding and support, or at least acceptance. Iraqis, I would soon vividly discover, wanted very much to learn about the document and discuss it—not simply to accept it and praise it but to dissect it, question it, debate it, and curse it.

Soon after I arrived, the Strategic Communications office (Stratcomm) prepared, for Bremer, a summary of local Iraqi media coverage of the TAL. Whereas the press from other Arab countries was dismissing the TAL as a U.S. document and were highlighting the Shiite-Kurdish division that almost derailed its acceptance, the summary of the local Iraqi coverage appeared more positive. Many Iraqi publications (most of them small, and many of them assisted by the United States) were expressing pride in the completion of the document, even with the delay. It marked, some papers editorialized, a "new Iraq," the guarantee of freedom and minority rights, "the birthday of the real united Iraq." One newspaper called it "the best achievement since the fall of Saddam's regime." But there was also criticism, skepticism, and concern. Iraqi commentators complained that the law had been drafted and negotiated in secret by the Governing Council and the CPA (which had allegedly manipulated the Iraqi body). They criticized the failure to consult the Iraqi people during the drafting process. And even while some were welcoming the provisions for federalism, others complained about the minority veto rights; one critic asserted, "The occupation took advantage of the situation to insert sectarian plans into the laws of the constitution." Similar criticisms surfaced in Mosul on March 12, when representatives from the CPA local office met with members of the Ninewa Provincial Council, including the governor and deputy governor. Most of the assembled officials had not seen the document, but they nevertheless denounced the provision reserving one-quarter of the assembly seats for women, and they wondered if their own opinions really mattered, since the document was already signed. One person who had read it argued that the Governing Council, because it was not an elected body, did not have the authority to adopt an interim constitution. When told it was just a temporary document, he replied, "They keep saying it's temporary, but if it's temporary long enough, it becomes permanent. This looks permanent."

By then, a very different document was already circulating on the streets of many cities. Well before we could distribute our beautifully produced leaflets explaining the key principles of the TAL, and weeks before the radio and television ads were set to roll out, a detailed critique of the TAL—crudely produced, but devastatingly effective— began shaping the terms of public debate. The document, apparently produced by the political organization around Ayatollah Sistani, asked, as its title, "What do you know about the TAL?" It read in part (as it was translated for us):

IN THE NAME OF ALLAH
MOST COMPASSIONATE MOST MERCIFUL

You Enthusiastic Iraqis

You who are concerned about the unity, independence, and stability of Iraq and are interested in keeping the rights of the Iraqi people from different sects and ethnicity.

Let us explain to you the tragedy of [the TAL.]

This law paves the way to divide Iraq and deepen sectarianism in its future system and makes Iraq [fall] into a stage of instability and violence, which cannot be estimated, but by our Maker.

This law was made in coordination with the occupying power; we can see the fingerprints of that power clearly on its articles and sources.

This law was made behind doors under pressure of the occupiers on many of the Governing Council members so as to finish it before the election campaign of Bush.

The occupiers didn't allow to show the TAL to the Iraqi people to be discussed through public seminar and the media before assigning it; many Iraqis didn't know anything about it till it was passed.

The handbill went on to criticize a number of provisions of the TAL. It gave substantial powers (including power over foreign policy and negotiating treaties) to an unelected interim government "whose members will be appointed by the occupiers." The government could "make military treaties to keep the foreign forces for 30 years." It was almost impossible to amend, requiring three-quarters of the assembly and unanimous approval of the presidency council. "Even 74% of [the assembly] will not be able to amend any Article of this law, which was passed by people not elected!! . . . Is this the democracy they promised the Iraqis?!" The TAL, the handbill claimed, mentioned but then restricted the role of Islam as a source of legislation, so as "to pave the way to pass any law that contradicts Islam. Is that the way to respect the religious underpinning of the Iraqi people?!" The TAL gave Iraqis who had been deprived of their citizenship, for political or religious reasons, the right to reclaim it. "This means giving back Iraqi citizenship to the Jews who left Iraq to Palestine half century ago." Israelis could come back to Iraq. "Maybe we will find some of them in some government positions later." It granted freedoms without requiring "observance of public morals," which could "cause public obscenity. . . . Is this the freedom they want us to enjoy?!" In providing for a three-member presidency council that had to act unanimously, it threatened to paralyze the country. Finally, in enabling any three provinces (by a two-thirds vote in each) to reject the draft constitution in the referendum, Article 61(c) might make it impossible to adopt a constitution and thus risked making the TAL permanent. The TAL was "a great performance for the occupiers" but not for Iraqis, who were implored to "raise your voices loudly to ask to amend this (Law) . . . in the annex which will be made in the coming months."

I would soon encounter many of these objections firsthand, as Ghassan Al Atiyyah had asked me to speak at two half-day seminars that his Iraq Foundation for Development and Democracy had scheduled for March 13 and 14 at the Babylon Hotel, near the CPA headquarters in Baghdad. Each meeting was well organized and drew a stimulating mix of about forty professionals and intellectuals from all over Iraq. Lawyers, engineers, doctors, professors, judges, business people, and tribal leaders came to listen and, most of all, to debate. Each participant was given both the English and the Arabic versions of the TAL. As they picked the document apart article by article, line by line, they challenged one another—and me. I opened each meeting with a brief explication of the key themes of the TAL: human rights, the rule of law, separation of powers, checks and balances, and power sharing. I stressed the importance, in a divided society, of providing democratic mechanisms to protect minority rights, avoid power monopolies, and create a system of "mutual security," in which each group feels that it has a stake in the system and that its most basic interests are protected. I explained how the federalist provisions of the TAL were designed to achieve these objectives, as a means of strengthening national unity and stability, and I underscored the significance of including women and ethnic and religious minorities.

Then came the debates. For several hours each day, these articulate, politically aware Iraqis let loose a torrent of questions, objections, and passionate opinions. Many of the participants appreciated some aspects of the TAL, particularly the guarantees of individual rights, the checks on government power, and the ability to choose their leaders in free elections. Our internal CPA polling data also showed strong popular support for these principles. One person offered the lukewarm endorsement that it was "better than nothing." But most of the commentary was critical, and at times heated. Repeatedly, often emotionally, people questioned why the draft of the TAL had not been submitted for consideration by civil society organizations, political parties, religious leaders, and the general public. Some wondered about the point of discussing it after it had been signed. One commented bitterly, "The Iraqi people are absent; they gave no consent to this." A woman suggested that the real purpose of the TAL was to constrain the permanent constitution. Reflecting the view of Ayatollah Sistani, a Shiite civic leader said that the TAL could not be legitimate until it was approved by a vote of the people or their elected representatives. Another put it more forcefully: "That this law should bind a future elected body is a crime against democracy." There was sentiment among some participants for strengthening the role of Islam as the basis of law—and sentiment among others for weakening it. There was praise (especially from women) for the 25 percent quota for women's representation—and protest that it was not enough, or not appropriate at all. There was both support and opposition to judicial review of government laws and actions. A Shiite politician sought compensation for the families of human rights victims under Saddam's rule. A Sunni demanded that the TAL affirm Iraq as an Arab nation.

As I expected, some of the strongest opinions (pro and con) concerned federalism. Some Iraqis insisted that federalism could not be consistent with the unity of the country. A sociologist reflected a widespread skepticism about the concept, which was alien to Iraq. "Freedom and equality are not new to Iraqis," she said, "but federalism is." Some were willing to accept federalism as the devolution of power to geographical units, but objected strenuously to having a unit of government that was based on ethnicity (the Kurdistan Regional Government). A few Iraqi Arabs felt that "the Kurds have the right to their ethnicity" and should be accepted "as brothers." Several protested the minority vetoes that were implicitly granted to the Kurds—allowing the Kurdistan Regional Government to "amend" the application of federal laws in its region, making it difficult to amend the TAL, and enabling any three provinces to reject the draft permanent constitution in the referendum. These provisions were denounced as a "dictatorship of the minorities," while they were vigorously defended by some Kurdish (and a few other) participants. A Kurd in the first session explained they were not seeking separation from Iraq but protection against another massacre. Another confessed, "I want separation but I don't want to shed blood." A Kurdish participant in the second session warned, "The majority of people in Kurdistan wanted separation, but we [the Kurdish political leaders] did not want that. The Kurdish people need to decide their own fate." As tensions rose, many of the participants started shouting down a Kurdish speaker. At this point, Atiyyah eloquently intervened:

> We should listen to what the Kurds want and we should help them. I am an Arab. But we displaced the Assyrian Christians and the Jews. We have persecuted the minorities for fifty years in this country. Arabs need to correct their mistakes.
>
> Many people in Kurdistan are not demanding separation. This includes the most educated Kurds. But they feel their fate is inse-

cure, even though they got rid of Saddam. We should search for
something together, not exchange accusations. Democracy can be
built only by democratic methods. Our exchange should be con-
structive, and build confidence between one another. We should
find a way to live together without persecution.

His words silenced the room and brought an end to the shouting. But
the questions about the TAL remained, and, as I would discover, there
was much more criticism to come.

★

Back in the palace, we were planning in earnest for the campaign to sell
the TAL and prepare the country for the handover of sovereignty on
June 30. The project had many components. The first was the preparation of a set of talking points that CPA officials, military officers in the
field, and Iraqi facilitators could use in trumpeting the virtues of the
TAL and responding to questions and objections. This internal document went through several refinements, because we wished to provide
cogent responses, in question-and-answer format, to the criticisms
posed in the handbill that was circulating all over the place.

To the criticism that the TAL had been drafted by a small, unelected body of Iraqis, we emphasized that the document was "only
the first step on the path to Iraq's democracy" and that an elected body
would write the permanent constitution (conveniently ignoring the
fact that the CPA's original plan had resisted this procedure as well).
The Governing Council, we argued, was "an appropriate body to write
this transitional law" because the UN recognized it as "embodying the
sovereignty of the Iraqi people," and because it was a diverse group
that included a wide range of political interests. Likewise, the Kurdish
veto provisions were "the result of intense bargaining and careful
compromise among Iraqis." More to the point, we noted that a two-
thirds vote in three provinces was a "very high" threshold and that
some degree of consensus would be necessary if democracy was to be
viable in Iraq. Forcing sections of Iraq "into a constitutional order
against their will and interests" would only lead to instability. We also
defended the three-person presidency and federalism as necessary

mechanisms to ensure broad representation and to protect the interests of the major groups in the country.

We had other questions and replies as well. To the demands for amendment of the TAL before June 30, we said in essence, look, this was a difficult compromise; if one group demands changes, others will as well, and the whole thing will unravel. It's just a temporary law for a transitional period. It would be more productive, we argued, for Iraqis to focus on the debate over the permanent constitution. To the complaints over the fact that the caretaker government would be unelected, we said, again in truth, that credible elections could not be organized by June 30, and that the selection of the interim government—which was yet to be decided—could still benefit from the participation of many Iraqi groups. In any case, the interim government would have only limited powers and would not be able to conclude a treaty. Only the new transitional national assembly could ratify a treaty, we reassured Iraqis—neglecting to mention that the CPA had expunged the provision that would have required a two-thirds majority to ratify a treaty. To these various replies, I added the point that I hoped would get circulation and that I would air in dialogues with Iraqis later in the month. Protecting minority rights is not a matter just of fairness but of self-interest, because, in a democracy, groups that constitute the political majority today could find themselves in the minority tomorrow.

As we labored over these questions and answers, we prepared to release one million copies of a pamphlet highlighting the key themes of the TAL. This pamphlet would immediately precede the launch of our civic education campaign of weekly flyers with a series of one-paragraph themes on democracy, which we had prepared in January. The attractively produced, four-page TAL pamphlet stressed, first, the June 30 date for the end of occupation and the transfer of sovereignty to an interim government, with a new constitution to be written and adopted and a new government elected by December 2005. Then it emphasized four themes, each developed in a concise paragraph: the bill of rights, which would guarantee all Iraqis basic freedoms; the separation of powers, which would ensure an independent judiciary that could protect the rights of all Iraqis; executive powers, which were to be split between a prime minister and a presidency council, and then checked by the assembly, to prevent the abuse of power; and federalism, which would prevent any region or group from dominating the others, and thereby strengthen, rather than undermine, the commitment of all groups to national unity.

The pamphlets on the TAL themes, along with copies of the document itself in booklet form, were distributed by Iraqi civic organizations like Just Read, the Free Prisoners Association, and the Iraqi Athletes Rights Association, as well as by the various CPA offices, military commands under the U.S.-led Coalition, and aid contractors. In addition, these materials, along with our questions and answers, helped guide the town hall meetings and small neighborhood discussions that were then taking place around the country as part of the democracy dialogues. In the dialogues, Iraqis had not taken well to the CPA propaganda about the November 15 agreement, but they were eager to learn about the TAL and the opportunities for democratic choice and control that it would provide. By early March, the USAID contractor Research Triangle International (RTI) was well on its way to hiring, training, and deploying 550 Iraqi facilitators to lead the discussions about principles of democracy, institutions and practices of democracy, and related CPA policies and initiatives. At the peak of the democracy dialogue activities were the national agenda conferences that would bring together Iraqis from around the country, across ethnic and regional lines, on the basis of occupational, personal, and social traits: for example, women, youth, farmers, lawyers, journalists, and the disabled.

Alongside the print materials and the dialogues, a comprehensive communications enterprise was being developed, with the aid of opinion polls and focus groups, to sell the TAL and to create public understanding, acceptance, and ownership of the transition process. The media campaign consisted of public service announcements, some recorded by Bremer himself; the televising of town hall meetings; television and radio talk shows; and radio, television, print, and outdoor advertisements (in both Arabic and Kurdish), all designed to generate a sense of momentum and optimism about the process. The key medium for the ads was television, which reached about 90 percent of Iraqi households, either through the Iraqi network, Al-Iraqiya, or through

Arab satellite outlets like Al-Jazeera, which about half of Iraqi households received. The London-based advertising agency Bell Pottinger, in
collaboration with the Dubai-based Bates Pangulf, had won the contract to produce the ads, which were to run in three waves, each with
two commercials. The mock-ups for the television ads impressed us
with their artistic and symbolic qualities. The first ad featured a young
Iraqi mother (with covered head) rocking a crib with a baby, singing the
emotional Iraqi lullaby "My Homeland." It was a tune that tugged at
the hearts and memories of Iraqis, no matter their ethnicity or religion,
and the ad ended by displaying the logo of the TAL and the words "An
Iraq of Hope and Peace," with a voice-over saying, "This message is
brought to you by the TAL." Its companion ad showed a small Iraqi boy
dragging a stick in the dirt. As the camera panned back, he was drawing
something, perhaps the outline of a house, while humming the same
lullaby. Panning back farther, the ad revealed the image in the dirt to
be the map of Iraq, with its two mighty rivers; the spot concluded with
a similar message about the TAL being the foundation of Iraq's future.
The radio ads used the same lullaby, and the print ads played on the images of the mother and baby, and the little boy with the stick. Later ads
trumpeted the interim electoral commission and the preparation for
the June 30 handover.

The TAL ads were imaginative, moving, and technically sophisticated. There was only one problem: as with so much of what Stratcomm did, the campaign came too late. It was not until the second half
of February that Stratcomm awarded the contract to the British-led
consortium, and hence the team did not even arrive in Baghdad until
March 3, to be briefed on the context and substance of what the agency
would be working with. During the first two weeks of March, the team
members developed the strategic and conceptual thrust of the campaign, generated creative options for the first two waves of ads, and
tested mock-ups with CPA staff and Iraqi focus groups. Finally, on
March 16, they got approval from Bremer. But by then, the TAL was
more than a week old; anti-TAL leaflets were flooding the nation; confusion, suspicion, and resentment were mounting; and it would still be
weeks before the ads could be produced, booked, and aired. In the last
two weeks of March, the consortium began casting, locating, and shoot-

ing the first TV spots, prepared the parallel ads for radio and newspapers, booked the necessary airtime, and moved the ads into the distribution pipelines. The first were aired on April 2, an impressive feat given the time constraints, and the logistical and security obstacles the team members encountered (which required production to be done outside the country).

Within a few days of the ad launch, however, Iraq fell into a paroxysm of insurgencies, in the Sunni center and Shiite south of the country, that threw all of the CPA's operations into crisis, and the ad campaign was temporarily suspended. The TV and radio spots eventually resumed, in the three phases in late April and May, and they apparently had some impact. But by then, the CPA had—once again—lost the initiative to a less technically sophisticated but shrewder, more nimble set of Iraqi opponents, who understood their society and culture to a degree that we never even approached. As the crisis deepened in early April and Bremer demanded action, the advertising team proposed a set of slick flyers to counter the crude opposition slogans with similarly catchy themes. But as someone close to the process later commented to me, "The CPA decision makers weren't interested in snappy communication; they wanted to win the argument and beat Iraqis into submission with the rightness of their cause and the power of their logic." The denunciations of the TAL caught on in part because they were easier to understand than the didactic TAL leaflets and talking points. However, as I would soon realize anew in my travels around the country, there was some substance behind the slogans and the outrage.

*

One of the first national agenda conferences, for Iraqi youth, was held in Baghdad on March 15 and 16; on the second day, I went with a few colleagues from USAID (which was funding the conferences and the dialogues) in an armored car to the heavily barricaded hotel in the Karrada district of Baghdad, where the meeting was taking place. The district had been the site of car bombings and considerable violence, and there were black-clad guards with automatic weapons everywhere—the front entrance, the back entrance, the lobby, the parking lot, the gate to the parking lot, the hotel roof, and places I am sure I did not even see. None of this seemed to faze the 140 young people who had gathered from all over Iraq to discuss the TAL, the country's political future, and the role of youth.

The final session was devoted to synthesizing the ideas and suggestions, and then developing an agenda for civic action by young people. The organizers (from the Just Read group) presented the tentative conclusions from the first day and a half: establishing television stations for youth, encouraging the networking of young people's NGOs and providing them with financial support, offering jobs and training for youth, and so on. Discussion, quarrels, and objections ensued. "Who authorized you to present these points?" one person asked us. "We didn't agree to that," protested another. Patiently, one by one, the moderator took the audience through each point. There was debate. There were amendments and further recommendations, such as establishing an Internet chat site for Iraqi youth, creating a "parliament" for youth, and, of course, holding another conference, with several delegations bidding for the right to host it. The give-and-take went on until everyone who wanted to speak had had a chance. As the suggestions were offered, the organizers entered the points into a notebook computer connected to a projector, which displayed them on a big screen in a Powerpoint-type presentation. All the technology had been provided by RTI, and these young Iraqis took to it like fish to water. Then the organizers revised the list and projected it on the screen again. With each point, the participants voted as a group. In the end, most of the suggestions passed almost unanimously. The conference concluded with a short musical interlude written and performed by the delegation from Al Amarah, in the largely rural, conservative Shiite province of Maysan. The music and lyrics, performed by five men and five women (conservatively dressed, with black scarves and long dresses), celebrated the conference, the nation, and the willingness of these young Iraqis to help. With the group playing, the audience clapping, and the Just Read volunteers filming, a praise singer rose from the audience and chanted in Arabic, "There is no country like you, Iraq. We will find no equal in civilization, culture, and religion. You will remain the great Iraq, land of palm, land of oil. We are ready to give our lives for you, Iraq!"

It was a remarkable session, democracy at work, with flair. It showed me, again, that the culture of the country could change, that new practices and habits of the heart could emerge. It was easier with young people, but it was happening with other groups as well. Many of the youths had ambitions for social and political leadership. The final session was moderated by a handsome, impressive Just Read organizer. I told him, with a kind of wry irony, that I had once organized a national youth conference in my own country (in November 1971, with Representative Allard Lowenstein, in Chicago). I thought it was a wonderful thing for students and young people to be involved in politics. He said something funny and touching: "Then I will be another Larry Diamond in the future." And we both laughed.

★

Shortly after I returned to Iraq in March, the weekly governance staff meeting pondered the implications, for our operations, of the recent murders of Holland and Zangas. It was a grim session, especially for me—as I was preparing to travel around the country. We had eighty to one hundred trips going out from CPA headquarters each week, most of them with no security. Most CPA officials had given up trying to get armed escorts because it was so damned difficult. Governance still had no dedicated hard vehicle. Within a month, the CPA would get some help. Forty new hard cars were to be delivered, but twenty-four of them would be going out to the provincial offices, leaving just sixteen cars for the headquarters, in addition to the handful we had available for the hundreds of officials traveling from the palace. Moreover, within the next month, another five hundred people would be coming to work for the CPA. And then the UN would be returning, placing a severe demand on the limited supply of hard cars and personal security details (PSDs), or what used to be called bodyguards. The supply was so short that Bremer told a meeting of CPA military and civilian leaders from around the country that once the UN returned, "unless we get more PSDs, CPA as a mission will essentially close down in order to support the UN." In the same meeting, we learned from our security chief that seventy-five more armored cars were in production, but that "the threat is going up, the targeting is going up." So we were asked to calculate carefully which trips would be worth the risk. Obviously, careering through the darkened streets of Baghdad at night, looking for a good pizza, would not be one of them.

In fact, the risks were multiplying. Violence was rising throughout the country, and so were attacks on Americans and Europeans. On March 14, a CPA adviser in the Ministry of Labor was ambushed in Mosul; he survived, but a high Iraqi official in the ministry was killed in the attack. The atmosphere in Mosul was becoming increasingly tense. The landlord of RTI's offices asked the contractor to leave, after posters popped up there and in three other cities alleging that it was an organization of "Zionists" and agents of the Israeli intelligence organization, the Mossad. The next day, four American Southern Baptist relief workers were killed and another critically wounded in the Mosul area when a hail of automatic weapons fire hit their unarmored truck, just hours after they had visited the local U.S. Army base to consult on how to improve their security. That same day, an Iraqi translator for the U.S. military command in the Mosul area was assassinated. And on March 16, two contractors (a Dutch and a German) were killed in an ambush in the south, not far from where Fern Holland and her companions had been gunned down the previous week.

An American army officer who knew Iraq well had warned me, before I returned, to be particularly careful in Mosul, which the U.S. military regarded as one of the most dangerous areas. I wanted very much to visit there, and the CPA provincial office had scheduled an extensive program for me on Friday, March 19, that would include meetings with political party leaders, a question-and-answer session over lunch with 125 sheikhs, a similar session with university students and professors, and a dinner with local NGO representatives. There was a C-130 flight from Mosul back to Baghdad the next morning. But we had to figure out a way to get to Mosul, two hundred dangerous miles north of Baghdad by road. Derek Berlin worked frantically to arrange the journey, but no armored vehicles or convoys were available, and every effort to book us a place or two on a helicopter failed. In frustration, at the last minute, unable to find any transportation other than the soft vehicles that civilians were dying in, we canceled the trip. Moreover, we had received recently a message from the Local Government Program in Basra, which wanted me to speak at a conference there, advising us that we had better get a flight down because "our project does not have adequate force protection, let alone armored vehicles." Late one night, after striking out at every turn, Derek slammed his notepad down in disgust. "This mission has been underresourced from the start," he exclaimed angrily, to no one in particular. It was one of the most memorable understatements of my time in Iraq.

Another trip, to Balad and Tikrit, in Saddam Hussein's home province of Salaheddin, was scheduled for Sunday, March 21. The CPA provincial coordinator, Mark Kennon—another extremely able career diplomat, fluent in Arabic, who had worked hard to cultivate ties to the local population—had arranged an extensive day-and-a-half-long program for me. We were determined not to cancel this trip as well. For several days Derek searched, begged, beseeched, and implored, but failed to locate an armored vehicle. Finally, late on Saturday afternoon, I returned from a meeting and he informed me that he had failed to find an available armored car anywhere in the sprawling CPA complex. Facing the prospect of a second cancellation, after days of planning, I got fed up and went to see Bremer. Just two hours earlier, Bremer and I, along with a hundred other CPA officials, had attended a moving memorial ceremony for Fern Holland and the six other CPA employees and international aid workers who had been murdered on the roads in the past couple of weeks. The gravity—and, I felt, in my anger, the needlessness—of the loss still hung in the air. What was the point of Bremer's asking me to travel around the country to promote the TAL if there was no way for me to do so with some minimum level of safety— the very minimum standard that he himself had insisted on in his latest memo? Bremer wasn't in, but I talked to his savvy, efficient executive assistant, Jessica LeCroy, who immediately swung into action. We struck out with several offices that did not have an armored vehicle to spare, but she finally persuaded the central logistics office to come to our rescue. It agreed to lend us a large armored van—the vehicle that was used in transporting members of the Governing Council and other dignitaries to and from the airport. There was just one catch: we had no driver for the mammoth vehicle, and no security detail. Now, already into the night, the search began again. Another governance staffer, Ali Khedery—an Iraqi American liaison to the Governing Council, who looked as though he was sixteen but operated as if he had been through a dozen of the hardest-fought political campaigns—somehow pulled a rabbit out of the hat. He persuaded four private security guards from Blackwater—the private company that was providing personal protection for Bremer and other key CPA officials—to help us on this mission.[1] Two drove us up in the armored van, and two drove a backup vehicle. Both vehicles were loaded with arms and communications gear. By coincidence, a military convoy was headed to Balad Sunday morning, and we arranged to join it. This escort was as much protection as any ordinary civilian was going to get in Iraq.

Despite my initial worries about traveling to Saddam's home area, and despite the name—Camp Danger—of the military base that headquartered both the U.S. Army's First Infantry Division and the CPA office in Salaheddin Province, we were secure and well accommodated in Tikrit. The provincial headquarters of the American occupation was a mammoth, decadent complex of palaces along the Tigris River that Saddam had built for himself and his Baathist and military cronies. The former dictator had five personal palaces in this one sprawling compound, and a huge mosque that was no doubt rarely used. On the grounds were numerous other mansions, only slightly less oversized and ornate, most with balconies, terraces, and picture windows that commanded sweeping views of the river, across which Saddam could see, in the distance, the place of his birth. The CPA's Tikrit headquarters were in one of these lesser houses, the ground floor of which soared some two and a half stories high, all marble and windows, looking out over the Tigris. A wide wooden spiral staircase rose to the second floor, with several bedrooms. The house, which was probably meant to accommodate five or six people, now slept twenty in divided and bunked-up rooms, not including the six of us visitors. Like the other Baathist palaces and mansions I had seen, this one was grand but cold, ostentatious, and uncomfortable, with sloppy workmanship and without a single room in which one could just sit down and feel comfortable reading or watching TV. It was all about quantity, might, and muscle. The CPA had turned the tables on the quantity theme by stuffing the building with staff and turning the sunken living room into a main office with six desks and computers.

Before visiting Tikrit, we stopped in Balad, a predominantly Shiite city thirty miles north of Baghdad, which hosted one of the largest air bases in the country. (I would later discover that it had also been the frequent site of deadly ambushes and roadside bomb attacks on American military convoys.) We arrived in the late morning at the city's Youth Center, where we were greeted by the president of the city council and then ushered into a public meeting room. The room was full: there were, altogether, 140 city council members, lawyers, professionals, sheikhs, and other citizens from around town and the surrounding area. I saw no women, though I was told there was one, maybe two, in the audience. As I would also do the next day at the meeting with the provincial council (and, the following week, in various dialogues in the south), I concluded my standard presentation on key themes and principles of the TAL with an attempt to defuse some of the objections I knew would come, regarding the lack of public involvement in the drafting. I explained the urgency of time, with the imminent approach of the handover, and the steps before June 30 that depended on having a completed interim constitution. More lamely, I noted that there had been public discussion of constitutional principles in meetings large and small around the country, although in fact I had seen no effort to integrate those discussions into the drafting process. Following my talking points, I referred to the compromises that all sides had made in the final TAL negotiations, and the opportunity, which Iraqis would soon have, to debate and draft a permanent constitution. And I suggested that since the TAL was purely a transitional law, Iraqis would do best to focus on the future constitution. All my efforts were to little avail, as I proceeded to receive (and also diligently note) the litany of familiar criticisms and complaints.

The questions were tough. For two of them, especially, I had no good answers—and would continue to have none, as I heard them, repeatedly, around the country. First, what was *I* doing there? "How can we discuss this law?" I was asked. "You are not a representative of the Governing Council." The complaint, again and again during my travels, was: Where is the Governing Council? Why aren't the members out selling and defending this law?[2] The loudest ovation during the public session in Balad—indeed, the one moment when the room burst spontaneously into applause—came when a speaker from the floor declared: "The members of the Governing Council do not represent the Iraqi people. They represent just a small segment of the Iraqi people." Second, why bother discussing the TAL now, when it was signed and could not be changed? Everywhere I went during the month of March—in Balad and Tikrit, then down to the south in Basra and Nasariyah, and finally in Hilla, just as in Baghdad—I heard not only substantive objections but, no less passionately, procedural ones: "Why weren't we consulted?" Many Iraqis took pride in the TAL and its provisions for civil rights and the rule of law. But most were upset that the people had not been given an opportunity to debate, amend, and approve the provisions of their interim constitution. I could say, in effect: Look, you want your sovereignty back on June 30; we are up against severe deadlines to meet that goal; there wasn't time. But it was difficult to argue with people who were saying, as the members of the Salaheddin Provincial Council said to me the next morning in Tikirt, "You are speaking about democracy, but the Governing Council was not elected. We were elected and this transitional law is being forced on us."

For the fourth or fifth time—I was losing count—the United States was finding itself on what appeared to be the *less* democratic side of an argument with Iraqis over transitional procedures. Sistani had called for an elected constitution-making body. Bremer said an appointed body would do. Iraqis (and many CPA officials) wanted to conduct direct elections for local governments. Bremer and the top governance officials vetoed them. The CPA proposed an opaque, convoluted process for choosing a transitional government, and Sistani, along with many Iraqis, again demanded direct elections. Now the CPA and the Governing Council were saying to Iraqis—and I myself was saying—Here is your wonderful interim constitution, and a great many Iraqis were responding, Don't we have a voice in shaping the rules that will govern us for the next eighteen months and will guide the making of our permanent constitution? Beyond the exigencies of time and practicality, there was no good answer.

The other most strongly felt objections were also those I had heard in Baghdad. Many speakers protested the provision that made it so difficult—indeed, nearly impossible—to amend the TAL, especially since it was written by "a small group in a closed room." More than any other provision, they objected to Article 61(c), which allowed any three provinces to reject the draft permanent constitution in the referendum. Most people did not seem to like the three-person presidency or at least opposed the requirement that all its decisions be unanimous. "We reject all these items, and we request amendments in the next steps," declared one speaker from the floor in Balad. The problem was that there were no clear next steps—except for the annex that would be added to the TAL and would specify the means for constituting the interim government that would take power on June 30. Most Iraqis seemed confused about the role of the annex and about the way the country would be governed between June 30 and the election of the transitional national assembly, scheduled for January 2005. I explained that there was a contradiction: Iraqis wanted their sovereignty back as soon as possible, but elections weren't feasible until December or January, so an interim government would have to be chosen in some other way. I said no decisions had been made yet on how this would be done, and they should convey their ideas and concerns to the Governing Council, the CPA, and the UN mission that would be returning soon to help mediate a solution. A few savvy lawyers and political leaders were suggesting (to me, and to other Iraqis) that the annex to the TAL go further, to amend the most objectionable provisions of the TAL.

I did my best, in these sessions, to navigate between representing the CPA and representing the democratic principles I was also working for. Sometimes I could only listen and note, as in the exchange between two provincial councillors in Tikrit, about U.S. forces. A man asked, "No one can make claims against coalition forces now. Will this persist after June 30?" And a woman replied, "All over the world, no one can make a claim against American soldiers." However, when the provincial councillors complained that the TAL could allow the unelected Iraqi interim government to negotiate a treaty with the United States that would bind an *elected* Iraqi government, I said flatly that I didn't think that my government would be so foolish as to try to negotiate a long-term treaty with an unelected Iraqi government—and that if it did so, I myself would oppose it. That seemed to reassure them, or at least win their confidence. And of course I was sincere. But I knew that I couldn't speak definitively for the Bush administration.

The meeting with the Salaheddin Provincial Council that Monday morning was a memorable one. The forty members included not only the once-mighty Tikritis—among them, the council chairman, a short, mild-mannered lawyer who nevertheless bore a familial resemblance to Saddam—but also other Sunnis from around the province, representatives of the province's Shiite minority, three women, and two Kurds. In addition to the complaints I'd been hearing, the members offered scattered criticisms of the quota for women's representation, the permission for dual citizenship, and the failure to establish Islam as the main source of legislation. But the most divisive issue concerned the Kurds. Several councillors objected to Kurdish as an official language and, most of all, to federalism—particularly because it was perceived to be structured on an ethnic rather than a geographical basis, thereby giving many "special powers" to the Kurds. Some members specifically protested the preservation of the Kurdistan Regional Government. "The Kurds are our brothers," said one councillor, "but no one should take more rights than the others." A Kurdish member replied, "There are Kurds in every province. Why don't you want to give me my rights?" Once again, as had happened in Baghdad when the issue of the Kurds arose, the room erupted into angry exchanges, and the chair had to appeal for civility, tapping his pencil on the table with a lawyerly calm that in no way resembled Saddam. The next speaker, another Arab, defended the Kurds and their right to some special form of government, and then the second Kurdish council member reflected, "We didn't feel we were Iraqis until we signed this law, reclaiming our membership in the country."

The two meetings, in Balad and Tikrit, were exhausting and sobering, as I confronted, in the raw, the deep divisions, frustrations, and resentments simmering in Iraqi society. The cable I drafted to Washington summarizing the meetings noted how the discussions had reflected "some of the emergent vigor of Iraqi democracy," as participants "expressed their views in a spirited way," with frequent reference to their rights and to principles of democratic legitimacy. But as I also observed, "spirited debate sometimes descended into shouting, and the Salaheddin Provincial Council meeting repeatedly descended into such a din of cacophony that it was difficult to determine who had the floor or what was happening." I had seen Kurds and Arabs yelling at one another. I had seen the explosiveness lurking beneath the competing visions of what Iraq is. There in Tikrit—in the heart of Sunni Arab nationalism, at the core of what had been Saddam Hussein's communal power base, near the village of his birth—members of the provincial council, whom the CPA itself had selected, said they wanted to amend the TAL to eliminate Kurdish as an official language, to erase or largely vitiate the federalist provisions, and to declare all Iraqis, not just Iraqi Arabs, "an inseparable part of the Arab nation." I knew that if Iraq went down the road of unraveling the pluralist, power-sharing spirit of the interim constitution, the result would have alarming implications for the country's stability and unity (not to mention its prospects for democracy). I remained hopeful that the steep slide to separation and catastrophic violence could be averted. But for the immediate future, I felt that something had to be done to address the objections to the most controversial provisions of the TAL, or we would see a crisis explode at some point down the road.

★

Immediately on returning to Baghdad from Tikrit and Balad, I began working on a memo to Bremer, which I sent him the next day (March 23), along with a draft of my long cable to Washington summarizing my meetings in the two cities. The memo, which I titled "Addressing Iraqi Objections to the TAL," followed one I had sent him four days earlier, reporting on the objections I had heard to the TAL in the Baghdad meetings. I warned Bremer more emphatically now: "We have some serious problems with the legitimacy and content of the TAL." We needed to do much more work, I argued—hear more feedback and obtain more public opinion data. But we would discover, I conjectured, that no amount of outreach or explanation would erase the Iraqis' fundamental objections, and I therefore suggested that something concrete had to be done to address them in the last remaining opportunity, the TAL annex. In a dire warning, I described what would happen if we failed to do so:

> I envision one of two scenarios. Either there will be growing challenges to the legitimacy of the entire transitional enterprise, or there will be a practical resolve on the part of key actors to wait until the election of the National Assembly, then declare the entire TAL illegitimate, and amend certain key provisions of it by a process well short of a three-quarters vote and unanimous presidential consent. It is not difficult to imagine that two-thirds of the members of the new National Assembly would, for example, vote to remove article 61(c), and perhaps even to change voting in the Presidency Council to a majority rather than unanimity, and then declare this new TAL the "legitimate version." Any such move would provoke a profound crisis of domestic and international legitimacy that could threaten the entire transition, but if two-thirds of the [transitional national assembly] voted to adopt a new interim constitution that amended a few key provisions of the TAL, would domestic and international legitimacy be with us, or with a democratically elected body that was acting by a large majority to amend a document that was adopted by manifestly less democratic means? It is not at all clear that we could prevail at that point, or that the Kurds would be in a stronger position then than they would be now to negotiate some new provisions that could garner broader societal consensus. Perhaps cooler Iraqi heads would prevail in February, but I would not want to witness the rising popular drumbeat that could be generated.

The coming negotiations over the annex to the TAL (to set the structure of the interim government) could provide a narrow opportunity to amend some of the most objectionable provisions, I suggested, through a refashioned consensus within the Governing Council; even a limited amendment of one or two widely opposed provisions "could let off popular steam that is gathering and provide a symbolic concession to public opinion." In my previous memo, I had advised Bremer of an intriguing potential compromise, which had come from Mowaffak al-Rubaie, the Shiite member of the Governing Council who had served, from time to time, as an intermediary to Ayatollah Sistani and his son.

In a meeting with me two nights previously, Rubaie had expressed concern about the rising disaffection on the Shiite street with the TAL, and especially Article 61(c). He suggested offering the Kurds, in an amendment to the TAL introduced in the annex, a substitute form of veto over the permanent constitution that would protect their interests but without the injury to national sensitivities that derived from a veto in a national referendum. In return for giving up Article 61(c), the Kurds could have a veto over any provisions relating to their regional rights in a federal system, which they could exercise in the assembly's constitutional deliberations. The revised language, I suggested to Bremer by way of example, might state that no such constitutional provision could be adopted if it were opposed by two-thirds of the delegates from Kurdistan (or, more generally, by two-thirds of the delegates from a bloc of any three provinces). As I wrote: "This would have two advantages: (1) it would avoid the possibility of a national train wreck [leading] toward civil war if a constitution clearly supported by the rest of the country in a referendum was vetoed by the Kurds; and (2) it would avoid the completely unanticipated possibility (which should not be dismissed, given the unpredictability of any election) that three other provinces outside Kurdistan might vote down the constitution, because, for example, it was not sufficiently Islamist."

Not long after he had read my memo, I raised the issue with Bremer directly, and he shut the door firmly on the discussion. The TAL was finished, he said. The negotiations had been excruciating. It was one of the CPA's most important achievements. He was not about to open up a can of worms. Using the annex to introduce substantive amendments was out of the question. And that was the end of it.

In many respects, amending the TAL in the annex would have been difficult. A member of our excellent CPA legal team had informally offered me the opinion that such a move would be of questionable legality but would be viable if it garnered a moral and political consensus. That would be a challenge, because, as I would soon discover, the Kurds were not the only stakeholders in the constitutional veto. A leading Sunni Islamist politician warned me that his party would walk out of the Governing Council if Article 61(c) was revised. And among many Governing Council members, there was a certain intellectual exhaustion with the whole process. Nevertheless, I felt confident that when the UN special envoy to Iraq, Lakhdar Brahimi, returned with his team to begin consulting on a means to assemble the interim government, he would hear the same criticisms of the TAL I had heard; there was a chance he could craft a compromise. On the basis of both democratic principle and my experience with similar projects, I had thought all along—and had told Bremer weeks previously—that the place to establish a threshold for adoption of the constitution was in the national assembly and not in the referendum. If the veto could be transferred to the assembly, it might be acceptable to everyone, at least as a face-saving compromise. That move would also have required, however, an agreement on the electoral system, so that the political figures could calculate the regional representation they might have in the assembly. And we were a long way from that.

I continued to feel that the annex was the last best chance to address the concerns I was hearing from Iraqis and to produce a broader national consensus behind the TAL, while retaining instruments that would enable the Kurds to defend their minority rights and regional autonomy. In the ensuing months, I would continue to worry about the nightmare scenario I had outlined to Bremer in my March 23 memo.

★

On March 26, Bremer met in the palace with his regional and provincial CPA officers, in a monthly conference of military and civilian leaders. They generally painted a rosier picture, of popular acceptance and even enthusiasm for the TAL, than I was encountering in my meetings, although in the Kurdish provinces there was genuine delight at the federalist articles, and I knew that Iraqis generally valued the provisions on rights, elections, and the rule of law. Even these officials, however—who had a sense of what Bremer did and did not want to hear—frequently reported the problem with Article 61(c), the frustration at the lack of participation, and the grumbling that members of the Governing Council never came before the people to explain and defend the document. The CPA leader in Mosul was particularly blunt in reporting "a difficult time in selling the TAL," with the Sunni Arabs questioning its legitimacy because of the lack of participation and electoral endorsement, and the smaller ethnic groups (such as the Yazidis and the Sabians) anxious about their future because they were not mentioned in the TAL. Concerns were also raised about the difficulty in amending the document, the role of Islam, and the power to negotiate treaties—all criticisms that I had heard in my travels. Bremer grew irritated. "We will not be susceptible to appeals to deal with these issues in the annex," he snapped. "Article 61, Article 59, Article 7, Article 3—these issues are settled. The annex is not a Christmas tree." Toward the end of the meeting, my head started spinning when one of my governance colleagues praised the process by which we got the TAL as "very participatory . . . within the GC," emphasizing that the members had "consulted their constituencies." If that was the case, their constituencies were either very narrow or had quickly developed a case of collective amnesia. But by now I had become accustomed to this kind of internal spin and groupthink. Months after I left Iraq, when by chance I ran into one of my younger CPA colleagues at a restaurant in downtown Washington, I learned the catchphrase for this self-delusion: "drinking the Kool-Aid."[3]

Later that day, I met with the Iraqi Higher Women's Council for the third time, at the Convention Center in Baghdad. I had promised to strategize with the group more specifically about how women might pursue opportunities, in the democratic political system, to get elected and expand their influence. Here I spoke only briefly about the TAL, as these women were knowledgeable and sophisticated; several of them were on the Governing Council or in the government in some capacity. The concern of our meeting was how to push forward. I described several ways in which the electoral system could be organized and how each choice might affect the attainment of women's representation. In all likelihood, some type of proportional representation (PR) would be adopted in electing the parliament. Under this system, each party or coalition nominates a list of candidates, and it sends to parliament a percentage of those candidates equal to its percentage of the vote. But PR systems vary widely, in intricate and complex ways. Most use some form of districting, so that parties present slates of candidates in districts that might each elect, say, five to ten candidates. Some countries have both a series of multimember districts and a set of nationwide lists, drawing from the latter as necessary to ensure that each party's share of seats in parliament matches, as closely as possible, its share of the national vote. Two democracies—the Netherlands and Israel—have no districts, but only nationwide slates of candidates. Then there is a variation in who decides which candidates from the lists go to parliament—the voters (in "open lists") or the party leaders (in "closed lists"). I suggested to the women the value of having district lists and, if possible, open lists, so that the voters in each community, rather than the (entirely male) national party leadership, could decide which women would be elected. This prospect resonated with them. At the same time, we discussed technical ways, by law, to ensure that women filled no fewer than one-quarter of the seats. I also stressed the importance of political organizing and funding for female candidates, and mentioned the example of the American political organization that provides financial support for women candidates, Emily's List. When I explained to them that "Emily" stands for "Early Money Is Like Yeast," we all had a hearty laugh. They got the message instinctively.

The women appreciated the suggestions and considered several issues. What about independent candidates? What about proxy voting? They were concerned about the sorry state of the Iraqi media. They felt a desperate need to educate women as voters and as potential candidates. "Most of our women here," one participant commented, "have been imprisoned—they have never been out of the country. They take orders from their fathers and sons." Too many Iraqi women stayed home; many had never come out to vote. Politically active women would have to work hard to lure them to the polls.

Then Salama al-Khufaji asked a question that froze me: "What is the relationship between our political progress and our personal security?" I didn't know how to answer. At first, I wasn't sure I had heard the translation correctly. I probably looked dumb. She continued more bluntly. A key challenge was that women should feel safe in running for office and in voting. There was inadequate security for women—they were still subject to retribution. Probably no one in the room was in a better position to speak to the danger than Dr. Salama, who had been appointed to the Governing Council only in December 2003, after another female member, Aquila al-Hashimi, had been assassinated in an ambush. Dr. Salama was a study in contrasts: a highly religious Shiite woman, who covered herself in black and did not shake hands with men, she was also a professor of dentistry at Baghdad University and a strong advocate of women's rights. In fact, she was one of the most interesting and appealing people I met in Iraq, and her question deeply troubled me. None of us knew then just how personal her question would become. In May, just two months later, she survived an assassination attempt herself, when the car in which she was traveling was ambushed and her son and several of her bodyguards were killed.

★

After a few days in Baghdad, my speaking tour resumed as a few of us flew to Basra for a conference on decentralization, and then continued on to Nasariyah for a meeting with the Dhi-Qar Provincial Council. I would finish up with a second trip to Hilla soon thereafter. In these meetings, I heard most of the same questions, concerns, and complaints, the same denunciations of Article 61(c), the presidency council, the high threshold to amend the TAL, the unelected interim government, and the ability of exiled Iraqis to return and reclaim their citizenship—the last item was condemned in part because it would allow "Israeli Jews" to return. By now the reaction sounded like a script, and indeed much of it had been scripted by the first strike in the propaganda war, the crude "What do you know about the TAL?" leaflet. In Nasariyah, however, I encountered stronger Islamist sentiment, as well as resentment that there was no one from that province on the Governing Council. And more than elsewhere, I sensed an absorption with the problems and needs of an extremely poor, neglected area, even by the standards of the deprived Iraqi south. The council members pressed me and the other CPA officials: "What is the authority of the provincial council until July 1? We are just talking and meeting with no authority." Their concerns were entirely valid; the Local Government Order, initially drafted by the CPA five months previously, was still waiting to be promulgated; without such a law, local and provincial councils had no real power. Much of our efforts to promote effective, local government was vitiated as a result. Moreover, the councillors were frustrated with the progress of the democratic component—namely, that local elections had been vetoed by the minister of municipalities. I did not have the nerve to tell these people who had really done the vetoing.

★

As with so much of what we did in the CPA, our grand ambitions for promoting the TAL and educating Iraqis about democracy were ground down by the harsh realities of the situation we faced—the shortage of resources and people, the makeshift character of our organization, the cumbersome pace of our deliberations, the economic and civic devastation of the country, and, most of all, the relentless and escalating violence. Our timetable for rolling out the weekly civic education leaflets slipped as we struggled to get the texts approved, translated, and printed. Not until after the TAL was signed, on March 8, did the published materials begin to be distributed. The plan had been to distribute from twelve to as many as twenty weekly paragraphs on elements of democracy by the time of the handover, June 30. In fact, fewer than half a dozen would get out by then. In an impressive organizational effort, over five hundred facilitators were recruited and trained to mediate the democracy dialogues. The enterprise got off to a good start, as ordinary Iraqis seemed eager not only to learn about democratic institutions and the provisions of the TAL but to express their views. However, just as the facilitators were spreading out around the country and the feedback mechanisms were starting to work, twin insurgencies erupted in early April, in the Sunni Triangle and in the Shiite south. The widespread fighting and insecurity made it difficult to hand out the leaflets—transportation and distribution depended heavily on Coalition military units that were engaged in combat—and it also threatened the safety of the Iraqi dialogue facilitators, two of whom would be murdered in the southeastern part of the nation during the summer. Administrative control and feedback would break down as staff members were recalled from provincial and regional offices around the country, including the entire south. Some of those who had developed the civic education program fought to extend the dialogue process, unsuccessfully, and RTI cut its local staff for the project almost in half. When the director of RTI's dialogue program went on R & R that spring, he did not return.

"It was sad," reflected one former staff member of the civic education effort. "The core of the process in Iraq is democratization. But the people at USAID and in local governance [on the ground in Iraq] just didn't sufficiently buy into this. There was no strong consensus on democracy building in Iraq."

And yet there were accomplishments. By the time of the handover, USAID reported that it had held more than 15,000 democracy dialogues, and a reasonable estimate is that 300,000 Iraqis participated, many of them attending more than one event. Because the participants came from the most educated stratum of Iraqi society—doctors, lawyers, teachers, government workers, and other professionals—one could argue that the dialogues never cracked the tougher challenge of engaging the mass of poor Iraqis in the rural areas and urban slums who lacked education, exposure to the West, and secure employment. Nevertheless, the political culture of the country had been so brutalized that we had to start somewhere, and the dialogues at least put some key democratic issues into circulation, by reaching a segment of opinion leaders.

One of the most valuable aspects of the dialogues was their potential to provide a two-way flow of communication, in which we could talk to Iraqis and they could respond, in each case through the medium of the facilitators. In fact, the Iraqi facilitators were diligent in reporting the questions raised and comments made during the dialogues. At the end of March, USAID sent the Governance Office an initial summary of feedback from the first round of democracy dialogues on the TAL. The report, based on perhaps a thousand small-scale discussions around the country, closely tracked what I had heard and conveyed to Bremer and my colleagues. Reaction was "mixed, but generally more critical than supportive." Iraqis were disillusioned and frustrated "with the process used to develop and adopt the TAL." Many noted the contradiction—which pervaded many aspects of the American occupation—between the declared democratic intent and the lack of opportunity for democratic participation. Frequently the Iraqis expressed concerns that the TAL would permit the interim and transitional governments to enter into binding treaties with the United States that the permanent, elected government would not be able to revisit. Article 61(c) remained "a contentious issue"; federalism was viewed skeptically and poorly understood; dual citizenship opened another source of conflict; and there were strong positions for and against a greater role for Islam. In the

South Central region, particularly in Najaf and Karbala, two-thirds of the Iraqis who were contacted refused even to discuss the TAL because of the reservations expressed by Ayatollah Sistani. In addition, many Iraqis felt the TAL could do little to achieve the rule of law if security was not improved. All of this information was precious feedback, but the CPA lacked the mechanisms—or the will—to adjust its actions and policies in response. The game remained one of trying to find more effective ways to communicate. Those were surely needed, but not enough.

The national agenda conferences did go forward; by the end of June, seven had taken place, bringing together not just young people but women, lawyers, journalists, health care workers, and disabled citizens from around the country.[4] If, in the context of violence, intimidation, and social disruption, the conferences did not meet the lofty goals of jump-starting the civil society networks and promulgating national agendas, they did provide an opportunity for constituencies to come together freely, for the first time, to talk about their common interests. As one USAID official who worked with the process later commented to me, "You have to accept that the initial stages of democratization are horribly inefficient. You need to allow a lot of time for people to talk." And the talking at least yielded the prospect of action. The conferences generated proposals for activities that led to about seventy-five USAID grants totaling $1 million.

Support continued to flow to a variety of other civil society organizations as well, and more than $2 million was committed for the civic education campaign. But as with so many aspects of the reconstruction effort, the campaign struggled constantly against the bureaucratic and security challenges of operating in Iraq, and was then thrown back on its heels by the insurgency. If a civic education campaign must be reinforced by what people experience in real life, then what Iraqis observed during the first half of 2004 was an interim constitution drafted and adopted without national debate, a postponement of elections, another round of appointed government, and a perpetuation of control by the forces on the Governing Council. To be sure, elements of political pluralism emerged, as independent media outlets appeared and NGOs and parties formed. But in the quest to create a democratic, tolerant, and participatory culture, we had only halfheartedly broken the ice.

8

THE SECOND WAR

★

Early in the morning of Wednesday, March 31, Mike Gfoeller drove up
to the front portico of the palace with his heavily armed security detail,
to bring me to Hilla for a day of lectures and discussions. I had promised Sayyid Farqad al-Qizwini that I would return to Hilla, and I was eager to do so. I was nervous about driving down to Hilla on roads that
had become frequent sites of ambushes and bombs, but Gfoeller traveled in an armored Chevy Suburban with a significant accompaniment
of U.S. government security specialists. On the ninety-minute drive
down to Hilla, Gfoeller briefed me on the deteriorating situation in the
South Central region in recent weeks. The information, which had only
been trickling in to CPA, was deeply disturbing.

On March 12, a mixed band of Iranian-backed Islamist militia fighters had attacked and razed the Gypsy village of Qawliyya, just outside
the city of Diwaniyah in the southern Shiite province of Al Qadisiyah.
The fighters—from Muqtada al-Sadr's Mahdi Army, SCIRI's Badr
Corps, and a militia of the Da'wa Party—assaulted the village after an
earlier altercation, during which some fighters from the Mahdi Army
and the local Iraqi police tried to arrest a woman on a morals charge, at
the instruction of Sadr's illegal Sharia court in Diwaniyah. The villagers,

many of whom were Gypsies, resisted the illegal arrest, gunfire was exchanged, and one of the zealots who had come to arrest the woman was killed. A little while later, the Mahdi Army returned with heavy weapons and a much larger force of fighters. After pumping round upon round of automatic rifle fire, mortars, and rocket-propelled grenades into Qawliyya, the militia set the buildings ablaze. Later they brought in bulldozers to demolish what remained of the settlement. As the villagers had received warning, most of them were able to flee for their lives. But a community of some 150 homes and several shops had been left in total ruins, and approximately one thousand people lost their homes and possessions. By the time American officials came to investigate, not a single building was standing. Wild dogs scavenged through the rubble of burned homes and broken furniture, while looters carted off everything salvageable that remained. Some hours after the destruction, eighteen of the village's survivors were arrested at a Mahdi Army checkpoint and detained for ten days in Sadr's illegal prison in Diwaniyah, where they were held in restraints, blindfolded, and tortured. Then they were transferred to Sadr's prison in Najaf, where they were tortured again for several days before the Najaf police chief took custody of them and turned them over to the local CPA office, which had learned of the incident and intervened. Without bothering with the niceties of legal authority, evidence, and warrants, Sadr's fighters had condemned the village as a den of immorality (bars and brothels), and when the village refused to submit to their vigilante justice, they wiped it off the face of the earth.

The event was alarming at a number of levels. Though often competing with one another, the three Islamist militias had now demonstrated their willingness to collaborate in an offensive operation. The destruction of Qawliyya occurred during a period of increasingly brazen exhibitions of power and intimidation by Sadr's growing ranks of fanatical young followers, political and pseudo-judicial agents, and paramilitary thugs. During my brief time in Iraq, I had been hearing alarming reports that they were seizing public buildings, beating up university professors and deans, taking over classrooms and departments, forcing women to wear the *hijab* (the traditional scarf that covers the head, neck, and throat), setting up illegal Sharia courts, and imposing their own brutal penalties—in other words, becoming a law unto themselves.

Muqtada al-Sadr was no clerical authority. Though he claimed to be thirty years old, many in Najaf believed he was no more than twenty-five, and in any case he lacked the Islamic scholarship that would qualify him for the role of religious leader. Short, pudgy, and crude, he did not seem to fit the image of a charismatic insurgent. However, he "was heir to a family tradition of martyrdom,"[1] and heir, as well, to an underground political and religious network in East Baghdad and throughout much of the Shiite south of Iraq. His father, Grand Ayatollah Mohammed Sadiq al-Sadr, had built a following of roughly two million adherents for his militant brand of Shiism, before being killed in Najaf, along with two other sons, by agents of Saddam Hussein in 1999. And his father's cousin Mohammed Baqir al-Sadr had been a leading Da'wa Party theoretician advocating Islamist government for Iraq; he was hanged by Saddam's regime in 1980.[2] Even before Saddam fell from power, on April 9, 2003, Muqtada al-Sadr's militant followers in East Baghdad had driven out the Baath Party and renamed the slum Sadr City. Then, in the words of Juan Cole of the University of Michigan:

> Muqtada's young clerical devotees reopened mosques and other Shiite institutions, established neighborhood militias, captured arms and ammunitions from Baath depots, took over hospitals, and asserted local authority in East Baghdad, Kufa, and some neighborhoods of Najaf, Karbala, and Basra. They engaged in crowd politics, calling for frequent demonstrations against the Anglo-American occupation in Baghdad, Basra, and Najaf, sometimes managing to get out crowds of 5,000 to 10,000.[3]

For some time, Sadr did not launch a military resistance against American troops. But his movement—drawn from the legions of young slum dwellers who had gotten nothing but oppression from Saddam and saw little more in the way of jobs and reconstruction from the U.S.-led occupation—constantly maneuvered for position, not only against the occupiers but against Ayatollah Sistani and other Shiite religious and political forces. His followers fought Sistani's for the right to preach in the sacred mosque of the Imam Husayn in Karbala. They struggled for control of the shrine of Imam Ali in Najaf as well. In late July 2003, Sadr's mobs, demonstrating in front of the Imam Husayn shrine in Karbala, provoked a group of U.S. marines into firing on the crowd, and a month later they stirred up anti-Coalition rioting in Basra.[4] In late October, Sadr's forces staged their most daring maneuver, an attempt to seize the area of the two holy shrines in Karbala. When the CPA got wind of the plot, the U.S. Army's Fourth Infantry Division was dispatched to block the road from Baghdad to Karbala, intercepting 362 buses with thirty fighters each. Sadr's ten thousand well-armed fighters had come within three hours of seizing the sacred central district of Karbala; had they done so, it would have taken urban combat to dislodge them.

Perhaps the closest parallel to Sadr's militia was the Taliban of Afghanistan, but like his father, Muqtada al-Sadr favored an Islamist theocracy according to Ayatollah Khomeini's philosophy of *vilayat al-faqih*—rule by the jurist, meaning the Islamic judicial authority. In fact, the younger Sadr drew religious inspiration and legitimacy from Grand Ayatollah Kazem al-Haeri, a hard-line Iranian cleric based in the holy city of Qum, who had been a longtime student of Mohammed Baqir al-Sadr—indeed, saw himself as Baqir al-Sadr's successor—and was explicitly calling for an Iranian-style Islamic government in Iraq. Though lacking significant clerical rank, Muqtada al-Sadr was brilliantly exploiting eschatological religious symbolism to motivate a fanatical following. The very name of his militia had chilling, millenarian overtones, because for Shiites the Mahdi is the hidden Twelfth Imam, a messianic figure who is expected to return to the temporal world one day.[5] In his rhetoric, Sadr claimed that the Americans knew of the impending reappearance of the Mahdi and had invaded Iraq to seize and kill him. His supporters were chanting Sadr's name at rallies in a manner that implied he was the son of the Mahdi. And he insisted he could not disband his army, as the CPA was demanding, because it "belongs to the Mahdi."[6]

Sadr's operation of illegal Sharia courts in Najaf and Diwaniyah was alarming to those who understood the philosophy of *vilayat al-faqih*, because the move signaled a bid to establish an alternative system of government. Mike Gfoeller explained to me that under Khomeini's system of clerical rule, governing authority grows out of judicial power. God has already legislated through the Koran, the Sharia (traditional Islamic law), and the Hadith (the sayings of the Prophet Muhammad as recorded by his companions and preserved and transmitted by subsequent generations of the faithful). The *qadi*, or Islamic judge, interprets the law, and the executive, the army, and the police implement the *qadi*'s rulings. By establishing Sharia courts and using his Mahdi Army to implement their decisions, Sadr was, in essence, attempting to establish a sovereign government, in competition with that of the occupation and the Iraqi civil authorities. If the seed of such a theocratic government could be firmly planted before June 30, it might well establish its dominance in parts of the Shiite heartland after that date.

Yet Sadr's movement was not just about religious fanaticism. It was also about the struggle to fill the vacuum of power. There was a fascist tone to all the street action and thuggery, which was meant to terrorize enlightened people, to persecute ethnic minorities, to cow opponents, to create the sense of an unstoppable force, and to strike fear into the heart of those who would be so naive as to think they could shape policies and determine the future of Iraq through peaceful, democratic means.

As news of the destruction of Qawliyya filtered in, some saw it as another warning of what would happen if the U.S.-led military coalition did not move vigorously to disarm the Iranian-backed militias. Investigations by CPA staff indicated that the assault was a calculated escalation of the intimidation campaign by the Mahdi Army (and by like-minded militias), designed to demonstrate its strength and daring to its political competitors and to the CPA. Qawliyya was a convenient target, because the local Arab prejudice against its Gypsy population provided fertile soil for an act of ethnic cleansing. So rapidly were Sadr and his Mahdi Army rising in power and audacity that Ayatollah Sistani's supporters were in the process of forming their own militia— Ansar al-Sistani (supporters of Sistani)—to defend the moderate grand ayatollah against a possible assault from the militant young cleric. In fact, Sadr, along with a dozen of his top henchmen, had already been indicted in Iraqi courts for complicity in the murder, the previous spring, of Abdul Majid al-Khoei. Perhaps the most important democratic Shiite cleric, al-Khoei was, in the view of Yitzhak Nakash of Brandeis University, "a man who exemplified the sober and moderate face of Iraqi Shi'ism."[7] In fact, the United States and Britain had just brought Khoei back to Iraq from London to counter the radical, pro-Iranian Islamist forces among the Shiites. His revered father, Abulqasim al-Khoei, had preceded Sistani as the grand marja, the leading grand ayatollah in Najaf, while profoundly shaping Sistani's beliefs on the separation of clergy from politics. For Sadr, there was also a score to settle. In assuming his position of religious leadership on the death of Khoei's father in 1992, the quietist Sistani had eclipsed Muqtada al-Sadr's radical father, who had coveted the role. By ordering the assassination of Khoei outside the Imam Ali shrine in Najaf on April 10, 2003, just one day after the fall of Saddam Hussein, Sadr was making an unambiguous statement about his power. It was, Mike Gfoeller later said, tantamount to shooting a cardinal on the steps of Saint Peter's Basilica.

Others were beginning to mobilize against the Mahdi Army as well. In the towns and villages of Iraq, every male over the age of fourteen had some kind of gun, but in response to the assault on Qawliyya, tribal sheikhs throughout the region were now acquiring heavier weapons. Fearing that what happened to Qawliyya could happen to any one of their villages, they were telling CPA officials that they had to arm, to prepare for war. One even volunteered, "If you won't do it, I'll kill Sadr." Gfoeller was deeply worried that the region was drawing close to civil war between the tribes and militias, or among the militias themselves. If all-out fighting did break out in the South Central region, the CPA would be instantly in trouble. Virtually everyone at the palace knew that we did not have adequate forces in the area. Since September 2003, the region had been secured not by U.S. troops but by the Multinational Division (MND), consisting of nine thousand soldiers from Poland, Ukraine, and Spain, along with smaller contingents from a dozen other nations, including Bulgaria, El Salvador, and the Dominican Republic. This force was to guard an area of five provinces in the Shiite heartland that included the sacred and politically strategic cities of Najaf and Karbala, and which by some estimates had as many as

25,000 militia fighters. The officers and units of the MND did not want trouble and had not come to Iraq to fight. Their rules of engagement, set by their home governments, were highly restrictive. Hence, they did not sustain early American military efforts to erode Sadr's organization and arrest his lieutenants. Instead, they looked the other way when problems or threats occurred—which was why, as I was driving down to Hilla almost three weeks after the destruction of Qawliyya, there had been no legal action, no military maneuvers, and no press coverage in response to it.

As we drove up to the headquarters of Qizwini's University of Scientific, Humanistic, and Theological Studies inside the largest mosque in Hilla, we passed a building down the road where the Mahdi Army was teaching new fighters the arts of firing automatic weapons and making car bombs. In full view of the MND and the CPA, the Mahdi Army was recruiting and training for the coming war in Iraq.

★

My speech in Hilla this time was not at the university but behind the mosque in the two-hundred-seat auditorium of the gleaming new Regional Democracy Center, which had been dedicated at the beginning of the month. Once again, Qizwini and a large retinue of turbaned clerics and religious students, along with tribal sheikhs in their characteristic black-and-white kaffiyeh headdress, were waiting to greet us as we drove up to the new compound. I gave a short speech about the TAL and the upcoming phases of political transition and, as in my previous sessions around the country, received comments and answered questions. There were the usual points of objection and confusion concerning the TAL, and resentment of a distant Governing Council that did not represent them, but there was also concern about the challenges, more generally, of democracy building. In particular, these Iraqis voiced anxiety over the rising threat of armed militias. After the event, Gfoeller and I were treated as guests of honor at a sumptuous traditional lunch in a tent adjoining the auditorium. The tent was stifling on a day that already had what many Americans would take as the heat of summer, but in a couple of months, temperatures here would rise another forty degrees. I joined my hosts and audience in feasting on abundant platters of rice, chicken, lamb, and unleavened bread. The mood was festive and welcoming, marking a kind of reunion from the January gathering.

After lunch, Qizwini gave us a tour of the impressive new Regional Democracy Center, with its tasteful, well-equipped, high-tech facilities for training, meetings, research, and networking, including a total of thirty-six computer workstations. I asked who used all the computers, meeting rooms, and offices. Qizwini was ready with a long list of groups: "Tribes, farmers, women, youth and sports unions, martyrs of the 1991 uprising, researchers, and human rights groups." After viewing both floors, Qizwini led us to the roof of the center, which offered a view of the magnificent cream-colored mosque. Beside it stood the worksite of yet more construction for the complex, including a cafeteria, classrooms, and separate dormitories for up to three hundred men and women who would, it was hoped, come to the center in steady streams over the coming months and years to be trained in democratic principles and organizational skills. The center itself was not an entirely new building. Before the war, Saddam's regime had begun constructing it as the new regional headquarters of the Baath Party. Now it was being established as the hub of a network of eighteen democracy centers in the region—one each for women, human rights, and tribal groups in each of the region's six provinces, all linked in a computer network through the wonders of Arabic Messenger, a service of Microsoft. The South Central CPA had invested several million dollars in the centers, which had been built, on schedule, by local Iraqi firms. The figure was just a fraction of the more than $100 million it had spent on roads, schools, sewers, water treatment plants, and other infrastructure. But it could prove to have one of the greatest long-term impacts.

From the democracy center we crossed back to the mosque and saw how much work had been done since I last visited, in January. The radio studio—for the new Iraqi Democratic Independent Voice—was almost completed. In the translation center, a sizable crew of Iraqis sat at computers translating a number of books on democracy, including two of mine. Qizwini's vision was advancing, and he was proud. We turned a corner and the huge cleric pointed to a stone square of the mosque's wall. This, it had only recently been discovered, was the movable facade of a secret chamber where Saddam could bury, without a trace, those who resisted him. Since it was a new mosque, he hadn't had time yet to start piling up bodies there. Qizwini then took us up to the roof of the mosque, where he had constructed his large traditional *mudheef*. We removed our shoes and entered.

The huge tented, reed-frame room was warm in the heat of the early afternoon (particularly so with my bulletproof vest drawn closed beneath my shirt, coat, and tie), and the only seats were rough burlap pillows on the woven straw floor. Qizwini had a well-appointed, air-conditioned office in the mosque, but this is where he most enjoyed receiving and engaging visitors. Over the next hour, with his enormous feet sticking out past his robe, the Sayyid proceeded to unload to me (as he had previously done to Gfoeller) his mounting worries about the Islamist militias that were running amok in the region. He believed in debate and rational dialogue—it was what his university was all about. But the militias, he warned, were "using only force, fighting people who oppose their opinions." Iran was pouring in arms, money, and advice to support them. Some of them worked for Ayatollah al-Haeri, who was close to Iran's supreme leader, Ayatollah Ali Khamenei. In Najaf and Karbala, he alleged, there were six thousand Iranian intelligence agents, and another two thousand to three thousand in Basra. In the last seventy-two hours, he told us, the Badr Corps and the Mahdi Army had obtained numerous weapons, both from Iraqi Army supply depots and from across the border in Iran, to prepare for violence during the transition. And then he described the letter he had received the previous day from the Sadr Martyrs, threatening to kill him and ten tribal leaders of his movement. Things had reached the point, he advised us gravely, where they would either have to surrender the eighteen democracy centers to the armed groups who were preparing to seize them, or form their own militia in self-defense. His movement, he claimed, had four thousand former army officers. "We could form one of the largest militias," he told us. But he did not want to go that route. "You must press on all the militias to disarm," he said, "so as not to create another Lebanon here in Iraq." And we had to do it soon, in the next week. "Give the militias ten days to disarm, and tell them if they fail to comply, you will arrest them and disarm them by force." I doubted that we had enough troops in Iraq to confront every militia at once, but clearly something had to be done. Otherwise, the region's high-tech democracy centers would soon become the Muqtada al-Sadr centers for the making of Islamic revolution.

There was another reason for Qizwini's sense of urgency. In ten days, Iraqis would be observing the Shiite Muslim holiday of Arba'een, which celebrates the end of the traditional forty-day period of mourning over the death of the seventh-century Shiite martyr and saint Imam Husayn ibn Ali, the grandson of the Prophet Muhammad and son of the first Shiite imam, Ali ibn Abi Talib. The first day of that mourning period, marking the actual anniversary of Imam Husayn's death, is Shiite Islam's holiest day, Ashura. This year Ashura had fallen on March 2, one of the bloodiest days in Iraq since the end of the war; 171 people were killed and hundreds more wounded in Baghdad and Karbala by car bombs believed to have been organized by the Al Qaeda mastermind, Abu Musab al-Zarqawi. As a result of those deadly attacks, even America's allies within southern Iraq were warning they would stop cooperating with the CPA and "go to war" if the United States failed to stem the violence. As the tension rose from militia attacks and bombings, the local tribes were starting to stockpile arms. Many experts believed that Arba'een, on April 10, could see even worse eruptions of violence, as hundreds of thousands of Shiite pilgrims were trekking for days from across Iraq and beyond to visit the Shrine of Imam Husayn in Karbala, as well as the Shrine of Imam Ali in Najaf. (Indeed, Gfoeller and I had already seen some of them walking, clad in black, on the roads around Hilla.) Tens of thousands of pilgrims were also coming from Iran, and CPA officials worried that a small but significant number of them would not be religious visitors but agents of the Iranian Ministry of Interior and the Revolutionary Guards, smuggling more money and instructions to the militias. Gfoeller detected a "pervasive sense of fear and foreboding" building up in the region, and a feeling in Karbala, especially, that they were on the edge of a takeover by terrorist forces. There was even concern that Sadr's Mahdi Army would cooperate with Sunni radical Islamist groups in order to sow chaos and destabilize the region.

As we sat in his office after dinner that night, Gfoeller expanded on his apprehensions, offering as trenchant an analysis of the problem of

Sadr as I would hear from anyone. "Muqtada reminds me of the Mafiosi in the former Soviet Union," he said. "He fits a certain type. The exercise of cruelty untrammeled by any law or custom has a certain intoxifying effect. And he is suffering from that intoxification. Like a drug addict, he requires ever larger doses of violence and mayhem to sate himself."

It was not only Sadr's Mahdi Army on the loose, and not only ethnic minorities or even Iraqis who were targets. The South Central region, and indeed the entire Shiite south, was rife with well-armed militias, many of which were as extreme in their religious fanaticism as they were in their criminality and brutality. In February, the commander of the Badr Corps in the Najaf area, Haji Hassan, a hard-line advocate of *vilayat al-faqih*, had threatened to assassinate the local CPA provincial coordinator, Rick Olson, after Olson confronted Hassan over his effort to bribe the Najaf Provincial Council in order to gain control of it. Then, on March 5, as Olson was traveling back with his personal security detail to Najaf from a meeting of civilian and military leaders at CPA headquarters in Baghdad, some fifteen Iraqis opened fire with AK-47s. Olson and his colleagues survived only because all three of their vehicles (recently procured) were armored; their bodyguards returned fire on the attackers with a heavy machine gun, killing three of them; and they were able to radio for help after their tires were shot out. The response of the CPA was not to go after Haji Hassan but rather to dismiss the incident as a "target of opportunity" attack by bandits, and to transfer Rick Olson back to Washington. "There is willful blindness in Baghdad," one of Olson's CPA colleagues lamented to me. Many other CPA officials were privately appalled.

As I learned during my travels through the Shiite south (and subsequently), the Islamist parties and militias formed a confusing patchwork of shifting loyalties and alliances, with Iran playing a significant role but with no one really in control. SCIRI's Badr Corps had been trained and armed in Iran by the Islamic Republic's Revolutionary Guards, growing to over ten thousand fighters by the late 1990s. But as they reestablished themselves in Iraq after the fall of Saddam, they took on different local colorations. The brutal, unpopular Badr Corps in Nasariyah and Najaf was not the same as the Badr Corps and the SCIRI in Basra;

the latter was more moderate, less violent, and had a stronger base of support. Da'wa had even more factions, having splintered into many pieces, both in exile and within Iraq, during the 1980s and 1990s. The leaders of some Da'wa branches (especially in Tehran) subscribed to Khomeini's philosophy of clerical rule, while others, including Ibrahim Jaafari, who sat on the Governing Council, appeared more moderately Islamist. And beyond the nationally known, party-linked militias, there were numerous shadowy groups building up their strength.[8]

What many of these groups appeared to have in common were ties to one or another faction of the Islamic Republic of Iran. From Iran, the Shiite militias received money, sometimes arms, tactical assistance, and other forms of guidance. Thus backing several (violent) horses, the Iranian regime maximized its prospects of achieving its strategic goals in Iraq: preventing the emergence of a democracy; bringing about, instead, some form of their Islamic clerical rule; assuming control over the Shiite holy cities of Najaf and Karbala; and eventually establishing a sphere of influence over all the Shiites in the Persian Gulf region, stretching from southern Iraq to Kuwait, northern Saudi Arabia, and Bahrain. Sad to say, during the occupation the Iranian mullahs would wind up promoting their goals far more effectively than the United States would promote democracy in Iraq.

★

The CPA understood that the militias constituted a threat to the future of democracy in Iraq and that something needed to be done to defuse that threat. Since early February, the "something" we had sought to achieve was a comprehensive plan, called Transition and Reintegration, for all the militias.[9] Such militia demobilization plans are an essential component of any postconflict reconstruction effort. Their common strategy is to get most irregular armed forces to decommission and disarm their fighters and turn in their weapons, in exchange for a variety of individual and group incentives. The group incentive is not to be attacked, crushed, and forcibly dismantled—a last resort that neither side wants. The individual fighters receive a flow of positive incentives. They are either reintegrated into the civilian economy and society, through job training and placement programs and in some cases the provision of pensions, or they are integrated into the new armed forces—in this case either the army, the Iraqi Civil Defense Corps (ICDC, subsequently renamed the National Guard), or one of three lighter forces managed under the Ministry of the Interior, the Iraqi Police, the Department of Border Enforcement, or Facilities Protection (local guards) services. The plan had been to require all forces to disband, beginning with the two largest, best-equipped, and most organized armed groups, the Kurdish *pesh merga* and the Badr Organization (previously known as the Badr Corps). Once it took effect, the TAL banned "armed forces and militias not under the command structure of the Iraqi Transitional Government," unless "provided by federal law." But because the TAL granted the Kurds responsibility for internal security in the Kurdistan region, half of the *pesh merga* were to be restructured into three new internal security services: a counterterrorism force, a rapid reaction force (a kind of gendarmerie), and mountain rangers (in Kurdish, *pesh merga*), while the other half were eligible for integration into the army and other Iraqi armed forces. On paper, it looked as though the members of the *pesh merga* were enlisting in the new forces as individuals, but in fact they were doing so as battalions. "We are taking *pesh* units and slapping an ICDC label on them," one U.S. Army officer told me in candor.

The Transition and Reintegration plan was expensive and ambitious. It was estimated that some 102,000 fighters in various militias would be involved: about one-third to be retired with pensions, one-third to be integrated into one of the new security forces, and one-third to be reintegrated into civilian employment. Millions of dollars would be required for additional job training and placement centers. The programs would have to include basic education for many of the fighters. Then there was the problem of the more than 300,000 cashiered army soldiers, who had been receiving stipends. Massive job training or continuing financial support would need to be factored into the security transition plan. If the plan was to succeed over time, there would need to be a significant commitment from Iraqi ministries like Labor and Social Affairs, and an international team with professional experience (perhaps from the UN Development Program), deployed in regional centers around the country, monitoring compliance and tracking the progress of the individuals designated for reintegration into the civilian sector.

The intention was to finish the negotiations over the Transition and Reintegration plan in April, and to announce it by May 1. Toward that end, military and civilian security specialists had been traveling around the country, negotiating directly with militia leaders.[10] But to persuade the mainstream militias, like the Badr Organization, to cooperate with the plan, the CPA believed, Sadr's militia would have to be dismantled first—almost certainly by force. Otherwise, the other militias we were seeking to bring into the political process—who were in several cases Sadr's competitors and directly threatened by him—would be engaging in unilateral disarmament at great risk, and the implicit threat by the U.S.-led military coalition to use force to dismantle them would not be credible. Therefore a CPA order—that all armed organizations outside the legitimate control of the government were illegal and had to be disbanded—would be issued. And of course, if such an order was issued, it would have to be enforced, or the program, and indeed the CPA itself, would lose credibility.

Not everyone thought it was feasible or necessary to arrest Sadr. Some specialists felt that if we cracked down quickly against his organization, he could be driven into exile in Iran, which could generate credibility problems for him and for his Iranian sponsors. Others within the CPA and the U.S. military were wary of any confrontation, noting Sadr's capacity to mobilize large numbers of fervent believers. In the palace, CPA officials guessed that the Mahdi Army numbered no more than three thousand to four thousand fighters, but if he could mobilize ten thousand people to try to seize central Karbala by stealth, how many could he call to arms in open rebellion against the occupation? It was this concern about what would happen in the slums of Sadr City (which contained one-third of Baghdad's 5.5 million people) and in other Shiite cities that had led American officials and commanders—in Baghdad and in Washington—repeatedly to veto or back away from plans to crack down on Sadr's organization, or to unseal and execute the warrants for the arrest of Sadr and his henchmen for the murder of Khoei. Instead, CPA kept the arrest warrants sealed, as a veiled warning to Sadr not to cross some unspecified line of outrage. But if CPA viewed the sealed warrants as a cudgel to keep Sadr in line, both the firebrand junior cleric and his opponents saw the failure to act on them as emblematic of the Coalition's impotence. Some senior Shiite religious leaders did urge restraint, in order not to make the young upstart a martyr. Some Iraqis felt the best course was to co-opt Sadr into the political game, but that option had essentially been lost in July 2003, when Sadr was excluded from any representation on the Governing Council. Subsequently, he took a radical turn, condemning the occupation, demanding American withdrawal, forming his Mahdi Army, and then flexing its muscles ever more brutally. Sadr kept pushing, and the United States kept waiting, warning, wavering, delaying, and debating.

Within the CPA, the Governance Office had grasped the inseparable link between improving security and completing the transition. It was the first substantive theme in a March 28 memo to Bremer conveying our collective thinking on the challenges for the remaining ninety-five days until the handover. Improving security, the memo stated, involved not only combating the insurgency and terrorism but also "addressing the militia problem." Since the end of the war, the number of militias had multiplied, destabilizing politics and "feeding a climate of intimidation across the country." Particularly in the south, the militias were "coercing women to veil themselves and convincing people to remain silent about crimes and injustices." If we did not dismantle or phase out the militias, we argued, they not only would destabilize the near-term political climate but would bias "the outcome of elections in 2005 to the favor of radicals and those against democracy." The memo concluded, representing our consensus view, "Tackling the militia challenge means we must choose to take actions that in the short term will be disruptive and could spark unrest." While continuing to negotiate with the *pesh merga* and the Badr Organization to bring them into the Transition and Reintegration plan, we had to "be prepared to combat with the force of law those with which we have no political relations or hope for cooperation." The memo did not name names, but it was clear that Sadr and his organization topped the list of the recalcitrant. For those close to the security reform effort, the entire Transition and Reintegration plan hinged on dealing with Sadr's Mahdi Army fighters. "If we can crack that nut and take them out, it would be a turning point," one official told the *Washington Post* in March.[11]

★

I returned to Baghdad on the morning of April 1 stunned by what I had learned from Qizwini and Gfoeller in Hilla, the conversations crystallizing the signals of a gathering storm. I had already largely drafted a memo to Ambassador Bremer on the political transition and institution-building challenges we needed to tackle before June 30. And I was due to see him that night, after he returned from Mosul and just one day before I was scheduled to return to the United States to attend to my other work. Now I concluded my memo with the problem of the militias:

> Nothing else we do in our transition program can succeed unless the problem of the militias in general is vigorously tackled, and the problem of Muqtada Sadr in particular very soon. If we move well into May with no action on this front, I believe the downward spiral of fear, anxiety, deceit, and competitive armament will take on a new and unstoppable momentum, leading ultimately to civil war. It is important for the Administration to understand that if this descent occurs, it will begin quite visibly, and perhaps horrifically, well before November 2 [that is, by the date of the U.S. presidential election].

I also prepared a detailed set of confidential reflections, titled "Militias and the Transition." In it, I said the most urgent challenge ahead was security. "The road to democracy in postconflict situations is littered with the corpses of transitions that failed because they could not establish this most basic condition of a viable state," I observed. "A common reason why is the presence of independent armed groups who refuse to play by the democratic rules of the game and who use force, fraud, thuggery, and intimidation to impose their will and conquer power." Our progress on training the Iraqi Army and police, I argued, had been overshadowed by the growth of the militias. (In fact, it was widely known that the establishment of the Iraqi police had been a disaster, as they were rushed into service poorly trained and ill equipped, and thus often melted away or defected in the face of the insurgencies that were about to explode.) Our Transition and Reintegration plan lacked a sense of urgency in demobilizing by force those groups that could not be won over through negotiations, especially Muqtada al-Sadr and his Mahdi Army. I summarized their reign of mayhem and what I had learned in Hilla. These forces had "metastasized like a malignant cancer in the body politic of Iraq." Every time we prepared to perform surgery to remove it, some reason emerged for a postponement. Now we were running out of time. If we didn't act soon, I warned, the Shiite south of Iraq might well explode; or, at best, it would become too late politically to contain this menace, and after the handover we would leave this part of the country to the mercies of Sadr's (and other) militias, as they seized both secular buildings and mosques, set up more illegal Sharia courts, terrorized communities and campuses, assassinated opponents, and extended their control over more and more communities. I didn't see how democratic elections could be conducted in that kind of climate.

Sadr's menace, I warned, played neatly into the hands of the Sunni insurgents, whose strategy was not only to exploit Sunni fears of minority status in an Iraq ruled by the majority Shiites but also "to turn the Shiite population against the Coalition, through its sin of omission—its inability to protect them against terrorist violence. This turn, Al Qaeda seems to believe, will spark a second front of resistance against the Coalition, along with a civil war in the Shiite south, and make Iraq ungovernable for the occupation." To prevent this from happening, Sadr had to be arrested in a "well coordinated strike in the very near future." I urged that his Mahdi Army be ordered to disband; that their headquarters, bases, and training facilities be seized and closed down; and that an investigation be opened into the ethnic cleansing at Qawliyya. Then, I said, we should move vigorously to put the smaller recalcitrant militias out of business while we completed negotiations on the Transition and Reintegration plan with the bigger and more cooperative ones. Finally, I warned, the Multinational Division had "proved manifestly incapable of confronting this slide toward chaos in South Central." If order was to be restored and much wider violence prevented, "a more capable and willful force" had to be "inserted into key places in the region immediately." I did not say so in the memo, but I planned to make clear to Bremer in person what I felt this meant: sending in the Marines.

When I entered his office at around eight-thirty that night, Bremer was eating dinner from a cafeteria tray. The meal that an aide had gathered up from the mess hall and put away for him had long since grown cold. His tie was off and he had traded his blue blazer for a blue fleece vest that he frequently wore over a white dress shirt open at the collar. He was tired, and in many ways worn out. As he ate, I briefly summarized for him what I had learned on my recent travels, and the contents of my two memos. I urged that we move quickly to execute a comprehensive plan to arrest Sadr and disable his militia. Bremer said that General Ricardo Sanchez, the commander of U.S. troops in Iraq, owed him an operational plan for precisely that purpose, but that Washington was reluctant to confront Sadr. There wasn't much else we could do in the near term because the MND's rules of engagement would not permit those troops to launch offensive operations.

I said that the MND was ineffectual and could not hold the region, and I recommended deploying five thousand marines to South Central: a thousand each in Hilla, Najaf, and Karbala, and another two thousand to secure roads and smaller towns. Only a force of that size and toughness was likely to keep a lid on things, I told Bremer. I knew I was not an expert on military strategy, but I had had extensive discussions with a CPA official who made this recommendation on the basis of an acute understanding of the situation. The First Marine Expeditionary Force, commanded by Lieutenant General James T. Conway, had just returned to Iraq to take over in Al-Anbar Province from the army's Eighty-second Airborne Division. The First Marines had fought many key battles in Operation Iraqi Freedom (while conducting the longest overland assault in the entire history of the Marine Corps) and had been responsible for security in southern Iraq. So they knew the terrain. If we could (as my CPA colleague had suggested) move one-fifth of these 25,000 marines down there quickly, they might stabilize the region. That would send a clear message to the Iranians and others that they couldn't shake the Coalition's resolve in the Shiite heartland.

Bremer became irritated. There was no chance of getting any marines down to South Central, he told me. "I don't know if you've noticed," he said, "but there is a war going on in the west." Indeed, Fallujah, the site of tenacious violence, had erupted the day before in one of the most gruesome episodes of the occupation. Four American security contractors working for Blackwater were ambushed and killed, and then an enraged mob jubilantly dragged their burned and bullet-ridden bodies through the streets of the city before hanging two of the corpses from a bridge over the Euphrates River. Every one of the marines was needed there, in Al-Anbar Province, Bremer said; there were none to spare. I said we *had* to get more troops in Iraq; everyone knew there weren't enough. Bremer implied that it was not politically possible, and anyway, with deployment lead times, "significantly more U.S. troops couldn't get here until September."

Then I pressed too far. The man was tired, and his youthful face was beginning to show the strain. Behind the conversation were months and layers of frustration that I could only guess at. Still, I had one more obligation I felt I had to discharge. The Coalition military command, CJTF-7, had recently cut in half the number of American military police supporting CPA operations in the southern provinces. The move was extremely untimely, coming precisely when violent attacks were increasing; some civilians within the CPA privately felt that the decline in protection had been a contributing factor in Fern Holland's death. In my recent travels, I had learned of a CPA headquarters in one of the provinces that had repeatedly come under attack and felt physically vulnerable. A CPA official there (I will call him Roger) had felt compelled to acquire additional security equipment for the guard force, to defend the compound against terrorist attack. Even so, he felt he needed "two Humvees and twenty marines" to bolster security for his convoys on the roads and at the compound. During the last two months, as the roads had become more murderous, that CPA office had been operating without any military security for its convoys. Roger had asked for twenty troops from the MND but was flatly turned down. "Unless we get more people," he had told me, "we will take more casualties." Now I thought, if I can't get five thousand marines down to the region, maybe I can at least get twenty down to that headquarters. I told

Bremer of Roger's concern and asked him if we could find two Humvees and twenty troops to help him out.

Then Bremer snapped. "We don't *have* any more troops," he said testily. "Eighty percent of all the available MPs are already here in Iraq. If Roger feels unsafe, tell him to go home."

It was the first time during my stay in Iraq that I had seen the smooth diplomat lose his composure, and the cavalier remark shocked me. This was coming from a man who had recently told a town hall meeting of CPA staffers, "Your security is our highest priority." Even allowing for his exhaustion and frustration, I was dismayed by his abrupt dismissal of the vulnerability of his own field staff. I thought, "You can't be serious that we can't find twenty troops *somewhere*. We can't be *that* short." But I did not utter the words, or much of anything else. Shaken, I returned the conversation to superficial pleasantries and bid him good-bye. I did not realize it at the time, but it would be my last meeting with Ambassador Bremer, and my final substantive moment as an adviser to the CPA.

★

The next day, Friday, April 2, I left Iraq on an Air Force C-130, not knowing whether I would return, as planned, later that month. Someone needed to speak out about the drift in the American posture—the lack of troops, the lack of will, the lack of a clear plan to establish the minimum security necessary for a transition to any kind of decent political order. I knew that the Bush administration would not welcome open criticism. And I also worried that conditions in Iraq might soon decline to the point where it would be impossible for me to play what was now my most valuable role—getting out of the Green Zone to engage Iraqi groups in discussions on the transition to democracy. As I headed out to the airport in a soft SUV on the morning of April 2, with the security situation deteriorating on multiple fronts, I held my breath and said a prayer.

At that moment, Muqtada al-Sadr was using his Friday prayers at a mosque in Kufa (a small city neighboring Najaf) to call for open rebellion against the occupation: "I and my followers of the believers have come under attack from the occupiers. . . . Be on the utmost readiness, and strike them where you meet them." The "attack" Sadr was referring to had occurred at the beginning of the week. On March 28, three days before Bremer told me that he was still waiting for an operational plan from the military to deal with Sadr, he had ordered the closure, for sixty days, of Muqtada al-Sadr's weekly newspaper, *al-Hawza*,[12] charging that it had spread false allegations that were inciting Iraqis to violence. One of its articles had accused American forces of firing rockets at a mosque. Another charged Bremer with deliberately starving the Iraqi people. In fact, Sadr himself was becoming more openly confrontational. On the previous Friday, he had delivered an ugly sermon praising the September 11 attacks as a "gift from God."[13]

In the days following the closure of his newspaper (which had a circulation of about ten thousand), Sadr generated a rising tide of anti-American protests among his followers. On March 31, the same day that the four American contractors were murdered and their bodies mutilated in Fallujah, thousands of Sadr's followers marched past the entrance to the Green Zone in Baghdad, chanting, "Just say the word, Muqtada, and we'll resume the 1920 revolution," a pointed reference to the uprising against British colonial rule. Then, on April 3, Sadr's deputy Mustafa Yacoubi was arrested on one of the warrants for involvement in the murder of Khoei—apparently on orders from a local Coalition military commander acting ahead of the CPA.

Immediately, Sadr lashed back. Hundreds of his supporters started flooding south from Baghdad to Kufa. By Sunday, April 4, they had seized the police station and a key government building in Najaf without a fight, while launching a withering assault on the CPA headquarters in Najaf. Though that siege was repelled, the Mahdi Army—its numbers rapidly swelling from hidden reserves who raced to battle on instructions of their leaders, and from other downtrodden young Shiites who simply claimed the offered cash to fight—quickly seized control of Najaf, as well as Kufa, Nasariyah, and the sprawling East Baghdad slum, Sadr City. "The occupation is over! We are now controlled by Sadr!" many of his black-clad insurgents yelled. That afternoon, Sadr issued a call to all-out war: "Terrorize your enemy. God will reward you well for what pleases him."[14] Shortly thereafter, Mahdi Army fighters ambushed a military patrol in Sadr City, killing eight

American soldiers. That night, Bremer declared, "This morning, a group of people in Najaf have crossed the line, and they have moved to violence. This will not be tolerated." The next day, he canceled a trip to Washington and declared Sadr an "outlaw," announcing a warrant for his arrest. An American military spokesman lamely called on Sadr, who was holed up in Kufa surrounded by hundreds of his fighters, to surrender himself in order "to calm the situation."[15] Yet according to press reports, U.S. officials decided to hold off on trying to capture or kill Sadr, for fear of igniting even worse violence.[16]

Brilliantly manipulating the imagery of resistance and martyrdom that suffused his family history—and thirteen centuries of Shiite suffering—Sadr vowed, "We don't fear death, and martyrdom gives us dignity from God." He also declared himself Sistani's "military wing in Iraq." However, Sistani, who privately feared and scorned Sadr, did not embrace his cause but rather appealed for a peaceful solution while urging Shiites to remain calm. In the subsequent days, Mahdi Army fighters seized more cities and towns in the Shiite south, including Kut, the capital of Wasit Province, where they drove Ukrainian troops of the MND to cede control after twenty-four hours of combat, in which a Ukrainian soldier was killed. In the process, after a terrifying siege, the CPA's compound in Kut fell to Sadr's fighters, who systematically looted, burned, and destroyed every room and computer in the six buildings.[17] It was the first post that the CPA had to abandon in Iraq, but it would not be the last. The CPA facilities in Najaf, Karbala, Hilla, and Diwaniyah soon came under fierce Mahdi Army assault, while the compound in Nasariyah was also overrun, with fatalities among the Italian troops protecting it.[18] In Karbala, Bulgarian forces had to appeal urgently for U.S. troops to help hold the city. As Sadr's forces quickly overran "government buildings, police stations, civil defense garrisons, and other installations built up by the Americans," they stripped them of "files, furnishings, and even toilet fixtures," while taking over policing and other government functions. Less than a week into the uprising, one CPA official glumly commented, "Six months of work is completely gone. There is nothing to show for it."[19]

The CPA was now moving against Sadr without a plan. First the Americans closed down his weekly newspaper, then they arrested his top lieutenant—but without any comprehensive strategy for disabling him or his organization. It was like punching a big bear in the eye without any idea of what to do next. Of course, the bear got angry and lashed back in a vicious way; Sadr was now implementing plans for the revolutionary seizure of power in key Shiite urban centers that he had probably had for some time. A smarter strategy would have been to move against Sadr with a sudden, devastating strike: arresting him and his top deputies and closing down his courts, his newspaper, his paramilitary bases and training camps, and his political headquarters all at once, while deploying massive force in or around key urban areas to deter or contain any violent reaction. The next step, one expert advised, should have been to cleanse the Old City of Najaf of illegally held arms. But everything seemed to be lacking for this approach: the strategic imagination, the tactical intelligence, the political will, and, most of all, a sufficient number of troops. So the Coalition stumbled piecemeal into all-out confrontation with Sadr—just as a war was erupting among the Sunni population in and around Fallujah.

A city of about a quarter of a million, Fallujah had been a Baathist stronghold during Saddam's rule and (with Mosul) a primary source of military officer recruitment going back to the Ottoman era. With the dissolution of the Iraqi Army and the far-reaching scope of de-Baathification, it was thus not surprising to some analysts (including in the U.S. Army) that it had been a "no-go" area and an operating base of the Sunni insurgency for months prior to the March 31 ambush. As the Marines assumed responsibility for Al-Anbar Province in mid-March, an offensive operation to restore order seemed imminent. Two days before Bremer closed Sadr's newspaper, the Marines killed fifteen Iraqis during a raid in Fallujah. The eruption of mob violence against the American contractors five days later seemed, to some observers, to mark a turning point in the deepening of the insurgency. "After Fallujah," the *New York Times* reporter John F. Burns wrote, "fewer Westerners here than ever, outside the American military and civilian establishment, could still believe that the American vision is likely to triumph over an insurgency that has featured recurrent acts of inhumanity, including suicide bombings that have killed more than 1,000 Iraqis."[20]

The Coalition didn't see it that way, however. The shocking events of March 31 stiffened its resolve to go after the insurgents embedded in the city. On April 4, the Marines cordoned off the city in what would become a weeks-long siege. Many residents now rallied to the cause of the Fallujah insurgents, and, on April 5, a new battalion of several hundred Iraqi soldiers refused to join the Marines in assaulting the city. The American occupation now faced its worst nightmare: "not just a two-front war . . . , but one in which each side was drawing strength from the other," as the *Washington Post* reported.[21] The two wings of the mushrooming insurgency now realized that American forces were seriously overstretched, and they started cooperating with each other tactically. Pictures of Muqtada al-Sadr began showing up in Sunni mosques. In the Sunni Triangle, the fighting spread to Ramadi, where twelve marines were killed on April 6 in an ambush and five-hour street battle. Ambushes, kidnappings, and roadside bombings sharply escalated. By the second week of April, the Coalition was facing an escalating uprising against the occupation that was feeding off a swelling tide of anti-Americanism. In response, the Pentagon delayed the departure of some 25,000 American soldiers who were due to be replaced, giving it a desperately needed boost in troop strength to wage this second war.

In Fallujah, fighting became intense, as American forces went on the attack, deeply embedded, well-armed insurgents resisted, and Shiite fighters slipped into the city from the south, on instructions from Sadr to "fight as one" with the Sunnis—"increase the killing and drive the Americans out."[22] On April 8, the Marines fought their way into the center of the city, while U.S. air power bombed the outer walls of a mosque in which snipers were hiding. As the fighting continued, casualties mounted on both sides. Doctors in Fallujah reported hundreds of Iraqi dead (including noncombatants), more than one thousand wounded, and a rupture in water, electricity, and food supplies.

The images of the siege of the city—dramatically portrayed, by the local and regional media, as American aggression and heroic Iraqi resistance—brought widespread condemnation from many American allies both inside Iraq and in the region. On April 9, Iraq's interim human rights minister, Abdel Basit Turki, resigned, calling the Fallujah escalation a "clear violation of human rights." Abdul-Karim al-Muhammadawi, who had led the Shiite marsh Arabs in a daring campaign of resistance against Saddam, suspended his membership on the Governing Council, and two other members of that body publicly threatened to quit. A wave of resignations seemed imminent, as council members bitterly lambasted Bremer for not consulting them on the decision to assault Fallujah (which they would have strongly opposed). Adnan Pachachi, one of America's best friends on the Governing Council, called the offensive "mass punishment" of the people of Fallujah, "unacceptable and illegal." The mission of the UN special representative, Lakhdar Brahimi—who had recently returned to Baghdad to mediate the construction of the interim government—appeared in danger of collapsing. "If you continue doing this," he told Robert Blackwill of the National Security Council, "there will be nothing for me to do here." From the Arab press—which had been silent through Saddam's worst atrocities—spewed a chorus of condemnations. "Freedom, democracy, the rule of law and other such promises have been transformed in the occupation's lexicon into violation, invasions, sieges, curfews, bombardments from Apache helicopters and the terrorization of a people," the United Arab Emirates' daily *Al Khaleej* wrote in what *New York Times* correspondent Neil MacFarquhar described as a "typical editorial."[23]

Seeing that the political transition program was now under threat, and facing the prospect of prolonged, bloody urban combat, the United States backed off. On Friday, April 9—one year to the day after the fall of Saddam—Bremer ordered a cease-fire in Fallujah. The purpose, he said, was "to give a political track an opportunity to reduce the violence," while allowing urgently needed medical supplies and food to reach the city, and the residents to bury the dead.[24] Negotiations with local leaders, mediated by representatives of the Governing Council, ensued, in an effort to find a political solution to pacify the city. The Iraqi insurgents agreed to a cease-fire two days later. By then, Fallujah residents claimed, some six hundred Iraqis had been killed, and the United States reported forty-eight Americans dead—the highest weekly toll since formal combat operations had ended almost a year earlier.

★

Down south, the United States was faring no better. In a hastily mounted strike, U.S. forces began to retake Kut. Eventually, they regained control of that city (and other towns in Wasit Province) with help from the Bani Zubayd tribal confederation, but Sadr's forces tightened their grip on Kufa and the holy cities of Najaf and Karbala. Sadr vowed to turn Iraq into "another Vietnam for America," while the chief U.S. military spokesman, Brigadier General Mark Kimmitt, promised that the troops would "destroy the Mahdi Army."[25] In the first week of Sadr's insurgency, American troops were forced to hold back while hundreds of thousands of religious pilgrims flocked to Najaf and Karbala to celebrate the Shiite holy day of Arba'een. But with the end of the holiday at sunset on April 11, American forces began massing outside the cities, and counterassaults seemed imminent. The next day, a delegation of leading Shiite clerics representing the four grand ayatollahs (collectively known as the *marjaiah*), including Sistani's highly influential son, Mohammed Reda Sistani, met with Sadr in Najaf, and the outlook appeared to change. Mahdi Army fighters started to withdraw from police stations and government buildings in the holy city, as some Najaf residents distributed leaflets implicitly denouncing Sadr, calling the prospect of his rule a threat to "return us to an era of slavery."[26] The following day, April 13, the Mahdi Army began to retreat from some of the centers of authority they had seized in Kufa and Karbala. The Shiite members of the Governing Council urged the CPA to negotiate a solution with Sadr, who said he was ready to "implement any order" from the religious establishment. According to a spokesman for the clerics who met with Sadr, a tentative deal had been struck, in which Sadr would dismantle his militia if the Americans did not send forces into Najaf and did not arrest him. The U.S. military said that it was "up to Sadr" to meet its conditions (dismantling the militia and giving himself up), and, in Washington, a Pentagon official stressed that Sadr had to be arrested. "Nothing is being considered in which he goes free."[27] And in fact no deal emerged.

By then, the U.S. death toll in April had risen to seventy, and the month was not yet half over. The insurgency had thrown the political transition into crisis while virtually freezing economic reconstruction. The democracy dialogues and other civic education activities were suspended throughout much of the country. Negotiations on the Transition and Reintegration plan were likewise thrown into disarray. The Brahimi mission had difficulty in consulting the necessary range of stakeholders on the formation of an interim government. Many of the CPA headquarters around the country had been shut down under siege. CPA officials and private contractors were now at unprecedented risk of assassination or kidnapping if they traveled outside the fortified zones of safety. Supply chains dried up as trucking became perilous. Two major contractors, General Electric and Siemens, suspended their operations in Iraq. Thousands of workers for private contractors were confined to their quarters in the Green Zone, unable to repair power plants, water-treatment facilities, and other decaying infrastructure. With the insurgency reaching a new scope and ferocity, scores of Iraqi translators and support staff in the Green Zone stopped showing up to work. Disillusionment with the occupation mounted, as did anti-American sentiment throughout the country.[28] "Four American people were killed in Fallujah," said an Iraqi shop owner in Baghdad. "Because of that, 500 people were killed in Fallujah. The message of the Americans is that 'we have the power.' Iraqis will never accept that."[29]

On April 19, the first outlines of a longer-term deal in Fallujah surfaced. American forces would end their offensive, relax their cordon of the city, and let local leaders pursue the killers of the four Blackwater security workers, if civic leaders would persuade insurgents to stop attacking the Marines and turn in their heavy weapons. At the same time, Sadr's militiamen continued their pullback from buildings they had seized, and the United States began to draw down the 2,500 troops it had rushed to the perimeter of Najaf. However, the prospects for peace quickly frayed. American commanders complained that the insurgents in Fallujah were not honoring their promise to hand over heavy weapons; exchanges of gunfire and shelling resumed; and on April 21, General Conway, of the First Marines, warned that a full-scale assault on the city could come soon. Two days later, in a lengthy television address to rally support from the Iraqi public, a grim Bremer vowed that the Coalition would do its part to restore security. "But you must do your part, too," he told the Iraqis. "If you do not defend your beloved country, it will not be saved." Yet senior American officers knew the risks of a military solution in Fallujah. "We have the potential to turn this into the Alamo if we get it wrong," said one.[30]

In Fallujah, the United States faced an impossible dilemma, for which there would be no decisive answer until it emptied and destroyed the city later in the year. If it launched an invasion, it risked massive civilian casualties and a disastrous political backlash—not only in Iraq but regionally—that might derail the transition and recruit many more fighters for the insurgency. On the other hand, the security of the entire country and the credibility and resolve of the Coalition were on the line, and the insurgents were emboldened by each new delay and retreat. Fallujah had become a base of the violent resistance, a factory for roadside and car bombs, and a haven for terrorists, including (it was believed) the worst foreign jihadists, such as Abu Musab al-Zarqawi, the diabolical engineer of many car bombings. Most American military commanders believed that the insurgency could be eliminated or contained only with a series of large-scale assaults. Every option had a compelling logic and a dreadful downside. As one senior American official lamented in Washington, "All the choices are unpalatable."[31]

On Sunday, April 25, with Iraqi leaders urging more time for a peaceful settlement in Fallujah, and with top American officials nervous about the political and military risks of an assault, U.S. commanders once again postponed the assault and announced that they would attempt to conduct joint patrols of the city with Iraqi security forces. This represented, said General Kimmitt in Baghdad, a shift to a "political track." Similarly, a political solution would continue to be pursued in Najaf. Military officials privately expressed skepticism, however, expecting that the Fallujah insurgents would fire on the joint patrols. And, in fact, the new plan was essentially derailed the next day when insurgents, violating the cease-fire, attacked the Marines from a mosque in Fallujah, and the Marines responded with heavy air support, toppling the mosque's minaret. Fighting and air strikes continued through the subsequent two days. But in Najaf, a hopeful sign came as residents grew disgusted with the presence of Sadr's fighters—who were reviled among the locals as thieves, thugs, fanatics, and drug addicts—and began launching vigilante attacks, killing five insurgents.

On April 29, the standoff in Fallujah was broken when General Conway, taking the initiative, brokered a deal in which responsibility for security in the city would be handed over to a new 1,000-man Iraqi militia, the Fallujah Protection Army (later renamed the Fallujah Brigade), headed by former Iraqi Army officers and staffed by former soldiers. In return, the Marines were to withdraw from the city and from their frontline positions surrounding it, lifting the monthlong siege. The expectation, expressed by one Marine officer, was that the new militia, which would be subordinate to the First Marines and would report to General Conway, would be "committed to fighting and maintaining the peace in Fallujah." The reality would prove very different. The Marines did withdraw, but the city remained an operational base of violent resistance. Within a few days, the Iraqi general the Americans selected had to be replaced because of alleged involvement in repression under Saddam. Within a month, the Fallujah Brigade would be camped outside the city in tents and the police would be cowering in their patrol cars while masked insurgents ran the city.[32] The heavy guns would not be surrendered, the foreign fighters would not be captured, and the killers of the four Blackwater contractors would not be apprehended. Across the Sunni heartland, hatred of the United States would harden as radical Sunni clerics extended their influence. But for the time being, the military confrontation in Fallujah had ended with what some outside observers called a "face-saving solution."

April had been a cruel month for the United States military in Iraq, claiming, in all, the lives of 130 American soldiers (122 in combat). This number was more than had died in combat and about as many dead overall as during the six-week invasion to topple Saddam's regime. Iraqi casualties were much higher, probably more than 1,000 dead, and by no

means only from American fire, for the terrorist war on Iraqis continued unabated.

★

Back in the United States, I watched with anger and sadness as much of
what I and many other people had been working for in Iraq unraveled.
In mid-April, I wrote to the head of the Governance Office, Scott Carpenter, telling him I would not be returning to Iraq as scheduled the
following week. With the dramatic deterioration in the security situation, I would clearly not be able to leave the Green Zone to meet and
talk with Iraqis about democracy, which was one of the main points of
my being there. I did not tell Carpenter, but I felt that since my advice
did not count for much within the CPA, engaging Iraqis directly was
the *only* purpose that could justify the risks of returning. I left open the
possibility of returning later if the security situation improved, but I privately suspected that my service as a CPA adviser was over. Still, I felt I
had something to offer, and something I owed to the friend who had
asked me to go to Iraq in the first place—Condoleezza Rice. On April
26, I sent her a long, confidential memorandum offering my views. I
titled the memo "Stabilizing the Situation in Iraq." It began:

> During the past month, the prospect for a successful transition in
> Iraq has deteriorated significantly. The current crisis is fed by but
> also overshadows serious political problems we confront. These
> derive most of all from the enormous legitimacy deficit of our oc-
> cupation, and also from fears that the U.S. intends to remain in
> Iraq indefinitely. If we do not find ways to enhance the legitimacy,
> or at least popular acceptability, of the political process, and to ease
> pervasive Iraqi suspicions and anxieties about American motives
> and intent, we will face a widening resistance that we will not be
> able to defeat militarily. We need a politically led strategy to con-
> tain the insurgency.

I congratulated the administration for reaching out to the United
Nations and for giving a substantial role to Brahimi in structuring the
transition, and for the recent decision to narrow the de-Baathification

campaign and thus make it possible for more civil servants to return to work. But I felt we needed to pursue a more comprehensive strategy to improve the political and security climate, and I made several recommendations. The first was that we should "disavow any long-term military aspirations in Iraq." The United States should clearly state to the Iraqi people and to the world that we would not seek permanent military bases in Iraq—one of the fears feeding the insurgency. Second, to take further steam out of the insurgency, I recommended establishing a target date for the withdrawal of our forces—even if it was three or four years down the line—again so Iraqis could see that the occupation would end at some point and that we were serious about leaving once the country was secure. Third, we must respond to the concerns about Iraqi detainees—at least give their families more information and more access. (This was two days before the prison abuse scandal at Abu Ghraib was revealed by CBS's *60 Minutes II*, and at the time I had no knowledge of those outrages.) I also suggested that we stop talking about the post–June 30 interim government as having only "limited sovereignty" and provide the level of authority necessary to make it credible and effective. And I reiterated a number of the recommendations on transitional issues that I had made in my final memo to Bremer: get more money flowing to our Iraqi allies (by paying the Governing Council members and security officials on time, and increasing their salaries); proceed vigorously with the plan to disarm, demobilize, and reintegrate the militias; invest in supporting moderate, secular Shiites; and establish a transparent political party fund to level the playing field.

My last recommendation, on which so much else depended, was this:

> We need to send significantly more troops and equipment. Perhaps it is already too late for this as well. But in my weeks in Iraq, I did not meet a single military officer who felt, privately, that we had enough troops. Many felt we needed (and need) tens of thousands more soldiers, and at this point (within the limits of the possible) at least another division or two. If we are going to secure the neighborhoods and roads and facilities, and create a minimally safe environment for voters to register and vote, for parties and

candidates to campaign, and for election observers to watch all of
this, we are going to need many, many more security forces than at
present—and many, many more armored cars, and other equipment. Hopefully some of this will result from accelerated training
of Iraqi Army and police units; there is a general feeling that police
training has been woefully slow and ineffective to date. Hopefully,
after the transfer of governing authority on June 30, more international actors will again contribute troops.

Then I concluded:

> I know many of these suggestions are difficult, and that the tone of
> this message is rather blunt. But I believe we are in serious and
> mounting danger of failing in Iraq. If we do not develop soon a co-
> herent counter-insurgency plan combining political and military,
> Iraqi and international initiatives, we will creep closer and closer
> to that tipping point, beyond which so many Iraqis sympathize
> with or join the insurgency that we cannot prevail at any bearable
> price.

To make sure that she received the memo, I contacted Rice's personal assistant. Yes, she told me, she had given Dr. Rice the memo, and
Ambassador Blackwill as well.

Since I never heard back from them, I don't know if any of my recommendations were seriously considered.

★

Muqtada al-Sadr's insurgency would drag on for many more weeks,
perhaps because he thought that the Americans would leave him in
control of Najaf, Karbala, and Kufa, in the same way they had drawn
back from a fight to root the insurgents out of Fallujah. But there were
big differences between the two rebellions. In contrast to Fallujah,
where the radical Islamist and Baathist insurgents were in firm control,
Sadr's forces were spread more thinly across a much wider terrain, and
had much less support from the local populations, who quickly lost all
patience with his fighters and the physical chaos and economic disloca-
tion they had wrought. Whereas Sunni Muslim clerics largely sympathized with the insurgency and united with Baath Party loyalists in its

cause, the most prestigious Shiite clerics increasingly signaled their contempt for Sadr and their desire to see his fighters leave the holy cities of Najaf and Karbala. While these senior clerics made clear that they did not want to see American forces in their cities either, their opposition quietly diminished as Sadr's intransigence and duplicity deepened. Many other Shiite figures were more open. "Najaf is not Mecca," said one tribal leader. If the Americans wanted to "get rid of criminals and thieves," he was all for it.[33] Even as Sadr mobilized antipathy toward the American occupation, while exploiting a wave of popular outrage over the prison abuse scandal at Abu Ghraib, antipathy toward Sadr's own occupation of Shiite cities grew.

As Sadr and his captains rebuffed the appeals of Shiite clerics and politicians to withdraw their fighters from the holy cities and disband their militia, American forces went on the attack, slowly closing in on the core strongholds of the Mahdi Army. The assault began on May 5, when American troops struck at Sadr's enclaves in Karbala and Diwaniyah. In the Karbala attack, the tragedy of the past several weeks turned to farce when 450 American soldiers in armored vehicles crashed through a neighborhood amusement park to an area near the Ferris wheel and bumper car ride, where the Mahdi Army had been storing weapons. In a heavy firefight, they killed an Iraqi "who had been lobbing grenades from the area of the pirate ship ride," as the *New York Times* reported.[34] Over the next several weeks, numerous attacks followed in Kufa, Karbala, Najaf, Amarah, Nasariyah, and Sadr City, as U.S. troops gradually routed the Mahdi Army, destroyed its urban headquarters, seized large caches of its weapons, and reclaimed strategic buildings. Hundreds of Sadr's fighters were killed, but only a few Americans. With heavy weaponry and increasing guile, Sadr's militiamen fought back and staged attacks of their own, but they were no match for the Americans, with their training, technology, and awesome firepower.[35]

The military victory over Sadr, however, was very much an Iraqi victory as well. Throughout the South Central region in the spring of 2004, Iraqi tribes played a major role in defeating the Mahdi Army. When much of the regular police deserted the fight in al-Qadisiyya Province, Governor Hazem Shaalan (who would become defense minister in the interim government that succeeded the occupation) personally led fighters from his al-Khuza'i tribe in battle, thus preventing the province from falling. In Babel Province, the Witwit tribe and the Bani Hasan tribal confederation rallied against Sadr's forces. Sheikh Ahmad Khabut al-Abbasi Bani Hasan, the mayor of al-Kifl, who had been my host when I visited the town and the Shrine of Ezekiel in March, led his tribesmen in three days of fierce fighting against the Mahdi Army and defeated them. Thanks to the efforts of the tribes in Babel, Sadr's forces in Najaf were never able to link up with their fellow fighters in Karbala—a development that might have made his insurgency unstoppable.[36] A former CPA official later observed that these Iraqis "were willing to fight to the death at the Coalition's side to defend the idea of a democratic future for Iraq. They recognized that Sadr was trying to establish another ruthless dictatorship and they mobilized to stop him."

On the propaganda front, Sadr and his forces tried to foment a mass Shiite uprising against the occupation forces, screaming at one point on the streets of Najaf, "They are Jews! They are Jews!" But those tactics fell short as well. On May 18, after Sadr appealed to Iraqis to come to his aid in Najaf, Sistani quickly issued his own statement, calling on all forces to leave Najaf and urging his fellow Shiites not to join the uprising. The American military now seemed to have implicit consent from Ayatollah Sistani and other Shiite religious leaders to root out Sadr's insurgents, provided they did not attack or damage the three Shiite holy shrines of the Imam Husayn and the Imam Abbas in Karbala and the Imam Ali in Najaf. As the days went by, the fighting drew nearer to the shrines, which the Mahdi Army tried but failed to seize (thanks to local guards from within the mosques and discreetly placed American snipers outside). From the precincts and gravesites of the shrines, Sadr's forces fired at American troops, hoping to lure them into a disastrous misfire that would rally masses of Shiites to their cause. But with clear instructions, strong discipline, and sophisticated targeting, the Americans avoided the political catastrophe of attacking or damaging the shrines. When it was over and Sadr's forces were evicted, a journalist would find, "The blue and white marble and tile walls that surround the Hussein Shrine were pocked by a handful of bullet holes. And yet less than 50 yards away, entire buildings had been obliterated."[37]

By late May, Sadr's decimated forces had largely withdrawn from Karbala, as if melting away in the night. They left behind a shattered city center, a wrecked local economy, and a community as disgusted with them as they were with the American occupation. U.S. forces then closed in on Sadr in Kufa, his home base, and tightened pressure on his forces in Najaf. Increasingly isolated politically, and with hundreds of his fighters dead, Sadr agreed, on May 27, to a deal with Iraqi leaders, approved by U.S. officials (under pressure from Sistani). Sadr would pull his forces off the streets of Najaf and Kufa, withdraw his nonresident fighters from both cities, and close down his Sharia courts, while the Americans would withdraw most of their forces from the two cities as well. Sadr was not required to surrender or disarm, though the CPA would not admit this publicly.[38]

Sporadic bloody clashes persisted for a week, and by late June, as more-moderate Shiite figures tried to draw him into the political process, Sadr endorsed the Iraqi interim government and ordered his fighters to put down their arms and go home to their provinces.

Sadr's insurgency thus came to a temporary end in an informal truce. For a time, a certain uneasy normalcy returned to the Shiite cities, as the police reasserted authority and people struggled to revive economic and religious life. Despite repeated American vows to kill or arrest Sadr and dismantle his Mahdi Army, he remained free, and his militia, though badly defeated, survived.

9

HANDING OVER

★

On April 4, the UN special envoy Lakhdar Brahimi returned to Baghdad to begin the delicate task of constructing the interim government, to which the CPA would hand over governing authority on June 30. The Transitional Administrative Law (TAL) had defined the structure and powers of the authority that would rule until a government was elected under a permanent constitution, by the end of 2005. But with the compromise that Brahimi had forged in February, deferring elections for the transitional parliament until the end of 2004 or early 2005, some means had to be found to constitute an interim caretaker government that would serve as a bridge between the June 30 handover and the transitional elections, probably in January 2005. The nature of this interim body also had to be defined. Once agreed upon, provisions for the interim government were to be codified in an annex to the TAL.

It was to be Brahimi's first trip back to Iraq following his mediation with Sistani in early February. The Bush administration considered his involvement vital if the interim authority was to have the international and domestic legitimacy it would need to govern postwar Iraq, prepare the country for elections, and reduce the nation's crippling international debt. "We're very dependent on him to develop a plan—and then to help legitimize it among Iraqis," a senior State Department official conceded in late March. "This is a time-sensitive process, and time's not something we have a lot of."[1] The White House and the CPA understood, too, that the UN's administrative expertise and international credibility were essential in helping to prepare Iraq for the January 2005 elections.

The Governing Council, however, did not see it that way. The core of the council's Shiite caucus—which included Ahmed Chalabi, Abdul-Aziz al-Hakim, Ibrahim al-Jaafari, and Muhammad Bahr al-Uloum—strongly resisted Brahimi's return. These Shiite leaders worried that as a Sunni Muslim who had been a moderate Arab nationalist through his long career, Brahimi would seek to ease de-Baathification provisions and to give more power to Sunnis in the transitional government—and that Brahimi would largely sideline them in the interim government, in favor of new political leaders. Seeking to preserve their dominance after June 30, they judged that their best option was to craft the interim government themselves in direct negotiations with the Americans.

The UN was ready to return to Iraq to mediate the transitional challenge and to help prepare the country for elections—but not without a formal letter of invitation from the Iraqis. "We are not begging for a role, but if we are needed, we will help," Brahimi said on March 16.[2] As the Americans pressed the Governing Council to issue a letter to the United Nations inviting Ambassador Brahimi to return, the Shiite hardliners dug in their heels. Seeking to fan support for their cause, they sought to impugn Brahimi's reputation with whispers and photographs implying he had once had friendly visits with Saddam—a charge that could have disqualified a wide swath of international diplomats and politicians from playing a role in Iraq, including a number of Americans. At the same time, the UN was struggling with more serious stains on its reputation. Reports suggesting massive corruption surrounding the UN-supervised oil-for-food program, which had enabled Iraq to sell $10 billion a year in oil in order to import food and other essentials during the sanctions on Saddam's regime, were circulating. And in early March, an independent investigative panel appointed by Kofi Annan found that lapses in the UN security management had contributed to the death toll in the August 2003 bombing of the world body's Baghdad mission.

In anticipation of Brahimi's imminent arrival, and to escalate pressure on the Governing Council to issue the requested invitation, Condoleezza Rice's NSC deputy for Iraq policy, Robert Blackwill, arrived in Baghdad on March 13. The plan was for him to stay for several weeks to help guide the discussions on the construction of the interim government, but he was also to shadow Brahimi, as a way to get information and assert American interests. Blackwill joined Bremer in pressuring the Governing Council members to invite the UN back. "We are trying to get the Governing Council to cough up a letter," one U.S. official put it bluntly.[3] On March 16, after several days of stalemate, the problem seemed to ease when the UN announced that Ayatollah Sistani had sent a letter to Secretary-General Annan, dissociating himself from reports that the Shiites did not want a return of the UN mission. The next morning, in a tense meeting with the Governing Council, Bremer warned the members of a "confrontation" with the United States if they did not come up with the letter. Several hours later, the body produced a draft letter to Annan, asking the UN to assist Iraq in forming an interim government and holding elections by January for a transitional government. The letter was not overflowing with enthusiasm, but it was good enough. Annan replied in letters to the Governing Council and to the CPA that Brahimi would lead the delegation to Iraq.

The following day, March 19, the political game shifted once again when Sistani's office wrote to Brahimi and informed him that the grand ayatollah would not consent to any meetings with him unless the Security Council agreed not to impose the TAL on a newly elected transitional assembly. With this letter, Sistani was signaling that he did not intend to drop his principled objections to the interim constitution and that when he relented and permitted the key Shiite members of the Governing Council to sign the document on March 8, his concession had been purely tactical. Sistani's letter came in response to information—entirely accurate—that the United States planned to seek formal recognition of the TAL in the next Security Council resolution on Iraq, which would also endorse the interim government and the transition process. The Kurds considered UN recognition of the TAL to be vital in nailing down their autonomy within the federal system. But it was precisely such entrenchment that Sistani opposed, believing, as he had repeatedly declared, that an unelected body could not bind an elected body. A UN endorsement of the TAL, Sistani advised, "would not be accepted by the general public of Iraq, and it would have serious consequences in the future."

★

As Brahimi prepared to return to Iraq, American officials in Baghdad and Washington were busy debating options for how the interim government would be appointed and what its structure and powers would be. The discussions were not meant to confine Brahimi, as Meghan O'Sullivan explained in a March 20 staff meeting. "We want the UN to engage on this," O'Sullivan said. "We are going to take more of a partnership approach with the Brahimi team this time." And if Brahimi was going to consider all points of view, surely one perspective he would want to weigh would be the CPA's.

There were basically four options for constituting the interim government. The simplest one—and the one that the leading members of the Governing Council most strongly supported—was to convert the council into the interim government, letting the twenty-five-member body select all of the officials and then constitute a limited legislative body. A variant of this approach was to expand the Governing Council modestly, perhaps by another ten to twenty-five members (or, under some scenarios, to a total of seventy-five or one hundred). The question was, then, who would choose the additional members. The Governing Council, of course, had a ready answer: "We will do so." Blackwill and some other American officials envisioned an expansion to no more than fifty, with the new members selected jointly by the existing Governing Council, the CPA, and the UN. A second option, suggested by some CPA officials, particularly from the regional offices, would incorporate a role for the provincial and local councils. Each provincial council and the biggest local ones might choose (in proportion to its province's share of the population) members of a selection body that would then pick the interim prime minister, cabinet, president, and deputy presidents. One regional coordinator suggested that all the provincial governors simply be added to the Governing Council. There were two more broadly participatory options, rumored to be the ones that Brahimi and his closest advisers favored. One would constitute a national conference—a kind of "mini–Loya Jirga," on the analogy of the 1,500-member traditional-style assembly that selected the interim government in Afghanistan. This option raised the question of how the delegates to the national conference would themselves be chosen—and whether the gathering could meet in time to select an interim government before June 30. Those who liked the concept but doubted the practicalities urged a fourth option: a smaller roundtable dialogue of some thirty to one hundred key stakeholders from around the country. But this approach also raised the thorny question of selection.

Although the Bush administration (through Blackwill) vigorously pressed the option of expanding the Governing Council, Bremer was more sensitive to the inefficacy and legitimacy problems of the council, and open to alternatives that would put it out of business. Bremer understood, and repeatedly made clear, that the interim government would have to be more representative than the Governing Council had been. What neither the U.S. government nor Bremer wished to see, however, was any kind of standing legislative body in the interim government. At a meeting of the Coalition's military and civilian leaders from around the country on March 26, Bremer explained that most Iraqis wanted the unelected interim government to have a limited scope of authority. But, in addition, he (and his superiors in Washington) worried about "the potential for this body [an interim legislature] to pass resolutions that could be very harmful to Coalition interests—such as calling for the withdrawal of the Coalition." For this reason, top American officials were wary of a significant expansion of the Governing Council (to anything more than about fifty members), or of a national conference that might veer out of control and challenge the U.S. presence in Iraq.

The opposition to a legislative branch contradicted a position that the Governance Office had staked out in two memos to Bremer, one in February (after we had gotten wind of Brahimi's idea of having a caretaker government installed before a transitional government could be elected), and the second on March 22 (written in collaboration with the CPA's Office of the General Counsel). We worried about the implications, even for six or seven months, of having an interim government that was not accountable to anybody (except, informally, to the Americans). Thus we emphasized the importance of having institutional checks and balances during the interim period, to deter the possible abuse of power by the interim government and especially the prime minister. While some checks could be exercised within the executive branch, we felt (going back to classic constitutional principles) that separate branches of government were needed, including a legislature or a "consultative council." (I was among those who also favored at least temporary appointment of supreme court judges for this purpose as well.) Bremer had spoken explicitly about the need for checks on the powers of the interim government, but he did not see the contradiction between that principle and his opposition to a legislative body. Following what we (and the UN) had been hearing from Iraqis, we stressed that a consultative body—and the interim government itself—ought to have limited powers. It should not be able to tamper with the TAL, adopt any treaties or agreements that would bind Iraq beyond the interim period, or otherwise alter the country's legal and economic structure. Such alterations required the legitimacy of an elected body. We even suggested borrowing from Sistani's language forbidding the interim council to take decisions "that would affect the destiny of Iraq."

Back in March, some of us in the palace sought to make the process of selecting the interim authority as democratic and participatory as possible, if the government was to have the breadth, legitimacy, and popular support it would need in tackling the tough challenges ahead. We therefore pondered ways of convening a national conference that would elect the key interim leaders. Our thinking was shaped by dozens of conversations that CPA officials had had, in the preceding weeks, with a wide range of Iraqis, who strongly favored a national conference to play this role, which would also foster national reconciliation. Many of these conversations were conducted by Thomas Warrick, the career diplomat who had organized the Future of Iraq Project at the State Department and who was now in Baghdad working with the CPA's Office of Provincial Outreach. In late March, Warrick pulled together the various ideas into a plan for a national conference, with participants chosen from across Iraq in the following manner: 400 to be elected by the provincial councils in numbers proportional to each province's population; 230 by broad-based professional associations and labor unions that drew from all ethnic and regional groups, in elections supervised by Iraqi judges; 250 by women's groups; 50 by tribal representatives selected by the CPA and UN in consultation with tribal leaders; and 30 by ethnic minorities. Rounding out the conference would be the 25 Governing Council members and 20 people appointed by Brahimi and Bremer to ensure overall balance. The large size of the national conference—1,005 participants—offered greater scope for ensuring a broadly representative body. But there was another consideration as well. A body of 1,000 members (or even 700) would be too large to preserve itself as a standing representative council.

In the plan Warrick developed, the national conference would meet for three days at the end of May, with Bremer and Brahimi as cochairs, to elect a three-person presidency council. The council would then nominate a prime minister, who would, in turn, need to be approved by a majority of the conference. Just before the conference formally convened, the delegations from each province would meet separately in Baghdad for three days to prepare for the meeting and to interact with Bremer, Brahimi, and other CPA and UN officials. The plan offered two structural options: one without an interim legislative body, and one with it. Reviewing the pros and cons, Warrick recommended that the national conference elect a 200-member consultative council with strictly limited powers. It would be able to debate only legislation drafted and submitted by the prime minister; but as an unelected body, it could not address constitutional questions like federalism and the role of religion. However, it would provide a forum for discussion and a possible check on the prime minister.

The plan was daring in several respects. In particular, it promised to put the CPA under formidable time pressure. Warrick reasoned that if the plan could be refined and then agreed upon by April 16 (which was only about three weeks away), the final two weeks of April would provide time to prepare the selection procedures with the CPA, UN, and Iraqi staff, and then to have the various Iraqi bodies elect their delegates in the first half of May. Following those indirect elections, preparations could be made to send all the delegates to Baghdad for the deliberations in late May. There was not much margin for delay here, as an interim prime minister would have to be selected by the beginning of June in order to assemble a cabinet and prepare it to assume governing authority on June 30.

I was impressed by the scope of Warrick's plan, and I liked it. In my dialogues with Iraqi groups and invididuals, I, too, had been hearing strong sentiment for a transparent, participatory political process, and specifically for some kind of national conference. The plan was risky—but the risks of not having an inclusive process were also great. Several of us in the palace met, debated, and tinkered with the composition and mechanics of the plan. In my view, any conference or selection body should meet the TAL's minimum goal of having women fill at least one-quarter of the seats. But I suggested that the provincial councils and professional bodies be required to select some minimum proportion of women among their delegates, rather than assuming that female delegates would be chosen only by women's groups. I also agreed with the proposal to have a legislative or advisory council, but by then top American officials seemed to have ruled out a standing representative body.

The plan to select the interim government through a representative national conference had significant support from among CPA and UN officials, as well as the enthusiastic backing of a variety of Iraqi groups and parties outside the Governing Council. But in the end, it fell flat—for three reasons. First, top administration officials in Washington didn't like it. Second, the Governing Council adamantly opposed it. And third, Brahimi himself was apprehensive about organizing a national conference and then having it select an interim government in so short a time. As a compromise, Brahimi's staff considered choosing the interim government through a smaller roundtable dialogue, which might draw fifteen Iraqis from the Governing Council and fifteen from alternative and opposition forces outside it. But Brahimi wasn't sure that the right people could be found to sit at the table, and, more important, U.S. officials rejected this option, too. As one participant who was close to the deliberations observed, "Washington wanted a clean outcome and to have control of the process. So we ended up with a process that was not transparent, choosing the interim government through backroom negotiations with the main players on the Governing Council." In the end, Brahimi and his team agreed to return to Iraq for a third round of consultations to select the leaders and ministers of the interim government, in "consultation" with the United States and the Governing Council.

As for the structure of the interim government, Brahimi opposed having a legislative component; like Ayatollah Sistani, he and his UN colleagues believed that major decisions should be deferred until the country had a sovereign, legitimate government, chosen by the Iraqi people. At the conclusion of his initial mission to Iraq, in February, Brahimi had stressed that the interim government would be a temporary, provisional body and, therefore, would not have extensive powers. In the written report of his fact-finding mission, Brahimi hinted further at what he had in mind, through his Socratic method of posing a question based on what Iraqis had suggested to him: "Many Iraqis have queried whether a legislative assembly would even be necessary during a short transition period. Would it not be simpler and more effective to develop consensus on establishing a provisional, caretaker government, with clear and limited powers [to prepare the country for elections and manage the country during the interim period]?" In addition, he noted, "many Iraqis further stressed that what is needed is a broad-based government that is not based on [ethnic] quotas, one that ideally would be primarily composed of competent technocrats."[4]

These were the key elements of the interim government with which Brahimi left Iraq in February and returned on April 4. His consultations over the subsequent ten days confirmed, for him and his advisers, the outlines of what they had established. In a press conference on April 14, Brahimi laid out his thoughts. The interim government would have an executive structure like the elected transitional government that was to follow it: a prime minister and a council of ministers, a president to act as head of state, and two vice presidents. As for the ministers, Brahimi restated his preference for a technocratic government not based on parties or ethnic quotas; it should consist, he said, of "Iraqi men and women known for their honesty, integrity, and competence." Without going into details on the process, Brahimi said the interim government would be chosen "in a timely manner, i.e., during the month of May 2004." He underscored, again, the limited, temporary character of the interim government, noting that Iraq would have "a genuinely

representative government" only after January 2005. "There is no substitute for the legitimacy that comes from free and fair elections," he
said.[5] The UN electoral team would assist that process, but urgent steps
were required on the Iraqi side.

The idea of a national conference was not completely jettisoned;
rather, it was transformed from a means for choosing a government before the handover into a less risky deliberation that "could take place
soon after the restoration of sovereignty, in July 2004." Such a conference, Brahimi said, "would serve the all-important aim of promoting
national dialogue, consensus building and national reconciliation in
Iraq." In a concession to those who felt that an advisory body was
needed outside the executive branch, Brahimi announced that the conference would elect a consultative assembly. As for the Governing
Council, it would "cease to exist on 30 June 2004." To many Iraqis who
watched Brahimi's press conference live on television, the plan seemed
promising, but still they worried. As one Iraqi told a reporter, "It
sounds good. But how strong is Brahimi? How strong is the UN?"[6]

The broad structure of the interim government had now been set.
The Governing Council would not be preserved, much less expanded,
as Washington had sought. The new government would largely be a
new cast of nonpolitical technocrats—or at least that is how Brahimi
envisioned it. There would be a national conference and a consultative
assembly, but only after the handover. This approach would allow time
to prepare for the selection of these bodies while greatly reducing the
political risk to the United States. It was the kind of pragmatic compromise that Brahimi had become known for, and the next day Condoleezza Rice and Colin Powell hastened to endorse the plan.[7] And a
day later, President Bush and British Prime Minister Tony Blair, meeting in Washington, enthusiastically did the same. Bush also took the opportunity to explain, finally, to the confused American people how the
interim government would be chosen: It would be "decided by Mr.
Brahimi."[8]

However, at his April 14 press conference, Brahimi had a few
thoughts to express that may not have been quite so welcome to the administration. In addition to the preparations for the interim government and the elections, he said, "confidence building measures" ought

to be undertaken. During his April consultations, as in February, Brahimi and his team heard numerous grievances about detainees being held without charge or trial. "They should be either charged or released, and their families and lawyers must have access to them," he declared. Furthermore, the scope of de-Baathification had to be reconsidered. "It is difficult to understand," he said, "that thousands upon thousands of teachers, university professors, medical doctors and hospital staff, engineers and other professionals who are needed, have been dismissed within the de-Baathification process, and far too many of those cases have yet to be reviewed."[9] Finally, in his view, the status of former military personnel required attention. The Governing Council did not dispute Brahimi's recommendations on the interim government, but several members vowed to resist any effort to trim de-Baathification.

Other questions and controversies remained. How much power would the interim government have? And what would become of Bremer's decrees? They now had the force of law. If the interim government could not adopt any laws, then it could not amend or remove Bremer's decrees—a dramatic diminution of its authority. And if it could not exercise some power over the foreign forces on its soil, how could it be said to possess sovereignty? In late April, Bush administration officials testified before Congress that the interim government would be receiving only "limited sovereignty," including partial control over its armed forces and no authority to enact laws.[10] But it quickly became apparent that such constraints would not fare well in Iraq or in the international community, and the administration dropped the word "limited" in front of "sovereignty."

★

While the structure of the interim government was now more or less defined, the leadership positions still needed to be filled. To complete this delicate task, Lakhdar Brahimi and his team of advisers returned to Baghdad in early May. The subsequent month would be the longest and most trying phase of their effort to mediate the transition in Iraq, filled with complex negotiations, political posturing, personal betrayal, and Machiavellian scheming for power.

The most difficult challenge was the selection of the interim prime minister, the most powerful leader in the new government. The position was expected to go to a Shiite, given the group's demographic weight in the country and political clout in the transitional arrangements. But the question was who? Three members of the Governing Council maneuvered intensely for the job: SCIRI's chief political operator and second-in-command, Adel Abdel Mahdi; the Da'wa leader Ibrahim Jaafari; and Ayad Allawi, the former Baathist leader of the London-based Iraqi National Accord, who was widely known to have been paid for many years by the CIA. (By this time, the fourth major Shiite power broker, Ahmed Chalabi, had alienated many of his colleagues and had fallen sharply out of favor with U.S. authorities, who would order his home and party headquarters raided, on May 20, in search of evidence of fraud and other crimes.) Brahimi, however, had repeatedly made clear his desire for a government of nonpolitical technocrats, and in speaking to the Security Council on April 27 (shortly before his return to Iraq), he said that the leading officials of the interim government should separate themselves from partisan politics by agreeing not to be candidates in the coming elections. For the three Shiite party leaders, such an act of self-sacrifice was hard to imagine. Shortly thereafter, in the first of a constant stream of leaks and speculations that formed part of the intricate political game, the *New York Times* reported that the UN favored Iraq's planning minister, Dr. Mehdi al-Hafidh, a well-respected Shiite and a member of Adnan Pachachi's Iraqi Independent Democrats, to be the next prime minister. But Hafidh, a former Communist and fiercely secular, was unacceptable to the critical Shiite religious parties, and thus became an early casualty of the maneuvering.

As Brahimi arrived in Baghdad to begin consultations, several factors started to complicate his work: the behind-the-scenes involvement of the strong-willed Robert Blackwill; the campaign of key Shiite members of the Governing Council to undermine and discredit Brahimi; the Governing Council's further bid to establish itself as the final arbiter of the major choices and to perpetuate itself as a legislative body after June 30; and then, later in the month, the Kurds' insistence that they be given one of the two top jobs (president or prime minister). Because many Governing Council members were petrified of being left without a position in the interim government, they proposed that the council be rekindled as an interim, lawmaking national body, which would have control over the budget and the right to appoint cabinet members. Here, Brahimi and the United States saw eye to eye in rebuffing the proposal. But other matters did not go so smoothly.

During April and the early part of May, Brahimi and his team consulted energetically with a range of Iraqi civic groups, to include these outside constituencies in the selection process from beginning to end. But when the negotiations to form the interim government entered their final phase, in late May, only three parties were at the table: the UN, the CPA, and the Governing Council—and the council, with its core of gifted and cynical power players, proved a surprisingly adept and tenacious player. In keeping with his search for a nonpartisan interim government, Brahimi had settled on an intriguing choice for prime minister: Dr. Hussein Sharistani, a sixty-two-year-old nuclear chemist who had spent ten years in Abu Ghraib prison for refusing Saddam Hussein's demand that he develop a nuclear weapons program. Sharistani was appealing, as well, because he was a religious Shiite, close to Ayatollah Sistani, who nevertheless was considered politically moderate and sophisticated. In addition, he had built up a popular following in Najaf and Basra through extensive charitable work in those cities. For several days, Sharistani seemed to be the pick, and on May 25 he expressed a reluctant willingness to "serve my people."[11] Then, the next day, he withdrew, with a spokesman for Brahimi stating, in some of the classic diplomatic verse of the drama, that Sharistani had "clarified that he would prefer to serve his country in other ways."[12] In fact, Sharistani had been vetoed by all the powerful forces on the Governing Council. The Kurds and the Sunnis saw him as too religious, and perhaps too close to Sistani. And the three leading Shiite players— SCIRI, Da'wa, and Allawi—claimed he was inexperienced, which was another way of saying they wanted the job for themselves. "They feel they are a kind of club, and this was a person who is outside their club," said an Iraqi official close to Sharistani.[13]

With Sharistani out, the three remaining candidates for prime minister were Mahdi, Jaafari, and Allawi. Neither of the two Shiite religious parties, SCIRI and Da'wa, would yield for the other, and in any case neither the Americans nor Brahimi was eager to have an interim prime minister from their ranks. This left Allawi—who was Blackwill's favored candidate from the beginning—as the last man standing. The Kurds liked him because he was secular; they were opposed to a prime minister from one of the religious parties, which they did not trust to preserve their minority rights. The Sunnis also found him more palatable than the Shiite religious politicians who, they feared, would press for greater political dominance. Sistani found Allawi acceptable, at least. Egypt and Jordan, crucial regional allies of the United States, had good relations with him. And the Bush administration itself was enthusiastic in its support. After all, Allawi had spent years on the U.S. payroll and could be trusted (to a degree that few other Iraqi leaders could) not to go against America's most vital interests. And so, as one person who was part of the negotiations told me, "We wound up with the lowest common denominator between the Kurds and the religious parties."

By Friday, May 28, the drama had run its course. The Governing Council was informed that Allawi was the choice for prime minister of the interim government, and they unanimously endorsed it.[14] The decision was made by Blackwill and Bremer and reluctantly accepted by Brahimi. In an unguarded moment during a telephone interview the next day, Brahimi said, "You know, sometimes people think I am a free agent out here, that I have a free hand to do whatever I want."[15] Later, at his final press conference in Baghdad, he was more direct in answering a question about the process of selecting the prime minister: "I'm sure he doesn't mind my saying it—Mr. Bremer is the dictator of Iraq. He has the money. He has the signature. Nothing happens without his agreement in this country."[16]

As the selection of the prime minister entered its final phase, maneuvering intensified in the search for a president and two deputy presidents, largely ceremonial posts for which, Brahimi felt, it would not be unreasonable to appoint party politicians. Though a much less powerful position than the post of prime minister, the presidency in particular was coveted by several groups and individuals for its symbolic stature and informal leverage, which some Iraqi political blocs thought could be forged into de facto power. It had long been assumed by many, inside and outside Iraq, that since the post of prime minister was going to a Shiite, a Sunni Arab would be selected as president, with a Kurd and a Shiite each taking one of the deputy slots. The Sunni that many Iraqis and outside observers expected to get the job was Adnan Pachachi, who had impressed CPA officials and many Iraqis with his statesmanship and integrity during the preceding ten months, and especially during the difficult process of drafting the interim constitution. Pachachi also enjoyed considerable respect among Iraqi professional and civil society groups who stood outside the big political parties. For these reasons, Brahimi resolved to offer him the presidency.

Again, however, the UN envoy encountered resistance. Although Bremer (who personally admired Pachachi) was neutral, and insisted, throughout, that he was representing the American position, Robert Blackwill had a different agenda.[17] He told several members of the Governing Council not to support Pachachi, and his staff began floating the name of Ghazi al-Yawer, a forty-five-year-old, American-educated engineer who was the nephew of the leader of the powerful Shammar tribe; Yawer currently held the monthly presidency of the Governing Council. (The State Department was apparently unaware of Blackwill's machinations.)[18] By then, powerful political forces on the council—led by Ahmed Chalabi, a nemesis of Pachachi's since before the war—were already opposing Pachachi for the presidency. To Kurdish members, he was an Arab nationalist who had not been supportive enough of their bid for federalist devolution of power; moreover, the Kurdish leader Jalal Talabani wanted the job himself. Key Shiite members feared that Pachachi, with his international reputation and connections, might draw too much effective power to the presidency, overshadowing the Shiite prime minister. They also liked the fact that Yawer was prominent in the Shammar tribe, which spans the Sunni-Shiite divide. I can only speculate why Blackwill backed Yawer instead of Pachachi, but his views may well have reflected the neoconservatives' campaign against Pachachi for not actively backing the efforts of Iraqi exile groups to overthrow Saddam, for his association with other Arab regimes in the Persian Gulf, and for not resisting Arab criticism of Israeli policies in the Middle East. Typical of the type of attacks was a column by William Safire in the *New York Times* that dismissed Pachachi as "having long been in the pocket of the Saudi royals" and "receiving instructions from Sunni central," by which he meant the Arab League.[19]

By late May, Yawer was actively maneuvering for the position; he suggested, for example, that Pachachi was too old for the job, even though he outworked colleagues half his age and did not intend to serve in the position beyond the seven-month interim period. In openly challenging Pachachi for the presidency, Yawer turned on the very man who had helped to promote him politically. When the Governing Council had been constituted the previous July, Pachachi took the relatively youthful, politically inexperienced Yawer—who had been running a cell phone company in Saudi Arabia before the war—under his wing. In April, when the Governing Council's presidency council had completed the monthly rotation among its nine members, Pachachi had suggested adding two names to hold the post for the final two months—Ezzedine Salim (who would be murdered in a car bombing in May) and Yawer. Had Yawer waited, he stood to inherit Pachachi's liberal mantle and support for the presidency in the transitional period. But with the apparent backing of Washington, he decided to go for the prize immediately, and won the nearly unanimous backing of the Governing Council, whose power brokers complained to the foreign press that in their endorsement of Pachachi, Brahimi and Bremer were trying to impose a president on them. For several days, the announcement of the interim government was delayed as the various parties sought to resolve the standoff.

This time, however, Brahimi did not yield. He was convinced that Pachachi was the more deserving choice, with wider support and respect from the Iraqi public. Early in the morning of June 1, Brahimi and Bremer informed a visibly upset Yawer that their choice for the presidency was Pachachi. Shortly thereafter, Brahimi offered Pachachi the position. By then, however, Pachachi felt he had been so undermined by the Americans and by his colleagues on the Governing Council that he could not operate effectively in the position, and he declined it. "The president should be a force for unity, not division," he reportedly told Brahimi.[20] Frustrated again, Brahimi offered the position to

Yawer, who readily accepted. Ironically, press reports had framed the outcome as one of the Governing Council resisting American pressure in order to choose an interim president who was "more independent and less supportive of U.S. policies," but to the extent that any of these considerations really mattered, the reverse was nearer the truth.[21] In his public statement, the bruised Pachachi could only insist, "I was never the occupation's candidate."[22]

The Governing Council also flexed its muscles in determining other key appointments. The two Shiite religious parties each got a high-profile position. Da'wa's Ibrahim Jaafari was named as one of the vice presidents, and SCIRI's Adel Abdel Mahdi got the finance ministry. As expected, the Kurds got the other vice presidential slot, which was filled by KDP leader Massoud Barzani's deputy Rowsch Shaways. To placate the Kurds for their failure to obtain one of the top two posts, a new position of deputy prime minister, with responsibility for foreign and defense policy, was created at the last minute, and given to a high-ranking PUK leader, Barham Salih (who had been expected to become foreign minister). Another prominent Kurdish figure, Hoshyar Zubari, was retained as foreign minister, while the prominent Shiite tribal leader Hazem Shaalan, who had heroically rallied resistance to the Mahdi Army in al-Qadisiyya Province in the spring, was named defense minister.[23] Beyond the politically sensitive top posts, the thirty-two ministers were chosen largely by Brahimi and his team on the criteria he had sought to impose on the entire interim government: integrity, professional experience, and technical competence. Only six of those named had ties to large political parties. Iraqi ministers who were considered corrupt or poor performers were dropped from the cabinet, while those who had built up a record of accomplishment retained their jobs. The new oil minister, Thamir Abbas Ghadban, was a petroleum engineer and longtime ministry official who had been demoted under Saddam Hussein for supporting reforms. Significantly, not a single member of the interim government was a member of Ahmed Chalabi's party. That was one thing Brahimi and the Americans seemed to agree on.

On June 1, as the thirty-six-member interim government (including six women) was introduced, the Governing Council finalized the annex to the TAL. The structure of the interim government was largely as outlined by Brahimi on April 14, with a few refinements. The Council of Ministers was empowered to "issue orders with the force of law," if they received the unanimous approval of the presidency; that body was also temporarily assigned the powers of the national assembly to make appointments and approve international agreements, but the wording of this section appeared to rule out (though not explicitly) concluding a formal treaty. The interim national council, to be chosen in July by a national conference (which, in the event, would take place in August), was to be composed of one hundred members, including all the Governing Council members not holding positions in the interim government. Nineteen council members were thus automatically selected into the new body, giving them the status they had craved. The new council had vague monitoring authority, but also the power to veto, by a two-thirds vote, laws adopted by the Council of Ministers. Following on our earlier recommendations from the Governance Office, the annex did indeed forbid the interim government "from taking any actions affecting Iraq's destiny beyond the limited interim period." This constraint, it was hoped, would reassure critics of the government's legitimacy. With the completion of the last major steps on the path to the transfer of sovereignty, the Governing Council officially went out of business.

The June 1 ceremony announcing the interim government lacked the theatrical staging and emotional drama of the March 8 signing ceremony for the TAL. Drained by the months-long, ruthless campaign of assassinations and terrorist attacks, the last two months of guerrilla war, and the bruising political battles, the participants seemed more of a mind just to get on with it than to celebrate. Predictably, the milestone was marred by violence, as a car bomb exploded just outside the Green Zone, killing several and wounding dozens, while a mortar shell landed so close to the Convention Center "that it shook the walls and sent a white mushroom cloud spiraling upward," according to a report in the *New York Times*.[24]

Back in Washington, President Bush and national security adviser Rice effusively welcomed the new government. "I can tell you firmly and without any contradiction, this is a terrific list, a really good government, and we are very pleased with the names that have emerged," Rice said. "These are not America's puppets." Secretary-General Kofi

Annan was also welcoming but more circumspect. He acknowledged that "the process wasn't perfect and it was a difficult environment. . . . [G]iven the circumstances, I believe Mr. Brahimi did as best as he could."[25]

★

Among the tasks that remained in the final weeks of occupation rule, one of the most important was to secure a UN resolution blessing the transitional steps and interim arrangements and giving some legal basis for the continued presence of American and other international forces. Just hours after the interim government was announced, the White House circulated a draft of what would become Resolution 1546. With the handover near and the interim government selected, the negotiations lacked the stridency of previous UN debates. A particularly sensitive matter concerned the treatment of the TAL. Sistani had explicitly warned the UN—and implicitly the Americans—not to enshrine recognition of the TAL in a UN resolution. By now the Americans had learned that they would defy Sistani at their peril. The United States did not want a major crisis in the final weeks before the handover— especially now that the military confrontation with Muqtada al-Sadr was finally drawing to a close, thanks in part to Sistani's refusal to endorse the uprising. Thus, the draft resolution that Washington circulated omitted mention of the TAL, leaving its legal status ambiguous—to the dismay of the Kurds. The one point that the Kurdish leader Rowsch Shaways had stressed in his remarks at the June 1 ceremony was the necessity of observing the interim constitution, in order to preserve national unity.

As adopted unanimously by the Security Council on June 8, Resolution 1546 offered something for everyone. The United States and its Iraqi partners got the international endorsement they sought of the interim government and the remaining timetable and process for political transition. The Iraqis and those opposed to the American-led occupation got a clear statement that Iraq would be reasserting "its full sovereignty," with undiminished authority over all funds, finances, and resources. The United States received authorization for the "multinational force . . . to take all necessary measures to contribute to the maintenance of security and stability in Iraq," and recognition of a "security partnership" between the (largely American) multinational force and the recently deployed Iraqi forces. Baghdad obtained recognition that its security forces "are responsible to appropriate Iraqi ministers," and not under multinational command. The strongest Security Council opponents of the war—France, Russia, and China—won a time limit to the authority of the multinational force, which would be reviewed in twelve months or at any time at the request of the Iraqi government, and which would come to an end once an elected government took power under a permanent constitution (as expected by December 31, 2005). The UN mission in Iraq was authorized to assist in convening the national conference and to advise and support the new independent electoral commission as it prepared for voting by January 2005. The mission was also to assist the Iraqi government on reconstruction and administration, and eventually help "promote national dialogue and consensus building" in the drafting of a permanent constitution, once that task got under way. Finally, the UN repeated the mantra that the interim government was to refrain "from taking any actions affecting Iraq's destiny beyond the limited interim period." The only real losers seemed to be the Kurds, who, intimating that they felt betrayed by the United States, threatened to withdraw from the central government and the January elections (and in effect the country) if the TAL was nullified.[26] Nine days after the adoption of Resolution 1546, the U.S. deputy secretary of defense, Paul Wolfowitz, helicoptered up to Kurdistan to assuage their concerns, while Prime Minister Ayad Allawi pledged that the interim government would respect the TAL.

★

In the final weeks before the handover, as the intrigues over the interim government were unfolding, numerous other tasks needed to be addressed. Efforts to promote democratic values, to assist emerging parties and civil society organizations, and to sell the TAL to the Iraqi people continued. These projects were sidelined when the twin insurgencies erupted in April, but as the Coalition began to reassert control in more areas, the dialogues, ad campaigns, and other promotional work resumed, albeit on a limited basis.

In particular, the legal and administrative infrastructure for the national elections to be held by January 2005 had to be prepared. Bremer, aware of the importance of getting the mundane matters right, gave them a good deal of attention. If elections were to take place by January, an electoral commission would need to be appointed, and laws drafted defining the system of voting and the legal status of political parties. He was adamant that the laws be issued before June 30 and not deferred to the interim government. At the same time, he understood the depth of Iraqi feelings of nationalism, and so he rejected suggestions that one or more of the members of the electoral commission come from the international community.

During the second half of March, we began in earnest to identify Iraqis who could serve as members of an electoral commission that would be responsible for preparing and administering the elections and counting the votes. Among the democracies of the world, there are four models for structuring such commissions. The first is purely administrative, with civil servants running the elections. The second taps senior judges to oversee the electoral functions. The third model, conceding that the process is inevitably political, puts a balance of political party representatives on the commission, so that no single party dominates. In the fourth approach, electoral administration is strictly nonpartisan, and therefore only technocrats who have no ties to political parties can serve as commissioners. Any of the four models can, in theory, produce a commission that treats all candidates and parties equally. But the first two were not realistic for Iraq, because of the need to reconstruct both the civil service and the judiciary after the long period of Baath Party rule, and the likelihood that the existing civil service would have, and would be seen as having, a political orientation. Politicizing an electoral commission (the third approach) is a dangerous game, I have always felt, and professional, nonpartisan electoral commissions (the fourth approach) have a better record of administering free and fair elections.

Not surprisingly, the Governing Council wanted to politicize (and control) the electoral commission, by naming its members. I argued emphatically for a nonpartisan, professional body. Fortunately, Bremer shared this view, which had been advocated by outside experts on electoral administration and by other CPA officials. There was a risk that if the politically powerful members of the Governing Council did not get their way, they might denounce the commission as American stooges. But we believed that the greater risk was to politicize the commission, undermining its domestic and international credibility. Moreover, a potential political backlash could be averted by involving the UN electoral assistance team in the selection of the commission members. So we began looking for names of Iraqis who had the stature, integrity, and independence to lead and staff such a commission. Unfortunately, many of the civil society leaders whom we thought might qualify planned to run as candidates for the transitional national assembly. As a result, we focused on senior judges who had maintained political neutrality and a degree of judicial independence even during Saddam's long, brutal rule. Here we encountered a different problem, however: the judges who were the most impressive candidates for the electoral commission were the same ones whose integrity, neutrality, and competence recommended them for leadership of the higher courts, for membership on the special tribunal that would try Saddam and other former regime officials, and for roles in other important transitional institutions, such as the Public Integrity Commission and the Iraqi Property Claims Commission.

We continued compiling lists of possible candidates both for the electoral commission and for provincial offices, but the effort was slowed by the competing demands on a limited pool of actors who were well known, accomplished, and independent. In the end, the enterprise proved unnecessary. As part of Brahimi's efforts in April and May, a UN electoral team (under Carina Perelli) took over this process and invited Iraqis to apply for a seat on the seven-member electoral commission. During the first two weeks of May, hundreds of applications were received and then a three-member team of international experts reviewed them, interviewed finalists, and selected the commission (with the approval of the CPA and the Governing Council). All the commission members were required to renounce participation in politics for the period of their service. This method of seeking volunteers or nominees, rather than looking for candidates, led the UN team to select seven commissioners who appeared able and independent but were not known to the Iraqi public—which would later lead to suspicions in some quarters.

The UN team also had to recommend an electoral law for Iraq—principally, a method by which the members of the national assembly would be chosen. Without detailed, reliable census information, there was no possibility of using the American system of single-member districts, in which the candidate with the most votes in a district wins. And in any case, most experts, including me, thought it would have been a bad choice for Iraq. Although the method would have encouraged Iraqis to focus on individuals and their qualities—with the goal of bringing independent candidates to the fore—small, nongeographically based parties would have had difficulty winning seats. In some political systems, such groups may be extremist and worth keeping out of parliament. But in Iraq, these minor parties figured to be among the strongest advocates of democracy. In addition, a society like Iraq, with deep ethnic, regional, and religious divisions, is better served by an electoral system that ensures the fair representation of every group. This conclusion suggested the value of some form of proportional representation (PR), in which parties or lists win seats in proportion to their share of the vote, in conjunction with multimember districts, so that there is a geographical as well as a proportional element.

The big question was how Iraq could draw districts of any kind when it had no acceptable census data—and no time to conduct a census before the election. A natural solution presented itself. Iraq already was divided into eighteen provinces, each of which could constitute an electoral district. We had two sets of data—one from the most recent census and one from the more trusted food ration card system—on the distribution of the population by province. Such data could be used to allocate the parliamentary seats to each province. The allocation would not be perfect, but under the circumstances, it could be acceptable. Moreover, an adjustment mechanism to ensure a fairer alignment between seats and votes could be worked out. By this mechanism, in what is called a two-tiered system, the vast majority of the seats could be assigned to the provinces, with parties, groups, or individuals presenting lists of candidates in each province. Citizens would vote for a list within a province, and would be able to review the names of the candidates on each list. In each province, each list would get a proportion of the seats equal to its share of the vote. The problem, however, is that the smaller the district becomes, the more likely it is to exclude, from the distribution of seats, parties that won an appreciable number of votes but not enough to qualify for a seat. If there are only five seats to go around, for instance, then a party is at risk of being shut out if it does not win 10 to 15 percent of the vote. Two-tiered systems compensate for this situation by making an additional distribution of seats after the district slots are allocated. The second distribution, which normally comes from nationwide lists, gives each party or coalition the number of seats it needs to ensure that its overall representation in parliament matches, as closely as possible, its share of the national vote.

When I left Iraq in early April, I expected that a system of proportional representation based on districts (using mainly the provincial boundaries) would be adopted. After reviewing the situation, however, the UN team opted to forgo districts and use proportional representation in a single nationwide district, because of its administrative simplicity and because the team thought that assigning fixed numbers of seats to districts would be too controversial, given the absence of broadly accepted census data. Bremer accepted this decision and wrote it into the electoral law that he decreed in mid-June. The decision was understandable, considering the political, administrative, and time pressures, but it would prove to be a huge mistake. Without any district-based guarantee of a minimum number of seats in parliament, the Sunni provinces, which had been slowest to organize politically and were most affected by the insurgent violence, risked being vastly underrepresented in the new parliament. This situation threatened to generate (and in fact would generate) an electoral boycott, and even greater alienation, polarization, and violence.

★

Before I left Baghdad, I had also been preoccupied with two nagging issues: how political parties would be funded and whether former members of the Baath Party would be allowed to participate. On the question of money, the playing field was far from level. SCIRI, Da'wa, and many other Shiite parties drew massive financial support from Iran. The religious establishment in Iraq received generous contributions from the faithful. The two Kurdish parties had been running governments in Kurdistan for the past thirteen years, so they, too, had financial resources to draw on. But new and politically independent parties, including those with secular, liberal outlooks and those based in the Sunni heartland but led by opponents of the previous regime, were desperately short of cash.

In a number of conversations in Baghdad and elsewhere, I heard repeated complaints from party activists about their lack of financial resources and about what they perceived to be a tilted playing field. One prominent Sunni Arab politician was direct with me: SCIRI and Da'wa, he said, were getting lavish funding from Iran. The Kurds had so much money that one of their leaders was giving gifts of $10,000 each to a number of Arab parties, perhaps to build up goodwill for the future. As I told Bremer in a memo in late March, I had the feeling that some of these struggling party leaders wouldn't mind a foreign angel themselves—and indeed, rumors emerged of funds flowing to several Sunni-based parties, from Saudi Arabia and some of the Gulf states. "At least two or three times," I told Bremer in the memo, "I felt the discussion was approaching an implicit appeal for covert funding from the United States. Without acknowledging that this is what they were implying, I made in each case the general observation that we, the United States, of course can't provide funding, openly or covertly, to some parties and not others; we have to be neutral and open in what we do."

I proposed that we establish, fairly soon, "some legitimate and transparent means for funding the more serious political parties, and thus to some extent, leveling the playing field." It might be possible, I suggested, to establish a political parties fund, containing, initially, several million dollars, and then distribute equal amounts of money to every party that met certain criteria of public support—for example, at least 100,000 signatures of eligible voters, with at least 10,000 supporters in each of five provinces. The funding and the certification of signatures could be administered by the electoral commission. The suggestion attracted interest from some of my colleagues in the CPA, including Bremer's deputy, Ambassador Richard Jones, and when I wrote my memo to Condoleezza Rice in late April, I repeated my proposal, urging a fund of $10 million to $20 million. Nothing ever came of the idea, however. Most likely, the burden of verifying the signatures and administering the fund would have been at least as big an obstacle as obtaining the funding. With the deterioration of the security situation, the electoral commission was hard-pressed just to establish itself, elaborate its operating procedures, and begin to register voters. In these circumstances, moreover, any fund that was large enough to motivate parties to gather signatures would, as well, motivate opportunistic organizations to compile fraudulent signatures.

The other issue that concerned me was the scope of the de-Baathification program. I had been hearing many complaints about this from Sunni politicians, and even from moderate Shiites. They felt that the program had gone too far and that, in purging so many teachers, professors, and bureaucrats who had joined the Baath Party purely to advance their careers, we were alienating a strategic slice of society that could participate in the development of the political and economic order. As others had been saying publicly and privately for months, I suggested that the de-Baathification program be narrowed and that its principle be more one of individual responsibility for specific crimes and abuses. Yes, former high Baathist officials had to be kept out of the security apparatus. But if there was no evidence that a former Baathist had committed a crime, he or she should be allowed to run for office or seek a position in government. "Some visible progress in this regard," I wrote Bremer, "along with greater Sunni heartland inclusion in the interim government, could help to take some of the steam out of the insurgency."

In fact, Bremer had been coming around, for some weeks, to the realization that the de-Baathification program needed adjustment. He was also yielding ground to the American generals who had felt, from the beginning, that the disbandment of the Iraqi Army had been a huge mistake and that the United States should accelerate the rebuilding of the Iraqi armed forces by bringing back a number of officers who had not been political loyalists of Saddam and against whom there were no charges of specific crimes. In his April 23 televised address to the Iraqi people, Bremer announced three policy adjustments that responded to the concerns of U.S. civilian and military officials about the need to bring in the Sunnis. First, he expressed a willingness to welcome back officers and soldiers who had "served honorably," indicating that the top generals were now being "drawn almost entirely from the many honorable men of the former Iraqi Army." Second, he acknowledged as "legitimate" the complaints he had heard that de-Baathification had been "applied unevenly and unjustly," and he promised to expedite the review of appeals and the reinstatement of thousands of teachers and professors who had felt compelled to join the party. Third, he declared that the Coalition was streamlining the processing of detainees and was providing information about individual detainees at police stations, courthouses, and on the CPA Web site.

Each of these initiatives was intended, as well, to allay the concerns that Brahimi had articulated in his April 14 press conference, and Brahimi, in his April 27 presentation to the Security Council, openly praised the steps. The policy adjustments raised the prospect that hundreds of former army officers from the Saddam era and perhaps as many as ten thousand teachers and professors who had belonged to the Baath Party would be reinstated, even as the initiatives provoked outrage among Shiite hard-liners like Ahmed Chalabi (who, in overseeing de-Baathification until recently, had slowed the appeals process). Perhaps predictably, Chalabi described Bremer's move as "like allowing Nazis into the German government after World War II."[27] More moderate Shiites, however, quietly accepted the scaling back of de-Baathification as the price of stabilizing the country. Unfortunately, like much of what the CPA did, the adjustments would prove to be too little, too late.

★

By the beginning of June, the task of assembling the interim government had been accomplished, but much remained to be finished. State Department officials were hard at work completing arrangements, begun weeks before, for the transition of the American presence from an occupation authority into an embassy. Though billed to the Iraqi public and the world as a dramatic transformation, it would wind up having many elements of continuity, including the necessary preservation of the fortified Green Zone, with the Republican Palace remaining as the base of operations. Gradually, one ministry after another was trans-

ferred from CPA to Iraqi control. During the final weeks of the occupation, in addition to appointing an electoral commission, Bremer formed
commissions to regulate communications, public broadcasting, and se-
curities markets, and to monitor corruption, while also appointing inspectors general to five-year terms in each ministry. In the minds of the
Americans, the CPA was laying the legal and institutional foundations
to ensure good governance after the transition. But many Iraqis saw the
raft of orders and appointments as an effort to cast the long shadow of
control over the future. "They have established a system to meddle in
our affairs," said the former Governing Council member Mahmoud
Othman. "Iraqis should decide many of these issues."[28]

Of the one hundred orders Bremer decreed during the occupation,
many of the most important ones came in the final month. In addition
to the decree establishing the Independent Electoral Commission of
Iraq, they included the following:

- the creation of a task force to compensate victims of the previous
  regime (with an endowment of $25 million from Iraq's oil income)
- a far-reaching anti–money laundering act, running to sixteen
  pages and twenty-six articles, to criminalize the financing of
  crime and terrorism and the illegal transfer of money
- a sixty-eight-page law (with 108 articles) to "comprehensively establish a safe, sound, competitive, and accessible banking system"
  for Iraq
- a financial management law establishing another "comprehensive
  framework" for the Iraqi government to conduct fiscal and bud-
  getary policy and to report on its activities "in line with international best practices"
- the establishment of an ombudsman to hear appeals and protests
  on penal and detention matters
- the creation of a joint detainee committee, composed of representatives of the (predominantly American) Multinational Force,
  the Iraqi interim government, and the American and British am-
  bassadors, to coordinate on "all matters relating to the management of" Iraqi suspects detained by the Multinational Force
- a Political Parties Law establishing the legal basis for political

parties, their equality before the law, and the electoral commission's authority over them. The law also required parties to have a transparent statute governing their organization and operation, and forbade them to "have or be associated with an armed force, militia or residual element."

- the long-awaited order (Number 91) on the Regulation of Armed Forces and Militias Within Iraq.[29]

The final order, Number 100, was an omnibus measure, with detailed amendments of many of the previous orders to make them consistent with the TAL (and with evolving American requirements) and suitable to stand as law after the transfer of sovereignty. It also extended Order 17, giving U.S. and other international forces immunity from "any form of arrest or detention other than by persons acting on behalf of their parent states."

Although the initial plan called for the Transition and Reintegration program (regarding the militias) to be announced at the beginning of May, order Number 91 was not signed into law by Bremer until June 7. Still, it was an impressive achievement, at least on paper. The result of several months of negotiations with militia leaders, the order, implementing an agreement that was supported and announced by Ayad Allawi, banned all Iraqi armed forces and militias unless they agreed to a specific Transition and Reintegration plan, which required them to provide a complete list of their members qualified to participate; stipulated the process by which those members would be "transitioned" from the status of militia fighters and reintegrated into the Iraqi armed forces or civilian economy; and provided "clearly defined milestones" for this process. Members of militias participating in the plan faced one of three options: entry into the Iraqi armed forces (or other Iraqi security forces), retirement "with the same pension they would have received had they served" in the Iraqi armed forces, or reintegration into Iraq's civil society and economy, with the aid of "skills screening, education benefits, job training and placement, and a limited stipend program." A crucial part of the plan was the commitment of $200 million for the establishment of job training centers and placement programs in each province. While a militia's members were "transitioning" out of the militia, its "residual elements" were exempt from the ban so long as they did not recruit new members, conduct operations, engage in criminal activity, or fail to register their weapons. The order also banned the residual elements from supporting any political party or candidate, and it set up a transition and reintegration implementation committee, chaired by the interior minister and including other government officials and agencies, to manage the process—and to impose coercive penalties if it deemed necessary. All members of illegal militias were to be "subject to criminal prosecution" and "banned from holding any political office for a period of three years." This provision included Muqtada al-Sadr, whose Mahdi Army had spurned the Transition and Reintegration process. Nevertheless, as Bremer was signing the order, some Shiite leaders were attempting to draw Sadr into the political process. Although Sadr had agreed, three days before, to end his violence against the occupation, his spokesman immediately rejected the Transition and Reintegration agreement, saying it did not apply to his force. "The Mahdi Army is not a militia," the representative claimed. "It is the Iraqis legitimately resisting the occupation."[30]

The Transition and Reintegration plan covered nine militias, with an estimated 102,000 fighters, that pledged to disband before the January 2005 elections. The groups included not only the *pesh merga* of the two Kurdish parties and the Badr Organization of SCIRI but the smaller militias of the Iraqi Islamic Party, the Iraqi Communist Party, and Iraqi Hizbollah, all of whom came forward to reveal their numbers of fighters and develop timetables for their demobilization.[31] Da'wa, the Iraqi National Accord, and the Iraqi National Congress declared that they had already disbanded their militias and were therefore in compliance. Although a PUK leader said after the announcement that the *pesh merga* were not included in the agreement,[32] both Kurdish party forces agreed to restructure one-half of their fighters into the three new services that would provide internal security in Kurdistan; the other half would go into the local police or the national army, or into civilian life.

The Transition and Reintegration plan succeeded on paper but withered in the implementation, as the new Iraqi ministers of defense, interior, and labor lacked the commitment of their predecessors. In particular, the new defense minister, Hazem Shaalan, was a fiercely secular Shiite who did not want SCIRI fighters in the Iraqi military, and canceled their recruitment. The minister of labor and social affairs was also wary (and unhappy with the people running the program), so the job-training element fell away. The only leg of the transitional triad left was the payment of pensions, which depended on the cooperation of the militias that were now being deprived of the other transitional benefits.

★

By mid-June, the CPA was well advanced into lame-duck status. The Governing Council was gone, the big transitional issues had been settled, Ayad Allawi was increasingly asserting his authority as the incoming prime minister, and the majority of the ministries had been turned over to Iraqi management. The American advisers who had run the Iraqi ministries were now becoming consultants, though some two hundred of them were slated to remain on in this role. But foremost in everyone's mind was the deteriorating security situation in the country. Even before Allawi assumed formal power, word circulated that he was considering declaring a state of emergency.

The violence was surging in a grisly, daily progression, as insurgents targeted anyone cooperating with the occupation and tried to demolish confidence in the transition. The deputy foreign minister was shot to death in Baghdad on June 12. The following day, two car bombs detonated, killing thirteen people in a densely populated area of central Baghdad, while gunmen murdered a senior official of the education ministry. The day after that, three bombs killed a total of twenty-one people, including a number of foreign contractors, and wounded dozens in and around Baghdad. On June 15, an oil ministry official was killed in Kirkuk. On June 16, a car bomb outside an Iraqi Army recruiting station killed thirty-five and wounded over one hundred. Six more died outside a town council building. On June 24, insurgents killed an estimated 100 Iraqis and wounded about 320 in what seemed a series of orchestrated car bombings and armed raids on police stations and other facilities in Mosul and five other cities. In testimony to the Senate Armed Services Committee a few hours later, Deputy Secretary of

State Richard Armitage conceded that the insurgents had a "central nervous system" that was exhibiting growing coordination and effectiveness.[33] Two days later, a car bomb in Hilla killed several dozen people. Beyond the spectacular strikes was a steady onslaught of dispersed attacks, ambushes, and roadside bombs around the country that killed smaller numbers of American soldiers, Iraqi soldiers and police, civilians, and foreign contractors on an almost daily basis.[34]

Not wanting the handover ceremony on June 30 to provide a target for the terrorists, Bremer and Allawi agreed to forgo a grand ceremony and accelerate the transfer of power by two days. While President Bush was attending a NATO summit in neighboring Turkey, Bremer, "looking exhausted and almost dazed," according to one report, transferred sovereignty to the new interim prime minister in a subdued proceeding, closed to the press.[35] Soon thereafter, his motorcade departed from the palace in such a frenzy that it momentarily left behind his deputy, Ambassador Jones.

Iraqis appeared cautiously hopeful about the future and relieved to have the political occupation ended. But even among leaders sympathetic to the United States, there was more than a little resentment. "It was late," said Deputy Prime Minister Barham Salih of the transfer of power. "We should have had sovereignty the day after liberation. But better late than never."[36] A woman working in a computer store in downtown Baghdad reflected the wariness of much of the public. "Bremer has left, but the strings attached to the new government are very long. They can be pulled from Washington."[37]

★

The selection of Ayad Allawi as interim prime minister was one of the most significant decisions of the last six months of the transition. It answered the most vexing puzzle in the transitional process, in a manner that generated at least a grudging agreement among the Governing Council members. It gave the helm of the first Iraqi government after the fall of the Baath Party dictatorship to a self-styled tough guy and specialist on security issues who promised to crack down on the violence and terror but had resolutely opposed radical de-Baathification and believed he could, as a onetime Baathist, reel in part of the insurgency. His presence raised the possibility that Iraq would return to some measure of stability.

Most of these expectations, however, would prove illusory. While Allawi enjoyed considerable initial popularity, or at least acceptance, his unwillingness to challenge the United States on any important matter, and his inability to achieve any reduction in the violence, cost him credibility at home. Moreover, his efforts to reach out to the Baathists who were funding and orchestrating much of the insurgent violence failed. To them, Allawi was an American pawn, a CIA agent, the traitor to the party whom they had tried brutally to murder in his bed in London years back. As for the support of his political colleagues, it would wear thin as he concentrated power in the office of prime minister and essentially ignored the cabinet. But these problems would surface only months later, well after the transfer of sovereignty.

10

WHAT WENT WRONG?

I have chronicled here what I believe was an American failure in postwar Iraq, a squandering of a decisive, potentially historic military victory. Mistakes were made at virtually every turn, and as the principal nation promoting the conflict and managing its aftermath, the United States bears the chief blame. In the weeks leading up to and following the war, the Bush administration depicted a liberated Iraq welcoming our invading troops as liberators, quickly stabilizing the political order, regaining economic vitality, and making the momentous transition to freedom—a transition that would, in turn, set off pressures for democratic change throughout the Middle East. But from the moment the war ended, Iraq fell into a deepening quagmire of chaos, criminality, insurgency, and terrorism, which, even in the months following the January 2005 elections, showed no prospect of ending anytime soon. During the period of occupation rule, Iraq became a black hole of instability and a justification for neighboring regimes that insisted their societies were not culturally suited or politically ready for democracy. By the time of the handover, America's quest to stabilize and democratize Iraq seemed to be becoming one of the major overseas blunders in U.S. history. In Iraq we deployed huge ambitions, strong ideals, billions of dollars, and devoted people working ninety hours a week. What went wrong?

When historians seek to explain the course of politics and war at key decision points, they often resort to some version of path dependence, the idea that events move in a causal chain that is not easily reversible. The particular course of action that a leader, or a country, pursues initiates a chain reaction of events that prevents a return to the starting point and the implementation of an alternative course. A decision taken at a critical juncture sets in motion a trajectory of change in which, in the oft-repeated words of the economic historian Paul A. David, "one damn thing follows another."[1]

Once the Bush administration decided to invade Iraq, "one damn thing" did indeed follow another. From the standpoint of preempting an *imminent* threat to U.S. national security, we now know that the war was a mistake; Saddam Hussein did not have stockpiles of weapons of mass destruction, and he was probably years away from being able to reconstitute them, especially if sanctions remained in place. For many advocates of the war—including prominent neoconservative commentators, some assertive liberals, and British Prime Minister Tony Blair—the liberation of Iraq from tyranny (an outcome that would fan the flames of freedom throughout the region) was a paramount moral justification for the war. But those advocates underestimated the "one damn thing after another" theory of history.

Some months after I left Iraq, I asked a distinguished diplomat from the region (and a good friend of the United States) what had gone wrong. He offered a long list, but he began with the war itself—hasty and largely unilateral, without international authorization, and without the support of much of the world (including the populations of the more than thirty other governments that participated, in some way, in the Coalition). "The war itself was the original sin," he said. "When you commit a sin as cardinal as that, you are bound to get a lot of things wrong." And then he offered an analogy of pure path dependence: "When you enter a one-way street in the wrong direction, no matter which way you turn, you will be entering all the other streets in the wrong way."

When, at the beginning of 2003, a top Bush administration official asked this diplomat how the United States should conduct itself in postwar Iraq if it invaded, he replied, "Don't invade." The official pressed him, "But what if we decide we must, in order to disarm Saddam?" Again, he urged that the United States not resort to war but continue down the multilateral process of pressuring Saddam already under way. When the aide pressed a third time, he reluctantly offered a few suggestions. Prominent among them: Don't dissolve the Iraqi Army, and don't purge the entire Baath Party from government. These, too, were mistakes the United States would make early on in its occupation. One damn thing followed another.

In writing this book, I found that the hardest issue I had to struggle with was my interlocutor's assertion of "original sin." Yet here was the irony: Despite that sin, he (and those who agreed with his criticism) eventually became involved in assisting the United States and the Iraqi people to achieve a viable transition. The first step the United States took made it difficult to bring democracy to Iraq, because it brought a military and political occupation as the instrument of liberation. Yet without the invasion, there would have been no opportunity for democracy. And even with an unpopular occupation, the prospect for democracy was not foreclosed. Rather, a number of other decisions propelled the United States down the ill-fated path of "one damn thing after another."

Taking the invasion as a given, two of the most ill-fated decisions of the postwar engagement involved the extraordinary trust that President George W. Bush placed in the senior Pentagon leadership, beginning with Secretary of Defense Donald Rumsfeld. First, Bush accepted Rumsfeld's plan to go into Iraq with a relatively light force of about 150,000 Coalition troops, despite the warnings of the U.S. Army and outside experts on postconflict reconstruction that—whatever the needs of the war itself—securing the peace would require a force two to three times that size. Second, in January 2003, Bush gave the Pentagon the lead responsibility for the management of postwar Iraq. This decision, in the words of one U.S. official, "sent out the signal that they [the Pentagon] are really in charge and reinforced and amplified their mandate to say 'to hell with everybody else.'"[2] With Rumsfeld's Pentagon thus confirmed in its blithe arrogance, the United States surged— in James Fallows's memorable words—"blind into Baghdad."[3]

As I have argued in chapter 2, and as numerous analyses have compellingly documented, the United States invaded Iraq without an effective plan to secure the peace. The immediate manifestation of this failure was the inability—perhaps even the unwillingness—to establish order on the ground after Saddam Hussein was toppled from power. In the days and weeks that followed, Iraqis—in spontaneous acts as well as in orchestrated assaults—attacked and ransacked virtually every significant public building in Baghdad, while ravaging other cities such as Basra. As Ambassador Peter Galbraith would later explain to a congressional committee, "In the three weeks following the U.S. takeover [in Baghdad on April 9], unchecked looting effectively gutted every important public institution in the city—with the notable exception of the oil ministry."[4] That was the one secular structure that American troops defended. And what Iraqis saw, a Shiite cleric later explained, was that the Americans protected that building and "*nothing* else. . . . So what else do you want us to think except that you want our oil?"[5] The economic cost of the looting was estimated at $12 billion, not including the future costs in delayed reconstruction, and the political price of having Iraqis equate freedom with disorder and violence.[6] Many Iraqis assumed, from the start, that the Americans did not care, or that they even welcomed the destruction. One cleric told a journalist, "I simply cannot understand how your soldiers could have stood by and watched. Maybe, they are weak, too. Or maybe they are wicked."[7] To the criticism, Rumsfeld replied in his famously cavalier manner, "Stuff happens. . . . Freedom's untidy, and free people are free to make mistakes and commit crimes and do bad things."[8]

More than a year after the end of the war, Deputy Secretary of Defense Paul Wolfowitz acknowledged, in testimony to Congress, that the Pentagon had underestimated the tenacity of the resistance in Iraq. But that misjudgment did not arise from a lack of warnings about the potential for chaos after the regime was toppled.

For example, the State Department–sponsored Future of Iraq Project had cautioned that the restoration of law and order and the prevention of criminality would be postwar imperatives. Even the Iraqi Democratic Principles Working Group, which sought to demilitarize society and establish civilian control over the military, warned of the "substantial social and economic chaos" (including the explosive growth of organized crime) that could result from the rapid "de-commissioning of hundreds of thousands of trained military personnel." It thus urged that military reorganization be done gradually by an Iraqi committee for military reform, which would offer cashiered soldiers civilian reconstruction jobs, basic and specialized educational programs, low-interest loans to create businesses, better pensions, and other forms of compensation.[9] Warnings of possible civil disorder after the fall of Baghdad were also a recurrent theme in CIA projections of postwar Iraq, and in numerous testimonies and reports by both American experts and Iraqi exiles.[10]

Perhaps most striking of all, the Army War College's Strategic Studies Institute anticipated such sources of turmoil, in a well-researched, sobering analysis, *Reconstructing Iraq*. Published in February 2003, the unclassified report synthesized the lessons of other U.S. occupations and of Iraqi history, society, and politics. The report is breathtaking in its prescience and in its detailed examination of the "real and serious" "possibility of the United States winning the war and losing the peace in Iraq." Suspicion of U.S. motives was likely to increase in postwar Iraq, the study found, even if the war itself ended rapidly, with light casualties; problems would be acute if the United States had to handle the bulk of the occupation itself, rather than turn it over to a "postwar international force." Moreover, the analysis foresaw resistance to what would likely be viewed as imperial domination by the Judeo-Christian West. Warning of the dangers of tribal and ethnic conflict, the report noted the widespread presence of private, armed militias. It cited Shiite Islamist terrorism in Lebanon as an example of "strategies to alienate Iraqis who are initially neutral toward a US occupation," and it expected that terrorists in Iraq would utilize suicide bombings. In predicting that the exiled opposition would not be welcomed back as the country's new leaders, it quoted an expert warning that Ahmed Chalabi and his party were "extremely unpopular in Iraq." The report said the Iraqi Army could serve as a "unifying force" in the postwar period, and speculated that demobilized soldiers would affiliate with violent elements if the army was disbanded. The longer an American occupation persisted, the greater the possibility of terrorism by Iraqis trying "to hasten the departure of US forces." Yet it also anticipated the dilemma the United States would find itself in: "At the same time, a premature withdrawal from Iraq could lead to instability and perhaps even civil war." This is why it stressed mobilizing the "massive resources" that would "need to be focused on this effort before the first shot is fired," to prepare "for the postwar rehabilitation of the Iraqi political system."[11]

Indeed, many experts warned Pentagon planners of the likelihood of Iraqi resistance after the war, only to be cavalierly dismissed. One American official with long experience in the region recalled to me:

> Any effort at postconflict realism was met with indifference and hostility. I tried to point out that this would not be a two- or three-day war. There would be resistance. Perhaps not initially, but Iraqis would not swallow our being there. I remembered how, after the Iranians had pushed Iraqi forces out of Iran early in the Iran–Iraq war, Iraqis turned around and fought intensely in protracted trench warfare. Whatever their differences, Iraqis were Iraqis, and they were going to keep the Iranians out. I said if they did that with the Iranians, then they are not going to let us be in the country; we would face an insurgency. That simply didn't go down, because it wasn't part of the scenario of roses and sweets, which expected that we would be greeted as liberators, not occupiers.

High-ranking professionals in the military as well as civilian experts were concerned about the size and preparedness of the international force that would occupy Iraq. The U.S. Army's chief of staff, General Eric Shinseki, advocated a large invasion force (on the order of 400,000 troops) so as not to be "trapped in an untenable position during the occupation," according to Fallows.[12] Shinseki was rewarded for his forthright position when Rumsfeld announced his successor as chief of staff fourteen months before the end of the general's term, making him an instant lame duck. But Shinseki continued to speak his mind. At a Senate Armed Services Committee hearing in February 2003, just weeks before the invasion, Shinseki said it would take "something on the order of several hundred thousand soldiers" to occupy Iraq.[13] Two days later, Wolfowitz publicly dismissed Shinseki's figure as "wildly off the mark." And yet Shinseki was hardly alone in his estimate. A National Security

Council briefing for Rice and her deputy Stephen Hadley came to a similar conclusion.[14] And a study by the RAND Corporation observed that the initial ratio of international soldiers to inhabitants in Bosnia and Kosovo had been about 1 to 50. To reproduce that ratio in Iraq would have required a force of nearly half a million troops. A major lesson that the RAND study drew from previous nation-building efforts addressed this point: "There appears to be an inverse correlation between the size of the stabilization force and the level of risk. The higher the proportion of stabilizing troops, the lower the number of casualties suffered and inflicted."[15] The military knew this lesson well, but, according to a senior intelligence official, "Rumsfeld just beat up on the military. And so they just shut up and did what they were told."[16]

Why did the Bush administration plunge into Baghdad with what so many experts felt would be an inadequate force to secure the peace? Several speculations have emerged. Convinced that we were in an era of warfare that would privilege speed, surprise, maneuverability, and high technology over "boots on the ground," Rumsfeld believed that toppling Saddam would require, by historical standards, only a relatively small invasion force. The defense secretary had begun to reconceptualize war, in the words of one senior army officer, "outside its political and human dimensions,"[17] a posture that many in the Pentagon viewed as disastrous. The White House also expected, Condoleezza Rice later conceded, that after the Iraqi Army was defeated, "the institutions would hold, everything from ministries to police forces."[18] As James Fallows notes, Rumsfeld never much cared for "nation building" and didn't want to see the United States get bogged down in the effort. The large peacekeeping presence in Kosovo had created a "culture of dependence," Rumsfeld believed, and he saw the much scantier international presence in Afghanistan as a more appropriate model—even though, experts insisted, the former Yugoslavia, with its highly urban population, its protracted economic decline, and its history of centralized, totalitarian rule, was a better analogy to Iraq. Then, too, Rumsfeld and his colleagues expected that once the war ended, numerous multinational forces, from NATO, from other European countries, and from the Persian Gulf states, could be recruited to replace some of the departing U.S. troops.

Beyond this, however, were deeper political and ideological concerns—and constraints. The war planners were not willing to consider any options that would slow the rush to war, or require from the American people a larger mobilization and greater degree of sacrifice than the Bush administration's desire to have it all: a war to topple the pivotal figure in its declared "axis of evil," a normal life in the United States, and a sweeping program of tax cuts. With biting satire, the columnist Thomas Friedman called this approach, "We're at war—let's party."[19] The United States had, in total, only about half a million active-duty army troops and 175,000 marines. Committing anything approaching the number of troops suggested by Shinseki or by the RAND study would have necessitated an immediate mobilization of the military reserves and National Guard (which would come later, in creeping fashion), and might have alarmed the public into questioning the costs and feasibility of the entire operation. Indeed, Rumsfeld reportedly denied a request to send in several thousand more military police precisely because it would have prompted a further call-up of reserves.[20] Then, too, the Bush war council was convinced, in its moral righteousness about the "cause," that American troops would be welcomed as liberators by an Iraqi population joyous at their deliverance from the clutches of Saddam's regime, that resistance would be limited, and that the Iraqi state would remain intact. The United States could then hand the country over to the pro-American exiles, led by Ahmed Chalabi, and get out within a few months, leaving behind, in the words of one bitter U.S. official, "a democratic Iraq that was amenable to our wishes and desires."[21]

The same almost theological determination to go to war no matter what, and the same unshakable confidence in the inevitability and speed of America's triumph, drove the Pentagon's decision to ignore the entire Future of Iraq Project, to ban its coordinator, Thomas Warrick, from the postwar occupation, and to sweep aside experts in the State Department and elsewhere who had described what the postwar realities in Iraq would require. Extensive planning was done in anticipation of a humanitarian crisis that could involve huge refugee flows and food shortages. But there was no coherent planning for Iraq's postwar future. Senator Chuck Hagel, the second-ranking Republican on the Foreign Relations Committee, declared in frustration in November 2003, "We so underestimated and underplanned and underthought about a post-Saddam Iraq that we've been woefully unprepared. Now we have a security problem. We have a reality problem. And we have a governance problem. . . . And time is not on our side."[22]

★

To be sure, the United States and its Coalition partners accomplished a number of important things. A wide array of Iraqi civil society organizations and political parties—many of them democratic to one degree or another—were assisted in their efforts to organize. An extensive network of democracy centers was established in the South Central region, and most of them survived the insurgencies that gripped that area during 2004—in part because the thousands of tribal sheikhs who had received democratic training came out with their armed followers to defend the centers from the Mahdi Army.[23] In all, 300,000 or more Iraqis had participated in democracy dialogues and training sessions by the June 28 handover, and the civic education programs were still operating at the end of 2004. And in some substantial areas of Iraq, organizations for democracy were either strengthened (in the Kurdish north) or created largely anew (as in the South Central region, Baghdad, and Basra). Women were given a sense of political hope, purpose, and confidence, and the interim constitution ensures them significant representation in the assembly—more than women enjoy in the U.S. Congress. In many respects, the interim constitution was a remarkable achievement, though one marred by the lack of an Iraqi sense of participation in it and ownership of it. Markets were revived, a new currency was issued, and education resumed free of the stifling impositions of Baathist ideology and the relentless glorification of Saddam Hussein. More then 3,500 schools were refurbished, and more than seventy health care facilities were built.[24]

However, the collapse of public order in the aftermath of the war had devastating, long-lasting consequences. It undermined Iraqis' confidence in the United States and in the postwar order. It fanned suspicions that the United States did not want a strong, independent Iraq. It opened Iraq's vast borders to the infiltration of Al Qaeda and other Islamist terrorists, suicide bombers, Iranian intelligence agents, and other malevolent foreign forces. It left Iraq's vast stores of arms—an estimated one million tons of weapons and ammunition—substantially unprotected, and thus ripe for plucking by the criminals and insurgents. It gave an opportunity for every ambitious opponent of a democratic Iraq—domestic and foreign—to rush into the void. Moreover, the chronic disorder made it difficult to carry out the functions of economic, civic, and political reconstruction. As Ambassador Bremer would later concede in a speech to a business group on October 4, 2004, "We paid a big price for not stopping [the looting] because it established an atmosphere of lawlessness."[25]

What was more, the mistakes and miscalculations continued during the occupation. In particular, the failure to address the security deficit persisted. Even when we faced a growing insurgency without enough troops to combat it and maintain order; even when Iraqi confidence in the CPA plummeted with each car bombing and attack; even when foreign fighters, arms, and money were pouring across the country's unsecured borders, Secretary Rumsfeld and other senior administration figures blithely insisted that we had a sufficient military presence. The inadequacy of force and of resources meant that we could not secure the roads, we could not protect the courageous Iraqis who were coming forward to work for us, and ultimately we could not protect our own people. Nor did we feel confident that our military could preempt the insurgent threats to our democratization program.

We never had enough troops in Iraq—particularly at the beginning, when it was vital to secure public buildings, streets, and weapons depots; to hunt down the remnants of Saddam's forces; to seal the borders; and to establish decisive authority. The hapless ORHA administrator, Jay Garner, later conceded, "We did not seal the borders because we did not have enough troops to do that, and that brought in terrorists."[26] Nor did we have enough equipment. The top American commander in Iraq, General Ricardo Sanchez, warned the Pentagon in December 2003 that he was so short of spare parts for tanks, helicopters, and Bradley fighting vehicles that "I cannot continue to support sustained combat operations with rates this low." He even complained of repeated delays in getting his soldiers protective inserts to upgrade 36,000 sets of body armor.[27] The disgraceful shortage of armor for Humvees and transport vehicles finally seized the American public when a soldier in Kuwait challenged Secretary of Defense Rumsfeld before an international television audience on December 8, 2004. In another famously flippant reply, Rumsfeld said, "You go to war with the army you have, not the army you might want or wish to have at a later time." But the shortage, and its terrible consequences, had been known for months; and by then, almost two years had elapsed since we had gone to war with the army we had.

The civilian side of the mission was likewise underresourced. We never had enough civilian employees, or enough armored cars, body armor, helicopters, and other forms of secure transportation to move the staff members safely around. And even if we had gotten more armored cars, we would still have needed more personal security details to guard the CPA officials in them. We never had enough translators and interpreters, nor did we do even half of what we might have done to protect the lives of those brave, talented Iraqis who volunteered for this role. We never had sufficient expertise on the ground—people who knew the country, its culture, and its history, and who could speak its language reasonably well. Only a tiny percentage of CPA employees met all four of the requirements for an "A team" in postconflict reconstruction: area (including language) expertise, functional expertise, current responsibility at the level of previous experience, and willingness to deploy for at least a year. I myself met, at most, two of these requirements; none of my governance colleagues met all four, and few met even three. Consequently, the CPA relied heavily on a revolving door of diplomats and other personnel who would leave just as they had begun to develop local knowledge and ties, and on a cadre of eager young neophytes—some arrogant and others reflective, some idealistic and others driven mainly by political ambition. A twenty-four-year-old Yale graduate was given the task of reorganizing the Baghdad stock exchange. A Harvard graduate of similar age was one of the American negotiators on the constitution. A junior U.S. diplomat managed a multimillion-dollar budget to refurbish the National Assembly and train its staff. However talented and patriotic, these young people lacked the experience and often also the judgment for such awesome tasks. In a society that is conscious of age and status, youthful American brashness could not help but offend even our Iraqi friends and partners. Further undermining our effectiveness was the lack of institutional memory, both in the CPA offices and in the ranks of our senior advisers in the ministries. As one of my governance colleagues later observed to me: "With tours of six weeks and then three months being the norm, it was difficult for U.S. government staff to get up to speed and produce. By the time they got their feet wet, their time was up. This also gave the Iraqis a bad impression, as one set of Americans after another rotated in, many times with differing agendas from their predecessors. If the Iraqis did not like one set of Americans, they could just wait for the next group. This hampered the consistency of the U.S. 'message' and work plan."

We never listened carefully to the Iraqi people, or to the figures in the country that they respected. We never won their trust and confidence. We failed to move with the necessary dispatch to transfer power to an Iraqi interim government, chosen through an acceptable, consultative process that could have been mediated by the United Nations. We did not give the world body the kind of role that could have spared us from many mistakes, and from being perceived as an occupying power, until we ran into serious difficulty with our own plans—and by then it was too little, too late. Against the advice of most experts on Iraq and the region, we dissolved the Iraqi Army, purged from public life a broad swath of the existing elite, and indeed wound up alienating and marginalizing a whole section of the country—the best organized and best armed—until a series of readjustments that were, again, too little, too late. Against the advice of most people who knew Iraq well (including the politicians in exile with whom we had been working), and flying in the face of a proud and defiant national history that we barely studied, we established ourselves as an occupying power in every respect and so ensured that we would face a dedicated, violent resistance— without enough troops to cope.

As a result, an organized resistance emerged—as the UN mission had warned that it would—undermining postwar reconstruction at every turn. Electricity grids could not be revived, oil facilities could not be repaired, reconstruction jobs could not be commissioned, supplies could not be delivered, civil society could not organize, and a transition to democracy could not move forward because of the pervasive terrorist, criminal, and insurgent violence. America was simply overmatched in a postwar conflict for which it was grossly unprepared. "This thing evolved in front of us," Major General Paul Eaton (who had overseen the training of the Iraqi Army in 2003–04) told an American journalist in October 2004. "And each day it got incrementally worse until it exploded." [28]

★

Who bears the responsibility for America's failures in Iraq? Clearly, blame for the early blunders lies with the high officials of the Bush administration—including the president himself—who decided to go to war when we did, in the way we did, with the lack of preparation that has become brutally apparent. In May 2004, a senior general at the Pentagon who believed the "the United States is already on the road to defeat in Iraq," blamed his civilian superiors, Secretary Rumsfeld and Deputy Secretary Wolfowitz. "I do not believe we had a clearly defined war strategy, end state and exit strategy before we commenced our invasion," this general told Thomas E. Ricks of the *Washington Post*. "The current OSD [Office of the Secretary of Defense] refused to listen or adhere to military advice." [29] This problem pervaded the top ranks of the administration and persisted well after the invasion. As Warren P. Strobel and John Walcott of Knight-Ridder observed, "The Bush administration's failure to plan to win the peace in Iraq was the product of many of the same problems that plagued the administration's case for war, including wishful thinking, bad information from Iraqi exiles who said Iraqis would welcome American troops as liberators and contempt for dissenting opinions." [30]

The startling mismanagement of planning for the postwar did not result from a sudden emergency and a lack of time to plan. As has been extensively documented, many top administration officials, like Wolfowitz and Vice President Dick Cheney, came into office in January 2001 feeling that Saddam Hussein would have to be removed by force, once and for all. Following the September 11, 2001, attacks on the United States, a determination rapidly crystallized, within the senior ranks of the Bush administration, to bring down Saddam Hussein.[31] At the State Department, the Future of Iraq Project had begun planning, in October 2001, for a possible postwar democratic transition in Iraq. The hubris of senior civilian Pentagon planners, and their desire for total control of the U.S. policy, gutted the political planning effort and overrode professional civilian and military judgments about the necessary resources.

There are many who agree with the diplomat who told me, "The war itself was the original sin," and indeed, as I have indicated, I opposed going to war in Iraq when we did. The largely unilateral rush to war created predictable problems from the outset. But I now believe that the truly cardinal sin was going to war so unprepared for the postwar— despite all the detailed warnings to which the administration had access. To my mind, this was negligence on a monumental scale, what is called in the law "gross negligence," or "criminal negligence." I do not use the terms lightly; here, for example, is how one state, California, defines "criminal negligence":

> A negligent act [or acts] which is aggravated, reckless or flagrant and which is such a departure from the conduct of an ordinarily prudent, careful person under the same circumstances as to be contrary to a proper regard for human life or to constitute indifference to the consequences of [that] act. The facts must be such that the consequences of the negligent act could reasonably have been foreseen and it must appear that the . . . danger to human life was not the result of inattention, mistaken judgment or misadventure but the natural and probable result of an aggravated, reckless or flagrantly negligent act.[32]

As I was leaving Iraq in April 2004, a year into the occupation, the shortages of everything necessary to secure the postwar order remained disgraceful. As Coalition soldiers and civilians were being attacked and killed in growing numbers, we still did not have enough armored cars, trucks, and Humvees, and enough high-quality body armor.[33] Everyone knew we faced crippling shortages, but no one in authority viewed the situation as urgent. One CPA office grew so frustrated with the life-threatening delays that it quietly took a significant portion of its project money to buy used armored cars from a nearby Arab country. In at least one instance, this move wound up saving a number of lives. The central CPA operation lacked that kind of imagination, however, or the nerve to demand extraordinary measures from Washington. Americans were dying in Iraq in soft cars while some American embassies in the region were using armored cars to drive luggage in from the airport. "Why doesn't the State Department have the presence of mind to reallocate cars?" a CPA colleague asked me bitterly. CPA operations also lacked secure phones for the field operations. Amazingly, some CPA field offices had to communicate with headquarters via e-mail over insecure phone lines, using Yahoo. "The whole CPA project has been penny-wise and pound-foolish," my CPA colleague added. "We came out here without any assets."

Imagine that a person was about to go on a long car ride, took his car into a mechanic, and said, "Get me ready quickly for this long trip." Then the mechanic called back and said, "I am working on it, but your brake linings are gone—you really must have new brakes." And the driver said, "Forget it. There's no time and money for that. Just change the fluids and give me the car." Then imagine that the driver plowed through a crosswalk because he couldn't stop his car, and killed several children. His actions could be considered gross, criminal negligence, punishable under the law. Or imagine that a parent left a young child with a babysitter knowing that the child had suffered a series of unexplained injuries in the sitter's care, and on this occasion the child died after being beaten and shaken. Similar behavior, in fact, has resulted in the parent's felony conviction based upon criminal negligence.[34]

How, then, do we weigh "gross negligence" when the consequences are so much greater than one or a few lives? What do we tell the families of the more than one thousand Americans who have lost their lives *since the end of the war*, and the families of the many thousands of

Iraqis, Americans, and other foreigners who have been injured grievously or killed in the postwar chaos? There are laws against individuals
and corporations who take grossly negligent actions. There are no
laws—and there probably cannot be—against negligence, however
gross, on the part of government officials at the highest level. But in the
broader calculus of moral responsibility, which is the greater offense?

★

The blunders ran well beyond the mission's woeful lack of preparation
and of adequate resources and staff. Some share of responsibility for the
failures of the occupation lies with its remarkable and talented administrator, Ambassador L. Paul Bremer III. Soon after he arrived, Bremer
imposed three fateful decisions that collectively put the United States
down a treacherous path: dissolving the Iraqi Army, purging from public
office tens of thousands of Iraqis (including schoolteachers) with a level
4 or higher membership in the Baath Party, and converting the U.S.
presence into a formal occupation, with no clear timetable for transferring sovereignty back to Iraqis. These decisions he made, or at least implemented, with a high degree of confidence but little knowledge of the
country. High-ranking U.S. Army officers opposed dissolving the Iraqi
Army, correctly anticipating that it would leave a security vacuum, hu-
miliate a strategic, well-armed segment of society, and thereby stimulate
a violent backlash. But Bremer was convinced that demobilization was
the right course. And when the Iraqi Army was eventually reconstituted,
the project was done on the cheap. A U.S. Army officer told me in the
spring of 2004, "We had to fight Bremer tooth and nail for a paltry increase in salaries of the Iraqi military and police—and they still aren't
being paid enough."[35] Similarly, Bremer spurned the appeals of a wide
range of Iraqis—including many who were cooperating with us—and of
the UN mission to transfer authority quickly to an Iraqi interim government, and he proceeded to reshape Iraq through an occupation that he
led, and over which he exerted tight, indeed almost total, control. A
knowledgeable observer of Iraq told me:

> He didn't know what he was doing. When Chalabi came and said
> the Baath Party was horrible, it should cease to exist, that sounded

reasonable. But if you take the time to analyze the situation, you realize that the Baath Party was the state, and when you dissolve the party you dissolve the state. You then deprive yourself of the whole state. You deprive kids of teachers, people of doctors. You deprive the country of engineers who could fix the infrastructure.

As the CPA established its rule, four additional mistakes proved to be very costly. Some of these errors, as well, may have resulted, at least partially, from decisions and assumptions at the highest levels of the Bush administration, but Bremer's responsibility for them cannot be evaded. First, Bremer and his inner circle were too slow to grasp the importance of Ayatollah Sistani, and to reach out to him and the social and political forces he represented, as a way to find a broadly acceptable transition path. Second (and related), Bremer and his advisers did not allow for sufficient Iraqi participation in and feedback to the transition that was supposedly bringing them democracy. Third, Bremer waited far too long to embark on a strategy of outreach to disaffected Sunni elements to bring them into the political game. Indeed, he and other top American officials proved unwilling to incorporate the players—Baathists and Arab nationalists—who would have been capable of defusing the Sunni-based resistance, and who were, in fact, sending signals that they wanted to talk directly to the United States.

Fourth, Bremer could never forge a coherent strategy for addressing the insurgency, including the Shiite resistance of Muqtada al-Sadr. Although he seemed to understand, early on, that we did not have enough troops and was frustrated by this handicap, the fact remains that no additional troops were forthcoming from the Bush administration. At the same time, he balked at the kind of political dialogue that might have shown some of these stakeholders that they had a stronger interest in politics than in violence. There were two possible strategies for dealing with Sadr: to co-opt him, by giving him a place in the Governing Council and a voice at what passed for the table of Iraqi power; or to crush his organization with a swift, decisive blow. Repeatedly, plans were developed to take down Sadr, but for various reasons— including political calculations in Washington that the risks were too great—they were never executed. Yet the alternative approach, to seek an accommodation, was never pursued either, and Sadr was left free to build up his forces.

I believe there were compelling justifications to arrest Sadr and suppress his violent threat early on. One of them was simple justice. He and his organization were widely believed responsible for the brutal murder of the liberal Shiite cleric Abdul Majid al-Khoei. It was not just his moderate religious stance that had made Khoei so vital a figure. His father was the esteemed religious leader of Iraqi Shiites preceding Ayatollah Sistani, and the Khoei dynasty had played a significant role in Iraqi Shi'ism for generations. Moreover, we, the United States, had helped to bring Khoei back to Najaf to be a leading voice for democracy and toleration. Khoei's murder shocked Sistani. If this crude young thug—Muqtada al-Sadr—could kill Khoei, he could murder anyone, including Sistani himself. Some analysts think it was in part the fear of assassination by Sadr that pushed Sistani into an alliance with SCIRI, the most blatantly pro-Iranian political force in Iraq, and one that had a militia that could protect the grand ayatollah. More important, the murder and subsequent impunity was one of the first in a series of events that made the Coalition look weak and hypocritical in the eyes of Iraqis (including Sistani).

Late in March 2004, one of my CPA colleagues shook his head in exasperation and despair. "We haven't had the will to confront the security challenges," he told me. "In April [2003], this was ours to lose." He did not finish the thought, but it was: "And we are losing it." After the Mahdi Army seized control of much of the Shiite south in April, Major General Martin Dempsey, commander of the First Armored Division then fighting Sadr's forces, conceded, "Clearly, in the six months between October and April when he instigated this attack, he was training troops, gaining resources, stockpiling ammunition. And so when I say we missed the opportunity, we probably gave him six more months than we should have."[36] It is ironic—and tragic—that an administration so bold as to launch a war to topple Saddam Hussein blanched at the prospect of confronting a much smaller bully like Muqtada al-Sadr, who was reviled by the Shiite religious establishment and the bulk of the population. As a result, resentment and distrust built up to explosive proportions, the Coalition lost credibility, and an insurgency that might have been contained through clever politicking or the early, decisive application of force rapidly grew in ferocity and popular support.[37]

To be sure, Bremer inherited an awesomely difficult situation, which was riddled with the contradictions intrinsic to the postwar situation—and to any imperial occupation. If he went too far in accommodating the Sunnis and incorporating the Baathists, he risked losing the Shiites and the Kurds. If he did not go far enough, he faced an insurgency that he did not have the force to crush. If he sought more troops, he risked reinforcing Iraqis' fears that the United States was settling in for a long period of domination. If he did not have enough troops, he risked a bitter loss of Iraqi confidence in his administration, for its inability to meet the basic obligation of any political authority— to maintain order and protect the lives of its subjects.

★

The mistakes were ones not only of substance but of attitude and demeanor. On both the military and civilian sides of the occupation, I believe, our intentions were basically good. Yes, there were the racists and sexual sadists who tortured and defiled Iraqis, and the honor of the United States, at Abu Ghraib. There were soldiers who got ground down and nasty after months of being shot at, ambushed, and bombed. And there were civilian officials who did not give a damn what Iraqis thought. However, the most reprehensible aspect of the American presence in Iraq, and in particular of its central headquarters in the palace, was not colonial ambition or mean-spiritedness but rather the same combination of arrogance, ignorance, and isolation that had plunged America into the war in the first place. The thousand-plus officials at CPA headquarters lived and worked in an artificial bubble (indeed that was the term, "the bubble," that many outsiders gave to the Green Zone). The layers of security did an excellent job of keeping the insurgents and terrorists out, save for their nightly mortar rounds. But the fortress also kept us barricaded in. Given the shortage of armored cars, helicopters, and other security assets, most CPA officials in the Green Zone did not venture out much, and few of us had contact with ordinary Iraqis who did not work for the CPA. One independent Iraqi intellectual complained to me, "The CPA behaves as if it knows everything. It has never reached out to the Iraqis. It is easier to go to Washington than to cross the bridge over the Tigris into the CPA." An experienced diplomat who worked in the CPA later reflected to me:

> What struck me most about the palace was the completely self-referential character of it. It was all about us, not about them [the Iraqis]. People would walk around the palace with a mixture of venal and idealistic motives. None of them knew Iraq. They thought they did. They talked to people on the Governing Council who spoke English well, and they thought that was Iraq. They did not know the country beyond the Governing Council. They didn't get out except to see Governing Council members.

The isolation extended to the way Bremer ran the CPA. Bremer himself cannot be accused of not venturing out. He did so often, speaking and touring around the country, at great physical risk. The security detail around him was a sight to behold: armored Humvees with heavy machine guns on top, a number of black, armored SUVs loaded with advanced communications gear and professional, heavily armed private security guards (most of them former army Rangers or navy Seals), now and then accompanied by Apache helicopters circling overhead. Day or night, home or office, Bremer was never without well-armed, physically imposing bodyguards. During his time in Iraq, perhaps no American official on the planet, other than President Bush, had a more elaborate security detail—and needed one. While Bremer sincerely wanted to engage Iraqis, he did so mostly by speaking rather than listening, and when he moved about, he was enveloped in a miniature version of the bubble. His isolation was accentuated by the centralized nature of his administration, which relied primarily on a few trusted political appointees in the Governance Office (two of them quite young) who spoke no Arabic and had no prior experience in the Arab world. His choice of advisers did not reflect the want of expertise inside the palace. At one time, in fact, there were as many as five senior American diplomats with ambassadorial rank and, collectively, decades of experience in the Middle East. For the most part, however, they were severely underutilized. Why were they not the major negotiators at the bargaining table with the members of the Governing Council? My guess is that Bremer did not fully trust the career diplomats, and neither did the Pentagon and the White House—which is why the State Department was marginalized from the beginning in Iraq. Bremer was famous for wanting to be in total control—a penchant he may have picked up from the two secretaries of state in whose executive offices he had served, Henry Kissinger and Alexander Haig. Although he thought this attitude made him an outstanding manager, many who worked under him had a different view. One of his senior officials later reflected in frustration, "He stovepiped everything. Nobody knew what anybody else was doing." The military was equally frustrated, since one consequence of the compartmentalization was a lack of integration and joint planning between the civilian and the military components of the occupation.[38]

Bremer represented the best and the worst of the United States. He was brilliant and yet had only a limited understanding of Iraq. He was alternately (and at times simultaneously) engaging and domineering, charming and patronizing, informal and imperial, practical and inflexible, impressive in his grasp of detail and yet incessantly micromanaging. Although he was an eloquent, appealing personality, he was excessively image-conscious, and lost many opportunities to win over Iraqi constituencies by insisting on a centralized control of "the message." Thus he failed to consult often enough, widely enough with Iraqi constituencies (or even among the CPA staff), and when he finally made adjustments, they were limited and too late in coming. One relatively sympathetic Iraqi, who interacted with Bremer over many months on a number of sensitive political matters, commented after the administrator's departure from Iraq: "He had a very difficult job, and he was afraid to let go. He did not trust Iraqis. He thought the Iraqis were not competent enough to rebuild the country."

But it was not only Bremer who wanted to be in control. The Governance Office and the entire CPA oscillated between awareness of the need to discuss and negotiate, to generate Iraqi consent, and a desire, indeed a mandate, to steer the broad course of Iraq's future. For the senior officials at CPA, it was an awkward situation. There were Iraqi ministers, and there was in each ministry an American senior adviser. Who was really in control? The answer, in the end, was the message that Bremer constantly gave to the Governing Council, even as he implored and negotiated with them. He and the CPA were the supreme authority so long as the CPA existed. But this reality did not sit well with Iraqis, who did not like the very idea of occupation and expected to be regaining substantial control over their own affairs.

The difficulty hit me in stark relief three nights after I arrived, when one of our colleagues on the governance staff stormed into the office, exasperated from a late-night meeting of the Governing Council, uttering: "We have a problem. And no one wants to deal with it. The Governing Council is issuing orders and the ministers are starting to execute them." Several of us were standing around in a circle and burst out laughing. On the face of it, the statement was absurd. We were fostering a transition to sovereignty and democracy. We had established the Iraqi Governing Council. But God forbid its members should actually seek to start governing! Beneath the humor was a dilemma that was never resolved.

Bremer was the captive of the same imperial hubris that had landed the United States in Iraq with a democratizing mission but no real sense of how to accomplish it. He failed to see how the United States was viewed by Iraqis who believed they were falling under long-term occupation and wanted their country back, and by Sunnis who believed they would lose out and wanted guarantees of at least a share of power. Like senior figures in the Pentagon and the White House, he thought that the United States confronted, in Iraq, a struggle between good and evil, and he therefore resisted the idea of negotiating with representatives of the insurgent forces. His view, framed in his public remarks, was that the insurgents were "evildoers" who should be captured and killed—as if there were only a finite number of them and they were not being driven by a calculus of rational interest. It was, in the view of some within the CPA, part of the larger failing, by much of the American political establishment, to understand how we are perceived in the Muslim world, "how the powerful behave and how the powerless behave," as one of my former CPA colleagues later reflected. "It is driven across the Muslim world, this *huge* sense of injustice. They see Palestinians in the refugee camps, Iraqis in Fallujah . . . all being beaten by 'the West.' They are not angry about *our* freedom. They are angry about *their* humiliation." The sense of humiliation—in Iraq, and in the broader Arab world—only deepened with the exposure of the prison abuse scandal at Abu Ghraib, which was entirely about inflicting as much degradation and shame on Iraqi inmates as possible.

The indignation over occupation and domination by the West was not a new phenomenon but, rather, summoned up decades and indeed centuries of wounds. Because Bremer and his colleagues in the CPA and the Bush administration never grasped this history, they could not anticipate how viscerally much of Iraq would react to an extended occupation. One who understood—one of the best—was the *New York Times* correspondent John F. Burns, who wrote:

> Wherever a Westerner travels in the Arab world, there is a pervasive sense of injured pride, of people humiliated by centuries of powerlessness and poverty relative to the West. Steeped in the history of the early Caliphs, Iraqis know that Baghdad 1,000 years ago was a center of learning and military prowess. Since the modern state's founding in 1921, they have been under the boot of colonial rulers, imposed kings or brutish dictators. Now, it is America's boots they feel on their necks.[39]

An Iraqi told me of an encounter he had with a brash young CPA official with whom he grew increasingly exasperated, during repeated encounters. "You must have thoroughly studied the history of the British occupation of Iraq," the Iraqi said to the self-confident American.

"Yes, I did," the latter replied.

"I thought so," said the Iraqi, "because you seem determined to repeat every one of their mistakes."

Part of what the Americans lacked was empathy: the ability to see ourselves as Iraqis saw us. We needed to put ourselves in Iraqis' shoes, to understand their fear at the chaos and violence, their resentment of occupation, their shame in the face of American weapons and checkpoints, their powerlessness and outrage at having family members disappear into detention for weeks or months with no word on their status.

With some capacity for empathy, honed in part through facility with the language and knowledge of the history and culture, we might have perceived ourselves as a growing number of Iraqis saw us: not as liberators, but as occupiers, offending their national honor and pride even as we sought, sincerely, to help them.

★

It is reasonable to ask, Could anything have worked, after we invaded Iraq without much international support? Or after we allowed a climate of lawlessness to emerge? Or after we disbanded the army and at the same time purged tens of thousands of Baathists from the bureaucracy and the schools? Or after we turned our presence into an extended occupation? Did any of these decisions mark a point of no return for the construction of democracy—a hopeless thrust into a maze of wrong-way streets?

Every mistake the United States made in Iraq narrowed the scope and lengthened the odds for progress. That much is clear. Still, the effort at postwar reconstruction might have recovered if it had not converted itself into a long-term occupation. If the United States had asked the UN to assume the responsibility for organizing a national conference in July 2003 to choose an interim government; if, instead of sanctioning what became an Anglo-American occupation of Iraq, Resolution 1483 had provided for the transfer of authority (at least over most matters) to an Iraqi interim government, which would then have had international recognition, the political corner might have been turned. In Sergio Vieira de Mello, the United Nations had an accomplished, widely admired special representative, one of the three great figures in its system (along with Lakhdar Brahimi and the secretary-general himself, Kofi Annan). In the early period of its presence, the UN mission did not know Iraqi society as well as it would a year later, when Brahimi engaged in the consultations to select an interim government. It was learning, however, and had on its staff a number of people who knew the region and the language to a degree that few Americans did. Over several weeks, the UN mission, with help from the Coalition, might have drawn together a representative gathering of Iraqis to select an interim government. Although that body might still have been dominated by the same six or seven parties that came to dominate the Governing Council and the interim government, it would have had a greater acceptance in the country—and a greater ability to roll back the budding insurgency—if it drew in genuine Sunni representation. The key would then have been to devise—again with United Nations assistance and perhaps mediation—a reasonable timetable for transition to a constitutional, elected government. Local elections could have proceeded in a number of communities while other tasks were unfolding at the national level.

Iraq was beyond the capacity of the United Nations to administer whole, as it had done in East Timor. But with the UN in the political lead, and with the United States signaling a willingness to hand over power to an interim government chosen through a representative process, a different dynamic would have been launched. Much of the energy expended in violent resistance might have been invested in the emerging political system.

To be sure, this scenario would have had a better chance for success if order had not been allowed to collapse in the wake of the collapse of Saddam's government. Consider an alternative historical scenario, with the following steps:

1. Anticipating the chaos and looting that might transpire after the war, the United States deploys an invasion force of 250,000 to 300,000 troops.
2. Immediately on taking Baghdad, Coalition troops surround major public buildings, infrastructure, and cultural and historical sites with thousands of troops, armed not only with heavy weapons but with tear gas and other means of crowd control, and with orders to protect the structures from looting and sabotage. Public order is then reestablished relatively rapidly, with only moderate damage and loss of life.
3. Tens of thousands of Coalition troops and supporting aircraft are deployed along Iraq's borders to prevent the incursion of foreign fighters—and the exit of Saddam loyalists.
4. The Iraqi police are called back to duty, with promises of retention, increased pay, and professional retraining for all those who pass an extended vetting process.

5. All soldiers and officers (up to a certain level) in the Iraqi Army are told to report to regional centers, where they are processed to receive continuing pay and then considered for readmission to duty.

6. A policy is announced that bans a few thousand top Baath Party and government officials from public life, while subjecting the other top tiers of party membership to a vetting process that retains them in their public sector jobs, and their right to run for office, if they are not found guilty of serious abuses under the old order. The Baath Party itself is allowed to reemerge under a new leadership.

7. Immediately on establishing authority in Baghdad, the United States proposes to transfer to the United Nations the primary authority for constituting, within three months, an Iraqi interim government, beginning with the selection of national conference delegates from communities around the country and ending with the conference choosing the members of an interim government.

8. In the emerging political processes, Iraqi exile groups must compete for standing with leaders and social forces that remained in the country, and the resulting national conference runs the gamut of political tendencies, from mainstream forces to former Baathists and radical Islamists (a minority presence).

9. During the first six months after the war, local elections are conducted, to the extent possible, in communities across the country.

10. The United Nations and the United States ask the interim government, in interaction with the national conference delegates, to draw up a timetable for the election of a constitutional convention, the drafting of a constitution, and the election of a permanent government.

There is no guarantee that such a scenario would have been successful. But it might have taken the steam out of the resistance and focused Iraqis on peacefully reorganizing and rebuilding the country. The other cleavages—ethnic, regional, and sectarian—would have asserted themselves, as they inevitably do. Even so, the country might have been able to get on with the political challenges it faced.

★

It is too soon to know what verdict historians will render on the American invasion and occupation of Iraq. I believe they will judge our mistakes harshly. Despite the litany of blunders we have committed, Iraq may yet emerge slowly from political chaos, first into a troubled semi-democracy, and then, gradually, into a democracy. But the costs will be much greater than we had imagined, or than were necessary. And the damage to America's standing in the region and in the world has been immense. Moreover, there is still the danger that all our postwar aspirations for Iraq—to become a democratic, stable, federal, and unified state, respectful of human rights and of its regional responsibilities— could be lost.

Although the American people will have little appetite, in the coming years, for another nation-building venture of this scale, humanitarian and geopolitical circumstances are bound to compel us to become involved again somewhere, sometime, in postconflict reconstruction. What lessons can we learn from our experience in Iraq?

The first lesson is that we cannot get to Jefferson and Madison without going through Thomas Hobbes. You can't build a democratic state unless you first have a state, and the essential condition for a state is that it must have an effective monopoly over the means of violence. Until the state can establish this capacity, a transitional authority must maintain law and order. If a democratic system is to be constructed, of course, the task cannot be undertaken with flagrant disregard for human rights. This conclusion generates four imperatives: (1) a sufficient number of troops, (2) the right mix of troops, with (3) adequate equipment and arms, and (4) robust rules of engagement. Muscular force must be deployed in sufficient depth throughout the country, and particularly in potential hot spots, to preempt looting, secure key facilities, deter troublemakers, demobilize militias, confront spoilers, and capture and kill terrorist and diehard elements. Deploying adequate force early on—something much closer to the recommended ratio of one international soldier for every fifty people—can save many lives down the road.

It is not just a question of the number of troops. International stabilization forces must have the rules of engagement to enable them to fight and, if necessary, eliminate threats to peace from terrorists, militias, and organized crime. The experience of the largely ineffective Polish-led Multinational Division in the South Central region of Iraq shows that a sizable international force does not stabilize a region unless it has the authority to fight. Equally important is the right mix of forces. Large numbers of combat troops were needed in Iraq "to conduct combat patrols in sufficient numbers to gain solid intelligence and paint a good picture of the enemy on the ground," and then "to act on the intelligence" to defeat terrorists and loyalists of the old regime.[40] But we also needed more military officers with training and experience in civil affairs—the delicate noncombat task of reviving political and economic life while maintaining order. And we needed more military police trained to control crowds, protect facilities, and prevent looting, riots, and other forms of disorder. Experts had urged the formation of rapid-response units along the lines of the French gendarmerie or the Italian carabinieri, and some military planners had wanted such forces (even the carabinieri themselves) on the ground when Baghdad fell. We lacked them.

We also needed to fill, much more quickly, the vacuum of conventional policing. In a country the size of Iraq, international actors must deploy thousands of "armed international police to monitor, train, mentor, and even substitute for indigenous forces until the creation of a proficient domestic police force," according to the RAND study published shortly after the war.[41] We had no ready reserve of specialists in rebuilding civilian policing after conflict. Instead, in May 2003, President Bush sent a former New York City police commissioner, Bernard Kerik, whose tenure at the Iraqi Ministry of Justice was widely regarded as a disaster. The Iraqi police he left behind were outgunned by the criminals, severely short of cars and radios, dispirited, and so poorly vetted that they were penetrated by criminals and insurgents. There was virtually no capacity for higher-level police functions, such as criminal investigation and police management. After Kerik left, the U.S. military wanted to take over police training, but Bremer refused. The crippling shortage of trained international police and police advisers contributed not only to the rampant criminality and disorder but also, possibly, to the abuse of prisoners at Abu Ghraib.   .

The second lesson concerns resources. Success in these difficult circumstances requires a substantial commitment of international human and financial resources, delivered in timely fashion, and sustained over an extended period, lasting (through an international engagement) for a minimum of five to ten years. The resources required in rebuilding a failed state are daunting in any case, but the challenge increases with the size of the nation—and by comparison with other recent cases, Iraq represented a substantial undertaking. We must anticipate needs and have ready, for rapid deployment, adequate equipment, including armored vehicles and state-of-the-art body armor. Some of this reserve can be dispersed to U.S. embassies and military bases around the world and then called on in times of need.

It is not just a matter of getting enough people, equipment, arms, armor, and money. Resources must reach the people of the society—ideally, with local participation and ownership. The effort requires some decentralization of the mechanisms of delivery and distribution. In Iraq, the reconstruction project never got very far because it was heavily centralized under Bremer's office in Baghdad and the Pentagon in Washington. In addition, too much money was invested in fat contracts for American corporations that wound up not being able to deliver because of the insecurity on the ground in Iraq and the slow processing in Washington. We ought to have put much more money—raw cash—into the hands, early on, of civil affairs programs that could, in turn, have gotten Iraqis at the community level employed in rebuilding their country, one neighborhood at a time. And we should have further decentralized our assistance by giving the CPA's provincial and regional civilian authorities more budget authority to get buildings, roads, sewers, and other infrastructure repaired by local contractors, with performance incentives and simplified contracting procedures. Would there have been a risk of corruption seeping in? Yes. But local Coalition staff, working with independent Iraqi representatives, could have monitored the performance of the contractors, and the risk of some local corruption would be a small price to pay, if we could get

Iraqis employed in large numbers, communities mobilized for their renewal, and infrastructure repaired. As it was, we had mismanagement in the contracts on a grander scale—and little progress was made. By the June 28 handover, the CPA had been able to spend only a small fraction of the $18.4 billion appropriated by Congress in November 2003 for Iraqi reconstruction.

The third lesson is that the United States must organize itself effectively for postconflict reconstruction. The government is not set up institutionally to manage the challenges we have faced and will continue to face in the post–Cold War world. In the 1990s, it was the State Department that coordinated American engagement after conflict. In Iraq—a country many times larger than the conflict-ridden states of the 1990s—the Pentagon was given control, and it botched the task grievously, until, finally, responsibility was transferred to the National Security Council. Yet the NSC is even less of an operational body than the State Department, and it lacks the capacity to oversee such a complex administrative task. The Department of Defense has developed functional capacity for peacekeeping operations, but overseeing the political and economic reconstruction of a devastated nation is quite a different task, for which the Pentagon is ill equipped.

In August 2004, in response to the glaring institutional deficit in the U.S. government, the Bush administration authorized the State Department to create the Office of the Coordinator for Reconstruction and Stabilization. The office is expected to develop the capacity (including a cadre of policy experts and professionals with on-the-ground experience) to aid countries in transition from conflict to a stable peace, democracy, and a market economy. The operation should beef up our ability to carry out rapid, effective reconstruction after conflict, but its assignment does not go far enough.

A number of policy professionals recognize that we need a more comprehensive operational capacity, with extensive institutional memory, to manage and coordinate postconflict engagements. The last significant reorganization of the government's capacity to assist countries in need came in 1961, when the Agency for International Development was established out of several foreign aid programs that had emerged during the Marshall Plan in the late 1940s and early 1950s. The world today differs substantially from the way it was during the Cold War era, but we have not significantly revised the structure of our government to respond rapidly, intelligently, and systematically to postconflict or humanitarian imperatives. Although the State Department is the most logical cabinet department to take on this role, it lacks the expertise in relief, reconstruction, and development, as well as the operational capacity. While some diplomats in provincial and regional offices in Iraq proved adept at arranging for communities to be repaired, facilities built, and civic organization supported, such work is not what they are trained to do as diplomats.

The agency with the mandate that most closely approximates the task is USAID, the chief American instrument for delivering development and humanitarian assistance. Within the agency are several elements that belong in the postconflict mix, including the Office of Humanitarian Affairs, to deliver emergency relief and coordinate on refugee flows, and the Office of Transition Initiatives, or OTI, which, as noted in chapter 5, arrives rapidly, connects with local civil society actors, and provides small grants with less bureaucracy. However, USAID is not a cabinet-level department, and the lead agency should have this status in order to sit on the National Security Council and coordinate, authoritatively, the work of other agencies and departments. What is needed now is to enlarge, formalize, and integrate USAID's existing roles by elevating it to a cabinet-level department for international development and reconstruction. The new department should have a significantly larger staff than the current 2,000 USAID officers, only a thousand of whom are career professionals. Such a department, built around an enhanced USAID, could recruit, foster, and integrate the individuals and groups who could provide the necessary expertise, and establish the coordinating authority, to permit the United States to respond with maximum speed, experience, professionalism, and flexibility. The department would also give the United States an appropriate institution with which to engage the multilateral and bilateral assistance agencies, including the United Nations, that most often wind up on the ground in these situations. Until we develop such an infrastructure, we are likely to stumble from one postconflict crisis to another in piecemeal fashion, without the coherence, expertise, and institutional learning vital to success.

The fourth lesson from the Iraqi experience concerns the timing of elections. It is one of the most vexing questions confronting all postconflict reconstruction efforts. Ill-timed and ill-prepared elections do not produce democracy, or even political stability, after conflict. Instead, they may only enhance the power of actors who incite coercion, fear, and prejudice, thereby reviving autocracy and even precipitating large-scale strife. In Angola in 1992, in Bosnia in 1996, and in Liberia in 1997, rushed elections set back the prospects for democracy and, in Angola and Liberia, paved the way for renewed civil war.[42] There are thus powerful reasons to defer national elections until militias have been demobilized, moderate parties trained and assisted, electoral infrastructure created, and democratic media and ideas generated. If one takes these cautions too literally, however, national elections may end up being deferred for a decade or more, and the challenge then becomes how to constitute an authority that will have legitimacy in the interim.

International interventions that seek to construct democracy after conflict must balance the tension between prolonged domination for the sake of implanting democracy and early withdrawal (typically, after elections) in the name of democracy. A key question is how long international rule can be viable. In the case of Iraq, the answer—readily apparent from history and from the profound, widespread suspicion among Iraqis of U.S. motives—was "not long."

If a representative interim government had been constructed early on, national elections could probably have been delayed for as much as two years. The Shiites' demand for an elected government would have compelled elections sooner than what would have seemed prudent from the standpoint of experience, but some of the pressure might have been alleviated if Iraqis around the country had been allowed to elect local and even provincial governments.

The failure to hold early, direct elections for local and provincial governments was another mistake of the occupation. One person involved in some of the indirect selection processes for local and provincial councils reflected to me in December 2004, "I keep regretting that we did not go ahead with local and provincial elections. We talked about it late into the night, but there was anxiety about fragmentation. It would have been easier to hold elections in the three provinces around Baghdad [in early 2004] than it is today. Now, we have the worst of what we were trying to avoid and none of the benefits from elections for local leaders." The CPA could have learned an important lesson from past efforts at nation building: holding community or provincial elections first "provides an opportunity for new local leaders to emerge and gain experience and for political parties to build a support base."[43] That could well have happened in Iraq if local elections had been allowed to proceed during 2003 or early 2004, and if some meaningful authority and resources had devolved to the recently elected bodies. Then the United States would have faced a more diverse and more legitimate array of Iraqi interlocutors, and the elected local bodies could have provided one basis for selecting an interim government.

The final, overriding lesson of America's misadventure in postwar Iraq is not "don't do it" but "don't do it alone," and "don't do it with an imperial approach." The experience in Iraq cautions against the gung ho logic that a country can be quickly transformed from dictatorship to democracy by warfare and occupation. Without an international mandate and coalition for regime transformation, any such mission in the future would no doubt face crippling shortages both of resources and of domestic and international legitimacy. This is in part why the RAND study concludes: "Multilateral nation-building can produce more thoroughgoing transformations and greater regional reconciliation than can unilateral efforts."[44] In postwar Iraq, the Bush administration could claim that more than thirty countries were involved in stabilizing and rebuilding the country; hence the occupation was a *Coalition* Provisional Authority. However, what the Iraqis saw was not an international coalition but an occupation by the United States and Britain—the most powerful nation in the world, paired with Iraq's former colonial ruler.

Success at postwar reconstruction requires greater humility than the United States exhibited in Iraq, including a strategy for involving the people of the country as quickly as possible in rebuilding their society, economy, and political system. No international reconstruction effort can succeed without some degree of acceptance and cooperation—and, eventually, support and positive engagement—from the local population. If the people have no trust in the international administration and its intentions, the intervention can become the target of popular wrath, and must then spend most of its military (and administrative) energies defending *itself* rather than rebuilding the country.

In the final page of a wise and learned book on postconflict state building, Simon Chesterman of New York University's Institute for International Law and Justice writes: "Modern trusteeships demand, above all, trust on the part of local actors. Earning and keeping that trust requires a level of understanding, sensitivity, and respect for local traditions and political aspirations that has often been lacking in international administration."[45] The American occupation lacked these qualities, and the Iraqi people knew it. Confidence was squandered from the beginning, with the failure to impose and maintain order, and the heavy reliance on Iraqi politicians returning from decades in exile. The trust and goodwill of the Iraqi people were further diminished by the failure to develop a clear, sustainable plan for transferring, early on, significant governing authority back to the Iraqis.

All international interventions to reconstruct a failed state on democratic foundations confront a fundamental contradiction. Their goal is democracy—freely elected government in which the people are sovereign. Yet their means are undemocratic—some form of imperial domination, however temporary. How can the circle be squared? Chesterman advises that when international actors come "to exercise state-like functions, they must not lose sight of their limited mandate to hold that sovereign power in trust for the population that will ultimately claim it."[46] This task requires a balancing of international trusteeship or imperial functions with a distinctly nonimperial attitude and a clear, early specification of an acceptable timetable for the restoration of sovereignty. The humiliating features of an extended, all-out occupation should be avoided.

In recent years, a few bold thinkers have called for an era of "liberal empire," in which the United States, as the world's "indispensable nation," and perhaps Europe as well, would use its power to impose on the world's failed and failing states the institutions of political and economic freedom—even by renewed colonial administration. Perhaps the most audacious advocate of this approach is the British historian Niall Ferguson, who has suggested that "Liberia would benefit immeasurably from something like an American colonial administration," and that, even if formal sovereignty was transferred soon in Iraq (as it was in June 2004), the United States should retain effective control over "military, fiscal, and monetary policies" through a "viceroy in all but name for decades."[47] Reviewing the history of the British colonial empire, Ferguson concludes that the United States should resist the pressure for an early end to effective domination of Iraq: "[I]t is possible to occupy a country for decades, while consistently denying that you have any intention of doing so. This is known as hypocrisy, and it is something to which liberal empires must sometimes resort."[48]

Moral issues aside, however, we are not in the imperial era of the late nineteenth century. Moreover, as Ferguson notes—and as the British painfully encountered in Iraq after World War I—there was plenty of violent resistance in the imperial era. In today's world, nationalism and anticolonialism run deep, and gratitude for international protection or liberation can quickly turn into anger against the intervening force.

It was the failure to comprehend these dynamics—and, indeed, to ponder seriously the lessons of the British colonial experience in Iraq— that was perhaps the single greatest mistake of the U.S. intervention. From this failure flowed everything else: the glib confidence that the occupiers would be welcomed as liberators, the expectation that only a relatively light force would be required for the postwar era, and the decision to embark on a formal, extended occupation when U.S. plans for a rapid handover collapsed amid the mounting disorder.

Iraq may well be the last instance for many years to come in which the United States finds its troops on the ground after an invasion to topple a regime. But it will not be the last time that the United States intervenes to help end a conflict or a crime against humanity, and to help build a viable and democratic peace. On balance, America's political occupation of Iraq was a failure. If we learn from our mistakes, our next engagement to help rebuild a collapsed state might have a more successful outcome.

11

CAN IRAQ BECOME A DEMOCRACY?

★

Most of my colleagues in the Coalition Provisional Authority were dedicated people who believed in the mission of helping Iraq to become a democracy, and an effective state once again. But they confronted a set of challenges that were formidable to begin with, and were then made much more so by the staggering failures of preparation on the part of Bush administration officials in Washington, especially in the Pentagon. A few months after I returned from Iraq, a young American military officer, just back from a tour of duty there, said to me, "Most Iraqis are good people—in a bad situation." Can good people in a bad situation still bring about democracy?

I believe that the majority of Iraqis want a democratic system for their country. It is difficult to know for sure, because opinion polls have been contradictory, and in any case pollsters have not reached beyond the urban centers. When asked in February 2004 what type of government they wanted, 86 percent of Iraqis polled approved of democracy, but 81 percent also endorsed having a single strong leader, and 53 percent supported "a government made up mainly of religious leaders." When asked to choose between democracy, a strong leader "for life," and an Islamic state, half chose democracy and half one of the two authoritarian options.[1] The majority of Iraqis do not understand all the intricacies of separation of powers, checks and balances, and minority rights. One of the great threats to the prospect for democracy is precisely that so many Iraqis, particularly among the long-suppressed Shiite majority, view democracy as mainly consisting of rule by the majority. In a deeply divided country like Iraq, with well-armed minority groups, such a one-dimensional concept of democracy cannot be viable. But Iraqi knowledge of democracy and the options for structuring it remain, at this writing, fluid and open. That fact itself provides some cause for hope. Although they are cynical about political parties, Iraqis overwhelmingly express a desire to choose their leaders in regular, free, and fair elections. That is one reason for the large, courageous, and deeply moving turnout of voters in most parts of the country in the January 30, 2005, elections. Moreover, if Iraqis do not, by and large, have a refined understanding of habeas corpus and international human rights covenants, they nevertheless have an emerging concept of rights, and they value the political and civil freedoms that were at least formally established during the occupation.[2] The CPA did some good in educating the people about these values and in strengthening them. Moreover, after several decades of tyranny, Iraqis know what they do not want. They do not wish to live in fear anymore, having to hide what is in their minds and their hearts. Nor do they want to dread the knock on the door in the middle of the night from a state security apparatus that can make them disappear for good without a trace. They desire a state that must observe basic standards and restraint, and that can be held to account by the people. In other words, most Iraqis yearn for some kind of democracy and rule of law.

However, it is not only the state that can make citizens afraid for their lives. People can be robbed of their freedom by an overbearing political order, and by the absence of order as well. Since the fall of Saddam Hussein, Iraqis have grappled with the personal insecurity that derives from disorder—the proliferation of armed militias, pseudo-religious warlords, criminal gangs, and terrorist cells, which seek to impose their rules, demands, and political visions. Exhibiting such behavior was one reason why Muqtada al-Sadr was reviled by much of the population in the Shiite south, and why the tribes organized to resist him. Before Iraq can become a democratic state, as we noted in the previous chapter, it must first become a state, which establishes a monopoly over the means of violence. Doing so will require strengthening not only the capacity but also the discipline of its armed forces (including the police), so that they answer to the authority of the central state and fight as one to defend it.

Unfortunately, Iraq has a long road to traverse toward this goal. The country must develop ambitious programs for the recruitment, training, and equipping of its army, National Guard, and other units (for which international assistance is vital); it must also foster a political climate in which citizens with distinct regional, ethnic, and religious allegiances have an equal or higher loyalty to the nation. Moreover, political parties, movements, and leaders who represent the various groups must work out, among themselves, agreements for sharing power and for restraining its abuse. Another requirement is a strategy for thwarting the efforts of Iran to penetrate the Iraqi government, party system, and security apparatus. And, finally, Iraq needs the one thing that most disastrously eluded both the CPA and the interim government that followed it—a political accommodation with the bulk of the Sunni population that feels marginalized from the emerging political order.

★

In the political flux of a decaying or collapsed regime, or a long period of violence and civil strife, competing ethnic, religious, class, and political actors do not embrace constitutional democracy out of idealism or magnanimity. Typically, they would prefer victory to compromise, domination to toleration, and power monopoly to power sharing. Anxiety stalks all sides, each one fearing that if it does not maximize its position, it may wind up with nothing. Yet if all sides seek to entrench their power, the result will not be security but rather Hobbes's worst nightmare: a war of "all against all" until one side triumphs. This situation represents, in the language of political science, a massive "coordination problem." The only way to solve it is through the simultaneous commitment, on the part of all major actors, to a series of restraints.

In the wake of violent struggle, a democratic constitution provides what the Yale political scientist Robert Dahl calls a "system of mutual security."[3] Under such a system, power is diffused in a variety of ways. The influence of the majority is restrained, and the rights of political and ethnic minorities are guaranteed. Each side is given protections for its most vital interests. Groups gain confidence that, if they find themselves in political opposition, they will not be suppressed or abused by the government. Obviously, a sturdy constitution and honest court system are crucial here. But they can bear only so much of the load. Other institutions are also vital.

Democracies around the world pursue various institutional strategies for giving each group some sense of political security. One way to do this is through an explicit power-sharing system, in which each group is guaranteed a fixed share of cabinet posts and other government positions, all major groups are drawn into a grand coalition, and large minorities are granted some veto over major policies. In their most comprehensive form, such systems have not fared well in the developing world, but rather, as in Lebanon, have further polarized ethnic groups in a way that intensifies political instability and even violent conflict. It is therefore ironic and—to many Iraqis and outside observers—worrisome that Iraq has, in its interim arrangements, borrowed some of the most notable features of the Lebanese power-sharing system, such as the allocation of cabinet posts to groups through ethnic quotas, and the agreement that the prime minister will be from one religious group (Shiite) and the president from another (Sunni). An alternative approach generates structural inducements to moderation, by encouraging groups to align with one another on the basis of crosscutting interests.[4] Yet both approaches favor federalism and devolution of power as tools for managing conflict in a deeply divided society, and both recognize that if groups are going to commit to democracy, each one needs to see that it has a tangible stake in the emerging system. Thus, both approaches avoid constitutional arrangements that simply empower the majority at the expense of the minority.

To ask whether Iraq can become a democracy, then, is to determine whether it can arrive at the point where all the groups that have the potential to overthrow, sabotage, destabilize, or otherwise undermine the system accept it, instead, as in their best interest. Fortunately, it is not necessary, at the outset, that all major groups value democracy intrinsically as the best form of government. Often throughout history, democracy has been embraced by competing (even warring) political forces as a pragmatic compromise, a second-best alternative when each side realized it could not attain or preserve (at least not without an unacceptable cost) its real aim: total power. In this common scenario—which includes not only recent instances of democracy after conflict, such as in El Salvador, Nicaragua, South Africa, and Mozambique, but many earlier transitions to democracy in Europe and Latin America—liberalization follows a period of "prolonged and inconclusive political struggle" that leaves contending forces fearful or exhausted, ready to agree on new rules of the game. According to the "genetic" theory of democratization, as the late political scientist Dankwart Rustow named it, "What matters at the decision stage is not what values the leaders hold dear in the abstract, but what concrete steps they are willing to take."[5] If they can agree on constitutional measures that serve the interests of each group and set of leaders, and that wisely structure and limit power, then democracy may gradually take root. Sometimes this happens with the aid of agreements among key leaders that explicitly (though not always publicly) guarantee the vital interests of the different groups.[6] Over time, with good institutions and some luck, politicians will at least behave as if they were democrats, and the commitment to democratic values may seep in gradually, as "both politicians and citizens learn from the successful resolution of some issues to place their faith in the new rules and to apply them to new issues."[7]

If this vision of how democracy emerges is disheartening, in that many leaders may embrace it for selfish, cynical, and purely tactical reasons, it is also hopeful, because it expands the horizons of the possible. If democracy can be initiated only when all the major stakeholders believe in free and fair elections, justice, liberty, and the rule of law, then few democracies would exist in the world today. On the other hand, as James Madison observed, "If men were angels, no government would be necessary."

The genetic view of democracy—as something that takes shape gradually, often out of instrumental commitments—is hopeful in another sense as well. For some time, it was assumed that in order to be a democracy, a country must meet a number of social requirements: a degree of economic development, with an educated population, a large middle class, and limited inequality; a pluralistic civil society, with an array of associations and media independent of the state; a religious and cultural orientation that values individual initiative and questions authority; a relatively homogeneous population culturally, or at least one that is not deeply divided along ethnic or religious lines; and, finally, a culture in which informed, questioning, self-confident citizens participate in politics while evincing a commitment to moderation, tolerance, civility, and, of course, democracy itself.[8] Iraq, of course, is a long way from meeting most of these social, economic, and cultural conditions for democracy.

Three decades ago, the prospects for democracy in the world looked grim, especially if one took seriously these preconditions for democracy. If we define democracy as a system of government in which the people can choose their leaders and replace them in free and fair elections, then barely one-quarter of the independent states in the world were democracies in 1974. They were mainly in the West—Europe, North America, Australia, and New Zealand (with Japan by then an honorary member of the democratic "West"). Democracy had taken hold in a few low-income countries in what was called the Third World—for example, India, Sri Lanka, Costa Rica, Venezuela, and Botswana—but these nations were considered the exceptions to the rule. By some accounts, the prospects even appeared dim in predominantly Catholic countries—Portugal, Spain, Latin America—because of the autocratic structure of the church and the presumed authoritarian values of its believers. Nevertheless, a wave of transitions to democracy began—in Portugal in 1974, sweeping across southern Europe and then Latin America. By the early 1980s, most governments in the world still remained authoritarian in one form or another, and when the Harvard political scientist Samuel P. Huntington asked, in the title of a famous article, "Will More Countries Become Democratic?" his answer was, essentially, no.[9] Economic growth, a bourgeoisie, and a market economy were necessary for democratic progress, and not many countries seemed then, in his view, poised in the "zone of transition." Yet the 1980s and early 1990s turned out to be the period of the most explosive growth in democracy in human history. By 1994, just a decade after Huntington published his skeptical piece, three-fifths of the world's states were democracies.[10] By then, Huntington had written a book celebrating this unprecedented "third wave" of global democratization.[11] Today, every area of the world contains a significant presence of democracy, except the Arab Middle East, where not a single state is democratic.

★

Even with the difficulties and mistakes of the postwar period, it is possible that Iraq can gradually become a democracy through the kind of genetic process that Rustow describes. In building a democracy, Iraq would not be starting from scratch. As the political scientist Adeed Dawisha has shown, the country saw a robust if partial emergence of democratic institutions, and even liberal beliefs, during the first four decades of the modern Iraqi state, from 1921 until the overthrow of the Hashemite monarchy in the 1958 military coup.[12] Such progress could provide a historical foundation on which to build. But for a democratic evolution to unfold—even initially through an extended period of semi-democracy, in which elections are not fully free and fair and the rule of law is weak—three conditions are necessary: the political arena must be made more inclusive; there must be a balance of power among Iraqi groups; and Iraq's major politicians and parties must evince pragmatism and flexibility.

First, the Iraqi leaders of the transitional government must draw into the political system a wider range of relevant actors. In the harsh language of conflict-ridden societies, any group that can mobilize violence, or enough popular support to destabilize politics, is "relevant." Some of the actors responsible for the insurgent and terrorist violence cannot be brought into the emerging political system at any price. At a minimum, this restriction applies to the foreign terrorists, such as Abu Musab al-Zarqawi and his Al Qaeda followers, who have infiltrated Iraq and seek now to establish it as the kind of safe haven for jihad against the West that Afghanistan was before September 11. It probably applies, as well, to the most extreme homegrown Sunni Muslim fundamentalists—radical Wahabists and revolutionary Salafists—who are influenced and funded from outside the country and seek a puritan-ical state under Islamic Sharia law.[13] These groups felt nothing but con-tempt for Saddam, but they are happy to cooperate with his surviving loyalists in order to wage holy war on the United States. Those Saddam loyalists who are still wanted for arrest, in turn, are happy to cooperate with the religious extremists, because they see no future for themselves in Iraq other than through the sort of chaos that might enable them to return to power. If Iraq is to become a democracy, these diehard ele-ments, secular and religious, must be isolated—separated from their networks of sympathy and support—and either captured, killed, or driven out of the country for good.

These organizations are not the only components of the insurgency, however. By late 2003, some of the groups that were either behind the in-surgency or lending it critical support were signaling an interest in nego-tiating entry into the political game. These predominantly Sunni Arab Iraqis who back the insurgency but may be willing to abandon it fall into several groups. One consists of Baathists who were disillusioned with Saddam and his tyranny even before the invasion but who still subscribe to the nationalist, pan-Arabist, and socialist principles of the Baath Party. This group probably cannot be brought into the political process unless its members are permitted to reconstitute the Baath Party as a legal con-tender and to run for office under its banner. Supporters of democracy—in Iraq and in the United States—would no doubt find the reconstituted party still offensive. But that is not the point. The Baath Party is not going to be voted back to power in Iraq. In the same way that allowing a recon-stituted Communist Party to contest elections helped to stabilize politics in Russia after its democratic revolution in the early 1990s, so the inclu-sion of a Baath Party in Iraq would do the same. The second group con-sists of the predominant network of Sunni Muslim clerics, organized into the Association of Muslim Scholars, whose secretary-general, Harith al-Dhari, has been an outspoken supporter of the resistance against the oc-cupation. The third group consists of secular Arab nationalists, including many intellectuals and professionals, who are not Baathists but adamantly oppose the occupation in all its aspects and want Iraq to be a great Arab nation again. The fourth group (really a loose network) con-sists of Sunni tribal sheikhs who benefited from Saddam's largesse.

Finally, the fifth group consists of mainstream Islamist parties, based in the Sunni heartland, who equivocate between participation and protest (many in this group reject violence, however). The most important of these has been the Iraqi Islamic Party, led by Mohsen Abdul Hamid, who was a member of the Governing Council but then, late in 2004, withdrew his party from the January 2005 elections in protest, articulating many of the grievances that other Sunni groups had raised.

These Sunni groups are socially, politically, and ideologically diverse. But they share a core set of concerns. They regard the Sunnis as the big losers of the invasion and occupation, and in one sense they were, as they lost their monopoly over power and resources and were disproportionately affected by the de-Baathification campaign. They feel victimized and humiliated by the occupation, its treatment of detainees, the destruction of Fallujah, and the disbandment of the Iraqi Army. Looking to the future, they fear that the Sunnis will be marginalized in the new political order, as the majority Shiites—with support from Iran—gain control of the country and its resources.

It is always risky to predict the future, but most independent analysts of Iraq believe that the nation will not be stable—and the insurgency will not diminish—until the political concerns of the Sunni Arab minority are addressed. While democracy can tolerate, however tragically, some degree of terrorism and violence, it cannot establish itself amid violence on the scale that has plagued Iraq during the postwar period. If Iraq is to become a democracy—or even a decent place to live—in the next few years, negotiations must take place with many of the groups that are waging or supporting the insurgency. The aim of these talks would be straightforward: to craft a political pact, a system of mutual security, that would assure these varied Sunni groups of their most vital interests, so that they would agree to abandon violence and play the political game.

Could such an agreement be reached in a manner consistent with democracy? For both the Sunni groups and Muqtada al-Sadr and his network of fundamentalist Shiites it is a central question. I believe it is possible, for two reasons. First, many of the Sunni groups appear to understand that the days of Sunni hegemony in Iraq are over. Now they want to keep the Shiites from turning the tables on them. They want a guarantee of a minimum share of power and resources. Ironically, they have, in this respect, a common interest with the Kurds, who also wish to see the state structured in a way that will guarantee each regional group its share of national wealth and autonomy over its own affairs, while preventing any one group from dominating at the center. For this reason, many Sunni Arabs—including the Iraqi Islamic Party—despite their tradition of support for a centralized state, began to warm to some of the federalist guarantees in the interim constitution that were designed to check the power of the majority.

The second reason for hope lies in what some of the leaders of these groups have been saying in public. Stripping aside much of the overheated nationalist rhetoric, one finds in their statements denouncing and boycotting the January 2005 elections a set of practical concerns. Thus, when a group of religious and secular Sunni Arab nationalists (including prominently the Association of Muslim Scholars) surfaced on October 27, 2004, as the Iraqi National Founding Congress, they focused on "the essential requirements for the proper conduct of elections." They called for a postponement of the elections, but they did not demand the withdrawal of American forces or the dissolution of the interim government before elections take place. Rather, they recommended that the elections be supervised by an international body, including figures from the Arab and Islamic world "who have moral weight and an unblemished reputation," and that a "number of Iraqi judges known for their impartiality and independence" be appointed to the electoral commission. They wanted "freedom for all components of Iraqi society to stand as candidates," implicitly including former Baathists and a reorganized Baath Party. They sought the withdrawal of occupation forces from cities and towns a month before the elections, and "the release of all political detainees and prisoners." In other statements, Sunni Arab groups demanded a postponement of the elections to give them more time to organize and to permit a change in the electoral system, from the single nationwide district to one of multimember districts, based on the provinces. Either system would have utilized proportional representation based on party lists, but the latter one would have guaranteed each province a share of the seats in parliament, while the nationwide-list system opened the prospect that, with fewer

Sunnis voting because of the violence and disruption of social and political life in those areas, Sunnis would be underrepresented in parliament. The focus on the electoral system, the electoral commission, and the timing of elections suggests that important elements of Iraq's Sunni Arabs have begun thinking seriously about the mechanics of democratic politics. They need to be brought into the game with rules and referees they consider fair.

Muqtada al-Sadr and his followers might be brought into the political system as well—especially if Sadr realizes that his support will diminish if he defies a government led by Shiites and blessed by Ayatollah Sistani—but including Sadr would require making a place for him in politics and, in essence, dropping the murder charges against him. For anyone who believes in justice and the rule of law, this is a repugnant prospect. But if the Americans did not have the nerve to confront Sadr, it is unlikely that a much shakier Iraqi government would do so.

★

The second condition for democracy to proceed in Iraq is a balance of power among the political forces. If Iraq is gradually to become a democracy, no single group can be allowed to dominate. Much of this outcome will depend on the state of politics in the Shiite majority. In the January 2005 elections for the transitional national assembly, the two major Shiite political parties—SCIRI and Da'wa—joined with a variety of other Shiite Islamist and even nonreligious parties, including Ahmed Chalabi's Iraqi National Congress and Abdul-Karim al-Muhammadawi's Hizbollah Iraq, in a broad coalition, implicitly endorsed by Sistani, called the United Iraqi Alliance. In a sign of the fluidity we are likely to see in the coming years in Iraqi electoral politics—if peaceful politics survive—the list was drawn together by Dr. Hussein Sharistani, the same Shiite civic leader whom SCIRI and Da'wa had blocked from becoming interim prime minister. The list also had a smattering of Sunni Arab, Kurdish, and Turkoman religious parties, and some representatives from Muqtada al-Sadr's movement.

The results of the January 2005 national elections were announced just as this book was going to press, and well before the shape of the new government became clear. Still, the election results themselves underscore some of the points I have made in this book, and they permit me to speculate on the serious challenges that lie ahead for democracy, and peace, in Iraq. In winning close to half the vote (about 48 percent)—and thereby obtaining an outright, if bare, majority of seats in the new National Assembly—the United Iraqi Alliance won a stunning victory, and the quest of a variety of other groups to produce a more dispersed, pluralistic balance of power was largely thwarted. While the spectacle of so many Iraqis voting freely, courageously, and joyously on January 30 was a moving demonstration of democratic aspirations and possibilities, the election took on much of the character of an identity referendum. The predominant Shiite coalition—what was often referred to as "the Sistani list" because it claimed to have Sistani's backing and freely used his picture as its main campaign symbol— swept an estimated 70 percent or more of the Shiite vote, and seemed likely to convert that support into control of the new parliament and government. Almost all the Kurds voted for the common Kurdish list, the Kurdistan Alliance, which united the KDP and the PUK—and in such heavy numbers that the list captured slightly more than a quarter of the total national vote. While turnout was extremely heavy in the Kurdish north (about 85 percent) and the Shiite south (slightly more than 70 percent), relatively few Sunnis voted (probably less than a quarter of the total Sunni Arab population in Iraq) and in the areas most severely in the grip of violence, boycott, fear, and alienation, the turnout was less than 10 percent. In Anbar province, it was 2 percent. In fact, the low Sunni turnout was a major reason why the United Iraqi Alliance was able to win effective control of the assembly and the Kurdish list was able to win fully a quarter of the assembly seats. While the Sunnis may comprise 20 percent of the population, they may well have accounted for no more than 5 percent of the electorate. From the character of the election as an ethnic census it is possible to estimate that the Kurds accounted for roughly 26 percent of the electorate, and the Turkoman and Assyrian Christian minorities less than 2 percent. This means that if the Shiites comprise perhaps 58 to 60 percent of the population, they nevertheless made up two-thirds of the electorate.[14]

Most of this was predictable, given the decision to use the electoral system of proportional representation in a single nationwide district,

326 | SQUANDERED VICTORY

rather than provincial districts in which voters might have been able to pay attention to the individual candidates—and given the levels of violence and insecurity and the extremely tilted playing field, in which very few lists had any significant financial resources or ability to get their name, program, purpose, and leadership on radio and television. All of this made it impossible for most political parties to campaign. Liberals with no militias and no funds were particularly hard-pressed. As the journalist Lawrence Kaplan wrote in the *New Republic* just before the elections, "How can there be liberalism in a country where liberals cannot leave their homes?"[15] As a result, just three political lists—the United Iraqi Alliance, the Kurdistan Alliance, and Prime Minister Ayad Allawi's Iraqi List—won about 88 percent of the vote, and more than 90 percent of the 275 seats in the Transitional National Assembly. Nine other lists (of the 111 total that competed) shared 5 percent of the vote and the remaining 20 seats. Although many of the candidates on the Kurdish and Allawi lists clearly have liberal and secular leanings, it remains to be seen how they will weight these values against other political interests. A number of moderate, liberal, democratic, and/or independent actors were virtually shut out of the new political power game, such as Farqad al-Qizwini and his Iraqi Democratic Gathering. Adnan Pachachi won not even a single seat for his Iraqi Independent Democrats.

The election results thus dealt a severe blow to Iraqi liberals and to their aspirations for a new, more peaceful and democratic order. With the Sunnis marginalized by the election, the insurgency gained renewed momentum. By the time the results were announced, the *Washington Post* reported, the insurgents had "answered hopes for a postelection calm with a wave of carnage, capping two days of violence with a suicide bombing . . . in front of a hospital south of Baghdad that killed 17 people."[16] The new transitional government, which was set to be headed by the United Iraqi Alliance, appeared poised to launch a new campaign of de-Baathification, beginning with the security forces, and to stack the ministries it controlled with its own loyalists. This figured to pour still more fuel onto the fires of the insurgency, deepening the sense of most Sunni Arabs that they were losing out completely in the new Iraq.

To be sure, 50 percent was not a thumping majority. If the Shiite coalition was to lead the new Iraq, it would still need to win the support of other groups in order to govern effectively and in order to adopt a new permanent constitution—assuming it does not attempt unilaterally to void Article 61(c), the provision of the interim constitution that enables any three provinces to veto the constitution in the referendum. Much will depend on the degree to which the United Iraqi Alliance holds together on key questions, and on how its leaders opt to deal with other political and social forces in Iraq. Throughout the election and post-election period, major Shiite leaders such as Adel Abdel Mahdi, Abdul-Aziz al-Hakim, and Ibrahim al-Jaafari were acknowledging the need for compromise, inclusion, and the avoidance of even the appearance of theocracy. But to many Sunnis, and Iraqi liberals of various religious orientations, these assurances rang hollow and conjured up the belief that Shiite Islam justifies pretending and dissembling in order to perpetuate the faith. Indeed, during 2004, SCIRI had contemplated having Adel Mahdi leave the party and form his own independent force so that he would be viewed as a more acceptable leader, even though he would have remained fully loyal to SCIRI. The tactic reminds one of the communists' phony "popular fronts" during the 1930s (and indeed at one time Adel Mahdi was a Maoist).

If they do evince moderation and inclusion, SCIRI and Da'wa are likely to do so only for purely tactical reasons. SCIRI in particular is a highly sectarian political organization, which formed and grew up in Iran, and which remains linked to the security apparatus of the Islamic Republic of Iran. Whatever they may say publicly for the moment, the true powers in SCIRI, beginning with Abdul-Aziz al-Hakim (who was placed first on the United Iraqi Alliance list), probably still believe in the Iranian system of *vilayat al-faqih*. Like the Leninists of a previous century (and the radical Islamists of the Iranian Revolution), their real goal will be to seize full power when the time is ripe. But, like the other politicians in the United Iraqi Alliance, they will need to be responsive to the moral guidance and political instructions of Ayatollah Ali al-Sistani.

In the near term, much of the future of Iraqi politics will turn on who Ayatollah Sistani really is. How much will he seek to hold the United Iraqi Alliance together as a coherent political force? How often will he seek to instruct it, and toward what ends? During my time in Iraq, and during the writing of this book, I largely accepted the assessment of Sistani as a political "quietist" who rejects the Khomeini philosophy of *vilayat al-faqih*. Unlike the fundamentalist mullahs who control political power in Iran, and their sympathizers in Iraq, Sistani believes that government should be in the hands of elected leaders, not religious clerics. Nevertheless, since the downfall of Saddam Hussein, he has waded into politics—always choosing his timing and his words carefully. If he continues to do so, he may be able to enforce more solidarity on Shiite politicians than would be healthy for democracy in Iraq—but would he seek to impose a fixed political (cum religious) agenda, or a compromise? Certainly, Sistani showed during the period of occupation a capacity for patience and compromise. But it remains to be seen how much of this was tactical and how much an acceptance of basic principles of democracy. Sistani and his fellow grand ayatollahs among the Shiite *marjaiya* in Najaf have signaled a desire to see an "Islamic constitution" in Iraq.[17] To the extent they press for language in the final constitution (as they did in the interim constitution) making Islam the primary or sole source of legislation in Iraq, deep political fissures will be aggravated.

For some time to come, the political balance in Iraq will be heavily shaped by the balance of ethnic and religious groups. In the absence of a detailed, reliable census, no one can claim to know the demographic balance of Iraq's principal groups. It is conventionally assumed that the Shiites constitute, overall, about 60 percent of the population.[18] The Kurds and the Sunni Arabs are each estimated to account for 15 to 20 percent of the population, and ethnic minorities (such as Turkoman and Assyrians) another 5 percent (with Christians, cutting across the various nationality groups, perhaps 3 percent).[19] If the Shiites should vote as a bloc in elections and in the parliament, they could control the country's political life, restrained only by a sense of pragmatism and fairness, and by the limits to majority rule in the interim constitution— if they chose to respect those limits. One of the great hopes for democracy in Iraq is therefore that Shiite solidarity—and indeed the solidarity of the three major identity groups in Iraq—will erode, giving rise to a shifting set of alliances and a dispersed balance of political power.

Such an eventuality, in turn, would depend on a level of democracy that may, initially, be difficult to attain. Multiple centers of power in each section of the country, particularly in the Shiite south, require a sufficiently peaceful and free climate so that alternative political parties can mobilize support. It was precisely this concern—not just for the transitional period but well beyond—that led a number of us within the CPA to stress so heavily the importance of demobilizing the various militias. We knew that if the major parties retained their own substantial armed forces, they were likely to use them to intimidate and suppress opposition in their own areas of strength, as party militias have done in countless other transitional political systems. A balance of power also depends on having electoral administration that is sufficiently strong, disciplined, and resourceful to ensure that the voting and vote counting proceed largely free of fraud.

★

The third condition for the emergence of democracy in Iraq concerns the behavior and strategic choices of Iraq's new political leaders. Two choices could prove decisive, and in each case a positive turn for democracy in Iraq would involve the Shiite politicians of the ruling alliance consciously choosing to underutilize their power—a development for which there is little precedent in Iraq, or anywhere else in the Arab world. Restraint on the part of the Shiites would not spring from magnanimity but from the sober realization that in trying to win too much, they could also lose a great deal. One choice involves the Sunnis, and whether and how they will be incorporated into the emerging political system. The other involves the Kurds.

No doubt, the politicians of the United Iraqi Alliance will ensure that there is Sunni representation in the new government. The question will be whether the Sunnis who are in the cabinet are given some positions of real power, and whether they are Sunnis who are seen by powerful Sunni communities to represent them. Unless the marginalized Sunni constituencies and political associations, who boycotted the elections (and at least some of whom have also supported the insurgency), are drawn into the government and the constitution-making process in meaningful roles and numbers, there will be little hope of forging a sustainable political consensus on the rules of the game in Iraq—and of winding down the insurgency.

The other crucial decision the Shiite-dominated ruling alliance must make concerns the interim constitution, the Transitional Administrative Law. If the United Iraqi Alliance resolves to follow through on the vows that were made after several of its leaders signed the TAL on March 8, 2004—that it could not take effect until certain amendments were made—and on the pronouncements of Ayatollah Sistani that the document is illegitimate and can be finalized only by an elected body, the delicate compromises that have held Iraq together could quickly unravel. If the Kurds are going to honor their commitment to live within a unified, federal, and democratic Iraq, the federal element will have to be maintained and the minority veto in Article 61(c) will have to be preserved in one form or another. Kurdish resolve and bargaining power—already powerful before the January election—was greatly strengthened by the results, which not only gave the united Kurdish list almost all the votes in Kurdistan, but which, in a nonbinding and supposedly independently organized referendum in Kurdistan held outside the official polling stations, saw well over 90 percent of Kurds who participated in the referendum reportedly opting for Kurdistan independence. If the guarantees for federalism and minority rights in the TAL were simply to be revoked unilaterally by a new majority, the Kurds would likely withdraw from the political system in Baghdad, extend their grip over lands on the perimeter of prewar Kurdistan, probably accelerate the forcible expulsion of Arabs from Kirkuk, and then seek to exercise an autonomy that would resemble independence in everything but name. Terrorism and ethnic violence would escalate, including possibly what CPA officials long regarded as one of their worst nightmares—all-out war for control of Kirkuk. In this context, radical Sunni groups, including Islamists and former Baathists, might seek to establish or entrench zones of control of their own. Local Shiite warlords could also make power grabs. There could be so much violence on so many fronts that American and other international forces would find the situation impossible to control.

When Lakhdar Brahimi was concluding his first UN mission to Iraq, on February 13, 2004, he issued a warning that he hoped everyone would take seriously. Asked whether there was a danger of civil war in Iraq, this man—who had seen his native Algeria fall into bloody internal conflict and who had mediated the end of the Lebanese civil war—replied:

> I would like to appeal to every Iraqi in every part of Iraq to be conscious of the fact that civil wars are not started . . . through a decision that . . . tomorrow we are going to start a civil war. Civil wars happen because people are reckless, because people are selfish, because groups think more of themselves than they do of the benefit of their country. . . . If there is one country that nobody ever thought would be the theater of a civil war, it is Lebanon, and yet we have seen what happened. I myself come from a country, where, again, nobody thought that there would be a civil war and there was one. So I have appealed to . . . everybody I have seen to be careful.

If Iraq is to become a democracy, it must avoid becoming (in this sense) another Lebanon. When I was traveling around southern Iraq in March 2004, an experienced CPA hand pointed out to me that Iraq had "all of the major ingredients" for a Lebanon-style civil war: deep ethnic and religious divisions that were intensifying, a society with a power vacuum, strong neighbors interfering in the conflict for competing purposes, and (another) U.S. intervention. One could have added the absence of national leadership, the rise of militias, the economic implosion, and the struggle over resources—particularly between Kurds and Arabs for control of the oil around Kirkuk and Mosul. "This is heading toward Lebanon and the Congo writ large," he warned. It was not just Muqtada al-Sadr that he was worried about. It was the determination of all the radical Islamist militias in the Shiite south to impose some version of Iranian-style *vilayat al-faqih*, and the determination, no less resolute, of the tribes to resist it. In southern Iraq, most Shiites do not want an Iranian system, nor do they wish to see Iraq (or any part of it) dominated by Iran. But it takes only a small minority—disciplined, organized, well financed, and armed—to start a revolution or a civil war, and that militant, ideological minority, with generous Iranian backing, now constitutes a significant bloc in the United Iraqi Alliance. It is possible that harder-line Islamists in SCIRI and Da'wa would at some point try to swallow and spit out the moderates in the alliance the way the Bolsheviks destroyed the Mensheviks after the Russian revolution. One thing that may pre-serve the prospect for democracy in Iraq, however, is that, for some time to come, political power may be too dispersed to make such a maneuver feasible.

★

This raises again the broader question of the power balance. To what ex-tent can Iraq be spared from the machinations of outside states, which helped ignite and perpetuate the Lebanese civil war? And to what ex-tent can the nation be bolstered by independent organizations in civil society? Neither prognosis is encouraging.

There is a civil society emerging in Iraq, and, with luck, it could be-come a development of the occupation period that Americans will look back on with some sense of accomplishment. Independent media, many of them local, most of them small in scale and lacking experience, have blossomed. Many organizations—women's, youth, and human rights groups prominent among them—have formed, and professional associations have revived with new independence. But the emergence of civil society has been stunted by the continuing violence and insecu-rity, and by economic hardship, recovery from which is slowed by the violence. Thus, while promising in its potential, civil society is still too weak and fragmented to offset the political forces in the country. De-veloping such a democratic counterweight will take time, international support, and a benign set of circumstances on the ground.

International support for democracy is one thing, but the effort to manipulate Iraq's future is another. As long as the United States retains tens of thousands of troops in Iraq, it will inevitably be, and be seen to be, a significant factor in the country's politics. If the troops remain in Iraq for years to come, they will continue to be a lightning rod for resis-tance. Yet if they leave before a viable state emerges—with well-run armed forces and a broad political settlement among competing groups—then Iraq will slide into civil war, or Iranian domination, or very likely some of both. As a matter of principle and pragmatic interest, the United States should promote the kind of dialogue and accommodation with the insurgency that would enable American forces to withdraw sooner rather than later. In addition, we need to avoid the imperial temptation to shape Iraq's destiny to our liking. Such intervention is likely to backfire in the end.

American political leaders need to take a cold shower of humility: we do not always know what is best for other people, even when we think it is their interests we have in mind. And as I saw during my time in Iraq, it was frequently our interests that were driving decisions we were trying to impose on Iraqi politics. We will be more likely to promote democracy in Iraq if we focus on assisting the development of democratic institutions, political parties, civic groups, business associations, trade unions, and mass media, while leaving the political decisions to the people Iraqis elect to make them.

Of course, other external actors are attempting to shape the future of Iraq; unfortunately, some of them have no interest in seeing democracy emerge. The biggest challenge will be for Iraqi democrats to contain the influence of Iran, which, through the first two years of the post-Saddam era, was the outside power that had gained the most in Iraq. If a pluralistic balance can be preserved among Shiites, and thus in the country's political system, Iran's influence will be contained by the simple fact that most Iraqis do not want it. But if the pro-Iranian forces within the United Iraqi Alliance gain the upper hand, their fragile status could induce them to lean increasingly on Iranian muscle to impose their will. That would likely spell the end of democracy in Iraq, and could grease the slide to civil war. Or, in the words of one of my former CPA colleagues, it could leave the United States "in the absurd position of maintaining 135,000 troops in-country in order to preserve a pro-Iranian government working against our strategic interests." The American public would not stand for that situation very long.

★

Perhaps the likeliest scenario in Iraq (at least over the medium term) is the perpetuation of some uneasy, periodically rejiggered, continually crisis-ridden form of the Governing Council coalition. This could well produce an elite political pact to generate peace and stability, but with only very limited democracy and with quite a bit of corruption and bad governance. There was a positive element to the experience of the Governing Council. Iraqi political leaders did frequently broker compromises with one another that kept the political transition from falling apart. In fact, it was often the Americans who constituted the bigger problem. Two factors make such a sharing of power—albeit with Shiite religious forces in the lead—feasible. One is that the principal alternative—the imposition of Shiite hegemony—would obviously lead to civil war. The other is the promise and curse that lies, literally, just beneath the surface of Iraqi politics: oil. Even in the midst of its current strife, and after two decades of decay in its production infrastructure, Iraq still produces about 2.5 million barrels of oil per day, giving it an annual income in 2004 of $17 billion. Its proven reserves of 112 billion barrels constitute over 10 percent of the world's total and rank second only to those of Saudi Arabia. Industry experts believe Iraq's actual reserves could be twice the current total, and that the country represents "a boom waiting to happen."[20] With some degree of stability, Iraq could become wealthy again. Money does have its allure.

Especially if stability can gradually take hold and oil exports revive, Iraq's oil wealth could lubricate the strains of coalition politics. Then the ruling coalition in Iraq could well resemble the one in Nigeria: diverse in ethnic, regional, and religious composition; constantly under strain; and held together by the same interests that often threaten to split it apart—the desire of each group to get a fair share of the national pie. The political system in Nigeria is still one of the most corrupt in the world, despite the partial efforts of its president, Olusegun Obasanjo (a former chairman of Transparency International), to reduce criminality. With the localized violence and fraud that pervade elections, Nigeria's political system can be considered only a semidemocracy. Yet that is certainly preferable to the brutal military dictatorships that preceded it, and more desirable than the civil war that claimed perhaps a million lives in the late 1960s.

In recent years, Nigeria's civilian politicians have managed to work out power-sharing arrangements, formal and informal, that have at least avoided large-scale violence and preserved some degree of freedom and pluralism. Not coincidentally, federalism has played a major role in sustaining this fragile order. A venal semidemocracy cannot generate development nor hold indefinitely at bay the forces of disintegration. But when compared to the descent toward state collapse on which Nigeria was headed in the 1990s, the situation is at least a beginning.

One hopes that the mechanisms of accountability—the inspectors general and the public integrity commission and all the other governance reforms—instituted by the CPA under L. Paul Bremer will survive and function in a democratic Iraq. Iraq can become democratic and stable only if the quality and transparency of governance gradually improve. But "good governance" will have little meaning in Iraq if political order is not restored and preserved, through means that will need to be more political than military. The overriding initial task must be to fashion a political bargain in which all major Iraqi groups feel they have a stake in the country's political future.

In the months and years ahead, the answer to the question of whether Iraq can become a democracy will depend, most of all, on Iraqi political leaders, and the decisions they make to widen the political arena or not, to share power and resources or not, to build a system of mutual security or, instead, try to dominate and even crush their opponents. The record of the Governing Council does not inspire great confidence in their leadership, and yet an occupation is hardly the ideal context for cultivating statesmanship. Now Iraq's future is theirs to shape. If they choose pragmatism and accommodation, the political system they craft may be something less than true democracy but much more than dictatorship and civil war. From the soggy soil of that political pluralism and power sharing, and with continued international support, a genuine democracy could gradually emerge.

AFTERWORD

★

Over the course of the year 2005, both Iraq and the United States struggled with the legacy of the bungled postwar effort to bring democracy to that bloodstained land. Although the January 30 elections for a transitional government were hailed by the Bush administration as a historic success—the tipping point, it was said, toward democracy, peace, and stability—those goals proved elusive in the ensuing months. Strained by the polarizing consequences of an election that became an identity referendum, and by the daunting difficulties of fashioning a power-sharing government amid severe ethnic and political fragmentation, the victorious Shiite and Kurdish political coalitions required almost three months to form a new government. The protracted political infighting quickly took the bloom off the inspirational moment of the January elections, leaving many Iraqis frustrated and disillusioned with the politicians.

In several respects, the new transitional government that took office on May 3, 2005, was historic, giving the most powerful post of prime minister to a moderately Islamist Shiite politician, Ibrahim Jaafari, and the ceremonial presidency to a Kurd, PUK leader Jalal Talabani. Yet just as important was the symbolism of key Sunni figures skipping the swearing-in ceremony, most notably the former interim president and

new transitional vice president, Ghazi al-Yawer. Five posts were left un-
filled initially, including two deputy prime minister slots and the crucial
defense and oil ministries. The last was temporarily given to the canny
Ahmed Chalabi, who also landed one of the deputy prime minister positions.

The new government, like the preceding interim government led by
Ayad Allawi and the Iraqi Governing Council before that, included
Sunnis in rough proportion to their share of the population, and ultimately gave the Defense Ministry to a savvy and tribally well connected
Sunni scholar and pollster, Saddoun al-Dulaimi. But the new government did not include the Sunnis who mattered most politically—the
nationalist, tribal, and religious groups who were supporting and waging the insurgency. Unlike the Al Qaeda insurgents and the Saddam
loyalists, these much more numerous Sunni groups were fighting for
more limited objectives, including an eventual incorporation into the
new Iraqi regime. But with their decision to boycott the January 30
elections and their effective exclusion from the new parliament, that
was not forthcoming.

With the Sunni Arabs as a group holding only 17 of the 275 seats in
parliament, with strategic communities like Fallujah and Ramadi effectively unrepresented, and with leaders of real stature excluded, the
Sunnis remained bitterly on the margins of government and politics—
just when the new parliament was about to write a permanent constitution for Iraq. When the parliament appointed in early May a fifty-five-
member constitution drafting committee without Sunni representation,
their anger intensified. At the same time, their towns and cities (along
with many others in Iraq) continued to chafe under an American military occupation that they perceived as indefinite and imperialistic in intent. These comprised the conditions for a "perfect storm" of escalating
insurgent violence.

The number of daily attacks, which had declined to an average of
slightly more than fify in the first three months of 2005, increased to
about sixty per day in April and seventy per day through the long hot
summer of constitution writing. By the time the constitution was adopted
on October 15, insurgent attacks were averaging one hundred per day—
despite a reported doubling of Iraqi security forces over the course of the

year.[1] American troop fatalities, which had also subsided during the first three months of 2005, spiked up sharply thereafter, averaging nearly seventy per month between April and November 2005, for a pace of nearly a thousand a year.

But statistics alone cannot convey the anger, frustration, exhaustion, and terror that Iraqis suffered from the relentless violence, particularly the spectacular suicide bombings. As the terrorists grew more skillful, they managed to coordinate their attacks to maximum deadly effect, often staging a second bombing in precisely the spot to which people might be calculated to flee in panic from the shattered glass, pools of blood, and flying limbs and flesh. Police academies, military recruitment centers, and other institutions of the reemerging Iraqi state were favorite targets, but the terrorists also struck at hospitals, mosques, markets, restaurants, ice cream parlors, transport stations, crowded buses—any place where innocent people might be physically concentrated for efficient slaughter. In October 2005 alone, the American military documented fifty-two suicide operations in Iraq (forty-six car bombings, and six using a belt or vest of explosives).[2]

As it clearly intended to do, the brutal terrorist violence, targeted mainly at the majority Shiite population, inflamed the country's ethnic and religious divisions. Although Ayatollah Ali al-Sistani continued to appeal to Iraqi Shiites to remain calm, Sunnis became the target of a brutal counter-campaign of assassinations and abductions, which often ended in torture and death. By the fall of 2005, reports were accumulating of several hundred targeted assassinations and disappearances of Sunni Arabs, many of whom were being taken away in the middle of the night, "without warrant or explanation," by men in uniform claiming to be security forces or intelligence agents.[3] Numerous reports pointed to the Shiite Islamist militias—such as SCIRI's Badr Organization and Muqtada al-Sadr's Mahdi Army—who were believed to have infiltrated the new Iraqi army and especially the police. Suspicions of official complicity deepened in November with the discovery (by the American military) of a secret underground detention center run by the Ministry of Interior, whose minister, Bayan Jabr, was a former Badr leader. While Shiite government leaders, including Jabr, downplayed the charges, Sunni political parties and leaders demanded an international investigation and threatened to suspend their political participation if the death squads were not shut down. Meanwhile, sectarian hatred and dread seeped more deeply into the social fabric. Fearing victimization, large numbers of Iraqi Christians and other middle-class professionals emigrated, taking with them precious skills and capital. Towns and neighborhoods around Baghdad where Iraqi Sunnis and Shiites had lived side by side for decades suddenly segregated, with Sunnis moving out of predominantly Shiite settlements, and vice versa. The population transfers accelerated sharply with acts of violence and intimidation, while sectarian prejudice screamed from graffiti and leaflets.[4]

As had happened during the period of the CPA's rule, the widespread violence and criminality also badly slowed the country's reconstruction and economic revival. With the insurgency relentlessly sabotaging pipelines and production facilities, and killing and terrorizing skilled workers, crude oil production struggled during 2005 to stay above 2 million barrels a day, and never came close to meeting the stated goal of 2.5 million barrels a day—which is itself less than half what Iraq might be capable of with peace and investment.[5] Even at that, oil revenues still accounted for almost all of Iraq's national income. Iraq also remained well below Bremer's oft-stated goal of 6,000 megawatts of electricity generated, a goal it still had yet to approach in the postwar period. Throughout the hot, bloody summer of 2005, most Iraqi communities were lucky to have power (and thus air conditioning) half of the time. Per capita income recovered somewhat during 2005, but remained only a fraction of what it once had been before Saddam and sanctions ran the country into the ground.

At year's end, the United States was spending an average of $6 billion a month to sustain a military deployment that oscillated between 138,000 and 160,000 American troops. This did not include the billions it was still trying to spend effectively on the country's reconstruction. While a report to Congress by an inspector general's office found that about two-thirds of 2,784 American-sponsored rebuilding projects had been completed (schools, hospitals, roads, bridges, police stations, sports facilities, water treatment plants, electricity generators, and other public infrastructure),[6] it also found millions of dollars wasted or mismanaged. In a speech two months later, President Bush acknowledged that the rebuilding had been slowed by violence, corruption, and misplaced priorities.[7] By the time Bush spoke, only $12 billion of the $21 billion allocated for that purpose had been spent, and more than a quarter of that had gone to pay security costs, while some portion of the rest had been wasted or stolen through corruption. In one particularly egregious case, a convicted fraudster who was somehow hired to manage some $82 million in reconstruction contracts in Hilla was arrested in November 2005 for allegedly taking huge bribes to award construction contracts that were executed shoddily or not at all.[8] Wayne White, the head of the State Department's Iraq intelligence team from 2003 to 2005, observed: "Progress is running far behind Iraqi expectations in virtually every area. In their view, most Iraqis are not seeing 'amazing progress.' All too many of them live in constant danger, with less electricity in many areas than under Saddam Hussein."[9]

Given all of this, it is noteworthy that Iraqis seemed to retain some reservoir of optimism about the future, with a plurality (47 percent) telling pollsters in October that they thought the country was headed in the right direction. But that proportion was down from 67 percent in April,[10] and its upbeat tone was contradicted by the reported results of a secret poll by the British Ministry of Defense that found two-thirds of Iraqis feeling less secure because of the occupation, 72 percent lacking confidence in the coalition forces, 82 percent "strongly opposed" to the presence of coalition troops, 43 percent seeing worsened conditions for peace and stability, and 45 percent seeing attacks on British and American troops as justified.[11] A December 2005 ABC News poll found (not surprisingly) that Sunni Arabs viewed the situation much more negatively than Shiites.[12]

★

One reason Iraqis did not lose all hope is that the political process did move forward over the course of 2005, even while stumbling badly. Most Iraqis were disappointed with the lackluster performance of Ibrahim Jaafari's transitional government, particularly in controlling the violence and reviving the economy. But soon after that government finally took office in May 2005, the country's attention turned anxiously to the more enduring question of how the new Iraqi state would be structured constitutionally.

Unfortunately, when the new Constitution Drafting Committee got down to business, it did not have much time to do its work. The Transitional Administrative Law had envisioned a constitution-drafting process of six months, from the time the parliament would convene shortly after the January 30 elections until the August 15 deadline for adopting a draft. But a number of Iraqi legal drafters and political leaders, as well as some international advisers, believed that even a full six months might not be enough time to resolve the big existential questions about the future nature of the Iraqi state and political system. Time was needed not only to negotiate and draft the constitution, but to implement the requirement (in Article 60 of the TAL) for the Assembly to encourage "debate on the constitution through regular general public meetings in all parts of Iraq and through the media," as well as to receive "proposals from the citizens of Iraq as it writes the constitution." Clearly, the kind of far-reaching national debate envisioned by the TAL was going to take time.[13] Thus, a provision was written into the TAL allowing for a one-time, six-month extension of the August 15 deadline— an extension that had to be activated (through a majority vote of the Assembly) by August 1.[14]

In the end, Iraq did not have six months, or even three, to draft, negotiate, debate, revise, and adopt a permanent constitution. It was not until May 10 that the Constitution Drafting Committee was appointed by the Assembly—incredibly, without a single Sunni representative. Not until May 23—almost another two weeks—was a chairman appointed, Sheikh Humam Hamoudi of SCIRI. Soundings of Iraqi public opinion that spring indicated a very broad and palpable desire for public participation in the constitution-making process—a sharp departure from the "hasty and secretive" process, excessively shaped by the United States, that produced the TAL.[15] But even the closed-door process of drafting could not begin, as it quickly became apparent that the constitution would not have broad legitimacy—or any hope of reducing the chronic violence and instability—without meaningful Sunni Arab representation in the deliberations. The drift (both in government formation and then in launching the constitutional process) was aggravated by the absence of a high-level American envoy in Baghdad. Ambassador John Negroponte had departed on March 17 to become Director of National Intelligence, and his replacement, Zalmay Khalilzad, would not arrive until late July. With the sense of crisis deepening, the United States once again intervened. Under heavy American pressure, the Assembly agreed on June 16 to add fifteen Sunni members to the Constitutional Drafting Committee and to accept the principle that, even though the new members could not vote (since, unlike the original fifty-five, they were not members of parliament), decisions would be taken by consensus.

On July 8—less than six weeks before the August 15 deadline—the work of the Constitution Drafting Committee formally began, with the Sunni delegates attending their first meeting. Eleven days later, after one of their members was assassinated, they suspended their participation, vowing not to return until they received better protection. They returned, at least partially reassured with new security, on July 25. By then, the hard decisions on Iraq's constitutional future still lay ahead, with only three weeks until the August 15 deadline and six days until the August 1 deadline for extending the process.

By this point, a wide range of Iraqi actors, including the drafting committee chairman, Sheikh Hamoudi, had concluded the obvious: They had to have significantly more time to achieve a broadly acceptable constitution, and would need to request the six-month extension. By one informed account, the "preference for an extension was shared by Mahmoud Othman and other senior Kurdish negotiators, international advisors to the Kurds, and senior Shia List officials on the committee, including Abbas Bayati [a prominent SCIRI politician]. This preference also had private support among senior independent Shia leaders in the Assembly," and the public support of "most, if not all, important civil society organizations."[16] No doubt, some Shiite political leaders were ready to barrel forward to a conclusion, while Sunni delegates were wary of extending a process that left them without formal voting rights and probably favored dissolving the Assembly and holding new elections. But what most key participants opposed and even dreaded was a decision to hold to the

August 15 date come hell or high water. One key actor, however, was adamant about this date—the United States. And it prevailed. In the days before August 1, as the Assembly appeared headed toward a vote to extend the process, Ambassador Khalilzad "convened meetings with political party leaders to impress upon them the importance of meeting the August 15 deadline."[17] As with the January 30 elections, the American insistence on adhering to the timetable came directly and adamantly from President Bush.[18] With the American president once again dug in, the Iraqis had to yield.

The absolute insistence on adhering to the August 15 completion date would prove to be one of America's more serious blunders in postwar Iraq. With the committee having gotten started so late and across such a huge gulf of sectarian distrust, with the drafting work through the month of July having proceeded so slowly, and with the process of soliciting public input having barely gotten off the ground, the failure on August 1 to extend the committee's work plunged the constitution drafting process into a state of crisis from which it never recovered. One week later, with the Sunnis still struggling to define their positions on key issues and with barely any common ground yet established on such contentious issues as federalism, national identity, and the scope of de-Baathification, the drafting committee essentially collapsed. With just one week left to the August 15 deadline, the negotiations moved from the Committee to "a series of ad hoc meetings" between the principal Shiite and Kurdish party leaders that took place in the living room of President Jalal Talabani and other residences inside the Baghdad International Zone (formerly known as the Green Zone). From these meetings, which determined the final language of the constitution that the Assembly would adopt, the Sunni delegates were almost entirely excluded.[19] It was little wonder, then, that they would indignantly denounce the concluded draft on both procedural and substantive grounds.

With agreement among the principal parties still lacking, the Assembly had to vote to amend the TAL to allow for a special one-week extension of the August 15 deadline—a provision that the drafters of the interim constitution had by no means envisioned and that violated at least the spirit of the document. When that next deadline expired on

August 22, the Assembly granted itself a three-day extension, and then an indefinite further extension, without even bothering to vote. By then the key party leaders were "clearly unwilling to submit a series of rolling amendments of the TAL deadline to the Assembly, in circumstances where the negotiating text of the constitution was being withheld even from Assembly members."[20]

The drafting process was deadlocked over a few pivotal issues, none more crucial and bitterly contested than federalism. The problem this time—as opposed to the negotiations the previous year over the TAL— was not the Kurdish demand for regional autonomy, but the Sunni Arabs' continued rejection of the idea of federalism, which they associated with the break-up of the country. Yet increasingly, as they looked down the road to a national state they would no longer control, they accepted the logic of devolving power and resources to the provinces, so long as the stigmatized term "federalism" was not applied to such devolution. (Indeed, it was one of the few truly hopeful developments that most Shiite and even Sunni political leaders had come to accept the necessity of significant regional autonomy for Kurdistan if it was to remain within Iraq.) Complicating matters was a political bombshell from the SCIRI leader Abdul-Aziz al-Hakim, who on August 11 endorsed a proposal for one huge Shiite mega-region spanning all nine southern provinces, and (with apparent Iranian support) began to organize his party to demonstrate on behalf of it. The idea of an autonomous southern region had earlier been floated by some secular Shiite politicians like Ahmed Chalabi as a means to correct the Shiite south's historic neglect by the center. However, these proposals had initially envisioned a smaller region of three provinces, centered in Basra. Hakim embraced a far more radical vision, and in the process mobilized a surge of popular support behind it.

The proposal for a single Shiite southern region dramatically transformed the delicate balance of federalism in the TAL and in subsequent constitutional proposals. Whereas the TAL had allowed no more than three provinces to form new regions of their own, Hakim's proposal lifted that limit and so left the Sunnis facing the prospect of floating in the arid middle of an eviscerated Iraq, with a nearly independent Kurdistan to the north and a Shiite quasi-state (closely tied to Iran) to the south.[21] The impending vacuum of central authority was under-scored by the failure to modify any of the extraordinary regional powers granted to Kurdistan by the TAL and now conferred on the prospective "Shiastan" as well, including the ability to legislate on a wide range of is-sues, to control most government spending in the territory, to veto the application in the region of many federal laws, and to maintain, in essence, its own armed forces. On August 14, the leading Sunni mem-ber of the constitutional committee, Saleh Mutlak declared in refer-ence to the Shiites' proposal: "If we accept federalism, the country will be finished."[22] And so, he and his fellow Sunni members feared, would they be personally. "We already have a problem with our people," he said the next day. "This is one agreement we cannot make, because if we make it we cannot walk in the street anymore."[23]

Three provisions relating to Iraq's chief export added to the panic and outrage with which Sunnis greeted the proposed constitutional draft. One assigned to the federal government "the management of oil and gas extracted from current fields," implying that the management of future oil and gas fields (believed to contain tremendous new, un-tapped reserves) would fall to the regions, even though the constitution in principle assigned ownership of these natural resources to "all the people of Iraq." Second was a provision for the allocation of existing oil and gas revenue that appeared to punish the Sunnis by granting addi-tional revenue "for a set time for the damaged regions that were un-justly deprived by the former regime."[24] The third provision required a referendum by the end of 2007 to determine the status of the city of Kirkuk, with the presumption that the city, by then heavily resettled by Kurds who had been expelled under Saddam, would vote to join Kur-distan. As roughly 80 percent of Iraq's immense oil and gas reserves were located in the far south and most of the rest in and around Kirkuk, the cumulative implication of these provisions was that the Sunnis could soon be left not only without political power but without secure access to oil revenues as well.

The Sunnis also objected to the fact that the proposed constitution granted regional governments the responsibility for organizing "inter-nal security forces for the region." Kurdistan had drafted the *pesh merga* into the role, and the Sunnis assumed that in the south the Badr

Organization and other Shiite militias would be given a new basis of power, resources, and legitimacy. The Sunnis were also troubled by the constitution's assignment of sweeping legislative authority to the regions, including the power "to amend the application of national legislation" within their territory—which many Sunnis feared would pave the way for the creation of a de facto Shiite Islamist state in the south.

The final negotiations saw deep divisions on other issues as well, such as the relationship of Islam to the state, the national identity of the state, the scope of de-Baathification, and the role of women. As the August 15 deadline neared and passed, fissures deepened and new ones opened up. The Shiites rallied behind Hakim's call for a mega-region in the south, while the Kurds renewed their push for the right to leave the Iraqi state. As the Shiites sought to have the constitution entrench Islamic Sharia law and recognize the autonomy and influence of their most senior ayatollahs, the Kurds dug in their heels as well. In the end, the constitutional deadlock was resolved only with heavy American involvement after August 8. Ambassador Khalilzad and other American officials attended numerous negotiating sessions, shuttled incessantly among the principal actors, and pressed the Shiite and Kurdish parties to compromise and accommodate Sunni Arab concerns. As Bremer had done during the negotiations over the TAL, Khalilzad and his colleagues also pressed for a mainly geographical conception of federalism and for more liberal provisions on religion and the status of women. Mediation proved maddeningly difficult, not only because the dominant parties were deeply wedded to their positions, but also because the Sunnis lacked both cohesive political organization and a coherent sense of what they really wanted—a result of their having entered the political process so late. "Khalilzad would receive a list of demands from one faction, then a contradictory list from another," the *Washington Post* reported.[25] With the negotiations dragging on, President Bush personally phoned SCIRI leader Abdul-Aziz al-Hakim on August 25 to press for greater flexibility.

In the bargain that was struck at the end of August, the Shiites got the right to form a mega-region, but would have to go through a process of provincial votes to form it, a procedural delay that did little to mollify the Sunnis. The Kurds once again had to surrender their demand for a right to secede. The new language on religion was remarkably similar to that of the TAL, save that Islam was now not just "a source of legislation" but "a fundamental source." Both the TAL and the new draft forbade any law that contradicted "the established provisions of Islam," the principles of democracy, or the charter's bill of rights. The executive structure of government also was preserved, in the form of a parliamentary system with a three-member presidency council (the latter only for the first term of the new system).[26] Yet to some alarmed observers, this augured a perpetuation of the weak, paralyzed government of the transitional period, dominated by hidden parliamentary power blocs.[27] In one of the most important innovations, the new constitution vaguely provided for the appointment of an unspecified number of "experts in Islamic jurisprudence" to the Federal Supreme Court, opening the possibility of Islamization by judicial interpretation, though the law to specify the Supreme Court structure would require a two-thirds vote of parliament. The charter of individual rights was still substantial, though reduced in many ways from the more liberal TAL. Freedoms of expression, press, and assembly now had to be consistent with "public order and morality"—a qualification that Feisal Istrabadi had successfully resisted in drafting the TAL, fearing it could lead to almost any degradation. Moreover, the omnibus provision he had written into the TAL, granting Iraqis "all the rights . . . stipulated in international treaties and agreements" deemed binding upon Iraq, was entirely dropped.

In many respects, the constitution agreed upon at the end of August was a pretty good document, more liberal and democratic than any other in the Arab world. Putting the best possible cast on it, Ambassador Khalilzad observed in the *Washington Post* that it contained "an enlightened synthesis of universal values and Iraqi traditions." If the charter was more traditional than Iraqi and American liberals might like, it did hold out, on paper at least, genuine hope for a political system that would limit power and uphold individual and group rights. Moreover, it was not without some accommodation to Sunni sentiments, Khalilzad argued, as "Shiite Arab and Kurdish leaders partially accommodated Sunni Arab demands by reducing the margin needed in the Assembly to dissolve the de-Baathification commission—from two-thirds to an absolute majority."[28]

However, many Sunnis were still unsatisfied, despite winning some concessions with American assistance. Saleh Mutlak warned ominously, "The violence will go up, and the hope among the people will go down. And the extremists will be the ones who are in control of the country."[29]

★

Exhausted though they were by the task of mediating across the huge gulf of sectarian enmity and distrust, the Americans were drawn back to the task by the cold logic expressed in Mutlak's warning. On September 18, the new draft constitution was submitted to the United Nations to be printed and then distributed en masse around the country. The country now faced two chilling alternatives. Either it would be adopted in the October 15 referendum over the bitter and nearly universal opposition of Sunni Arabs, deepening the country's polarization and intensifying the insurgency, or it would be vetoed with a two-thirds "no" vote in three provinces, enraging the Kurds and the Shiites and forcing the new parliament to start from scratch. So the search for accommodation quietly resumed.

Seeking some explicit Sunni support for the new document and a softening of Sunni outrage, Ambassador Khalilzad drew into the new negotiations the most established Sunni Arab party, the Iraqi Islamic Party (which acted in coordination with a second Sunni group). On October 11, the two Sunni groups publicly endorsed the constitution in exchange for an agreement to establish a broadly representative committee of the new parliament that would have four months to review the constitution and propose amendments that would require only a simple majority of the parliament, as opposed to the two-thirds requirement for future amendments. These first amendments could also be vetoed (in the same way as the draft constitution itself) by a two-thirds vote in each of any three provinces.

For some Sunnis, these and other last-minute changes took a bit of the sting out of the constitution, even if they also created the bizarre situation of most Iraqis voting on a document whose final provisions they had not read. But the changes were not enough. Despite the tepid support of some Sunni moderates, the constitution was overwhelmingly rejected in the two predominantly Sunni provinces of Al-Anbar (where 97 percent voted no) and Salaheddin (82 percent). However, in two other provinces, Diyala (49 percent no) and Ninewa (55 percent no), Sunni Arabs accounted only for a more modest majority of the population, and so failed to reach the two-thirds threshold. In the country as a whole, the Electoral Commission reported that the constitution was endorsed by 79 percent of Iraqi voters. Many Sunni political leaders were bitter and felt cheated. In Ninewa in particular, some Sunnis alleged that there had been electoral fraud to suppress the "no" vote, but investigations by the U.S. embassy indicated that some attempted fraud was thwarted and that such practices were too limited to have affected the outcome.

Even more than the January 30 elections, the October constitutional referendum was determined by ethnic and religious identity. Most Sunni Arabs, perhaps as many as 90 percent, voted against the constitution. In the nine Shiite majority provinces of the south, the "yes" vote averaged over 96 percent, and in the three Kurdish provinces, it averaged 99 percent. The process left the country more polarized than ever, yet by establishing some plausible means for future constitutional compromise and revision, the October 11 agreement may have spared the country a descent into much worse violence—at least for a time. Angry though they were, the Sunni communities decided to move on to the biggest prize, the contest for power in the December 15 elections. Save for the die-hard Al Qaeda and pro-Saddam rejectionists, most Sunnis resolved not to repeat their ill-conceived electoral boycott of January. Instead, the Sunni provinces now buzzed for the first time with competitive party politics and widespread voter registration.

★

From late October through the first half of December, the struggle to shape Iraq's political future shifted from the negotiating rooms to the airwaves and election campaign trails, as 307 political parties, many of them grouped into 19 different coalitions, vied for the 275 seats in Iraq's new parliament, the Council of Representatives.

As in January, the three leading contending coalitions were again the United Iraqi Alliance of the Shiite religious parties, the Kurdistan Coalition List (uniting the KDP and the PUK), and Ayad Allawi's secular Iraqi National List. But there were some significant changes. The United Iraqi Alliance continued to encompass SCIRI, Dawa, and the Sadr Movement (along with fifteen smaller groups), and to enjoy or at least claim the implicit endorsement (though now with contradictory signals) of Ayatollah Sistani, whose photograph they once more plastered over their posters. But several smaller Shiite parties, including Ahmed Chalabi's Iraqi National Congress, broke off to run on their own, and the remaining coalition exhibited increasing strains, especially between SCIRI and the Sadrists (whose militias had fought one another for control of territory, and whose late patron clerics were religious rivals).[30] At the same time, Allawi fashioned a broader secular and pan-sectarian list than he had in January, drawing in the political formations of former interim president Ghazi al-Yawer, Adnan Pachachi (Iraq's most respected liberal), the Iraqi Communist Party, and an assortment of moderate Shiites, Sunnis, and ethnic minorities. Allawi thus figured to win significantly more than the forty seats he had won in January, and some (including a number of American officials) expected he might recapture the prime ministership. The Kurdistan coalition narrowed slightly with the departure of the Kurdistan Islamic Union. Most important, perhaps, was the addition of two significant Sunni Arab coalitions that had boycotted the January contest (along with a host of smaller Sunni lists that were now competing) and that figured to score well in the cities and towns associated with the insurgency. The Iraqi Consensus Front[31] was a coalition of three mainly Islamist Sunni Arab parties, led by the long-established Iraqi Islamic Party. The other Sunni coalition, the Iraqi Front for National Dialogue, led by Saleh Mutlak, grouped together Arab nationalists and secular Sunnis with links to the Baath Party. Both fronts promised to push for revision of the constitution's federal structure, the return of former army officers to duty, a rollback of de-Baathification provisions, and the withdrawal of foreign forces (a goal loudly pushed by Muqtada al-Sadr as well). When they and other Sunni lists vowed to "kick the foreigners out of our country," they were referring not only to the U.S.-led coalition troops but also to the Iranians they believed were backing and infiltrating the Shiite Islamist parties.[32]

In all, Iraqis had to choose among 231 political lists fielding some 7,000 different candidates. The effusion of political enthusiasm and ambition, however, was heavily dampened by violence and intolerance. A number of candidates were assassinated, including, in the last two weeks of the campaign, at least eleven people associated with Allawi's party, and at least two belonging to the Kurdistan Islamic Union.[33] Allawi himself had to beat a hasty and humiliating retreat from the Imam Ali shrine in Najaf in early December when a band of Muqtada al-Sadr's loyalists pelted him with rocks, tomatoes, and shoes (the latter a particularly grave insult in Iraqi culture). He and his bodyguards depicted the attack as an assassination attempt, a claim that was greeted with skepticism in some quarters but that could hardly be dismissed, given the Sadrists' involvement in the murder of the democratic Shiite cleric Majid al-Khoei at the very same holy site in 2003. So great were the dangers that many lists declined to reveal the identities of their candidates until the day of the election.

Despite the heavy investment of democracy assistance groups in training candidates and parties in campaign techniques, any kind of "normal" election campaign proved impossible. With campaign rallies and road travel heavily constricted by the terrorist, insurgent, militia, and criminal violence, and with many parties finding their posters defaced or torn down by opposing militants (particularly, it appears, those associated with the United Iraqi Alliance, sometimes in police uniform), the campaign had to rely mainly on electronic means: television and radio ads, press conferences, interactive web sites, and even cell phone text messaging. The Shiite and Sunni religious parties also sought to promote their campaigns through the sermons of supportive imams. With extensive funding from sources that were never disclosed, only three lists could compete fully on this electronic terrain: those of the religious Shiites, the Kurds, and Allawi, and during the final days of the campaign, ads poured forth. Lacking detailed programs, the contending coalitions fell back on appeals to identity, negative and positive, with the Shiite Islamist parties running ads showing Allawi's face morphing into Saddam Hussein's, while Allawi appealed to Iraqis to put their faith in Iraq and to resist a sectarian (and Iranian) takeover of the country.

In several respects, the elections were an unprecedented success. Voter participation jumped dramatically, from 9.8 million in the October 15 constitutional referendum to nearly 11 million in December (about 70 percent of registered voters), despite the continued efforts of Sunni jihadist groups to deter voting. A wide range of Sunni Arab groups—including the militant clerics gathered in the Association of Muslim Scholars—promoted a large Sunni turnout and successfully contained Al Qaeda ambitions to suppress the vote.[34] (For most of the groups associated with the resistance, however, the election marked not an end to violent struggle but "another front in the war," as one of their leaders told an Iraqi colleague of mine.) Sunni confidence in the elections was aided by a change in the electoral system that guaranteed each province a minimum number of seats in parliament.[35] Even more than in January and October, the comprehensive security blanket thrown over the country by American and Iraqi troops made for a largely peaceful day of balloting on December 15.

Although the conduct of the voting was bitterly protested by the Sunni alliances and the Allawi list—all of whom alleged widespread intimidation and malpractices—the United Nations' chief electoral officer in Iraq soon came forward to endorse the election as "credible." This outraged the protesting parties, who insisted there had been "huge fraud" that could not be assessed by "several international workers sitting inside the Green Zone."[36] To address their charges and ward off potentially crippling doubts about the election's legitimacy, the International Mission for Iraqi Elections (the principal external monitoring group) agreed on December 29 (with U.S. and UN support) to send a team of four observers into Iraq to investigate the charges of fraud.

As this edition went to press in January 2006, the charges of fraud were still being investigated and the final results had yet to be announced. It appeared that any corrections to the vote count might affect the distribution of ten to twenty seats, coming mainly at the expense of the United Iraqi Alliance. Without question, there were serious malpractices that diminished the climate of freedom, fairness, and neutrality that is necessary for truly democratic elections. In some cases, there were significant efforts to stuff ballot boxes and alter results. It is unlikely, however, that these specific transgressions significantly altered the broad shape of the outcome. How the election outcome might have differed if there had been real security and freedom for political candidates and campaigns is impossible to know—for that would require imagining a fundamentally different Iraq than what existed in 2005.

Once again, and even more so than in January or October, the voting became an identity referendum, in which about 90 percent of Kurdistan voted for the Kurdistan Coalition list, about three-quarters or more of Shiites voted for the United Iraqi Alliance, and about 90 percent of Sunnis voted for one of the two principal Sunni lists.[37] Consequently, the principal Kurdish list and the two Sunnis lists together each won about 20 percent of the seats, while the United Iraqi Alliance emerged again as the dominant political player, with about 45 percent of the seats.[38] Squeezed between these respective embraces of ethnic or sectarian identity, Ayad Allawi—representing the only viable nonsectarian political option—suffered a crushing defeat, apparently winning no more than 10 percent of the vote. Ahmed Chalabi was even more ignominiously routed, failing to win even a single seat for his list.

As the Shiite religious parties had anticipated all along, they were able to prevail by the sheer force of demography. In the early postwar period, one of their leaders had confided to a colleague of mine, "We love democracy, because we have the numbers." And indeed, they did. The election results appeared to confirm very rough estimates that the Shiites account for approximately 60 percent of the Iraqi population, the Kurds about 20 percent, and the Sunnis about 20 percent (with various minorities accounting for about 3 to 5 percent). Though many Sunni political leaders continued to believe that the Sunni Arabs were a majority in Iraq—or at least a plurality—this simply did not square with any possible construction of the results of an election in which Sunni Arabs finally turned out in great numbers to vote. When an election becomes an ethnic census, it does provide at least some crude sense of the size of each group.

★

The question that loomed large in the aftermath of the December election was not whether Iraq can become a democracy (a challenge that will be, at best, years in the making) but whether it can achieve any kind of political stability at all. Although the election succeeded for the first time in bringing the Sunnis squarely into the postwar political arena, that in itself offered no assurance of a reduction in the insurgent violence. Stabilization would require difficult and dramatic new developments on both the political and security fronts.

At the end of the electoral marathon year of 2005, the political imperatives remained what they had been at the beginning: to give the Sunnis a stake in the new political order, and to negotiate with the more tactical elements of the insurgency an end to the violent resistance, in exchange for an end to the occupation. The election went some distance toward achieving the first goal, as Sunni parties and candidates— representing mainly the hard-line constituencies that sympathized with the insurgency—won a meaningful share of seats and thus a legitimate place at the political bargaining table. Moreover, early postelection statements and talks signaled a recognition by the main Shiite and Kurdish political leaders of the need for a broad "national unity government" that would include at least the largest Sunni alliance, the Iraqi Consensus Front. But with the United Iraqi Alliance once again the dominant force in parliament and government, Sunni political and constitutional concerns could not be addressed without significant concessions from the Shiite religious parties. With the new parliament having in its first four months to appoint the constitutional review commission and then finalize the constitution, Iraq was approaching a historical fork in the road toward either accommodation or intensified violence and quite possibly civil war.

The crux of the issue would be whether the United Iraqi Alliance would continue to insist on the right to form a Shiite mega-region. It was conceivable, as the Carnegie Endowment scholar Marina Ottaway advocated, that the Sunnis might be mollified by the concurrent creation of a viable Sunni region, with guaranteed access to oil revenue.[39] But it was doubtful that the Sunnis would trust any such promises or that they would ever agree conceptually to such a radically decentralized system—a gross contradiction of the unified Iraqi state they still idealized. Moreover, even if they did accept such a region, a political structure consisting mainly of three ethnic regions would doom Iraq to disintegration and probably civil war. Or as Kanan Makiya of Brandeis University (one of the most influential Iraqi overseas intellectuals) cogently reflected, "The more Iraqi provinces opt for regional status, and get it, the more the federal state will shrivel up and die."[40] On the eve of the December elections, Makiya had called for a package of constitutional amendments that would have restored the three-province limit on the size of any new regions and set a ten-year moratorium on their creation, while also allocating oil revenue to the provinces on purely demographic terms.[41] It was far from clear that the relevant parties would embrace such reasoned accommodation, or that the United States and other external actors would possess sufficient leverage left to press them to do so.

With respect to the insurgency, there were new signs of political hope. From the beginning, the insurgency had mainly consisted of Sunni Arab tribal, religious, and nationalist forces who were fighting for limited, tactical objectives: a share of power and resources, an end to de-Baathification, a containment of Iranian influence, the release of detainees, and an end to foreign occupation. While many of these insurgent elements cooperated with the more lethal die-hard elements— Abu Musab al-Zarqawi's Al Qaeda in Iraq, and the surviving Saddam loyalists—there were growing signs that homegrown Iraqi resistance forces were turning against Al Qaeda and even fighting it on the ground.[42] This did not prevent the resumption of a new wave of devastating suicide bombings in January 2006, but it did enlarge the possibility that the Sunni Arab tribal and religious communities of Iraq could be broadly turned against their former tactical allies and enlisted in a new effort to stabilize Iraq, in exchange for political concessions. Under growing military pressure from coalition and Iraqi forces, increasingly alarmed by the growing power of the Shiite religious parties, and with a foot in the door of the political system through new legitimate political fronts, insurgent elements now signaled through international intermediaries a desire to negotiate with the United

States. Ambassador Khalilzad's statement late in 2005 (widely reported in the Arabic-language press) that he was willing to talk to anyone except for Al Qaeda and the Saddam loyalists helped to spur such contacts, as did Jalal Talabani's statement that he would meet with insurgents if they renounced violence. After two years of missed opportunities and mutual intransigence, the prospect emerged for the first time of serious negotiations between the United States and the Iraqi insurgency. By January 2006, American officials were engaged in "face-to-face discussions with insurgents in the field," the *New York Times* reported, and the American ambassador in Baghdad was vigorously pursuing avenues for higher-level direct talks.[43]

As the year drew to a close and President Bush acknowledged mistakes in America's postwar engagement in Iraq, the American administration was exhibiting a new and much needed pragmatism and flexibility. For the first time, it welcomed the involvement of the Arab League, which in late November 2005 hosted a conference in Cairo of one hundred Sunni, Shiite, and Kurdish leaders, representing the widest range of Iraqis to meet face-to-face since Saddam's fall.[44] But it was still not clear that Bush would welcome the kind of international mediation (from the Arab League, the United Nations, and European countries) needed to conduct serious talks with the insurgency or, if he did, that an agreement would be possible. Among the serious obstacles were the severe fragmentation of the insurgency into several dozen groups, requiring a comprehensive effort to identify and assess the key players so as to prepare for systematic negotiations, and the insurgents' pervasive, enduring distrust of the Americans. Neither of these obstacles is likely to be overcome without substantial international mediation.

The other imponderable concerned the security side of the equation. By the second half of 2005, observers and Iraqis themselves were increasingly characterizing the country as already in the grip of a kind of civil war—"a quiet and deadly struggle" of terrorist bombings, death-squad assassinations and kidnappings, brutal torture of detainees, sectarian executions of whole families, sabotage of critical fuel supplies, and ethnic cleansing of militia-dominated neighborhoods.[45] If Iraq were to stabilize to a degree that would enable the American military to withdraw without plunging the country from a low-intensity civil war claiming an estimated 1,000 Iraqi lives per month to an all-out confla-gration that might kill ten or twenty times as many, its security forces would need to bear the burden of maintaining order. After much lost time and several false starts, the United States made some significant progress during 2005 in establishing and training a new Iraqi army. But by even the most optimistic accounts, the Iraqi army still had few (if any) units capable of operating independently of the U.S. military, and it seemed likely to be years before the Iraqi armed forces would have not just the manpower but also the training, equipment, armor, weaponry, air support, medical relief, intelligence systems, and logisti-cal and technical capability to function fully and effectively on their own. Moreover, as James Fallows reported in the December 2005 issue of *The Atlantic Monthly*, the training of the Iraqi armed forces, which had been late in getting off the ground, was still being slowed by a lack of urgency on the American side and by massive corruption (costing hundreds of millions of dollars) on the Iraqi side.[46]

As Fallows notes, ethnic and sectarian tensions have seeped deeply into the Iraqi military, to the point where it is not clear to whom units really owe their loyalty. In the case of the *pesh merga* and Shiite militia fighters who dominate the most capable units of the new Iraqi army, it is very likely to be to their ethnic parties first and Iraq second.[47] More-over, he adds, "If an army has no stable government to defend, even the best-trained troops will devolve into regional militias and warlord gangs."[48] There is also a danger, in the absence of political progress, that the insurgency could infiltrate the Iraqi army and capture its modern equipment, which may account for the Pentagon's reluctance to trans-fer sophisticated arms and armor.

The Iraqi police are also plagued by the problem of conflicting loy-alties. During the second half of 2005, evidence mounted that Sadr's Mahdi Army, SCIRI's Badr Organization, and the militias of Dawa, Fadila, and other Shiite Islamist parties and factions were casting a long shadow of fear, coercion, murder, and other human rights abuses over life in the south. In the huge, sprawling Baghdad slum of Sadr City, "squad cars cruise openly with pictures of [Muqtada] Sadr taped to the windows," according to the *New York Times*.[49] As the Islamist factions stacked the police and government apparatus with their loyalists, they used their militias and their impunity from legal accountability to impose a harsh Islamic order, "firebombing internet cafes, alcohol and music shops, and attacking unveiled women," in the words of Rory Stewart, a trenchant British observer of the region who served as deputy governor of Maysan and Dhi Qar provinces during the CPA,[50] while imposing religious courts to deal with family law and banning alcohol, dancing, and concerts.[51] Stewart also reports an incident in March 2005 when "the Sadr militia in Basra attacked a group of engineering students from the local university who were having a picnic." Angry that the Christian women were unveiled, that some Christians had alcohol, and that men were mixing with women, "the Sadrists kidnapped some of them and shot dead a female student for wearing jeans."[52] That, it appears, may be the near-term future of southern Iraq, a future foretold in Muqtada al-Sadr's unchecked rampaging through the Iraqi landscape during much of the period of the CPA. If, as Stewart insists, security is significantly better now in the south, it is in many respects the security of an oppressive, quasi-Taliban order, or in the *New York Times* journalist Edward Wong's words, a "mini-theocracy under Shiite rule."[53] It is "not the kind of state the coalition had hoped to create," Stewart said, but rather an elected Islamist state that appears to match better than the liberal parties we tried to support the conservative religious and moral values of most Iraqi Shiites, "as well as their suspicion of non-Muslims and 'western decadence and colonialism.'"[54]

It may be that some scope for pluralism will emerge from the deep divisions among the highly factionalized Shiite Islamist forces or that the worst abuses of the militia forces and other incipient warlords and autocrats can be contained if the authority of the central government can be strengthened. But the Islamist parties and militias seem set to consolidate their control over southern Iraq for years to come, if judged by their tightening grip on government patronage, administration, and security in the southern provinces, by the broad political and philosophical support they have received from senior Shiite clerics (beginning, if rather more vaguely, with Ayatollah Sistani), and by their commanding performance in the December elections.

As of the end of 2005, American policymakers and independent analysts had hardly begun to ponder the consequences of this historic but deeply troubling development. "Victory," President Bush declared to the Naval Academy on November 30, would come "when the terrorists and Saddamists can no longer threaten Iraq's democracy, when the Iraqi security forces can provide for the safety of their own citizens, and when Iraq is not a safe haven for terrorists to plot new attacks on our nation." But what if the threats to democracy in Iraq come as much from the parties we helped to empower as from those that have resisted the new order? What if the safety and rights of Iraqi citizens are threatened by the very security forces we have helped to stand up? What if a Shiite Islamic government spanning the south of Iraq quietly allies with a militant Islamic government in Iran hell-bent on the pursuit of nuclear weapons? What if it remains the case for years to come that the only force capable of containing the slide to full-scale civil war is the American military—a force that cannot stay and cannot leave? As the first full-term government prepared to take office in Iraq, the United States had no clear answers to any of these questions—only the fervent hope that its quest for "victory" in Iraq would not again be squandered.

NOTES

Quotations that are not referenced in the notes are from conversations with the author or from interviews conducted by the author.

Introduction: The View from Babylon

1. Amatzia Baram, quoted in "Where Judaism Began," by Yigal Schleifer, *The Scribe*, Spring 2003. http://www.dangoor.com/issue76/articles/76056.htm.
2. Ibid.

1: The Call

1. Joel Brinkley, "The Struggle for Iraq: The Attacks; Despite Positives, More Negatives Are Predicted," *New York Times*, November 3, 2003, p. 10.
2. *San Diego Union Tribune*, October 25, 2003. In April, Iraqis had been about evenly divided (46 to 43 percent) in their perceptions of "occupiers" vs. "liberators."
3. Rajiv Chandrasekaran and Theola Labbe, "Blast Hits Red Cross Offices in Baghdad; at Least 2 Killed; U.S. Officer Dies in Earlier Attack," *Washington Post*, October 27, 2003.
4. Robin Wright and Anthony Shadid, "U.S. Seeks a Faster Transition in Iraq; Top Administrator Returns for Talks with White House," *Washington Post*, November 12, 2003, p. 1.
5. "Endgame: Why the United States Should Not Go It Alone," *Hoover Digest*, no. 1, 2003, pp. 82–85. http://www-hoover.stanford.edu/publications/digest/031/diamond. html.

6. Larry Diamond, "Can Iraq Become a Democracy?" *Hoover Digest*, no. 2, 2003, p. 10. http://www.hoover.stanford.edu/publications/digest/032/diamond.html.

7. Larry Diamond, *Developing Democracy: Toward Consolidation* (Baltimore: Johns Hopkins University Press, 1999), p. 25.

8. Larry Diamond, "Universal Democracy?" *Policy Review*, June 2003, pp. 3–25. http://www.policyreview.org/jun03/diamond.html.

9. Larry Diamond, Marc F. Plattner, and Daniel Brumberg, eds., *Islam and Democracy in the Middle East* (Baltimore: Johns Hopkins University Press, 2003).

10. The precise distribution of the Iraqi population is a matter of speculation, because of the lack of a reliable census in recent decades. Phebe Marr estimates the Kurds at 15 to 20 percent, the Arab Sunnis at 15 to 20 percent, the Arab Shi'a at 60 percent, the Turkish-speaking Turkoman at 2 to 3 percent, and the remaining 3 percent or so accounted for by Chaldean and Assyrian Christians, other small Christian groups, and two other small, distinct religious groups, the Yazidis and the Sabians; *The Modern History of Iraq* (Boulder, CO: Westview, 2004), pp. 12–18.

11. Marr, *The Modern History of Iraq*, pp. 200–202.

12. Peter W. Galbraith, "How to Get Out of Iraq," *The New York Review of Books*, vol. 51, no. 8, May 13, 2004, p. 8. http://www.nybooks.com/articles/17103.

13. Terry Lynn Karl, *The Paradox of Plenty: Oil Booms and Petro-States* (Berkeley: University of California Press, 1997).

14. James Dobbins et al., *America's Role in Nation-Building: From Germany to Iraq* (Santa Monica, CA: RAND, 2003), p. 166.

15. Adeed Dawisha, "Democratic Attitudes and Practices in Iraq, 1921–1958," *Middle East Journal* 59 (Winter 2005). I confess that I did not appreciate this democratic legacy until I read this fascinating essay by Dawisha well after returning from Iraq.

16. Diamond, "Can Iraq Become a Democracy?," p. 23.

2: In Search of a Plan

1. *The Telegraph*, November 13, 2003. http://www.telegraph.co.uk/news/main.jhtml?xml=/news/2003/11/13/wirq13.xml.

2. *The Telegraph*, November 11, 2003. http://www.telegraph.co.uk/news/main.jhtml;sessionid=OBTDY4D2SBLJRQFIQMFSNAGAVCBQoJVC?xml=/news/2003/11/11/wirq11.xml&secureRefresh rue&_requestid=7990.

3. "Skepticism About U.S. Deep, Iraq Polls Shows," *Washington Post*, November 12, 2003.

4. Democratic Principles Working Group, *Final Report on the Transition to Democracy in Iraq*, November 2002, p. 18.

5. A minority view held that only a fully elected constituent assembly should draft a constitution—a view that would be forcefully pressed by Ayatollah Sistani.

6. Michael R. Gordon, "The Strategy to Secure Iraq Did Not Foresee a 2nd War," *New York Times*, October 19, 2004.

7. David Rieff, "Who Botched the Occupation?" *New York Times Magazine*, November 2, 2003, p. 32.

8. Eric Schmitt and David E. Sanger, "Looting Disrupts Detailed U.S. Plan to Restore Iraq," *New York Times*, May 19, 2003.

9. http://news.bbc.co.uk/1/hi/world/americas/2924201.stm.

10. http://www.brainyencyclopedia.com/encyclopedia/2/20/2003_occupation_of_iraq_timeline.html.

11. Associated Press, April 28, 2003. http://www.iraqfoundation.org/news/2003/dapril/28_rebuilding.html.

12. George Packer, "Letter from Baghdad: After the War," *The New Yorker*, November 24, 2003 (p. 8 of Internet edition).

13. Interview with former senior ORHA official, September 26, 2004.

14. Fred Barnes, "Our Man in Baghdad: The Unsung Achievements of Paul Bremer," *The Weekly Standard*, July 26, 2004, p. 22.

15. Susan Sachs, "Iraqi Political Leaders Warn of Rising Hostility If Allies Don't Support an Interim Government," *New York Times*, May 18, 2003.

16. Anthony Shadid, "Shiite Denounce Occupation; Clerics Say U.S. Has Not Involved Them in Postwar Planning," *Washington Post*, May 20, 2003.

17. Patrick Tyler, "Iraqi Politicians to Issue a Protest of Occupation Rule," *New York Times*, May 21, 2003.

18. Security Council, May 22, 2003. http://ods-dds-ny.un.org/doc/UNDOC/GEN/N03/368/53/PDF/N0336853.pdf?OpenElement.

19. Michael R. Gordon, "Debate Lingering on Decision to Dissolve the Iraqi Military," *New York Times*, October 21, 2004. Abizaid was not alone in favoring a rapid reconstruction of the Iraqi Army, which could then take the lead in restoring security. He was joined by senior American military commanders in Iraq, and by Iraqi politicians and parties, who warned of the dangers of a prolonged American occupation.

20. Rieff, "Who Botched the Occupation?" p. 32.

21. Rajiv Chandrasekaran, "Iraqis Say They Will Defy U.S. on Council Plan," *Washington Post*, June 4, 2003.

22. With the exception of Chaderchi, who would soon be eclipsed in influence by Adnan Pachachi, these six leaders would remain the dominant political forces during the political occupation.

23. The panel urged "a major initiative to reintegrate 'self-demobilized' Iraqi soldiers *and* local militias," along with decentralization of authority, accelerated reconstruction spending, and massive public works projects. John Hamre, Frederick Barton, Bathsheba Crocker, Johanna Mendelson-Form, and Robert Orr, "Iraq's Post-Conflict Reconstruction: A Field Review and Recommendations," Center for Strategic and International Studies, July 17, 2003, pp. i, 1–2.

24. http://www.dod.gov/news/Jul2003/n07242003_200307242.html.

25. L. Paul Bremer III, "Operation Iraqi Prosperity," *Wall Street Journal*, June 20, 2003. Much of this agenda was implemented, including a flat income tax, but the privatization of Iraq's antiquated state-run industries would soon be dropped for fear of the political consequences of rising unemployment.

26. Alex Berenson, "Anti-U.S. Cleric Harangues, but Iraq's Shiites Heed Four Ayatollahs," *Washington Post*, October 22, 2003.

27. I am grateful to Laith Kubba for this interpretation.

28. "Coalition" here refers to the combined military of the U.S., Britain, Poland, Spain, Ukraine, and other nations, under overall U.S. command, known as Coalition Joint Task Force Seven. However, most of the international forces in Iraq were American or (to a much lesser extent) British, and in both its military and political aspects, Iraqis saw the "Coalition" as essentially an American (or at most Anglo-American) occupation. Throughout this book, I will use the term "Coalition" to refer both to the American-led international military forces and to the occupation presence in all of its political and mili-

tary aspects. When referring only to the political and administrative aspects of the occupation, I use the term for the formal governing authority of the occupation, the CPA.

29. "U.S. Presses New Iraqi Council to Begin Tackling Major Issues," *Washington Post*, July 15, 2003.

30. Bremer conference call with editorial writers, July 24, 2003. http://www
.dod.mil/transcripts/2003/tr20030724-0501.html.

31. Colum Lynch, "Annan Wants Plan for Iraqi Self-Rule," *Washington Post*, July 19, 2003.

32. http://www.juancole.com/2003_08_01_juancole_archive.html; August 29, 2003, comment.

33. http://www.cnn.com/2003/WORLD/meast/09/02/sprj.irq.main/.

34. http://www.cpa-iraq.org/pressconferences/Pressconference23AugwithQAs.html.

35. In the opinion of Professor Juan Cole, Ayatollah Mohammed Baqir al-Hakim was a believer "in Khomeini's theory of clerical rule" who was nevertheless "a pragmatist willing to accept a pluralistic, parliamentary government in Iraq" until an Islamic Republic could be achieved. http://www.juancole.com/2003_08_01_juancole_archive
.html; August 30, 2003, comment.

36. "Iraqi Public Has Wide-Ranging Preferences for a Future Political System," opinion analysis, Office of Research, Department of State, October 21, 2003.

37. Rajiv Chandrasekaran, "Shiite Demand to Elect Constitution's Drafters Could Delay Transfer of Power," *Washington Post*, October 21, 2003.

38. *The Telegraph*, October 29, 2003. http://www.telegraph.co.uk/core/Content/
displayPrintable.jhtml?xml=/news/2003/10/29/wirq129.xml&site=5.

39. Patrick E. Tyler, "Three Wars over Iraq: Staying the Course May Be the Hardest Battle," *New York Times*, October 5, 2003.

40. Ibid.

41. The survey was conducted by the independent Iraqi Centre for Research and Strategic Studies.

3: Mediation Efforts

1. Patrick E. Tyler, "Three Wars over Iraq: Staying the Course May Be the Hardest Battle," *New York Times*, October 5, 2003.

2. A suicide bomber drove a cement mixer loaded with 1,500 pounds of explosives into the side of the UN compound, wreaking devastation.

3. http://www.un.org/apps/news/storyAr.asp?NewsID=8543&Cr=iraq&Cr1=#.

4. The emphasis was in the original memo.

4: The Palace

1. George Packer, "Letter from Baghdad: After the War," *The New Yorker*, November 24, 2003 (p. 1 of Internet edition).

2. Rumor had it that the table was meant to represent a woman's spread legs, but an observer from the region told me that the structure allowed Saddam to sit in a unique place, with no peer.

3. Edward Wong, "Direct Election of Iraqi Assembly Pushed by Cleric," *New York Times*, January 12, 2004.

4. This occurred just three weeks after the deadly car bombing at the Assassin's Gate that killed twenty-five Iraqis at a similar security checkpoint. Rashid was only 100 meters away when that bomb went off.

5. A few weeks after my conversation, as I was exiting the Green Zone, I saw a long line of Iraqis waiting to pass through security at the entrance to the Fourteenth of July Bridge. I stared in disbelief at these helpless people. Six weeks later, on May 6, a suicide car bomb exploded at that very checkpoint as Iraqi cars were lined up. Five Iraqis and one U.S. soldier were killed in the fiery blast.

5: Promoting Democracy

1. The document is available on the center's Web site, http://civiced.org/PDFS/respublica.pdf.

2. The full text of these nine paragraphs, along with some of the speeches I gave in Iraq on principles of democracy, federalism, and civil society, are available on my Web site, http://www.stanford.edu/~ldiamond/iraq.html.

3. The selection process did not take place in the three predominantly Kurdish provinces, as only the Kurdistan Regional Government really mattered in that area.

4. In fact, the university was the latest manifestation of an ancient Shiite school of Islamic philosophy and scholarship known as al-Qizwiniyya. Sayyid Farqad has a collection of several thousand volumes (including handwritten works), amassed over the centuries by his family, of philosophy and Islamic learning.

5. Originally descended from the martyred Imam Husayn, the younger brother of Imam Ali, the founder of Shi'ism, the family took its name from the city of Qazvin in Iran, which was once the capital of Persia and remains an important center of Shiite learning.

6. Kevin Whitelaw, "Democracy 101: Travel with 'Mr. Mike' As He Sets About Winning Hearts and Minds in Southern Iraq," *U.S. News & World Report*, February 2, 2004.

7. Edward Wong, "U.S. Tries to Give Moderates an Edge in Iraqi Elections," *New York Times*, January 18, 2004.

8. United Nations, *The Political Transition in Iraq: Report of the Fact-Finding Mission*, February 23, 2004, p. 3.

9. The subsequent quotations are from *The Political Transition in Iraq*, pp. 3–12. In addition to the grand bargain Brahimi had worked out in Baghdad, scrapping the caucus system but deferring elections until December or January, the report recommended that an independent Iraqi electoral commission be established immediately—something that several of us in the CPA had been urging—and indicated that the UN stood ready to offer substantial technical assistance to the commission.

6: Constitutions and Compromises

1. Iraqis had insisted that the document not be called an interim "constitution" for three reasons. First, no Iraqi wanted a foreign civil administrator (Bremer) to be in the position of approving the nation's constitution. Second, Ayatollah Sistani had been adamant that only an elected body could draft a constitution. And third, Iraqi liberals

worried about having yet another document in a long line of "provisional" constitutions that never gained permanence.

2. Like many Iraqis, Istrabadi has a mixed family heritage that transcends the country's divides. His father's family is Shiite, of Persian origin, while his mother's family is Sunni, of Arab, Turkoman, and Kurdish origin. "So what does that make me?" he once asked. The identity he always insisted upon was "an Iraqi."

3. For a revealing portrait of the two men, see Yochi J. Dreazen, "Founding Fissures: Two Exiles Writing Law of Land in Iraq Reveal Its Divisions," *Wall Street Journal*, April 12, 2004. While the article is illuminating in many respects, it overstates the philosophical differences between the two men, as I explain below.

4. In the end, the section on fundamental rights in the TAL would occupy fourteen of the document's sixty-two articles, with far-reaching guarantees of freedom of thought, religious belief, expression, assembly, organization, demonstration, and movement. Historically, these provisions may prove to be one of the most important legacies of the TAL, not only for Iraq but for the Arab world.

5. This was a particular concern for the estimated half million Christians in Iraq.

6. The original compromise had simply perpetuated the type of language in previous Iraqi constitutions. During the final negotiations, the Shiite caucus demanded that Islam be established as "a principal source of legislation," dropping the words "among other sources." They said that the more moderate wording was a deal breaker. The liberals, led by Pachachi, said they were ready to break the deal. After hours of painstaking but respectful negotiations, the liberals and the Shiite Islamists agreed to drop the word "principal" and establish Islam (for the time being) as "a source of legislation." In return, the Shiite caucus demanded wording that "no law can be enacted which is contrary to Islam." But the liberals insisted on inserting "universally agreed tenets" of Islam, and Pachachi then added the provisions ensuring that no law contradict democracy or the bill of rights.

7. Our thinking was influenced by a study being prepared by the U.S. Institute of Peace. For some of its early key conclusions and the application to Iraq, see Jamal Benomar, "Constitution-Making After Conflict: Lessons from Iraq," *Journal of Democracy*, vol. 15, April 2004, pp. 81–95, an early draft of which we had in hand as we deliberated.

8. Soon after it was established in 1991, the autonomous Kurdistan government splintered in two, as a result of internal strife, but the Kurds nevertheless managed to hold democratic elections and generate a freer political climate than Iraq had known in decades. In June 2003 the two ruling Kurdish parties, the KDP and the PUK, agreed to unite their areas of administration into one regional government.

9. http://www.krg.org/docs/mb-federalism-kurdistan-dec03.asp.

10. The term "voluntary union" was used by Qabad Talabani, son of PUK leader Jalal Talabani; Rajiv Chandrasekaran, "Kurds Reject Key Parts of Proposed Iraq Constitution," *Washington Post*, February 21, 2004.

11. The TAL authorized the Iraqi Property Claims Commission to remedy the injustices of deportation and forced migration from Kirkuk and other areas by restoring the original residents to their homes and property or by providing them just compensation, while resettling and compensating those who had been newly introduced to the affected areas. Eventually, the IPCC was given an elaborate administrative and judicial structure to resolve all property claims from injustices done during the thirty-five years of Baath Party rule.

12. Dexter Filkins, "Iraqi Kurdish Leaders Resist As the U.S. Presses Them to Moderate Their Demands," *New York Times*, February 21, 2004.

13. Law of Administration for the State of Iraq for the Transitional Period (English version), 8 March 2004, Chapter 3, Article 25 (e).

14. Ibid., Article 9.

15. The key actors for the Shiite caucus were its five core leaders, Ahmed Chalabi, Adel Abdel Mahdi (again acting for the SCIRI leader, Abdul-Aziz al-Hakim), Ibrahim al-Jaafari, Muhammad Bahr al-Uloum, and Mowaffak al-Rubaie.

16. Originally, the proposed revision had referred only to the three Kurdish provinces, but an Iraqi Arab adviser to a Governing Council member urged Shaways to generalize the reference to make it more acceptable.

17. Rajiv Chandrasekaran, "Iraqi Shiites Fail to Sign Pact After Cleric Balks," *Washington Post*, March 6, 2004.

18. Rajiv Chandrasekaran, "Iraqi Council Signs Charter," *Washington Post*, March 9, 2004.

19. http://www.iraqcoalition.org/transcripts/20040308_signing_transcript.html.

7: Salesmanship

1. Within the palace, one office within the CPA often "persuaded" another to part with some scarce good or service by offering in return some kind of "favor" or token of appreciation—a case of beer, a couple of bottles of scotch, or a bureaucratic concession on some other issue. I never learned what, if anything, we offered to get the security detail at the eleventh hour, but I later discovered that these types of exchanges were known within the palace as "drug deals."

2. In truth, a few of them were doing so from time to time, but most of them weren't. A notable exception was Judge Wael Abdul Latif, who was also the governor of Basra Province. He spoke on behalf of the TAL in a number of public sessions in his home province, and gave an articulate, persuasive defense of the federalist provisions of the TAL, at a conference on decentralization that I attended on March 28.

3. This was a sardonic reference to the mass suicide at Jonestown, Guyana, in 1978, when the psychotic cult figure Jim Jones and 913 of his Peoples Temple followers drank a Kool-Aid fruit punch laced with cyanide.

4. By September, all ten of the planned national conferences had taken place.

8: The Second War

1. Juan Cole, "The Iraqi Shiites," *Boston Review*, October–November 2003, p. 8. www.bostonreview.net/BR28.5/cole.html.

2. For more on this contemporary history of Iraq's Shiites, see Yitzhak Nakash, "The Shi'ites and the Future of Iraq," *Foreign Affairs*, vol. 82, July–August 2003, pp. 17–26; and Cole, "The Iraqi Shiites." For the deeper history and sociology, see Yitzhak Nakash, *The Shi'is of Iraq* (Princeton: Princeton University Press, 1994).

3. Cole, "The Iraqi Shiites," p. 8

4. Ibid., p. 8.

5. Nakash, "The Shi'ites and the Future of Iraq," p. 21. In Shi'a Islam, the first eleven imams were lineal descendants of the Prophet Muhammad's cousin and rightful successor, Ali, and the Prophet's daughter, Fatima. "The twelfth of these vicars or

'Imams' was held to have disappeared into a supernatural realm, from which he would one day return." Cole, "The Iraqi Shiites," p. 5.

6. http://www.globalsecurity.org/military/world/para/al-sadr.htm.

7. Nakash, "The Shi'ites and the Future of Iraq," p. 21.

8. These included Fadl Allah, affiliated with Sadr's movement; 15 Shabaan (the date of the beginning of the 1991 Shiite uprising against Saddam), which originated as an arm of Iranian intelligence but now had strong popular support in Dhi-Qar Province; and Hassan al-Sari's Hizbollah Movement of Iraq—a SCIRI ally and not to be confused with the organization from which it split off, Iraqi Hizbollah, a resistance movement under Saddam (led by Governing Council member Abdul-Karim al-Muhammadawi, known by the nom de guerre "Abu Hatem").

9. Normally such plans are called "disarmament, demobilization, and reintegration," but the softer label was chosen in order not to stigmatize groups that had fought against Saddam, and because the militias were to face a gradual transition in status, rather than immediate demobilization.

10. A key figure was the RAND Corporation's Terrence Kelly, a former army lieutenant colonel.

11. Rajiv Chandrasekaran and Robin Wright, "Iraqi Militias Near Accord to Disband," *Washington Post*, March 22, 2004.

12. Named after the thousand-year-old Shiite seminary in Najaf that has been the premier center of Shiite religious instruction and authority.

13. Tony Karon, "Iraq After the Hand-Over," *Time*, March 30, 2004. http://www.time.com/time/world/article/0,8599,606092,00.html.

14. Rajiv Chandrasekaran and Anthony Shadid, "U.S. Targeted Fiery Cleric in Risky Move," *Washington Post*, April 11, 2004.

15. Christine Hauser, "Iraqi Uprising Spreads," *New York Times*, April 8, 2004.

16. Douglas Jehl, "U.S. Says It Will Move Gingerly Against Sadr," *New York Times*, April 7, 2004.

17. Derek Berlin, "Challenges to Democracy: The Struggle to Rebuild Iraq," unpublished paper, Columbia University, December 15, 2004. Berlin, who was among a small team that reestablished the CPA presence in late April, reports that, for good measure, the insurgents even put a nail into the compound's basketball.

18. Ibid., p. 36.

19. Hauser, "Iraqi Uprising Spreads."

20. John F. Burns, "The Long Shadow of a Mob," *New York Times*, April 4, 2004.

21. Chandrasekaran and Shadid, "U.S. Targeted Fiery Cleric in Risky Move."

22. The quotations are from a Mahdi Army foot soldier; Jeffrey Gettleman, "Ex-Rivals Uniting," *New York Times*, April 9, 2004.

23. Neil MacFarquhar, "Arabs Worry over Extremism While Evoking Vindication," *New York Times*, April 9, 2004.

24. John F. Burns, "Fighting Halts Briefly in Falluja," *New York Times*, April 10, 2004.

25. Rajiv Chandrasekaran, "Anti-U.S. Uprising Widens in Iraq," *Washington Post*, April 8, 2004.

26. Edward Wong, "Cleric's Militia Upends Shiite Power Balance," *New York Times*, April 21, 2004.

27. Bradley Graham, "U.S. Denies Raid on Najaf Is Imminent," *Washington Post*, April 15, 2004.

28. Even just before the uprising, 80 percent of Iraqis polled said they distrusted

the CPA, and 82 percent disapproved of Coalition forces; Thomas E. Ricks, "80% in Iraq Distrust Occupation Authority," *Washington Post*, May 13, 2004. The poll was conducted in selected cities in late March and early April.

29. Edward Wong, "Battle for Falluja Rouses the Anger of Iraqis Weary of the U.S. Occupation," *New York Times*, April 22, 2004.

30. Eric Schmitt, "U.S. General at Falluja Warns a Full Attack Could Come Soon," *New York Times*, April 22, 2004.

31. Rajiv Chandrasekaran and Robin Wright, "In Two Sieges, U.S. Finds Itself Shut Out," *Washington Post*, April 29, 2004.

32. Daniel Williams, "Despite Agreement, Insurgents Rule Fallujah," *Washington Post*, June 7, 2004.

33. John F. Burns, "Iraq Shiites Urge Cleric to Resist," *New York Times*, May 5, 2004.

34. Edward Wong, "U.S. Troops Start Major Attacks on Shiite Insurgents in 2 Cities," *New York Times*, May 6, 2004.

35. Much of the devastation of urban landscapes resulted from these massive cannons. Tank shells ripped through walls, "crumbling rows of houses sometimes two and three beyond the intended targets due to the force of the projectile"; Berlin, "Challenges to Democracy," p. 39.

36. Iraqi tribes also prevented the Mahdi Army from gaining a foothold in the countryside of Najaf Province (thus bottling up Sadr and his fighters in Kufa and Najaf) and helped prevent Sadr's forces from consolidating control of Karbala.

37. Dexter Filkins, "Two Shrines Intact, but U.S. Reputation Is Marred After Clashes with Rebels," *New York Times*, May 27, 2004.

38. Daniel Williams, "U.S. Calls Sadr Cease-Fire Intact Despite Clashes," *Washington Post*, May 29, 2004.

9: Handing Over

1. Robin Wright, "U.S. Relying on U.N. Help with Iraq Exit Plan," *Washington Post*, March 30, 2004.

2. Warren Hoge, "Iraqi Leader Reaffirms U.N. Role in Transition," *New York Times*, March 17, 2004.

3. Colum Lynch and Rajiv Chandrasekaran, "Shiite Leader in Iraq Wants Help of U.N., Envoy Says," *Washington Post*, March 17, 2004.

4. United Nations, *The Political Transition in Iraq: Report of the Fact-Finding Mission*, February 23, 2004, p. 7.

5. Joint Press Conference by Lakhdar Brahimi, Special Adviser to the Secretary General, and Mr. Massoud Barzani, President of the Iraqi Governing Council, 14 April 2004. http://www.un.org/apps/news/printinfocusnews.asp?nid=723.

6. Warren Hoge, "U.N. Is Wary of Dangers in Taking Lead Role in Iraq," *Washington Post*, April 18, 2004.

7. Secretary of Defense Rumsfeld, who was rumored to be hoping still for Chalabi to lead the next government, appeared more resigned to the plan than supportive of it.

8. Dana Milbank, "Bush, Blair Support U.N. on Iraq Plan," *Washington Post*, April 17, 2004.

9. Joint Press Conference by Brahimi and Barzani.

10. Josh White and Jonathan Weisman, "Limited Iraqi Sovereignty Planned," *Washington Post*, April 22, 2004.

11. Robin Wright and Rajiv Chandrasekaran, "U.N. Closes In on Choice to Lead Iraq," *Washington Post*, May 26, 2004.

12. Christine Hauser, "Top Candidate to Lead Iraq's Interim Government Says He Doesn't Want the Job," *New York Times*, May 27, 2004.

13. Rajiv Chandrasekaran, "Shiite Politicians' Objections Lead Candidate to Withdraw," *Washington Post*, May 27, 2004.

14. Rajiv Chandrasekaran, "Former Exile Is Selected as Interim Iraqi Leader," *Washington Post*, May 29, 2004.

15. Warren Hoge and Steven R. Weisman, "Surprising Choice Reflects U.S. Influence," *New York Times*, May 29, 2004.

16. Rajiv Chandrasekaran, "Interim Leaders Named in Iraq," *Washington Post*, June 2, 2004.

17. While some of the Iraqi and international participants in the selection process came to resent Blackwill's subterranean maneuvering, they praised Bremer for his decency, transparency, and open-mindedness.

18. This is from a respected Iraqi figure, who reports that a senior State Department official he contacted was dismayed to learn that Blackwill was pushing Yawer.

19. William Safire, "The Fourth Election," *New York Times*, December 1, 2004. Safire's evidence for the latter charge was: "At the Ambrosetti conference in Italy a year ago, I saw him with Amr Moussa, head of the Arab League, receiving instructions from Sunni Central." Moreover, Safire did not bother to explain why, if Pachachi was a tool of the Saudis and was taking instructions from the Arab League, he had drafted the most liberal and democratic constitution anywhere in the Arab world—one bound to be subversive of Arab authoritarian orders. Although Safire's column was written six months after the selection of the interim president, the tone reflected what pro-Chalabi neoconservative critics had been saying at least since early February 2003. From the start, the vitriolic assault on Pachachi reflected the strains between the State Department, which promoted Pachachi, and the Pentagon, which promoted Chalabi.

20. Chandrasekaran, "Interim Leaders Named in Iraq."

21. The quote is from the analysis by Rajiv Chandrasekaran, "Iraqi Council Members Oppose U.S., U.N. on President," *Washington Post*, May 30, 2004.

22. Dexter Filkins, "New Government Is Formed in Iraq As Attacks Go On," *New York Times*, June 2, 2004.

23. Shaalan had also come to the aid of the victims of the Qawliyya assault. The scion of a noble family that founded the city of Diwaniyah in the eleventh century, he had accompanied Ayatollah Abdul Majid al-Khoei from exile back to Iraq, and had narrowly escaped death himself when al-Khoei was stabbed to death in Najaf in April 2003.

24. Filkins, "New Government Is Formed in Iraq As Attacks Go On."

25. Chandrasekaran, "Interim Leaders Named in Iraq."

26. Dexter Filkins, "Kurds Threaten to Walk Away from Iraqi State," *New York Times*, June 9, 2004.

27. John F. Burns and Ian Fisher, "U.S., Seeking to Stabilize Iraq, Casts Baathists in Lead Roles," *New York Times*, May 3, 2004.

28. Rajiv Chandrasekaran and Walter Pincus, "U.S. Edicts Curb Power of Iraq's Leadership," *Washington Post*, June 27, 2004. Noting the absurdity of some of the decrees, Chandrasekaran reported that the CPA-imposed traffic code "stipulates the use of a car horn in 'emergency conditions only' and requires a driver to 'hold the steering wheel with both hands.'"

29. These orders and regulations were posted on the CPA Web site, http://www.iraqcoalition.org/regulations/index.html#Regulations.

30. Edward Cody, "Decree Outlaws Iraqi Militias," *Washington Post*, June 8, 2004.

31. The *pesh merga*, with 75,000 fighters, accounted for the bulk of these numbers; the Badr Organization, which reported that it had 15,000 fighters, was second.

32. Dexter Filkins, "9 Iraqi Militias Are Said to Approve a Deal to Disband," *New York Times*, June 8, 2004.

33. Josh White, "Iraqi Insurgents Are Surprisingly Cohesive, Armitage Says," *Washington Post*, June 26, 2004.

34. Scott Wilson, "Insurgency Leaves U.S. Forces Baffled," *Washington Post*, June 27, 2004.

35. Philip Kennicott, "America's Missed Photo Opportunity," *Washington Post*, June 29, 2004.

36. Eric Schmitt, "Insurgency and Able Government Prompted Transfer Decision," *New York Times*, June 29, 2004.

37. Edward Wong and Ian Fisher, "Wary Iraqis Face Changes with Silence and Hope," *New York Times*, June 29, 2004.

10: What Went Wrong?

1. Quoted in Ruth Berins Collier and David Collier, *Shaping the Political Arena: Critical Junctures, the Labor Movement, and Regime Dynamics in Latin America* (Princeton: Princeton University Press, 1991), p. 28. See the Colliers' text for further explanation of path dependence and the related concept they develop of critical historical junctures.

2. Gerard Baker and Stephen Fidler, "The Best Laid Plans?" *Financial Times*, August 4, 2003.

3. James Fallows, "Blind into Baghdad," *The Atlantic Monthly*, January–February 2004.

4. Quoted in Fallows, "Blind into Baghdad," p. 73.

5. David Rieff, "Who Botched the Occupation?" *New York Times Magazine*, November 2, 2003, p. 44.

6. George Packer, "Letter from Baghdad: After the War," *The New Yorker*, November 24, 2003 (p. 8 of Internet edition).

7. Rieff, "Who Botched the Occupation?"

8. http://www.cnn.com/2003/US/04/11/sprj.irq.pentagon/

9. Democratic Principles Working Group, *Final Report on the Transition to Democracy in Iraq*, November 2002, pp. 69 and 71.

10. Fallows, "Blind into Baghdad," p. 63.

11. Conrad C. Crane and W. Andrew Terrill, *Reconstructing Iraq: Insights, Challenges, and Missions for Military Forces in a Post-Conflict Scenario* (Carlisle, PA: Strategic Studies Institute, Army War College, February 2003). The extended quotations are from pages 42 and 37.

12. Fallows, "Blind into Baghdad," p. 65.

13. Quoted in Fallows, "Blind into Baghdad," p. 72.

14. Michael R. Gordon, "The Strategy to Secure Iraq Did Not Foresee a 2nd War," *New York Times*, October 19, 2004.

15. James Dobbins et al., *America's Role in Nation-Building: From Germany to Iraq* (Santa Monica, CA: RAND, 2003), pp. 165–66.

16. Warren P. Strobel and John Walcott, "Planning for After the War in Iraq Non-existent," Knight-Ridder Newspapers, October 16, 2004, posted at http://www .realcities.com/mld/krwashington/9927782.htm, October 15, 2004.

17. This was the view of one army officer with experience both in the Pentagon and in Iraq.

18. Gordon, "The Strategy to Secure Iraq Did Not Foresee a 2nd War."

19. Thomas L. Friedman, "Bush, Iraq, and Sister Souljah," *New York Times*, December 8, 2002.

20. Baker and Fidler, "The Best Laid Plans?"

21. Ibid.

22. Robin Wright and Thomas E. Ricks, "New Urgency, New Risks in 'Iraqification,'" *Washington Post*, November 14, 2003.

23. It was not uncommon for 1,000 sheikhs (among others) to show up at the lectures and classes on democracy. This may have helped to generate (or at least fortify) their resolve to resist Sadr's forces, because they had, in Gfoeller's words, "something to fight for."

24. "Blunders Worsened Iraqi Predicament," *Sunday Times* (Contra Costa), Knight-Ridder, October 17, 2004.

25. Ibid.

26. Gordon, "The Strategy to Secure Iraq Did Not Foresee a 2nd War."

27. Thomas E. Ricks, "General Reported Shortages in Iraq," *Washington Post*, October 18, 2004.

28. Ibid.

29. Thomas E. Ricks, "Dissension Grows in Senior Ranks on War Strategy," *Washington Post*, May 9, 2004.

30. Strobel and Walcott, "Planning for After the War in Iraq Non-existent."

31. On November 21, 2001, Bush asked Rumsfeld for a war plan for Iraq; Bob Woodward, *Plan of Attack* (New York: Simon and Schuster, 2004), p. 1.

32. California Jury Instructions—Criminal. CALJIC 3.36. Criminal or Gross Negligence—Defined.

33. For most of the occupation, CPA's Governance Office had few of the ceramic-plated body vests required for adequate protection (and routinely worn by the British and by USAID officials). "Towards the end of CPA, three more were acquired after months of requests, to be shared by roughly 25 members of the joint Governance Offices"; Derek Berlin, "Challenges to Democracy: The Struggle to Rebuild Iraq," unpublished paper, Columbia University, December 15, 2004, p. 28.

34. *People v. Valdez* (2002), 27 Cal.4th 778.

35. One reason for the high rate of desertions from the reconstituting Iraqi Army was probably the low pay.

36. Edward Wong and Dexter Filkins, "U.S. Strikes Mosque Held by Iraqi Cleric's Militia," *New York Times*, May 12, 2004.

37. Even after Sadr launched a full-scale insurgency in April 2004, the CPA continued to contradict itself, appearing weak and even ridiculous. Bremer declared Muqtada an outlaw and announced a warrant for his arrest. As the country then descended into a two-front civil war, American military commanders and civilian officials let it be known that they would not arrest or kill Sadr anytime soon, for fear of making the situation worse. Virtually at the same time, a "senior White House official" declared that Sadr would "be dealt with, and I don't mean through negotiation." Douglas Jehl, "U.S. Says It Will Move Gingerly Against Sadr," *New York Times*, April 7, 2004; and Douglas

Jehl et al., "U.S. May Delay Departure of Some Troops in Iraq," *New York Times*, April 8, 2004.

38. In the spring of 2004, a well-placed army officer told me, emphatically, about the source of the problem: "I fault Bremer. He is a control freak. There is no joint planning."

39. John F. Burns, "The Long Shadow of a Mob," *New York Times*, April 4, 2004.

40. These observations were made by Major General James A. Marks, U.S. Army, to Michael Gordon; "The Strategy to Secure Iraq Did Not Foresee a 2nd War."

41. Dobbins et al., *America's Role in Nation-Building*, p. 151.

42. Stephen John Stedman, Donald Rothchild, and Elizabeth M. Cousens, eds., *Ending Civil Wars: The Implementation of Peace Agreements* (Boulder, CO: Lynne Rienner, 2002). See, in particular, in this collection, Terrence Lyons, "The Role of Post-settlement Elections," 215–36.

43. Dobbins et al., *America's Role in Nation-Building*, p. 154.

44. Ibid.

45. Simon Chesterman, *You the People: The United Nations, Transitional Administration, and State-Building* (Oxford: Oxford University Press, 2004), p. 257.

46. Ibid.

47. Niall Ferguson, *Colossus: The Price of America's Empire* (New York: Penguin, 2004), pp. 198, 223, 225.

48. Ibid.

11: Can Iraq Become a Democracy?

1. ABC News Poll: "Iraq—Where Things Stand," released March 15, 2004, conducted February 9–28, 2004. Forty-nine percent of Iraqis chose democracy, 28 percent a strong leader, and 21 percent an Islamic state.

2. In a poll conducted by the CPA in August and September 2003, in seven representative Iraqi cities, 87 percent rated the "right to free and fair elections" as "very important," 73 percent did so for "the right to criticize the government," and 61 percent did so for press freedom; Department of State, Office of Research and Opinion Analysis, "Iraqi Public Has Wide-Ranging Preferences for a Future Political System," October 21, 2003.

3. Robert A. Dahl, *Polyarchy: Participation and Opposition* (New Haven: Yale University Press, 1971).

4. The chief proponent of the power-sharing, or "consensus," model of democracy has been Arend Lijphart. See his *Patterns of Democracy: Government Forms and Performance in Thirty-six Countries* (New Haven: Yale University Press, 1999). The most prominent advocate of designing institutions to "make moderation pay," as he puts it, is Donald L. Horowitz. See his *Ethnic Groups in Conflict* (Berkeley: University of California Press, 1985).

5. Dankwart A. Rustow, "Transitions to Democracy," *Comparative Politics*, vol. 2, April 1970, pp. 352 and 357.

6. Guillermo O'Donnell and Philippe C. Schmitter, *Transitions from Authoritarian Rule: Tentative Conclusions About Uncertain Democracies* (Baltimore: Johns Hopkins University Press, 1986), p. 37.

7. Rustow, "Transitions to Democracy," p. 360.

8. For an overview of this literature, see Larry Diamond, Juan J. Linz, and Seymour Martin Lipset, "Introduction: What Makes for Democracy," in Diamond, Linz, and Lipset, *Politics in Developing Countries: Comparing Experiences with Democracy*, 2nd ed. (Boulder, CO: Lynne Rienner, 1995), pp. 1–66.

9. Samuel P. Huntington, "Will More Countries Become Democratic?" *Political Science Quarterly*, vol. 99, Summer 1984, pp. 193–218.

10. Larry Diamond, *Developing Democracy: Toward Consolidation* (Baltimore: Johns Hopkins University Press, 1999).

11. Samuel P. Huntington, *The Third Wave: Global Democratization in the Late Twentieth Century* (Norman: University of Oklahoma Press, 1991).

12. Adeed Dawisha, "Democratic Attitudes and Practices in Iraq, 1921–58," *Middle East Journal*, vol. 59, Winter 2005.

13. Radical Salafists seek to restore, through holy war, the dictates of Islam dating back to the Prophet Muhammad and his followers. Wahabism is the puritanical, fundamentalist branch of Islam that officially predominates in Saudi Arabia. Both versions harbor strong prejudice against Shi'a Islam.

14. The numbers can be calculated as follows. The Kurdistan Alliance won 25.7 percent of the valid votes, and the Islamic Kurdish Society won 0.7 percent, for a total of slightly over 26 percent. The Turkomen Iraqi Front won 1.1 percent and the National Rafidain List (an Assyrian Christian list) won 0.4 percent, giving it a single seat. These four groups accounted for 28 percent of the vote, and I estimate that Sunni Arabs accounted for about 5 percent of voters, leaving the Shiites with about 67 percent of the electorate. A few Kurds and other ethnic minorities may have voted for Allawi's Iraqi List and perhaps a few for the United Iraqi Alliance, but these votes were probably negligible in percentage terms. The Shiites were split among the United Iraqi Alliance, the Iraqi List, and small parties like the Communists, but if the Shiites were 67 percent of the electorate, then this means that the United Iraqi Alliance won about 72 percent of the Shiite vote.

15. Lawrence F. Kaplan, "The Last Casualty: The Tragic End to a Liberal Iraq," *The New Republic*, February 7, 2005, p. 20.

16. Douglas Struck, "Insurgents Step Up Violence on Civilians," *Washington Post*, February 13, 2005.

17. This happened during the final phase of negotiations over the interim constitution, but it surfaced again almost immediately after the January 30, 2005, election. Thanassis Cambanis, "Top Shiite Clerics Begin to Press for an Islamic Constitution," *Boston Globe*, February 2, 2005.

18. A tiny proportion of this figure would be Iraqi Shiites who are non-Arab, primarily Kurdish.

19. If the election results were not seriously contaminated by fraud, if we assume that the Kurds had about an 80 percent voter turnout, Shiites 70 percent, and Sunnis 20 percent, and if we also assume that almost all Kurds who voted cast their votes for the Kurdistan Alliance or the Islamic Kurdish Society, then this would imply that the Kurds account for about 21 percent of the population. The United Iraqi Alliance vote would account for about 62 percent of the population, and I suspect most of these are Shiites, confirming the assumption that they are about 60 percent of the population. If ethnic minorities account for 3 to 4 percent, then the Sunnis probably account for no more than 15 to 17 percent of the Iraqi population. The one virtue of an election as an ethnic census is that (again with the assumption of reasonable accuracy in the vote count) it does provide a window onto the ethnic composition of the population.

20. James A. Paul, "Iraq: The Struggle for Oil," Global Policy Forum, December 2002. http://www.globalpolicy.org/security/oil/2002/08jim.htm. See also Lawrence Kumins, *Iraqi Oil: Reserves, Production and Potential Revenues,* Congressional Research Service Report for Congress, September 29, 2003. http://www.fas.org/man/crs/RS21626.pdf.

Afterword

1. http://www.brookings.edu/dybdocroot/fp/saban/iraq/index.pdf, pp. 20, 23.

2. Edward Wong, "Suicide Bombing Near U.S. Convoy Kills and Wounds Dozens at Iraqi Hospital," *New York Times*, November 25, 2005.

3. Dexter Filkins, "Sunnis Accuse Iraqi Military of Executions," *New York Times*, November 29, 2005. The methods of torture described by detainees and revealed on bodies of the deceased were hauntingly similar to those used by Saddam's state security forces.

4. Sabrina Tavernise, "Sectarian Hatred Pulls Apart Iraq's Mixed Towns," *New York Times*, November 19, 2005.

5. http://www.brookings.edu/dybdocroot/fp/saban/iraq/index.pdf, p. 27.

6. James Glanz, "Fund Fade, Deaths Rise, and Iraq Rebuilding Is Spotty," *New York Times*, October 31, 2005.

7. Peter Baker, "Bush Cites Setbacks in Rebuilding by the U.S.," *Washington Post*, December 8, 2005.

8. James Glanz, "U.S. Aide Accused of Graft in Iraq Had a Shadowy Past," *New York Times*, November 19, 2005.

9. Robin Wright and Saad Sarhan, "In Cities Bush Cited, Progress Is Relative," *Washington Post*, December 8, 2005.

10. Ibid. p. 34.

11. http://www.telegraph.co.uk/news/main.jhtml?xml=/news/2005/10/23/wirq23.xml &sSheet=/portal/2005/10/23/ixportaltop.html.

12. "Only 43% of Sunnis described life as good versus 86% for Shi'ites. Only 9% of Sunnis felt things in Iraq were going well versus 53% for Shi'ites. . . . Only 11% of Sunnis said they felt 'very safe' versus 80% for Shi'ites." Overall, 44 percent of Iraqis said things were going well in the country. Anthony H. Cordesman, "The Impact of the Iraqi Election: A Working Analysis," Center for Strategic and International Studies, December 21, 2005, pp. 16, 25.

13. Informed by the lessons of much previous experience in postconflict constitution making, as distilled by a joint UN and U.S. Institute for Peace study group, UN Security Council Resolution 1546 (adopted on June 8, 2004) directed the United Nations Assistance Mission for Iraq (UNAMI) to "promote national dialogue and consensus-building on the drafting of a national constitution by the people of Iraq" (p. 3, article 7 (a) iii). On the lessons in this regard of previous constitutional efforts in postconflict societies, see Jamal Benomar, "Constitution-Making after Conflict: Lessons for Iraq," *Journal of Democracy*, vol. 15, April 2004, pp. 81–95.

14. In my role as an adviser on the drafting of the TAL, I was one of the strongest advocates of the need for more time, and had told Ambassador Bremer as well as my Iraqi colleagues that I felt the timetable of three elections and a constitutional draft within the space of a single year was far too compressed. As they pondered the obvious need to fashion a consensus over contentious issues in the

drafting of a permanent constitution, and the imperative as well of broad public participation and debate, the Iraqi drafters of the TAL also became concerned about the possible inadequacy of time. Recognizing the potential danger of a short and inflexible deadline, but worrying about the repeated syndrome of Arab governments operating under perpetually temporary constitutions, Feisal Istrabadi proposed the idea of the one-time, six-month extension, which was eventually adopted with slight modifications.

15. Jonathan Morrow, "Iraq's Constitutional Process II: An Opportunity Lost," Special Report 155, United States Institute of Peace, November 2005, p. 5.

16. Ibid. p. 10.

17. Ibid.

18. Peter Baker and Robin Wright, "In Iraq, Bush Pushed for Deadline Democracy," *Washington Post*, December 11, 2005.

19. Morrow, "Iraq's Constitutional Process II," p. 9.

20. Ibid. p. 15.

21. In the drafting of the TAL, some Iraqi liberals and American advisers, including myself, had strongly opposed the option of creating any more regions beyond Kurdistan, favoring instead a geographical federalism based on the eighteen provinces. This was the American position generally, but opposition to new regions was not an American priority.

22. Dexter Filkins, "Iraqis Consider Bypassing Sunnis on Constitution," *New York Times*, August 15, 2005.

23. Dexter Filkins and James Glanz, "Leaders in Iraq Extend Deadline on Constitution," *New York Times*, August 16, 2005.

24. Article 111 of the Iraqi Constitution, as amended and adopted on October 15, 2005.

25. Peter Baker and Robin Wright, "In Iraq, Bush Pushed for Deadline Democracy," *Washington Post*, December 11, 2005.

26. So frenetic and chaotic was the final constitution-making process that the drafters had to append to the document a set of "Final and Transitional Provisions" (in Section Six) to accommodate all their last-minute compromises. One of these restored the three-member presidency council, which had been dropped in favor of a single, unitary president, but the unitary presidency was to be "reactivated one successive term after this Constitution comes into force" (Article 137).

27. Kanan Makiya, "Present at the Disintegration," *New York Times*, December 11, 2005,

28. Zalmay Khalilzad, "Politics Breaks Out in Iraq," *Washington Post*, September 4, 2005.

29. Ibid.

30. Other breakaway groups included Abdul-Karim al-Muhammadawi's Hizbollah Iraq and Oil Minister Muhammad Bahr al-Uloum's Gathering for the Future of Iraq. For a useful roadmap, see Edward Wong, "Iraq's Powerful Shiite Coalition Shows Signs of Stress as Parliamentary Elections Loom," *New York Times*, December 9, 2005. Chalabi was apparently rebuffed by the Alliance when he demanded more safe seats on the Alliance lists than the group was willing to give him.

31. Or by some translations, the Iraqi Accordance (or Accord) Front.

32. Anna Badkhen, "Sunnis Won't Boycott Again," *San Francisco Chronicle*, December 11, 2005. One Sunni politician warned ominously, "If Shiites connected to Iran rule our country, there will be fighting all over the country and blood up to the waist."

33. On December 6, gunmen stormed five offices of the Kurdistan Islamic Union in an apparently coordinated assault, burning down their offices and killing between two and four party members, while injuring numerous others. Robert F. Worth and Edward Wong, "Politics Iraqi Style," *New York Times*, December 11, 2005, and Jonathan Finder, "In Iraq, Signs of Political Evolution," *Washington Post*, December 8, 2005. The assault was reportedly staged by *pesh merga* soldiers loyal to the KDP in retaliation for the Islamic Union's campaigning on the allegation that the local KDP administration in Dahuk was corrupt. http://iraqthemodel.blogspot.com/, December 6, 2005.

34. According to preliminary results, Saddam's former province of Salaheddin actually had the highest voter turnout, of more than 88 percent (topping even the Kurdish provinces), and while Anbar was the lowest at 55 percent, that was dramatically better than its 2 percent turnout in January and its 32 percent turnout in October. Cordesman, "The Impact of the Iraqi Election," pp. 7–8.

35. Two hundred thirty seats were allocated among the provinces based on their relative shares of registered voters, while the other forty-five seats were to be awarded to parties and lists so as to make their overall seat total as closely proportional to their national vote share as possible. (This compensatory distribution was partly designed to help smaller parties that qualified for national representation but did not do well enough to win seats in any one province.) This system was similar to what I and several other election experts had recommended early in 2004.

36. The quotes are from Dhafir al-Ani, Iraqi Consensus Front spokesman. Sabrina Tavernise, "U.N.'s Observer in Baghdad Calls the Voting Valid," *New York Times*, December 29, 2005.

37. By one early estimate, "Nine out of 10 Iraqis in the Shiite Muslim provinces of the south voted for religious Shiite parties." Borzou Daraghi and Louise Roug, "Iraq's History Still Divides Children of Mesopotamia," *Los Angeles Times*, December 29, 2005. A small sliver of these southern votes went to a separate Sadrist party. Preliminary results showed the United Iraqi Alliance winning 75–87 percent of the vote in each of the nine Shiite-majority southern provinces. Most of the Kurdistan voters who did not support the DPK–PUK alliance voted for the Kurdistan Islamic Union.

38. Initial estimates were that the United Iraqi Alliance had won about 130 seats (47 percent of the total) but reports indicated this could be cut back perhaps to 120 seats as a result of the fraud investigations.

39. Marina Ottaway, "Back from the Brink: A Strategy for Iraq," Policy Brief 43, November 2005, Carnegie Endowment for International Peace. http://www.carnegie endowment.org/publications/index.cfm?fa=view&id=17724&prog=zgp&proj=zme.

40. Kanan Makiya, "Present at the Disintegration," *New York Times*, December 11, 2005.

41. Ibid.

42. Dexter Filkins and Sabrina Tavernise, "Americans Said to Meet Rebels, Exploiting Rift," *New York Times*, January 7, 2006.

43. Ibid.

44. The meeting, which produced a broad statement calling for a timetable for withdrawal of foreign troops and acknowledging a right to resist foreign occupation, was to be followed by another conference in early 2006.

45. John Daniszewski, "Iraqi Civil War? Some Experts Say It's Arrived," *Los Angeles Times*, January 1, 2006. See also John Burns, "If It's Civil War, Do We Know It?" *New York Times*, July 24, 2005, and the anonymous report from an American news professional in Baghdad posted on www.JuanCole.com, January 8, 2006.

46. James Fallows, "Why Iraq Has No Army," *The Atlantic Monthly*, December 2005, http://www.theatlantic.com/doc/print/200512/iraq-army. One civilian in Baghdad told Fallows that "corruption is eating the guts of this counter-insurgency effort," p. 2.

47. Tom Lasseter, "Kurds in Iraqi Army Proclaim Loyalty to Militia," *Knight Ridder Newspapers*, December 27, 2005, http://www.realcities.com/mld/krwashington/13495329.htm. Of the 203,000 soldiers, police officers, emergency workers, and prisoners who cast ballots in the December 15 election, fully 45 percent voted for the Kurdistan list, indicating the heavy *pesh merga* presence in the new security forces. Borzou Daraghi, "Skewed Loyalties in Security Forces," *Los Angeles Times*, December 27, 2005.

48. Fallows, "Why Iraq Has No Army," p. 14.

49. Edward Wong, "Shiite Cleric Wields Violence and Popularity to Increase Power in Iraq," *New York Times*, November 27, 2005.

50. Rory Stewart, "Losing the South," *Prospect*, Issue 116, http://www.prospectmagazine.co.uk/article_details.php?id=7111.

51. Thanassis Cambani, "Senior Cleric in Iraq Wields Great Influence over Election," *San Francisco Chronicle*, December 11, 2005.

52. Stewart, "Losing the South."

53. Edward Wong, "Shiite Morality Is Taking Hold in Iraqi Oil Port," *New York Times*, July 7, 2005.

54. Stewart, "Losing the South."

ACKNOWLEDGMENTS

★

I did not go to Iraq intending to write a book. However, I did want to keep in regular touch with friends and family, and the miracle that is the Internet enabled me to do so regularly from my computer in the Republican Palace in Baghdad. During my brief time in Baghdad, I sent back via e-mail thirteen long letters that described, to the extent I could, what I was seeing and experiencing in Iraq. I began by simply reporting what I was doing and feeling—the hopes and frustrations, the anxieties and achievements, and the succession of strange, funny, and frightening moments. These e-mails began to be passed from friend to friend, and a number of people who read them urged me to write a book.

After I returned home from Baghdad in April and decided not to go back, I sent these e-mails to my superb agent, Scott Mendel, asking if they might somehow be gathered into a short book on my experiences in Iraq. He was wisely skeptical and encouraged me to focus on my plan for a book on global democratization. Still, I could not get Iraq out of my mind and heart. My time in Iraq had been the most illuminating, inspiring, and disturbing experience of my life as a scholar and promoter of democracy, and I simply could not rid myself of the need to write about it. When I persisted, Scott encouraged me to craft a true book rather than a collection of letters, and the result is this account of the American occupation and the effort to bring democracy to Iraq.

I do not offer this as a definitive account of America's fifteen-month political occupation of Iraq. No book coming so soon after the termination of the Coalition Provisional Authority, by one of its own officials, and with the larger transition in Iraq still unfolding, can be definitive and unbiased. It will fall to a succession of historians, who are able to sift through mountains of documents and the varying accounts of American, British, Iraqi, and other actors, to generate more dispassionate and comprehensive assessments of the experience. Still, my story may be distinctive, at least for a time, in penetrating the thick walls of the CPA headquarters without feeling any particular obligation to justify or condemn what we did.

Unlike any other book I have written or edited, I am unable to thank here by name many of the people who have assisted me with this project. I owe a large debt to a number of Iraqis and Americans (and a few of other nationalities) who helped me enter, understand, and move around the country, as well as research and write the book itself, but who, for security or professional reasons, asked that I not thank them by name. Shortly before this book went to press, I learned anew and very painfully how high the stakes in anonymity could be. The Iraqi who had acted as interpreter for me and for others in the American effort—a man for whom I felt particular affection and gratitude—was assassinated after more than a year of threats. This is why I have used pseudonyms for all Iraqis who are not public personalities.

These difficulties notwithstanding, I do want to acknowledge a number of people who made this book possible. I am grateful to Dr. Condoleezza Rice and Ambassador L. Paul Bremer III for asking me to go to Iraq to advise on the political transition, and to Scott Carpenter for the opportunities and encouragement he gave me within our Governance Office. I owe a large debt to George Adair, Derek Berlin, and Nancy Alain for the personal support they gave me in Baghdad and for helping me to get in and out of the country (and the Green Zone) as safely as possible. George and Derek also introduced me (both during and after the experience) to aspects of the culture of the palace that I would not otherwise have grasped. Judy Van Rest and her democracy program staff made it possible for me to meet and engage a number of Iraqis in civil society, including the remarkable women leaders in the Iraqi Higher Women's Council. My interactions with these women were among the most fascinating and inspiring moments of my time in Iraq, and it has been particularly painful to learn of the continuing deadly violence targeted at many of them.

For their cooperation with me during my time in Iraq and/or subsequently in doing research for this book, I would like to thank, in addition to George Adair and Derek Berlin, Rahman Aljebouri, Ghassan Al Atiyyah, Jamal Benomar, Barbara Bodine, Lakhdar Brahimi, Salem Chalabi, Dana Eyre, Feisal Istrabadi, Ronald Johnson, Terrence Kelly, Michaela Meehan, Ahmed al-Rahim, Emma Sky, and Fareed Yaseen.

At times my story was also amplified, documented, or informed in important ways by the reporting of foreign correspondents in Iraq. Certainly, their work was not flawless, and in the course of weighing many news accounts against my own experience and other informed accounts, I discovered in the enormous flow of daily news reports a number of mistakes and inaccuracies, some of them quite glaring (and a few no doubt deliberately planted by some of the actors in this drama). Still, by and large, I think they got the story right in its broad contours and in many of its vital details. In portions of this book I have especially benefited from the work of *New York Times* and *Washington Post* reporters such as John F. Burns, Dexter Filkins, Edward Wong, Rajiv Chandrasekaran, Karl Vick, and Anthony Shadid, and from the occasional reporting of George Packer, as well as the retrospective assessments of James Fallows and David Rieff. I came to know and admire Chandrasekaran personally in Baghdad, and in the course of our conversations I gained an appreciation for the daunting obstacles and dangers facing foreign correspondents in Iraq. My time in Iraq deepened my admiration for these journalists as individuals and as representatives of a profession that is vital to democracy.

I would like to thank several people who helped prepare me to understand Iraq before I began my advising role there. Beyond some of those I have already named, these included Abdulwahab Alkebsi, Amatzia Baram, Adeed Dawisha, Ray Jennings, and Laith Kubba. My research for this book benefited from the energetic and conscientious assistance of three outstanding Stanford undergraduates, Jeff Allen, Juliet Frerking, and Michael Ortiz. My assistant of the past six years, Alice Carter, also provided invaluable research support; she also kept my professional life together while I was in Iraq, and while I was in retreat at home writing this book. A number of readers offered comments on portions of the manuscript, and among those who can be named I particularly want to thank Adeed Dawisha and Maen Nsour. Susan Joseph did a skillful and meticulous job of copyediting the manuscript.

Most of all, in the preparation of this book from conception to completion, I want to thank the enormously gifted editorial director of Times Books, Paul Golob, whose wise and creative work in helping to structure, focus, and trim the manuscript made this a much better book. I must confess that it was only after I signed a contract with Times Books that I began to realize how widely respected he is in the world of nonfiction book publishing. And it was not until I had finished the manuscript and we had both struggled through many long nights of work that I gained the full measure of appreciation for his talents and generous spirit.

Finally, I would like to thank my friends and family—even the ones who cursed me as I prepared to leave for Iraq. In putting up with my impossible hours and long stretches of invisibility, and in supporting, if in some cases reluctantly, what I was doing, they made it possible for me to tell this story.

INDEX

★

ABOUT THE AUTHOR

★

Larry Diamond is a senior fellow at the Hoover Institution and professor by courtesy of political science and sociology at Stanford University. He has also been the coeditor of the widely respected *Journal of Democracy* since its founding in 1990. From January to April 2004, he served as a senior adviser to the Coalition Provisional Authority in Baghdad. He lives in Stanford, California.